Monographs in Theoretical Computer Science
An EATCS Series

Springer
Berlin
Heidelberg
New York
Hong Kong
London
Milan
Paris
Tokyo

Martin Große-Rhode

Semantic Integration of Heterogeneous Software Specifications

With 78 Figures

 Springer

Author

Dr. Martin Große-Rhode

Fraunhofer Institut
Software- und Systemtechnik, ISST
Mollstr. 1, 10178 Berlin, Germany
martin.grosse-rhode@isst.fraunhofer.de

Series Editors

Prof. Dr. Wilfried Brauer
Institut für Informatik der TUM
Boltzmannstr. 3, 85748 Garching, Germany
Brauer@informatik.tu-muenchen.de

Prof. Dr. Grzegorz Rozenberg
Leiden Institute of Advanced Computer Science
University of Leiden
Niels Bohrweg 1, 2333 CA Leiden, The Netherlands
rozenber@liacs.nl

Prof. Dr. Arto Salomaa
Turku Centre for Computer Science
Lemminkäisenkatu 14 A, 20520 Turku, Finland
asalomaa@utu.fi

Library of Congress Cataloging-in-Publication Data applied for

Die Deutsche Bibliothek – CIP-Einheitsaufnahme

Bibliographic information published by Die Deutsche Bibliothek
Die Deutsche Bibliothek lists this publication in the Deutsche Nationalbibliografie;
detailed bibliographic data is available in the Internet at <http://dnb.ddb.de>.

ACM Computing Classification (1998): F.3.2, D.2.2, D.2.1, H.1.0, I.6.5

ISBN 3-540-40257-8 Springer-Verlag Berlin Heidelberg New York

Springer-Verlag is a part of Springer Science+Business Media

springeronline.com

© Springer-Verlag Berlin Heidelberg 2004
Printed in Germany

The use of general descriptive names, trademarks, etc. in this publication does not imply, even in the absence of a specific statement, that such names are exempt from the relevant protective laws and therefore free for general use.

Cover Design: KünkelLopka, Heidelberg
Typesetting: Computer to film by author's data
Printed on acid-free paper   45/3142/GF - 5 4 3 2 1 0

Preface

In October 1998 the German Research Council (Deutsche Forschungsgemein-schaft, DFG) launched a Priority Program on the Integration of Software Specification Techniques for Applications in Engineering. Thirteen research projects were coordinated in this program, working in an interdisciplinary fashion on the different aspects of integration of software specifications. From the engineering point of view the systematic development of control soft ware for technical systems was addressed, and computer scientists investigated the corresponding specification languages and techniques from the method-ological, pragmatic, and semantic points of view. The overall concern within the program has been the multiparadigm approach to software development, which is inherently related to the subject of the program: working in differ-ent disciplines, with different backgrounds, aims, and languages. But multi-paradigmatic views occur in industrial practice too, when teams of engineers and computer scientists work together on a common product and thus need to communicate with each other. The benefit of covering such a wide range of views in a research program, in spite of the communication problems each in-terdisciplinary project starts with, is that it corresponds with actual practice and thus enhances significantly the usability of the research results.

The main precondition for the definition of the Priority Program was that the multiparadigm approach to software development should not be avoided, but rather be supported. Instead of searching for the one language that serves all purposes, lets everyone understand each other, and makes every-thing unique, the use of established and tailor-made languages for the different concerns was supported as the only realistic and practicable way. This view is also broadly accepted elsewhere, and developments like the standardised Reference Model of Open Distributed Processing (RM-ODP) and the Unified Modeling Language (UML) realise these principles in different ways. The issue that arises immediately with the use of different languages, however, is the integration of these languages. Are the various specifications consistent with each other? Do some of their elements correspond to each other and, if so, in which way? Can specifications be translated from one language to another one or are there paradigmatic differences that prevent this? Questions like these have to be addressed in such projects, and, from a more fundamental point of view, it must be clarified whether these are the relevant questions at all.

The aim of this book is to provide a framework for the integration of heterogeneous software specifications and in this way to support the multiparadigm approach. The book addresses in the first line the fundamental issues of what integration in this context means and how it can be achieved in general. Following the old slogan *Semantics first!*, the starting point has been to make precise the semantic concepts of specification languages, which also provide the fundamental concepts for integration. Separating semantics from both syntactic and methodological aspects in this way has led to a general semantic integration framework that is now independent of specification languages and methods, and can be universally applied. The instantiation of the integration framework with concrete languages will still require significant application-specific effort, depending on the syntactic and semantic complexity of the languages: the more features a language has and the less clear their semantics are, the more difficult and complex the instantiation will be. But, having a guideline that tells one what to do obviously makes such an endeavour much easier than trying to achieve an integration without an explicit integration concept and guideline. Moreover, many smaller examples for instantiations of the integration framework are worked out in detail in the book. They cover a wide spectrum of specification approaches, showing how their different concepts can all be embedded into the conceptual framework and how an integration can be achieved. According to the meta-level approach of the integration framework, the envisaged readers of this book are researchers in the areas of rigorous software systems development methods and modelling, integrated formal methods, and the semantics of specification languages, and theoretical computer scientists working in the area of specification and semantics.

While developing the integration framework I was working in different situations. Most of the time I worked at the Technische Universität Berlin on various research projects, including the above-mentioned Priority Program. In between I had the pleasure of working at the Università di Roma *La Sapienza*, the Università di Pisa, and the Universitat de les Illes Balears, Palma de Mallorca. These research visits gave me the opportunity to discuss the topic with people from very different backgrounds and consider its problems from many different points of view. I am very grateful to all my colleagues who accompanied me along this way and gave me the opportunity to pursue my work over the whole period. I would also like to thank the two anonymous referees who made many helpful comments on the initial version of this book.

Berlin, August 2003   *Martin Große-Rhode*

Contents

1

Introduction

The common feature of model-oriented, model-based, and model-driven software development methods is to use models of the system under development as abstract representations of its desired properties. Models are used to determine the structure and behaviour of the system and to analyse its properties before it is realised in a deployed implementation. Also, for the maintenance and evolution of a system models are better suited as information sources than code or executables, which can only be inspected by running them. At least for larger projects, the usage of models for the construction, analysis, and evolution of systems is nowadays widely accepted as best practice.

Due to the complexity of large software systems, however, different kinds of models have to be constructed for these purposes. They represent different views of the system, corresponding to the different perspectives of the people involved in the process, and different formal aspects of the system, such as structure vs. behaviour, logical vs. technical design, or other classifications. In order to support this decomposition of the development process into various viewpoints, different languages and methods for the construction of the models are used, which offer those features that are needed for the definition of these views. Thus, whenever the complexity of the development process is reduced by using viewpoint models, this results in increased complexity of the models. Different languages are used, different aspects are specified, and different paradigms underlie these specifications, which necessarily lead to heterogeneous models.

The heterogeneous viewpoint models are conceptually kept together by being models of one and the same system. However, at least during the development phase, the system only exists as an idea, as an object of discourse. Therefore the development process must offer other means to tie the models together. It must be possible for instance to state whether or how elements of different viewpoint models correspond to each other and to check whether models are consistent with each other during the development. Since the system is not yet available, these issues must be directly addressed at the level of the models. Such a conceptual integration, which provides the means to consider a collection of models as one model of a system, is a necessary component of any development process that incorporates viewpoint models. In order to retain the benefits of the decomposition into viewpoint models, however, integration must not rely on the concrete construction of one integrated model, but provide the means to run a model-based development with a collection of viewpoint models as if these were one model.

Although the integration must be achieved at the level of the models without explicit reference to the system, integration is inherently a semantic issue. Correspondence of model elements means that these elements refer to the same element or part of the system, i.e., they have the same meaning. Consistency means that models are free of contradictions, which holds if and only if there is at least one system that conforms to all models. This means that there must be one common semantic interpretation of the viewpoint models. Thus, to introduce a model integration approach first the semantic concepts have to be made precise. Based on this, syntactic representations and concrete methods can be defined that would become part of an integrated model-based development method.

In the following sections the viewpoint model of systems development, the conceptual integration, and the reference model approach that is introduced here are discussed in more detail.

1.1 The Viewpoint Model of Software Systems Development

The viewpoint model of software systems development comprises two major aspects: model-based development on the one hand and viewpoints on the other. The first one means that the software development should be based on models; that is, before and beyond the implementation abstract models of the system that is to be developed are constructed in order to have an abstract representation of the required structure, functionality, and properties of the system. These models allow one to state features and properties accurately without delving into the implementation details of programming languages, or even without giving a solution of how these properties can be achieved.

As mentioned above, this usage of models as a necessary abstraction layer in the development process for larger software systems is nowadays generally accepted. Appropriate languages and notation for the construction of models are offered by a variety of methods. The Unified Modeling Language (UML, see [UML03, BRJ98]) for example provides a family of visual languages for the modelling of object-oriented systems. It is a result of the unification and standardisation of notation that had been introduced earlier within different streams of object-oriented development methods. The standard that is used in its current version UML 1.5 here (see [UML03]) describes the syntax of the language formally in a boot-strapping manner, using class diagrams with constraints for the description of the language that itself contains class diagrams and constraints. The semantics of the language is defined in natural language; the search for formal semantics of the whole language or parts of it is an ongoing research effort. Nevertheless, UML has already led to great unification within the field of object-oriented modelling concepts, and to widespread use of viewpoint models for the development of software systems.

But also more formal specification techniques are used to construct abstract models of software systems, such as the model-based techniques B [Abr96] and Z [Spi88, Spi92], process specification calculi like CCS [Mil89] and CSP [Hoa85], or the many variants of Petri nets [Pet62, Rei85, PR91]. Within the formal specification techniques a further distinction can be made between *specification formalisms* that formally define and clarify elementary notions of specification, including their formal syntax and semantics, and *formal methods* that are based on specification formalisms but have an elaborate concrete syntax and offer a method for the development of models. The model-based set-theoretic method VDM [Jon86, HW89] for example comes with an explicit development method, and object-oriented extensions of Z like Object-Z [DRS95, Smi00] introduce elaborate presentation and structuring concepts from object-oriented design. Also, the process specification formalisms CCS and CSP have been extended to formal methods, for instance in the process specification languages LOTOS [LOT87, Bri89] and ELOTOS [Que98]. Obviously, there is no clear frontier between specification formalisms and formal methods, but both can be distinguished from the more pragmatic *software modelling or specification techniques and languages* like UML, where syntactic extension is more important than precise formal semantics.

It is important to realise that for any model-based development process the models are not only auxiliary means in the early development phases before the real implementation of the system. On the contrary, they serve as adequate, readable information sources during the whole maintenance and evolution process. They have to be maintained as documentation of the system since important properties of the system and design decisions in its development process are most clearly documented by the models. Thus any further development of the system should be based on these abstract descriptions rather than on their realisation in the programming language code or the executable artefacts, where the desired structure will be hard to detect. In this way models help to reduce the complexity of developing and maintaining software systems by the abstraction of details.

The second main feature of the viewpoint model is that models are not developed for the system in its entirety, but, with each model, only a certain aspect or view of the system is represented. A class diagram for example only models the static structure of a system without giving information about its dynamic behaviour, use cases model the main functionality without revealing the structure of the system or the realisation of this functionality, process calculi focus on the temporal ordering of actions, neglecting the data types, etc. The consequence of focusing on designated viewpoints is of course that each model yields only a *partial specification* of the system, because all aspects that are not concerned with this viewpoint are also not specified or constrained by this model.

The different viewpoints that are addressed in a modelling process may arise from different classifications. For instance, the different people taking part in the system's development play different roles and thus have different interests and expertise. Domain experts, software developers, system engineers, process managers, and clients for example need different information about the system and require different abstractions. Another classification that is based on the formal structural properties of systems and models instead of their envisaged usage is induced for example by the different UML diagram languages. These viewpoints essentially concern the static structure, the dynamic behaviour, both within and in between objects, and the implementation and deployment of the system. Yet another classification has been defined in the Reference Model of Open Distributed Processing RM-ODP [ODP, Lin91], which can be seen as one of the main sources of the viewpoint model altogether. It introduces five designated viewpoints that should be addressed when developing open distributed systems. Clearly, this particular feature of ODP is relevant for all system developments and not restricted to open distributed systems. The five viewpoints of the RM-ODP are the

enterprise viewpoint, the overall view of the system's purpose and aims, its agents and its policies;

information viewpoint, the information model of the system;

computation viewpoint, the view of the system as a set of interacting objects, adhering to the system's policies and realising its flow of information;

engineering viewpoint, the abstract machine view of the system, comprising its (technical) interaction mechanisms; and the

technology viewpoint, the configuration of software and hardware objects.

These viewpoints are of course mutually related, but no temporal order of their development is implied, as opposed to the software development phases of analysis, design, implementation, and test. In the ODP standard it is emphasised, moreover, that each of the viewpoint modellings should be supported by an adequate language, i.e., a language that allows the representation of the desired features directly without artificial encodings. Furthermore, these languages should be as formal as possible to allow for precise modelling and support the formal checking of properties with corresponding tool support.

Viewpoints contribute to the separation of concerns in the software development and thus yield a reduction in its complexity orthogonal to the contribution of the model-based approach.

The different classifications of viewpoints mentioned above are independent of each other to a large extent. This means, for example, that both software developers and domain experts are interested in information models, or that class, sequence, and state diagrams are used in the computational viewpoint. On the other hand, some combinations may be useless or excluded, so that the matrix of viewpoint classifications might have some empty entries.

Finally it is important to separate viewpoints as understood here from other decomposition or abstraction means. The decomposition of systems into manageable parts like components, modules, or classes for example is orthogonal to the concept of viewpoints, and raises completely different integration questions than the one of viewpoints (cf. the discussion in [BSBD99]). Furthermore, the view concept of databases that yields restricted views of complex data or object compounds is conceptually different from the viewpoint concept in software systems development, although technically similar integration questions may be addressed.

1.2 Integration of Specifications

Being accepted as an essential contribution to the rational development of software systems, the viewpoint model on the other hand immediately prompts the question on the relationships of the different models, especially since these may be given in very different languages, and even based on completely different modelling paradigms. There are, obviously, semantic relationships that have to be taken into consideration and clarified before syntactic support for the integration of viewpoint specifications can be developed (*Semantics first!*). As a slogan, the situation arising from the viewpoint approach could be formulated as: '*Many* people use *many* languages to develop *many* models of *many* views of **one** system.'

How can it be assured that indeed *one* system is modelled? The problem can be divided into two parts. The first one concerns the conceptual integration of models, which clarifies how different models can be considered as one model of a system. A model may for instance supplement the information given by another model, i.e., it can be considered as a refinement, making the first model more concrete by adding further details or further aspects that have not yet been addressed. The sequence and collaboration diagrams of UML for example refine the information given via the use cases by making explicit the dynamic interactions of the objects that realise the functionality specified by the use cases. State diagrams add information on the dynamic intra-object behaviour to class diagrams that only specify their static structure etc.

In contrast with this supplementation models may also deliver mutually overlapping information, where the same aspect of a system is concerned, but seen from different points of view. To use UML models again as examples, sequence diagrams model the interaction of objects realising certain scenarios, i.e., requirements on the objects. Statechart diagrams on the other hand model the intra-object behaviour, i.e., the capabilities of the objects. The semantic demand is then to check whether the objects—according to their statechart diagrams—are able to satisfy the requirements stated in the sequence diagrams. As opposed to the supplementation case discussed above, where models can hardly be inconsistent with each other, the semantic correspondences in the case of overlapping models are much more involved and require a deeper and more precise semantic analysis.

The conceptual integration of models thus means to establish *correspondences* between model elements that express semantic relationships.

The second part of the problem concerns the *consistency* of the given models, i.e., intuitively, the question whether the set of models is free of contradictions. In the logical sense consistency means to have a common model or a common semantic interpretation. Before going into this discussion, however, a brief deviation concerning the usage of the terms *model* and *specification* is necessary at this point.

In the discussion above the term model has been used as usual in software engineering or computer science in general, where a model is an abstract representation of something made by somebody for some specific purpose (as defined in [Ste93b]). A model thus represents or describes something, a structure, a behaviour, etc., which is different from the model itself. A class diagram for example does not represent a class diagram, but possible states of objects. This distinction is made explicit in mathematical logic, where the (semantic) entities that are represented are called models, in contrast with the representing (syntactic) entities that are called specifications. Thus, beyond other distinctions that could be made, a software engineering model is a specification from the logical point of view, whereas the logical (model-theoretic) model does not have a common designation in software engineering, except perhaps the 'meaning' (or semantics) of the model. For that reason, and because to a large extent the terms model and specification are used as synonyms in computer science, I prefer to use the term specification instead of model in the sense of system modelling, and the term interpretation instead of model in the logical sense of a semantic entity.

Coming back to the question of the consistency of specifications, i.e., the absence of contradictions, its logical characterisation is given as follows. A set of specifications is consistent if there is a common model of all specifications. The problem with this definition in the context of heterogeneous specification languages is that the categories of models for different specification languages are often disjoint by definition, whence two specifications written in these languages may never be consistent, independently of their semantic content and intention. For example, the models of algebraic data type specifications are algebras (see for instance [EM85, BHK89, LEW96]), and the models of Petri nets are reachability graphs [Pet62, Rei85], processes, or occurrence nets [RG83, DMM89], or event structures [Win88a], depending on the chosen level of abstraction. Thus even if the data type of, say, lists is specified algebraically and some of its operations are expressed by Petri nets, the strict definition of consistency would in this case always lead to the conclusion that they are inconsistent, because an algebra is neither a reachability graph nor a process, nor even an event structure.

For that reason other definitions of consistency have been suggested. For example, a set of specifications may be considered as consistent if there is a common (physical) implementation of all of them. This rephrases the original definition by replacing 'common model' with 'common implementation', but has the disadvantage that, in spite of its pragmatic flavour, this condition will be hard if not impossible to check. Viewpoint specifications have been introduced to deal with complex situations in the development of large systems, thus checking for consistency in this sense would amount to finishing the entire development first. A more concise approach to consistency in the context of the viewpoint model, especially the ODP viewpoints, has been developed in [BSBD99, BD99, BBDS99, BBD⁺00].[1] Different types of consistency checks are distinguished, like inter- and intra-language consistency and global vs. binary consistency, and further types of consistency checks are introduced that may depend on the specific relationships of the specifications, according to their roles in the development process and the different relations to the target system. The major contribution concerning the definition of consistency in this approach is to replace the common model and the common implementation suggested by the other definitions by 'having a common refinement or a common development'. In order to support this approach development relations are investigated and presented in a universal formal framework that allows the study of consistency at a very general level, corresponding to the overall aims of the ODP standard. Whereas the formalisation of intra-language consistency checks, i.e., checks for specifications written in one language, is treated adequately, the inter-language check is more constrained and based on a translation between specific languages, Z and LOTOS in this case ([DBBS96]), which is not entirely satisfactory. The translation is too schematic to deal with language-specific modelling decisions and different modelling styles within one language. Recall also that for consistency checks of heterogeneous specifications correspondences need to be established first, which may depend on a specific comparison with other specifications, and usually cannot be obtained automatically. A fixed consistency check as in the mentioned approach does not offer the necessary flexibility for this purpose.

The approach to the integration and consistency checking of heterogeneous specifications introduced here claims to be as general as the consistency approach discussed, but is much more flexible, because it is based entirely on the semantics of the specifications. The basic contribution is indeed given by the definition of a common semantic domain that serves to interpret all languages that are used to construct specifications, whence each of the languages obtains its global semantics by referring to this domain. For this reason the semantic domain constructed here is called a *reference model* for the integration of specifications. With its usage the original logical definition of consistency can be taken up again; that means a set of specifications is consistent if there is a common interpretation of all specifications of the set in the reference model.

---

[1] See also http://www.cs.ukc.ac.uk/research/groups/tcs/openviews/.

In Figure 1.1 an example of an integration via a reference model is depicted. A small sample of a system is described by different specifications: a programming language construct, a class diagram with only one class, a statechart, and an algebraic Petri net. The class defines the structure, given by the

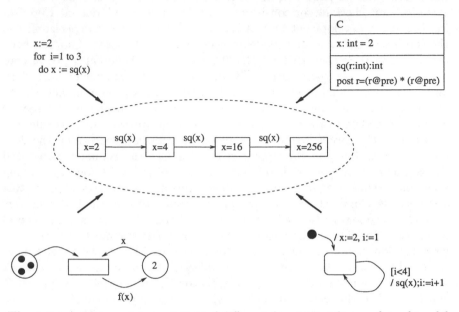

Fig. 1.1. A common interpretation of different descriptions by one formal model

integer attribute x and the operation sq of type *int*. Additionally it specifies an initial value $x = 2$ for x and a postcondition $r = (r@pre) \times (r@pre)$ for the operation, formulated in the object constraint language OCL of UML (see [WK98, UML03]). The expression $r@pre$ denotes the value of the parameter r before application of the operation. Beyond the pure structure, the behaviour is thus also partly specified by the class. It does not specify, however, when and how the operation should be applied. The program loop and the statechart specify the behaviour in very similar ways. Both the data states, given by the values of the attribute, and the control flow are modelled via variables whose values are manipulated. In addition to the implicit structure information given by the operations and the predicates that are applied to the variables, the dynamic behaviour is specified: the sq-operation is applied three times in sequence. The main difference between the two descriptions is that the program is textual whereas the statechart is mixed graphical and textual. Note that not only does the implicit typing of x in the program loop and the statechart overlap with the information given in the class, but so does its initialisation value. On the other hand, there is no information given about the effect of the operation sq on the variable x. Only its name indicates its intended meaning. Finally, the algebraic Petri net models the same dynamic behaviour on the same structure in a slightly different way. Instead of introducing a new variable such as i in the other specifications, the control flow is specified here via an additional place. It holds three tokens that are consumed when applying the function f, i.e., f is applied three times. The effect of f is also not specified in the Petri net. Relating it to the sq-operation specified in the class diagram adds the information given in its postcondition to the Petri net. That means the integration of the partial viewpoint specifications enriches them mutually.

Using the reference model the consistency of these four specifications can be shown by stating one common model in the reference model as the semantic interpretation of all of them. This interpretation is depicted in the centre of Figure 1.1. There are four states containing the actual values of the static entity x, connected by three transitions labelled by the operation application $sq(x)$. This model is an admissible interpretation of the operational semantics of the program loop and the statechart, abstracting from the control flow variable i, and, analogously, it represents the operational semantics of the algebraic Petri net when interpreting the function f as $f(x) = x^2$. Moreover, it represents the possible behaviour of an object of the class. Thus the four specifications have a common interpretation, whence they are consistent.

Since the class does not specify the dynamic behaviour it obviously admits a set of models in the reference model, whereas the other specifications are usually understood as describing a single behaviour. Nevertheless, the latter can also be interpreted in different ways. The behaviour of the function f in the Petri net for instance is not specified in the net, whence it can be interpreted arbitrarily as long as no further information is given. The decision for the interpretation $f(x) = x^2$ is determined by a comparison with the class diagram that contains a postcondition for the operation the function f might correspond to. Similarly, the variables x and i in the statechart and the program loop are treated differently in the model: x is interpreted as a static entity, whereas i is resolved into the dynamics. Obviously, this distinction is influenced by the comparison with the information given in the class diagram again, which only contains the attribute x. This shows that the semantic interpretation of a specification for consistency checking and integration may depend on the interpretation of the other ones considered within this test. These local decisions about the interpretation have to be taken into account of course when different groups of specifications are compared. This discussion again supports the statement made above: that consistency checks cannot be entirely automated, but require context-dependent correspondence information.

Further, the consistency check of the four specifications in the example already contained an implicit integration in the sense of a model correspondence. The syntactic entity x in all four specifications refers to the same item in the semantic interpretation, which yields the correspondence of the specifications at these points. This is a very simple correspondence induced by identical names, but in general correspondences may be much more complex and will hardly rely on the identity of accidentally chosen local names. The operation sq in the class, the statechart, and the program loop here correspond to the function f of the Petri net, and the three black tokens of the Petri net correspond to the loop condition *for* $i = 1$ *to* 3 in the program fragment, and the combination of the initialisation $i := 1$ and the condition $[i < 4]$ of the loop transition in the statechart.

1.2.1 Admissible Interpretations, Correspondences, and Consistency

Taking into account the above-mentioned incompleteness of viewpoint specifications that is due to their partial view of the system, a more general conception of integration is achieved. Instead of immediately searching for a common interpretation in the reference model, the following three steps in an integration process based on a common reference model are methodologically distinguished and treated explicitly.

Admissible interpretations The elements of the reference model are models of systems that cover all relevant aspects. Since a viewpoint specification constrains only one aspect of a system, it admits a set of interpretations in the reference model. The first step in an integration consists of the determination of the sets of admissible interpretations of the individual specifications. This may be induced by the language used for the construction of the specifications, for instance if these are formal specifications with formal semantics, but it might also depend on the usage, the application domain, etc. In Figure 1.2 sets of admissible interpretations are shown as subsets of the reference model, indicated by the arrows from the specifications.

Correspondences The viewpoint specifications may be developed within different name spaces, address different parts or scopes of the system, refer to different granularities w.r.t. behaviour and structure, and use different means to specify corresponding information. These semantic correspondences have to be made explicit for the integration. Within the reference model correspondences appear as transformations of the sets of admissible interpretations. System models, as elements of the reference model, may be projected onto common parts or scopes of the system, or adjusted to a common level of granularity, etc.

Consistency In order to check the consistency of the specifications, after their admissible interpretations have been determined and the correspondences have been declared, the intersection of the correspondingly transformed sets of admissible interpretations is considered. If it is empty the specifications are inconsistent w.r.t. the considered interpretations and correspondences. If there is more than one interpretation in the intersection the collection of specifications is still incomplete, i.e., the information given w.r.t. the considered level of granularity is still not sufficient. If there is exactly one model in the intersection the specifications are consistent and complete in this sense; that means, w.r.t. the interpretations and the explicit correspondences considered in this integration.

This complete view of the integration of viewpoint specifications by the transformation and intersection of sets of admissible interpretations is illustrated on another small example in Figure 1.2. A class diagram, a statechart dia-

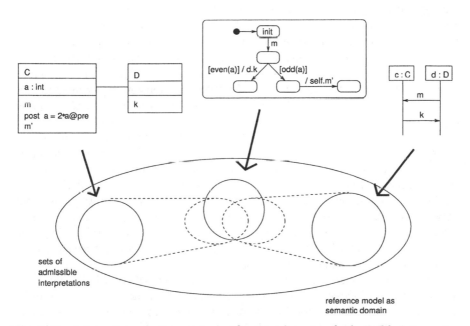

Fig. 1.2. Integration of viewpoint specifications by sets of admissible interpretations, transformations, and intersection

gram, and a sequence diagram are shown that together specify a (very small) system. The class diagram defines the structure of the objects and, by the constraint that defines the postcondition for the operation m in C, one aspect of their behaviour. The state machine specifies the simple reactive behaviour of the objects of the class. It is assumed that the state machine is associated with the the class C, one correspondence that is not explicit in the figure. This kind of correspondence is defined in the UML meta model for example as the context of the state machine, and realised for instance by hyperlinks in modelling tools. Finally, the sequence diagram specifies one interaction of objects of the classes C and D. For the integration all three specifications are interpreted by the full sets of system models that are admissible interpretations of the specifications. The class diagram for instance does not constrain the sequences of steps the objects can perform; that means all sequences of executions of the operations may occur (or not occur) in a semantic interpretation of the class diagram. On the other hand, the statechart diagram and the sequence diagram do not constrain or specify the side effects of the operations on the data states of the objects or whether operations are deterministic or not. All interpretations w.r.t. these aspects are admissible.

In the second step of the integration the correspondences of the specifications have to be considered. For this example we assume that equal names have equal meanings, i.e., C, D, a, m, and m' denote the same class, attribute, and operations respectively in all specifications. Furthermore, as mentioned above, the state machine is considered to specify the behaviour of objects of class C. Such a single name space might not always be assumed. In a larger development names may be chosen locally and only in the integration of the specifications do the correspondences between the name spaces have to be declared. As shown in the examples in the following chapters these need not be one-to-one correspondences of names, but more complex constructions might be required, mapping, for instance, names to descriptions.

A further correspondence relates the scopes of the three specifications. The class diagram specifies arbitrary collections of objects, the statechart diagram specifies the behaviour of a single object of class C, and the sequence diagram specifies one desired behaviour of linked objects of classes C and D respectively. Thus to compare and integrate their semantics appropriate projections have to be applied first that map the system models in the respective sets of interpretations to the same portion of the system. For example, all system models associated with the class and sequence diagram can be projected onto systems with exactly one object of class C.

An analysis of the intersection of the transformed sets of admissible interpretations of the three specifications then shows in which way they supplement each other. Obviously, in this example the intersection contains more than one system. On the one hand, the specifications do not contradict each other, which means that there is at least one common interpretation. On the other hand, neither the initial value of the attribute a nor the side effects of the operations m' and k are specified in any diagram, which means that they can still be consistently defined in different ways. Thus there is more than one common interpretation of the three specifications.

Considering now the class diagram and the state machine together yields that, due to the postcondition for m stated in the class diagram, only the left transition from the second state (the one with the guard $even(a)$) in the state machine can be executed. This implies that, due to the state machine this time, each object of class C can perform at most one macro-step: If m is called the object calls the operation k at object d and then terminates.

In Figure 1.3 some possible interpretations of the class and the state machine diagrams are sketched. The class diagram interpretations in these samples contain two objects, one of class C and one of class D. The state machine interpretations contain one object of class C, but these also refer to operations from class D. For the comparison the class diagram interpretations must now be projected onto systems representing a single object c of class C. On the other hand, the transition labels of the state machine interpretations must be projected onto the operations of class C. Only one system remains in the intersection of the transformed sets. This not only shows by its existence the consistency of the two diagrams, but incorporates and integrates the information spread over the two viewpoint specifications.

Taking into account the scenario specified by the sequence diagram then shows that the operation m will be called at least one time. Combining this with the information given by the state machine yields that the first message of the scenario can only be sent if the object c is in its initial state and has never done anything else before. Note that the sequence diagram describes arbitrary incomplete scenarios, i.e., ones that might not occur at the beginning of the life cycle of an object. That means, considered individually, it admits interpretations that contain the specified sequence of steps, but it also admits other steps before or after this sequence. In this example the sequence diagram does not add further information to the other two specifications. The integration, however, shows that the state machine together with the class correctly implements the scenario.

The results of such an analysis could be used to refine and develop the individual specifications, for instance by cancelling the right branch of the state machine's transition and adding the information on the initiality of c to the sequence diagram as an OCL constraint ($c.oclInState(init)$). This could be enhanced later on, when the initial value of the attribute a is known. However, the reflection of the results of the conceptual integration onto the specifications obviously depends very much on the languages they are given in. Since the overall integration approach introduced here is language independent, the reflection cannot be developed systematically in the general framework. For this purpose concrete languages or families of languages would have to be investigated in detail.

1.2.2 Language- and Method-Independent Integration

In the examples discussed just now viewpoint specifications have been compared and integrated out of context, i.e., without asking for their position or role in a development process. In fact, the viewpoint concept can be employed in many different ways in different contexts. Beyond being independent of specific modelling or specification languages, the viewpoint approach itself is also independent of any particular method that would state how to develop and use the viewpoint models. Instead, it can be deployed with a variety of methods, just as it can be instantiated with a variety of languages.

A strictly hierarchical method for instance would not only prescribe which viewpoints have to be specified, but also give an order for their development and rules that state how new viewpoint models are to be constructed based on the given ones. The advantage of such a strict hierarchy is that integration and consistency aspects can be incorporated and fixed in the method and

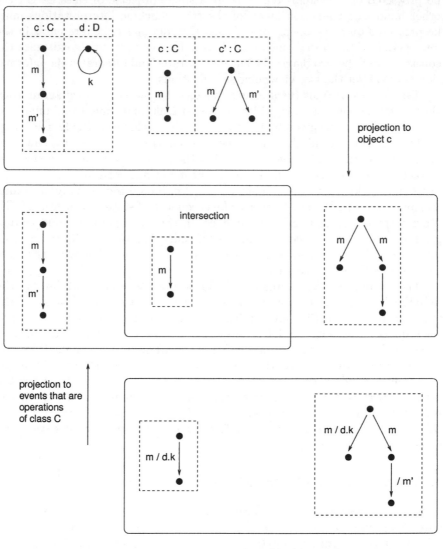

Fig. 1.3. Semantic integration of the class and the statechart diagram

need not be considered anew in each individual development. On the other hand, this does not allow deviations from the fixed order of development steps and thus limits the flexibility of both the development and the maintenance or evolution process. And if models are used continuously to support the system's evolution, new notation probably will have to be taken into account at some point and require an integration with that used so far. This concerns especially the integration of new components whose specification might not conform to the same strict development method and might not be given in the same notation.

Less strict methods allow at least different starting points for the development process. For example, instead of requiring either the structure or the behaviour of the system to be specified first, both views may be considered initially independently of each other. UML-based software development methods, for example Catalysis [DW98] and the development method for component-based systems presented in [CD00], support this flexibility. The models developed for the different views then have to be integrated at some stage. Thus the integration problem occurs again, although in a less drastic form since the basic conceptual relationships of the models are already determined by the method.

An entirely liberal approach, where all viewpoints are equivalent, is supported by the RM-ODP. It stresses that no order should be prescribed on the specification of the viewpoints. This allows for example the integration of assets, i.e., models that have been developed before, and the flexible adaptation of the development to the given requirements. Obviously, the integration task occurs here in its most general form, since even the viewpoint specification languages are not fixed.

Heterogeneous specifications and the corresponding need for integration also arise in processes where stakeholders are used to employ specific notation that is established in their domains. Developing software for embedded systems for example involves specifications of software systems, given for instance in a UML notation like statechart diagrams, and specifications of programmable machines, given for instance in the IEC 61131-3 language Sequential Function Charts [SFC]. A flexible method should support the usage of both languages and add integration mechanisms instead of forcing the users to agree on one of the languages.

In order not to constrain the application of the integration approach unnecessarily, methodological questions as well as specific languages are separated here completely from the semantics of integration. (Separation of concerns is as important in theory design as it is in systems design.) That means that viewpoint specifications are considered independently of their envisaged usage in a development process and independently of the language that is used for their construction. The contribution of the proposal thus amounts to a framework at a meta level that delivers the fundamental notions and concepts. For an application-specific usage, given by a definite set of viewpoints, the corresponding concrete viewpoint specification languages, and a method for the concerned development process, significant instantiation effort is still required. The generality of the approach, however, allows one to use, adapt, or specialise the proposed integration framework in any method that is based on viewpoints, or takes into account heterogeneous models and specifications for any other reason. Of course, the full generality of the concepts introduced here might not be completely exploited in a specific instantiation, due to its

constraints on the viewpoints, the languages, and the usage of viewpoint specifications. The proposed integration framework serves as a foundation for the
development of such methods.

1.3 Requirements of Reference Models and Their Usage

General requirements of the internal structure of a reference model for the
integration of heterogeneous specifications can be stated immediately. First
of all, the reference model must supply formal system models as elements that
serve as semantic interpretations of the specifications. On the one hand this
means that it must be possible to represent the structure and the behaviour
of the specified systems with the system models. On the other hand it must
be possible to adjust the granularity of the interpretation according to the
desired degree of abstraction. This may be induced by the specification level
(more abstract or more concrete specification) or by its scope (larger or smaller
system, subsystem, component, object, etc.).

Second, there must be relations expressing the development of system models in order to trace modelling decisions made within iterative development
steps. To operationalise the developments, there should be operations that
allow the constructive development of more refined or more abstract views or
versions of given system models.

Finally, orthogonal to the dimension of the development, there must be
composition operations that allow the construction of larger, more complex
system models from given ones. Defining the composition by operations in
the mathematical sense means two things. First, it has to be defined how system models can be connected in order to compose them, i.e., the definition of
relations on their structures and behaviours must be supported. These relations of the system models represent the *architecture* of the composed system.
Second, the result of executing the composition operation has to be defined.
That means the system model representing the whole composed system of
interconnected models has to be given. This second requirement implies compositionality in the sense of *structural transparency*: a composition of local
system models can be considered as a single system model again, and thus
the internal structure of the system can be hidden.

Note that this does not mean that the result of the composition always
has to be computed. Structured systems—architectures—may be retained in a
development stage as connected system models (as defined in the first part of
the definition of an operation). The second part of the operation's definition,
the computation of its result, only offers the possibility to consider the interconnected models as a single model again, which may be computed whenever
desired.

The two dimensions of development and composition must be brought
together by checking the *compositionality of developments*. This means conditions must be stated that guarantee that local developments of system models

can be composed in the same way as the system models themselves and that this yields a global development of the whole system that comprises the local developments conservatively.

As mentioned above, the intended usage of a reference model is to map viewpoint specifications to it in order to compare and integrate them semantically. This can be achieved in a uniform way by considering the specification languages and mapping them to the reference model. That just means to define their semantics in terms of the elements, relations, and operations of the reference model. If the formal semantics of a language is already defined then the redefinition in the reference model must be shown to be compatible with the given one. In general the two definitions will not coincide, because the structure of the elements of a reference model will be much richer than the one used before, due to the generality of the reference model. But it must be possible to recover the original semantics from its redefinition. It is not the idea of the reference model approach to define completely new, 'better' semantics with better properties. (Although a criticism of the language design or the semantics definitions may arise from their reconstruction in the reference model.) If the semantics of the languages has been defined only informally, a reference model may help to formalise them further by offering its elements and its structure as formal semantic objects. (This depends of course on the formality of the reference model itself.) Furthermore, languages may lack some of the structure or the properties of a reference model, for instance appropriate composition operations, development relations, or compositionality properties. Then the corresponding feature of the reference model might be reflected to the language by seeking syntactic representations in terms of the language or by appropriate extensions of the desired features. Analogously, the reference model may be used to investigate which of the operations support which compositionality properties.

1.4 The Transformation Systems Reference Model

In this section a first informal survey of transformation systems and their usage as a reference model for the integration of heterogeneous software specifications is given. The presentation proceeds along the requirements stated above in order to demonstrate how the different dimensions and features are covered in this approach.

A specific property of the transformation systems reference model is that it is fully formal, i.e., the elements, relations, and operations are defined mathematically. This allows us to give precise definitions, to state its properties explicitly, and to prove them. On the other hand, the correspondence of the mathematical constructions and the software specification concepts has to be established, which can be achieved only at an informal level. For that reason a large part of the book is devoted to examples, explanations, and discussions. Thus beyond the formal definitions of the reference model its basic notions and constructs are analysed and explained at an informal level. This allows us to carry over the integration method also to applications that cannot (or should not) be handled entirely at the formal level.

1.4.1 Transformation Systems

The elements of the transformation systems reference model represent the static structure and the dynamic behaviour of systems via a two-level structure. The behaviour of a system is modelled by a transition system, given by a set of abstract control states and transitions between these states (first level). The control states demarcate reference points to the systems, i.e., these are the states at which the systems can be inspected and accessed. The internal structure of a control state, i.e., the corresponding state of the data, is attached to the control state as a label, given in the second level. All data states of a transformation system adhere to the same static structure, but may be different instances of course. That means that the static structure is the schema of which the data states are instances. The other part of the second level consists of the labels for the transitions of the transition system. Whereas a transition from one control state to another one only states that it is possible to pass from the first state to the second one, the transition label indicates which actions are performed in this step. Actions might be assignments, method calls, passive actions like events, input and output actions, etc. Using an action or a set of actions as the label of one transition means that no inspection or access to the data state is possible in between the initial and the final state of the transition. In particular, invariants need not hold in between and no other communication may take place during the step.

A transformation system—an element of the reference model—is thus an extended version of a labelled transition system (LTS), where not only the transitions but also the states are labelled. LTSs are traditionally used for the definition of operational semantics for all kinds of languages and systems, like imperative and functional programming languages, process and data type specification languages, and others. Therefore transition systems are also chosen here as formal models of the behaviour part, representing the smallest common denominator of semantic models for this aspect. Defining the labels of transitions and states appropriately and choosing the right transition system allows a flexible adjustment of this structure to the forms required by the different integration tasks.

The data states attached to the control states have been introduced as instances of one schema representing their common static structure. In the simplest case the schema is given by a list of typed static entities like the attributes of a class, program variables declared in some program, or the variables of a Z schema, for example. The corresponding instances (data states) are given by type-compatible bindings of these entities to values, i.e., elements of the corresponding types. That means a data state is given by a list of values. Making the types and their data type structure explicit leads to the definition of data states as algebras. (This relates the transformation system approach to the states-as-algebras approaches, see [ABR99]). In addition to the data type signature there are then constants in the (static structure) signature, corresponding to the syntactic entities, such as attributes, variables, etc. Each algebra of such a signature is thus given by a data type or a collection of data types and a set of designated elements of these types. The latter represent the actual values of the static entities.

The usage of algebras then allows further generalisations, as for example parameterised constants like attributes of array types, which are programming language encodings of finite functions. (See for instance [CD00], where parameterised attributes for the specification of components and interfaces with UML are advocated.) Since data types are usually partial, and attributes/variables need not always be defined, partial algebras are used immediately as data states within transformation systems. They have essentially the same theory as total algebras (see [Bur86, Rei87, CGW95]). Finally, since the definition of transformation systems as elements of the reference model does not really depend on the choice of the labels, a generic (institution-independent) definition is given as a further generalisation that allows the usage of arbitrary data type models as data states, like first- or higher order logic structures, or order-sorted algebras, for example.

Analogous to the labelling of the control states, the transitions on the first level are labelled by sets of *actions* on the second level. The interpretation of these actions—as observations, method applications, operation calls, actions, events (passive actions), or whatever—is left open and must be taken into account when different models are compared. A set of actions attached to a transition is interpreted as the occurrence of all actions of the set in between the initial and the final state of this step. According to the interpretation of control states given above, no state inspection is possible between the initial and the final state of a transition. Thus there is no order on the actions attached to one transition, nor is it assumed that they occur at the same time. As for the control states there is also a generic version of actions, corresponding to the generic specification framework (institution) of the data state models. This allows for instance the incorporation of guards or composed actions, or distinctions of events and actions as in statecharts. For more technical reasons, implied by the generality of the transformation systems reference model, transitions are labelled furthermore by a second component, a *tracking relation*, that keeps track of the identity of data elements through state changes. (Tracking relations correspond to the partial tracking functions of *D-oids* introduced in [AZ93, AZ95].)

A transition t leading from a state c to a state d, written $t : c \to d$, is thus associated with three labels: the data states C and D attached to the control states c and d respectively, and the pair $T = (act_t, \sim_t)$ given by the action set act_t and the tracking relation $\sim_t$ attached to t. Thus a transition $t : c \to d$ can also be seen as a data state transformation $T : C \Rightarrow D$. This point of view, which distinguishes transformation systems from ordinary labelled transition systems most clearly and is also predominant in the states-as-algebras approaches, was decisive for the designation *transformation systems*.

In Figure 1.4 a transformation system is shown that models the possible behaviour of a point object that moves erratically on a 3×3 grid. The static structure of the system is given by two attributes x and y of type $\{1, 2, 3\}$, representing the coordinates of the point and their values. The data states are given accordingly by the nine possible different values of the attributes. The transformations are interpretations of the applications of the parameterless *move*-action. The underlying transition system is given by the nine states,

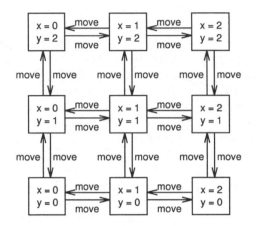

Fig. 1.4. A transformation system representing a point object moving on a grid

depicted by the rectangles, and the twenty-four transitions, depicted by the arrows. Data states and actions are given by the labels in and at the rectangles and arrows respectively.

1.4.2 Development Operations and Relations

The development of transformation systems is supported in the reference model in two ways. First, there are development operations that allow the construction of more abstract or more concrete systems from given ones. According to the two-level structure of transformation systems—the transition system level representing the dynamic behaviour and the label level corresponding to the static structure—the operations may be used to reduce or to refine the behaviour and the structure. Reduction and refinement or extension on the two levels can be combined arbitrarily. The behaviour can be restricted to certain actions, i.e., the other ones are excluded, or further steps can be added extending the behaviour. Analogously, only (public) parts of the data structure may be shown (i.e., private parts may be hidden), or further (internal, private) structure may be added. Furthermore, single actions or steps in one system may be refined by composed steps (transactions) in another system, and static functions may be refined or implemented by compositions of static functions of the refining type. For example, an attribute *Name:String* may be refined by the composition *concat(Title,LastName,',',FirstName)* in another specification. In the opposite direction this yields the means to define interfaces of systems in the sense of more abstract views. Note that these interfaces are semantic elements, too, and that they represent not only static structure information like interfaces in class diagrams, but also behaviour information.

From a less operational point of view development relations are more adequate than development operations. For this reason they are also provided in the reference model. Given two transformation systems it can be checked with these development relations if and how one of these systems can be seen as a development of the other one. Developments are so general as to include refinements, implementations of one transformation system by another one, and interfaces as views as mentioned above. The development relations are a generalisation of the development operations in the sense that the application of a development operation always yields a system which is in development relation with the old one.

In Figure 1.5 for example the static structure of the grid-point system is refined by adding a new attribute *next* that determines the direction in which the point can move. This refinement corresponds to an inheritance in a class diagram: the static structure may be enlarged and the behaviour may be redefined. In this case, the behaviour is restricted to only one possibility per state. Also in the context of process specifications, the reduction of non-determinism is an important refinement technique, leading from abstract specifications that allow non-determinism to concrete, deterministic implementations. Implementations, as a further development relation, may also require additional internal structure, represented as a refinement by extension at the structure level.

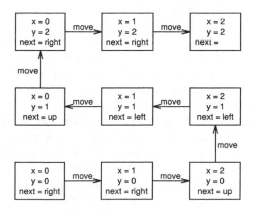

Fig. 1.5. A transformation system representing deterministic moves on a grid

1.4.3 Composition

Analogous to the development of transformation systems, their composition is based on composition operations for the two levels, transition systems (dynamic behaviour) and data state and action labels (static structure). As stated in the requirements above, the composition of systems is based on relations that describe how the local components are connected. For transformation systems these are given by two relations. A synchronisation relation on the transition systems expresses which states of the local systems can be entered simultaneously and which steps of the local systems can be performed simultaneously. An identification relation on the static structure expresses which parts of the local static structures are shared by the local systems, and thus identified in the global view. The synchronisation relation does not presume that the local systems are synchronised by a global system clock. Instead, transformation systems allow the formal synchronisation of transitions also with states, modelling situations where one component performs its actions whereas the other one remains idle in its state. Since one transition may be related to several transitions or states of the other component, synchronisation means that the transition *may be* synchronised with one of the related transitions or states. If there is exactly one related transition or state these *must be* synchronised.

Consider for example two systems M_1 and M_2, each of which performs two consecutive steps t_1, t_1' (in M_1) and t_2, t_2' (in M_2) respectively (see Figure 1.6, where only the transition system level of the two transformation systems is shown). Consider first the case where M_1 and M_2 are completely independent of each other, i.e., all states of M_1 and M_2 can coexist and all transitions of M_1 and M_2 can take place together in one global step of the composed system. This is expressed by the full synchronisation relation, i.e., each transition and state of M_1 is related to each transition and state of M_2. Then the composed system is able to perform the local steps in any order, including single and parallel executions, as shown in the centre of Figure 1.6.

To express that t_1 must be synchronised with t_2, while t_1' and t_2' may still be synchronised with each other or with the corresponding states, the synchronisation relation shown in Figure 1.7 has to be given. Then the global system behaves as shown by the dashed arrows in Figure 1.6. The steps depicted by the solid arrows are excluded because they consist of pairs that are not in the synchronisation relation of Figure 1.7.

With the identification relation the sharing of common (static) data types can be expressed, such as interchange data or pervasive types, shared variables as in the access to a common store, or shared actions like the input/output actions of process calculi. In Figure 1.8 for example the two components M_1 and M_2 share a variable, which is called x in M_1 and a in M_2, and each one has a private variable, y and b, respectively. This is expressed by the identification relation x id a on the signatures $\{x, y : int\}$ for M_1 and $\{a, b : int\}$ for M_2. As indicated in the transformation systems, M_1 has writing access to x, whereas

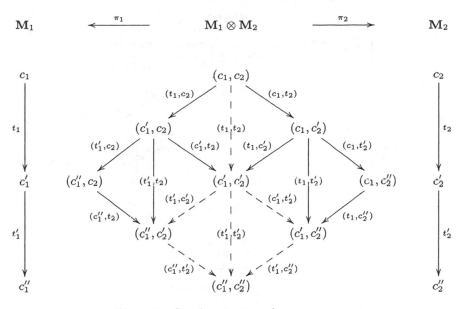

$$\mathbf{M_1} \quad \xleftarrow{\quad \pi_1 \quad} \quad \mathbf{M_1 \otimes M_2} \quad \xrightarrow{\quad \pi_2 \quad} \quad \mathbf{M_2}$$

Fig. 1.6. Synchronisation of two systems

$\mathbf{M_2}$ can only read a. In its first step it observes that the value of a has been changed.

The global data states of the composed system $\mathbf{M_1 \otimes M_2}$ are then given by a superposition of the local ones. Shared parts are identified, i.e., they are represented only once in the global state, whereas the local parts are kept apart, i.e., they are added disjointly. This yields the global data states in the upper row of Figure 1.8. The actions of a step in the global system are given by the unions of the local action sets, where again names that are related via the identification relation are identified. As mentioned above, this

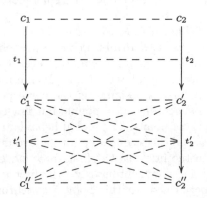

Fig. 1.7. A synchronisation relation on two transition systems

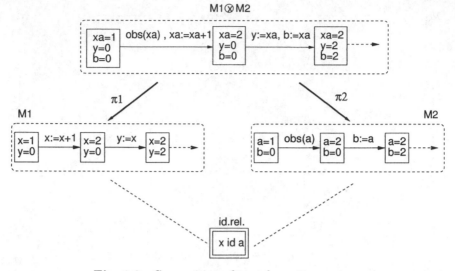

Fig. 1.8. Composition of transformation systems

sharing (identification) as well as keeping apart local parts of the structure does not depend on the names chosen in the local specifications. Instead, the identification relations are used to express arbitrary correspondences between the elements or derived elements of the local structures.

Synchronisation and identification relation need not be binary but may connect arbitrary numbers of local systems. Together they describe the connection of local systems, i.e., the architecture. This corresponds to the first part of the definition of composition operations as discussed in Section 1.3. The result of a composition, i.e., the global system seen as one transformation system again, is then given by the tuples of synchronous steps of the local systems and the corresponding superpositions of their data states and action sets as discussed above. In Figures 1.6 and 1.8 such global views have already been shown.

The abstraction mechanisms mentioned in the discussion of the development relations can also be used to obtain more asynchronous forms of behaviour composition. In Figure 1.9 for example several sequences of steps in the local components are encapsulated by introducing interfaces. Synchronising these abstract steps means designating the corresponding control states in the local systems as synchronisation points, but not constraining the local behaviour in between these points. The global behaviour induced by the synchronisation of the first and the second steps of the two interfaces is then given by two global steps. In the first one the first three steps of the left concrete system are performed and—asynchronously—the first two steps of the right concrete system are performed. At this point a synchronisation takes place. Then the last two steps of the left system and the last step of the right system are performed, again asynchronously. As opposed to the direct synchronisation (including synchronisations with states) there is no global state of the asynchronous system during the execution of the local actions that constitute one global step.

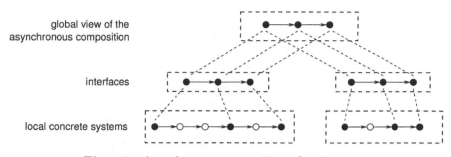

global view of the
asynchronous composition

interfaces

local concrete systems

Fig. 1.9. Asynchronous composition of two systems

The structural transparency achieved by computing the result of a composition operation, i.e., the representation of a composition of systems by a single transformation system as its global view, also allows the representation of refinements and developments at the architectural level. The direct composition of two systems by a synchronisation and an identification relation for example can be refined by first introducing interfaces for the encapsulation of local steps and then composing these more abstract views as discussed above. Since both sides, the direct composition and the asynchronous composition via the interfaces, can be considered as single transformation systems in turn, the definition of the development relations for structured systems can be reduced to the basic unstructured case discussed above. That means the asynchronously composed system is a development of the directly composed system if their global views are in a development relation.

Moreover, also due to the structural transparency, the architecture of the data states and the architecture of the behavioural components need not coincide. If, for example, two processes with different behaviours exchange complex data, then the architecture of the behaviour (the two linked processes) is completely different from the architecture of the data, which may be composed of many substructures (see Figure 1.10).

1.4.4 Granularity

The examples discussed above might have led to the impression that the representation of software systems or components as transformation systems in the reference model might be rather low level. In fact, however, the granularity of the formal model can be chosen arbitrarily according to the level of abstraction required for a specific view and offered by the corresponding specification technique. The reference model itself is entirely open w.r.t. modelling decisions concerning the granularity. That means the distinction between static data

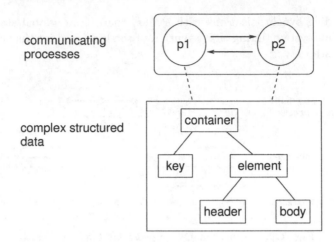

Fig. 1.10. Different architectures of behaviour and data

types and dynamic operations with side effects, and the distribution of the structure and the behaviour into local transformation systems in a concrete model are induced by the given specifications and specification techniques. They are not prescribed by the reference model.

Consider as an example the assignment of a result of a database query to an attribute of some object. If the purpose of the specification is just to state that this value is bound to the attribute, the whole query and the assignment can be considered as one data state of the system. The database query is then modelled as a static function within a static data type and the state is characterised by the equation $attr = query(par_1, \ldots, par_n)$. Thus, in this case, the query is identified with its result, as in the mathematical set-theoretic understanding of a function, which is a very high abstraction. If, however, the dynamic behaviour of the query has to be modelled, for instance its execution inside the database management system, the transition system level of transformation systems has to be used, too. Then the single steps are modelled by transitions and the data states now also may contain further internal variables to store intermediate results and control information. Finally, it could be necessary to consider also the architecture level, for example if the internal structure of the database management system needs to be considered or if the query is sent by a mediator to several databases. Then the local dynamics and data structures are coordinated by a specific component, sitting on top of the other ones.

The representation of one scenario may thus use the static data type level alone, a single transformation system, or a set of interconnected transformation systems. This depends only on the desired granularity of the overall modelling.

1.5 Organisation of the Book

In the following chapter first the formal definitions of transformation systems are introduced, comprising the basic notions of control states, transitions, data states, and transformations. Their intended meaning and usage is shown in a series of examples. In Chapter 3 the properties of transformation systems are classified and investigated, introducing abstract syntactic means to formulate such properties. These refer to the notions introduced above: data invariants refer to data states, transformation rules refer to data state transformations, and control flow properties refer to the whole control flow level, possibly even including their labels. The development operations and relations are introduced in Chapter 4. They are also based on the structure of transformation systems introduced in the first chapter. Data states and transformations can be developed by adding or refining structure, or by hiding some parts, or, dually, making only designated parts visible. The behaviour can be developed by decreasing or increasing the non-determinism, adding or constraining behavioural capabilities, or refining steps by sequential or parallel composition of steps. Also the relation of developments and properties of transformation systems as discussed in Chapter 3 is presented in this chapter. That is, it is investigated what kinds of properties are preserved by which kinds of development steps, and, conditions are given that guarantee the preservation of certain properties by the corresponding development steps.

In Chapter 5 composition operations are introduced. Their definition also refers to the two-level structure of transformation systems. As discussed in Section 1.3, the first part of a composition of systems consists of their interconnection. This is given by an identification relation that addresses the data states and action sets and a synchronisation relation on the control states and transitions. The result of the application of a composition operation is given by an integration of composition operations for the data states and transformations on the one hand and transition systems on the other. Beyond the compositionality in the sense of structural transparency as discussed above, this also yields *compositional semantics* (see Section 5.4). That means the composition operations on the abstract syntactical level of transformation systems induce compositions at the associated semantic entities. The relations to the different kinds of properties of transformation systems are expressed as conditions for the *compositionality of properties* (Section 5.5), the ones to the development relations as *compositionality of developments* (Section 5.6). The former guarantees that the properties of components that can be expressed in their local languages are preserved by a composition, i.e., in the resulting global system the property also holds. Compositionality of developments means that local development steps of the components of a system induce a global development step of the system that contains the local ones, provided the local developments are compatible with the connection of the components.

An application of the integration approach to semi-formal software specifications is discussed in Chapter 6. Different UML models—class, statechart, and sequence diagrams—are considered and analysed as viewpoint specifications. Their integration first requires them to be interpreted formally in the domain of transformation systems. Due to the complexity of the languages and the informal definition of their semantics, this obviously can be done only by examples. Moreover, the treatment will include certain assumptions on the intended meaning of the language constructs used, according to the idea of admissible interpretations. Since the idea of the chapter is just to demonstrate the integration approach and not to define a complete integrated UML semantics, this suffices, however. On the basis of the transformation system semantics the conceptual integration is then discussed. Different kinds of transformations of the semantics are presented that relate the specifications according to their relation to the global system specification. The transformations make possible the mutual adjustment of the specifications w.r.t. their name spaces, their structures, their levels of granularity, and their scopes, i.e., the parts of the system they address. These transformations thus define the syntactic and semantic correspondences of the specifications.

In Chapter 7 a conclusion and a short summary of the main concepts are given and possible further applications to concrete languages and methodological support are discussed. Then related approaches are discussed and compared with the transformation system approach. Finally some methodological issues are discussed that were crucial both for the development and the presentation of the transformation system approach.

2

Transformation Systems

In this chapter transformation systems are introduced as formal models of parts of software systems. The concrete understanding of the term *part* thereby depends on the desired granularity of the model, i.e., its degree of abstractness. Whether some portion of a system is considered as a part in this sense is not an objective property of the software system, but a design decision in the modelling process. A transformation system might be a model of an object, or a process as a part of the behaviour of an object, or a component in the sense of component-based software engineering (see e.g. [SP96, Gri98, Szy98, CD00]), or a whole software system. In the last case the transformation system will probably be constructed from smaller parts by appropriate composition operations, as discussed in Chapter 5.

The chapter is organised as follows. First the constituent parts of transformation systems, namely transition graphs and data spaces, are introduced. These represent the dynamic behaviour and the static structure respectively. Transition graphs are a slight extension of (unlabelled) transition systems with an additional structure that is essentially needed to support the composition operations later on. The term *transition graph* has been chosen instead of transition system to avoid overstraining the term *system*. A data space is a collection of all possible data states and data state transformations, i.e., a structured set of all instances of the structure schema. After these basic definitions two larger examples are presented, showing how transformation systems can be used in different application contexts. These examples are further developed in the following sections. In Section 2.3 a generalisation of the data state models and actions is discussed that yields a definition of transformation systems that is generic w.r.t. the specification framework used for the data spaces. In Section 2.4 this extension is used to obtain a formal model of object systems with data and object references. The chapter ends with a discussion of the concepts introduced so far and a first comparison with other approaches.

2.1 Transition Graphs and Data Spaces

A transformation system is a two-layered structure, given by a transition graph and a data space. The transition graph is given by a set of abstract control states, its nodes, and the possible transitions between these states, i. e., its edges. It models the temporal ordering of the steps of the system, i. e., its dynamic behaviour. The data space is given by the data states and their transformations, where the latter are induced by some given actions and furthermore adorned by relations that keep track of the identities of the data elements through state changes.

The data space of the system provides all possible data states and transformations, independently of whether they are ever reached or executed by a system. The selection of the data states and transformations out of the data space and their temporal ordering are represented by the transition graph, together with a labelling function that associates a data state to each control state and a data state transformation to each transition of the transition graph. Thus a transformation system is a labelled transition system, where both the states and the transitions are labelled. From the distinction of the two levels the control flow information can be separated from the data state information. Correspondingly, first the data space of a system might be defined, and then its transition graph to define how the atomic data transformations are composed to processes. The paths in the transition graph then model the sequential execution of steps; branching indicates non-deterministic choice.

In order to support the composition of components further structure is imposed on the transition graphs. First there is an initialisation and finalisation state that is used to enter and leave the model, for example when the thread of control is passed from one component to another one, or when objects are created or destroyed during the runtime of the system. Thus the initialisation and finalisation state represents a state *outside* the system, as opposed to the initial states of the system, which are the ones that are reachable from the initialisation state via a single step, and the final states, which are the ones that have a direct step to the finalisation state. (For the sake of brevity there is one such designated state, generally called the initialisation state, although it is used as above as an initialisation and finalisation state.) Finalisation allows us to distinguish the successful termination of a component's behaviour leading to the finalisation state from deadlocking behaviour, represented by a state inside the system without an outgoing transition. Second, there are idle transitions for all states. These are used in parallel compositions, where steps of different components are synchronised. Synchronisation with an idle transition then means that in fact only one component performs a step, whereas the other component remains idle. These idle transitions should not be confused with internal actions. As opposed to idle transitions the latter may change the state, but, like the former, they are not visible.

Definition 2.1 (Transition Graph). *A transition graph $TG = (CS, T, in, id)$ is given by*

- *a set CS of* control states,
- *a family* $T = (T(c,d))_{c,d \in CS}$ *of sets of* transitions,
- *a designated* initialisation *(and* finalisation*) state in* $\in CS$, *and*
- *a function id* : $CS \to T$ *that assigns an* idle transition $id(c) \in T(c,c)$ *to each state* $c \in CS$.

As usual a transition $t \in T(c,d)$ *is also denoted by* $t : c \to d \in T$. *A control state* $c \in CS - \{in\}$ *with* $T(in,c) \neq \emptyset$ *is called an* initial *state, and the corresponding transitions* $t_{in} : in \to c \in T$ *are called* initialisations *of TG. Analogously control states* $c \in CS - \{in\}$ *with* $T(c,in) \neq \emptyset$ *and transitions* $t_{fi} : c \to in$ *are called* final states *and* finalisations *of TG respectively.*

A morphism $h = (h_{CS}, h_T) : TG \to TG'$ *of transition graphs* $TG = (CS, T, in, id)$ *and* $TG' = (CS', T', in', id')$ *is given by*

- *a mapping* $h_{CS} : CS \to CS'$ *and*
- *a family of mappings* $h_T = (h_{T(c,d)})_{c,d \in CS}$ *with*

$$h_{T(c,d)} : T(c,d) \to T'(h_{CS}(c), h_{CS}(d)) ,$$

for all $c, d \in CS$, *such that*
- $h_{CS}(in) = in'$ *and* $h_{T(c,c)}(id(c)) = id(h_{CS}(c))$ *for each* $c \in CS$.

(The indexes CS and $T(c,d)$ designating the state and transition parts h_{CS} and $h_{T(c,d)}$ respectively of the morphisms h will be omitted in the sequel.)

The data states of a transformation system are partial algebras of a given algebraic signature. They contain the static data types, like integers, booleans, and strings, for example. Whether further data types like queues or arrays are taken up into the data states as static data types, or whether the operations are modelled as state transformers, depends again on the granularity of the model. If, for example, queues are just used to model more complex behaviour the queue operations might be considered as functions in the set-theoretic sense, i.e., they do not change the state, have no side effects, and need no time to deliver the result. (In this sense $enqueue(d, q)$ is *the same* as the queue dq.) The set of all queues with its functions corresponding to the queue operations is then a static data type. Otherwise, if the purpose of the model is to represent the dynamic behaviour of the queue operations, for example, a data state might be the state of a single queue and each operation is given by one or several transformations of this state.

Beyond the static data types a data state contains mutable types and functions. A constant symbol of the signature for instance can be bound to different values in different algebras (=states), thus modelling the updating of an object's attributes or a program variable. In this case the constant symbol delivers the identity of an entity that has different values in different states.

Data state transformations are just pairs of data states, i. e.,the input or initial state and the output or final state of the transformation, decorated by a set of actions that may indicate the cause of the transformation or its synchronisation or communication capability, and a tracking relation. Actions may have input and creation parameters. The input parameters can be instantiated by values from the algebra representing the actual state. The creation parameters denote the elements that are created by the action, and thus they are elements of the output state.

The structure of data states and actions is given by a data space signature that extends the algebraic data signature by an action signature. In this general definition no distinction is made between static data types and mutable parts, because these might not always be clearly separable (cf. the discussion at the beginning of Section 2.2).

Definition 2.2 (Data Space Signature). *A data space signature $D\Sigma = (\Sigma, A)$ is given by an algebraic signature $\Sigma = (S, F)$, the* data signature, *and a family $A = (A_{w,w'})_{w,w' \in S^*}$ of sets, the* action signature. *An action name $a \in A_{w,w'}$ is denoted by $a : w; w'$ for short.*

The following small example will be used throughout the next sections to illustrate the concepts.

Example 2.3 (A Program with Pointers). Consider a program that contains a declaration of pointers to natural numbers and a method to increment the value of a pointer by a given amount. A data space signature that specifies these ingredients is given by

> **prog = nat +**
>   **sorts** pointer
>   **funs** p: → pointer
>   !: pointer → nat
>   **acts** inc: pointer, nat

(Concerning the notation: Sorts, functions with their argument and result types, and actions with their parameter types are listed after the keywords *sorts*, *funs*, and *acts* respectively. Empty sort name strings are omitted according to the following conventions:

> *constants* $c :\to s$ instead of $c : \lambda \to s$
> *predicates* $p : w$ instead of $p : w \to \lambda$
> *actions* $a : w$ instead of $a : w; \lambda$

The import of another signature *sig'* is denoted by $sig = sig' + \dots$.)

In the signature *prog* a signature of the natural numbers is imported and extended by a sort of pointers. The partial dereferencing function ! yields— in each state—the actual values of the pointers. Furthermore there is one designated pointer p, but there may be more pointers in the model. The incrementation action *inc* has two parameters, the pointer whose value is updated and the amount it is incremented by.

The data space of a transformation system is given by all partial algebras of the given data signature as possible data states and all pairs of data states as possible data state transformations. The latter are labelled by all possible sets of actions, i.e., action names supplied with actual parameters, and all tracking relations. A set of actions represents the parallel execution of all its members, the empty set as a transition label corresponds to an internal action. Note that the data space itself has the structure of a transition graph. Its initialisation state is given by the empty algebra, representing a void state outside the system, and the idle transitions are given by the empty action sets and identity relations.

Since different algebras are used as states of one system the tracking relations have to be given as additional information on how these are related. That means they indicate which elements of the algebras should be considered as equal. An element may cease to exist after some step, or appear, or even split, although the last possibility will hardly be used. In most examples the tracking relation will be given by the identity on the carrier sets of some fixed static data types that are present in all states. (Thus in a first reading the tracking relation can be ignored.) In the categorical constructions, however, like the free construction of successor states (in Section 3.4) or composition by limits (in Chapter 5) the tracking relation must allow for more flexibility since the states are defined only up to isomorphism.

Definition 2.4 (Actions, Transformations, Data Space). *Let $D\Sigma = (\Sigma, A)$ be a data space signature with $\Sigma = (S, F)$.*

1. *Given S-sorted sets M and N the set of* actions $Act_{D\Sigma}(M, N)$ *is defined as*

$$Act_{D\Sigma}(M, N) = \{a(m; n) \mid a : w; w' \in A, m \in M_w, n \in N_{w'}\},$$

   i.e., an action is given by an action name $a : w; w' \in A$ and lists $m = (m_1, \ldots, m_k)$ and $n = (n_1, \ldots, n_l)$ of elements $m_i \in M_{s_i}, n_j \in N_{s'_j}$ as input and creation parameters respectively, where $s_1 \ldots s_k = w$ and $s'_1 \ldots s'_l = w'$.

2. *Given partial Σ-algebras C and D the set of* transformations $Tf_{D\Sigma}(C, D)$ *is defined by*

$$Tf_{D\Sigma}(C, D) = \mathcal{P}(Act_{D\Sigma}(|C|, |D|)) \times Rel^S(|C|, |D|),$$

   where $\mathcal{P}$ and Rel^S denote the powerset and the set of S-sorted relations respectively.

   That means a transformation $T \in Tf_{D\Sigma}(C, D)$ is given by a set of actions and a relation. A transformation $T \in Tf_{D\Sigma}(C, D)$ is also denoted by $T : C \Rightarrow D \in Tf_{D\Sigma}$.

3. *The* data space

$$\mathbb{D}_{D\Sigma} = (|\mathbf{PAlg}(\Sigma)|, Tf_{D\Sigma}, \emptyset, \langle \emptyset, id \rangle)$$

is the (large) transition graph given by the class $|\mathbf{PAlg}(\Sigma)|$ *as the class of control states, the set* $Tf_{D\Sigma}(C, D)$ *as the set of transitions from* C *to* D, *the empty partial* Σ-*algebra* $\emptyset$ *as the initialisation state, and the empty action set and identical relation as the idle transition for each control state.*

Example 2.5 (Data Space of the Program with Pointers). The data space of the program signature given in Example 2.3 consists of all partial Σ_{prog}-algebras as states, where Σ_{prog} is the data signature of *prog*. An algebra A that extends the natural numbers $I\!N$ by some set M of pointers with a designated element $P \in M$ and a partial function $e : M \dashrightarrow I\!N$ represents a state, basically given by the *environment* e. That means e defines the actual values $e(q) \in I\!N$ of the pointers $q \in M$. However, the data space also contains algebras whose *nat*–part is not isomorphic to the type of natural numbers and whose designated pointer is not defined. Furthermore, for *each* pair of algebras A and B, *any* set of actions is a transformation from A to B. Thus the data space contains many more states and transitions than might be expected. In Figure 2.1 for example the second row of states and transformations might be considered as a part of a sensible interpretation of the *prog*-signature (with pointers P, Q, R and actual values depicted by $P \mapsto n$, etc.). But also the other data states and transformations belong to the data space by definition. If no further information is given to constrain the interpretation of the syntactic symbols introduced in the signature, this is indeed the space of all possible states and transformations.

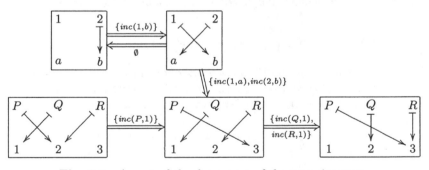

Fig. 2.1. A part of the data space of the *prog*-signature

In the transformation system given in Example 2.7, which is the intended (or at least a rather meaningful) model for this signature, only meaningful states and transformations are selected from the data space as labels of its transition graph. Moreover, in Chapter 3 specification means are introduced that allow us to reduce the data space by requiring certain properties of data states and transformations.

Transition graphs and data spaces, connected by labelling functions, yield transformation systems (see Figure 2.2). Thus the data space provides the labels for the transition graph.

Definition 2.6 (Transformation System). *Let $D\Sigma = (\Sigma, A)$ be a data space signature. A $D\Sigma$-transformation system $\mathbf{M} = (TG_{\mathbf{M}}, \mathbf{m})$ is given by a transition graph $TG_{\mathbf{M}}$ and a transition graph morphism $\mathbf{m} : TG_{\mathbf{M}} \to I\!\!D_{D\Sigma}$.*

The first and second components of the label $\mathbf{m}(t)$ for a transition t are also denoted by $act_t^{\mathbf{m}}$ and $\sim_t^{\mathbf{m}}$, i.e., $\mathbf{m}(t) = \langle act_t^{\mathbf{m}}, \sim_t^{\mathbf{m}} \rangle$.

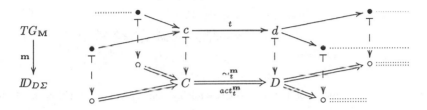

Fig. 2.2. Definition of transformation systems as transition graph morphisms to the data space

According to the interpretation of action sets above a system is called *sequential* if there is at most one action per transition, i.e., $\sharp(act_t^{\mathbf{m}}) \leq 1$ for all transitions $t \in T$.

Example 2.7 (Interpretation of the Program with Pointers). A *prog*-transformation system $\mathbf{X} = (TG_{\mathbf{X}}, \mathbf{x})$ that models a meaningful interpretation of the *prog*-signature of Example 2.3 can be defined as follows. Let X_n for each $n \in I\!\!N$ be the partial Σ_{prog}-algebra defined by

$$X_n|_{\mathbf{nat}} = I\!\!N, (X_n)_{pointer} = \{X\}, p^{X_n} = X, !^{X_n}(X) = n \,,$$

i.e., X_n is the state in which X has the value n. Then let $\mathbf{X} = (TG_{\mathbf{X}}, \mathbf{x})$ with $TG_{\mathbf{X}} = (CS_{\mathbf{X}}, T_{\mathbf{X}}, \Delta, idle)$ be defined as in Table 2.1.

In this model there is only one pointer, which is initialised with the value zero. In each state it can be incremented by any amount, and the system can be left in each state. It is a sequential system that contains as labelled paths all sequences of applications of the incrementation method (see Figure 2.3). The control states and transitions are given by the minimal information that is needed to recover the data states and actions respectively. The label function expands this information to partial Σ_{prog}-algebras ($n \mapsto X_n$) and actions ($k \mapsto inc(X, k)$). The method *inc* induces a function on states in this example that assigns to each data state X_n and each pair of parameters X and k a successor state X_{n+k}. In general, actions need be neither total nor deterministic; that is, they correspond to relations rather than functions.

control states	$CS_\mathbf{X} = I\!N \cup \{\Delta\}$
	where Δ is the initialisation state
transitions	$T_\mathbf{X}(n, n+k) = \begin{cases} \{k\} & (k > 0) \\ \{0, idle\} & (k = 0) \end{cases}$
	$T_\mathbf{X}(\Delta, n) = \begin{cases} \emptyset & (n > 0) \\ \{init\} & (n = 0) \end{cases}$
	$T_\mathbf{X}(n, \Delta) = \{final\}$
	with $idle : n \to n$ being the idle transitions
data states	$\mathbf{x}(n) = X_n, \quad \mathbf{x}(\Delta) = \emptyset$
actions	$act^\mathbf{x}_k = \{inc(X, k)\}$
	$act^\mathbf{x}_{idle} = act^\mathbf{x}_{init} = act^\mathbf{x}_{final} = \emptyset$
tracking relations	$\sim^\mathbf{x}_k = \sim^\mathbf{x}_{idle} = (id_{I\!N}, id_{\{X\}})$
	$\sim^\mathbf{x}_{init} = \sim^\mathbf{x}_{final} = \emptyset$

Table 2.1. Definition of the transformation system $\mathbf{X}$ as interpretation of the program with pointers

Remark 2.8. 1. Given a $D\Sigma$-transformation system $\mathbf{M} = (TG_\mathbf{M}, \mathbf{m})$, each action $a \in A_{w,\lambda}$ yields a relation on the data states of $\mathbf{M}$ with parameters, given by $(C, \bar{\gamma}, D) \in a$ if there is a transition $t : c \to d$ in $TG_\mathbf{M}$ such that $\mathbf{m}(c) = C$, $\mathbf{m}(d) = D$, and $act^\mathbf{m}_t = \{a(\bar{\gamma})\}$ for some $\bar{\gamma} \in C_w$. Thus actions can always be interpreted as non-deterministic operations, whose input parameters are provided by the actual states. A transformation system is *deterministic* if each operation induced by an action in this way is a partial function on data states, i.e., for each data state C and each parameter $\bar{\gamma} \in C_w$ there is at most one data state D such that $(C, \bar{\gamma}, D) \in a$. (Making this definition precise, the tracking relations should be taken into account, as well as the creation parameters, i.e., actions from $a \in A_{w,w'}$.)

2. Return values of operations can be modelled by including for each action a a constant *return_a* of the corresponding type in the data signature. Then in a transformation $a(\bar{\gamma}) : C \Rightarrow D$ the value $(return\_a)^D$ of *return_a* in D represents the return value of a. Actions as partial operations with return values are used in the D-oid approach [AZ95].

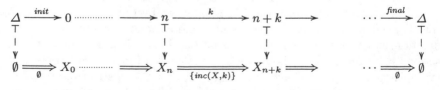

Fig. 2.3. A path in the *prog*-transformation system $\mathbf{X}$

3. Sets of actions have been interpreted as parallel occurrences of actions, with the empty set as an internal step corresponding to an invisible action. But in general the action sets need not be correlated uniformly, i.e., there might be a transition labelled $T \cup T'$ but no transition labelled T or T', or if there are such transitions, their underlying data states need not be correlated.

4. A syntactic representation of a tracking relation, which is more general than the identity on static data types contained in the data states as discussed above, can be obtained by designating a subsignature Σ_0 of the data state signature Σ and defining $\gamma \sim_t^m \delta$ for $\gamma \in |C|$ and $\delta \in |D|$ if there is a term $r \in Term_{\Sigma_0}$ such that $\gamma = r^C$ and $\delta = r^D$. If states are defined up to isomorphism, for instance via a free construction or a colimit, this more flexible definition is more adequate.

A formal comparison between transformation systems as formal semantic models and approaches that use LTSs as operational semantics can be achieved by forgetting the state labels and tracking relations.

Definition 2.9 (Underlying LTS). *The underlying LTS of a $D\Sigma$-transformation system $\mathbf{M} = (TG_{\mathbf{M}}, \mathbf{m})$ with $TG_{\mathbf{M}} = (CS, T, in, id)$ is defined by*

- $LTS(\mathbf{M}) = (S, A, \rightarrow)$

where

- $S = CS - \{i\}$,
- $A = \mathcal{P}(Act_{D\Sigma})$, *where $\emptyset$ corresponds to τ, and*
- $c \xrightarrow{l} d$ *iff there is a $t : c \rightarrow d$ in $TG_{\mathbf{M}}$ such that $l = act_t^m$.*

If there is exactly one initial state in $\mathbf{M}$ this also yields the initial state of $LTS(\mathbf{M})$, otherwise LTSs with sets of initial states have to be allowed or the initialisation state has to be used as the initial state. Note that all LTSs obtained in this way are reflexive, i.e., each state has a designated idle transition. This corresponds to taking label–partial morphisms as in [WN97]. Another possibility would be to remove the idle transitions from the transformation systems when mapping them to LTSs.

Transformation systems w.r.t. a given data space signature $D\Sigma$ are defined as transition graph morphisms to a fixed transition graph. This yields their categorical structure as objects of a comma category. The corresponding morphisms are given accordingly by those transition graph morphisms that preserve the data space labels. In the following let **TG** be the category of transition graphs and transition graph morphisms, with component-wise composition and identities of state and transition mappings.

Definition 2.10 (Category of Transformation Systems). *Given a data space signature $D\Sigma$ the category $\mathbf{TF}(D\Sigma)$ of $D\Sigma$-transformation systems is defined as the comma category $(\mathbf{TG} \downarrow I\!D_{D\Sigma})$, i. e., its objects $\mathbf{M} = (TG_{\mathbf{M}}, \mathbf{m})$*

are pairs of transition graphs $TG_{\mathbf{M}}$ *and transition graph morphisms* $\mathbf{m}$: $TG_{\mathbf{M}} \to I\!D_{D\Sigma}$, *and its morphisms* $h : \mathbf{M} \to \mathbf{M}'$ *are transition graph morphisms* $h : TG_{\mathbf{M}} \to TG_{\mathbf{M}'}$ *such that* $\mathbf{m}' \circ h = \mathbf{m}$.

Remark 2.11. The mapping from $D\Sigma$-transformation systems to their underlying LTSs can be extended to a functor from the category of $D\Sigma$-transformation systems to the fibre of the category **LTS** of LTSs over the action set $\mathcal{P}(Act_{D\Sigma})$, i.e., the subcategory of all LTSs whose actions are given by the set $\mathcal{P}(Act_{D\Sigma})$.

2.2 Examples

In this section two examples are developed in order to show in more detail how systems or their parts can be modelled by transformation systems. Therefore some methodological distinctions are also discussed that are not reflected in the formal definitions. For example, very often data states are defined as mutable extensions of some fixed static data types designated by some subsignature Σ_0 of the data signature Σ, or control states are obtained as abstractions of data states in the sense that the definition of a specific constant or function for instance characterises the data state w.r.t. a given static data type. This constant or function can then be used to represent the whole data state and serve in this way as a control state. Concepts like these have not been included in the formal definitions in order to keep the theory logically clear and maintainable. Moreover, these methodological distinctions need not be valid for all applications. For example, in a radical object-oriented approach *nothing is static.* Furthermore, control states may also contain more information than their underlying data states, in cases where the control flow information is not encoded in (or deducible from) the data states (cf. Example 2.13).

In the first example a part of a simplified version of a class of linked lists is modelled, following the presentation in [Mey88] where a corresponding class is implemented in the object-oriented programming language Eiffel. The second example presents a model for the CCS specification of the sender component of the alternating bit protocol given in [Mil89] as a transformation system. In addition to the dynamic behaviour modelling, the transformation system makes explicit the inherent data state structure. Since CCS has full formal semantics, given in terms of LTSs, in this case also a formal comparison between the CCS semantics and the corresponding transformation system can be achieved by restricting the latter to the underlying LTS, i.e., by abstracting from the data states again.

Example 2.12 (Linked Lists). Linked lists are constructed by connecting linkable cells that contain the data elements and pointers to other cells for their dynamic connection. To handle lists efficiently four designated list pointers are introduced, pointing to the first and actual cell of a list, and the predecessor and successor of the actual position respectively (cf. [Mey88], p. 184 ff.). The actual cell pointer thus serves as a list cursor. The end of a list is marked by a void cell that contains neither a data element nor a pointer (see Figure 2.4).

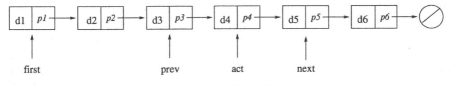

Fig. 2.4. A linked list

In the data space signature *linked-list* given below, sorts for data, pointers, and cells are introduced, with constructors for cells given by a binary constructor and a constant *void*, and the four list pointers. Note that the binary cell constructor is partial, which allows us to have in each state only the cells that are actually used in the list. Corresponding to the binary constructor there are two (partial) projections (destructors) *fst* and *snd* to data and pointers, and the cells can be tested for being not void. The values of the pointers are obtained by the partial dereferencing function !. Finally a derived function *right* is introduced that returns the right neighbour of a cell in the actual list, if it is defined. (All the informal semantic explanations given so far are made precise in the formal definition of the model following below.) Then two elementary actions are declared, both without parameters. A *move* action moves the list cursor one position to the right, or to the first position if the actual position is the last one in the list. With the second action the actual cell of the list is deleted. In both cases the list structure has to be rearranged to obtain a consistent setting of all pointers again, as described in the formal semantic definitions below.

> **linked-list =**
> **sorts** data, pointer, cell
> **funs** void: $\rightarrow$ cell
> $\langle \_, \_ \rangle$: data, pointer $\rightarrow$ cell
> fst: cell $\rightarrow$ data
> snd: cell $\rightarrow$ pointer
> nonvoid: cell
> first, prev, act, next: $\rightarrow$ pointer
> !: pointer $\rightarrow$ cell
> right: cell $\rightarrow$ cell
> **acts** move, delete: λ

To develop the formal model, i.e., the desired *linked-list*-transformation system, first the data state signature is decomposed into a static and a mutable part. The first one contains the parts that never change, like the data set and the set of list pointers. (Also the set of pointers could vary dynamically. It is modelled as a fixed set here, e.g., the set of all possible addresses, to keep the example smaller.) Let the static subsignature Σ_{ll}^{static} be accordingly defined by the sorts *data* and *pointer*, and the constants *first*, *prev*, *act*, and *next*. Let L be a Σ_{ll}^{static}-algebra with $L_{data} = D$, $L_{pointer} = P$, for some given sets D and P, and $first^L = f, prev^L = p, act^L = a, next^L = n$ for some fixed elements $f, p, a, n \in P$.

The remaining parts of the *linked-list* data signature are the ones that constitute the mutable part of the states. These parts are determined by the dereferencing function that yields the actual values of the pointers and thereby defines an *environment*. Depending on the environment also the set of cells changes dynamically. The void cell is always present, but a cell $\langle d, q \rangle$ is only present if it is referenced by a pointer.

An environment for the algebra L is given by a partial function $e : P \dashrightarrow (D \times P) \cup \{\oslash\}$ that satisfies the following consistency properties.

1. The list pointers always have a value (which, however, might also be *void*):

$$\{f, p, a, n\} \subseteq dom(e) .$$

2. If a points to the first cell, then p is void, and vice versa:

$$e(a) = e(f) \text{ iff } e(p) = \oslash .$$

3. The value of a is the right neighbour of the value of p, if this is not void, and vice versa:

$$e(\pi_2(e(p))) = e(a) \text{ iff } e(p) \neq \oslash$$

(where π_2 denotes the second projection, i.e., $\pi_2(\langle d, q \rangle) = q$).

4. The value of n is the right neighbour of the value of a:

$$e(\pi_2(e(a))) = e(n) \text{ if } e(a) \neq \oslash .$$

The value of n might be void, indicating that the actual position is the last one.

5. As opposed to the original model in [Mey88] the actual position is required to be within the list whenever there is at least one cell in it, i.e., it must not be *offleft* or *offright*. This restriction saves some case distinctions and is only imposed to make the example a little shorter:

$$e(a) \neq \oslash, \text{ or } e(x) = \oslash \text{ for all } x \in dom(e) .$$

6. The other pointers are set in such a way that the cells yield a list of finite length ending in a void cell, and the four designated pointers are not used in the list:

$$\exists\, p_1,\ldots,p_r,q_1,\ldots,q_s \in dom(e) - \{f,p,a,n\},\ (r,s \geq 0)$$
$$\pi_2(e(p_i)) = p_{i+1}\ (i = 1,\ldots,r-1),$$
$$\pi_2(e(q_j)) = q_{j+1}\ (j = 1,\ldots,s-1),$$
$$\pi_2(e(f)) = p_1,\quad \pi_2(e(a)) = q_1,$$
$$e(p_{r-1}) = e(p),\quad e(p_r) = e(a),$$
$$e(q_1) = e(n),\quad e(q_s) = \oslash.$$

Let Env be the set of all environments for L.

Environments represent the relevant information contents of the states. The other parts of the data states are either static or can be deduced from the actual definition of the environment, like the set of cells existing in a state or the right neighbour function. Therefore environments are also used to represent the control states, at least in the part of the model dealing only with the move actions. (To model the delete action further control flow information will be added, which cannot be derived from the data states.)

The part $\mathbf{LL}^{move} = (TG_{\mathbf{LL}}^{move}, \mathbf{ll}^{move})$ of the *linked-list* transformation system that models the *move* steps can now be defined. The complete system $\mathbf{LL}$ will then be given by the union of $\mathbf{LL}^{move}$ with the delete part $\mathbf{LL}^{del}$ defined below (compare Example 5.14). As mentioned above, the control states of $\mathbf{LL}^{move}$ are defined by

- $CS_{\mathbf{LL}}^{move} = Env \cup \{\Delta\}$,

where Δ is the additional initialisation state.

The definition of the transitions $T_{\mathbf{LL}}^{move}$ for the *move* action formalises the consistent stepwise movement of the list cursor (see Figure 2.5). The set $T_{\mathbf{LL}}^{move}(e,e')$ with $e,e' \in Env$ contains an element *move* if the following conditions hold.

- If $e(n) \neq \oslash$ then

$$e'(p) = e(a)$$
$$e'(a) = e(n)$$
$$e'(n) = e(\pi_2(e(n)))$$
$$e'(x) = e(x) \qquad \text{for all } x \in dom(e) - \{p,a,n\}.$$

- If $e(n) = \oslash$ and $e(p) \neq \oslash$ then

$$e'(p) = \oslash$$
$$e'(a) = e(f)$$
$$e'(n) = e(\pi_2(e(f)))$$
$$e'(x) = e(x) \qquad \text{for all } x \in dom(e) - \{p,a,n\}.$$

- If $e(n) = e(p) = \oslash$ then $e' = e$.
  (The list contains at most one element.)
- If $e(a) = \oslash$ then $e' = e$.
  (The list is empty.)

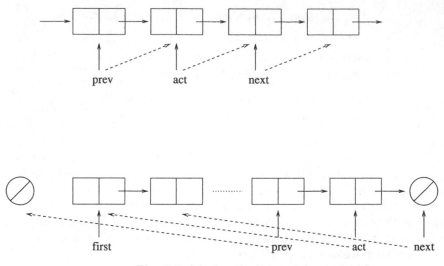

Fig. 2.5. Moving the list cursor

Furthermore

$$idle \in T_{\mathbf{LL}}^{move}(e,e)\,,\ T_{\mathbf{LL}}^{move}(\Delta,e) = \{enter\}\,,\ T_{\mathbf{LL}}^{move}(e,\Delta) = \{leave\}$$

for all $e \in Env$. That means there are the required idle transitions and the *move* model can be entered and left in any state.

The data states $L[e] = \mathbb{ll}^{move}(e)$ belonging to the control states $e \in Env$ are given by the extensions of the partial Σ_{ll}^{static}-algebra L to the complete data signature Σ_{ll} of *linked-list* as follows.

- The set of cells is given by the actual values of all pointers and the void cell:

$$L[e]_{cell} = \{\langle d,q \rangle \in D \times P \mid \exists q' \in dom(e)\,.\,e(q') = \langle d,q \rangle\} \cup \{\oslash\}\,.$$

- The cell constructors and destructors are defined accordingly:

$$
\begin{aligned}
void^{L[e]} &= \oslash \\
\langle\_,\_\rangle^{L[e]}(d,q) &= \langle d,q \rangle \quad \text{if } \langle d,q \rangle \in L[e]_{cell} \\
fst^{L[e]}(\langle d,q \rangle) &= d \\
snd^{L[e]}(\langle d,q \rangle) &= q \\
nonvoid^{L[e]}(\langle d,q \rangle) &
\end{aligned}
$$

for all $\langle d,q \rangle \in L[e]_{cell}$. The domains of the partial functions are given implicitly here. In particular, the predicate $nonvoid^{L[e]}$ holds for all pairs $\langle d,q \rangle \in L[e]_{cell}$; and it does not hold for $\oslash$.

- The dereferencing function is given by the environment itself:

$$!^{L[e]} = e .$$

- The right neighbour of a cell is the value of its pointer:

$$right^{L[e]}(\langle d, p \rangle) = e(p) \text{ if } p \in dom(e) .$$

The data state $ll^{move}(\Delta)$ is the empty partial Σ_{ll}-algebra by definition. Finally the actions and tracking relations are given by

- $act^{ll^{move}}_{move} = \{move\}$

  $act^{ll^{move}}_{idle} = act^{ll^{move}}_{enter} = act^{ll^{move}}_{leave} = \emptyset$

- $\sim^{ll^{move}}_{move} = (id_D, id_P, id_{L[e]_{cell} \cap L[e']_{cell}})$

  $\sim^{ll^{move}}_{idle} = (id_D, id_P, id_{L[e]_{cell}})$

  $\sim^{ll^{move}}_{enter} = \sim^{ll^{move}}_{leave} = \emptyset$

This means that the tracking relation is given by the identity on the static data type part (D and P) and the cells that exist before and after the step. This concludes the definition of the transition graph morphism $ll^{move} : TG^{move}_{LL} \rightarrow I\!\!D_{linked\_list}$, and thus of the transformation system $\mathbf{LL}^{move}$.

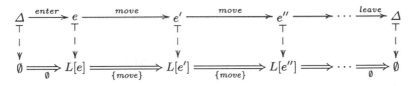

Fig. 2.6. A path in the *move* model

The paths in the *move* model represent the continuous movement of the cursor through the list (see Figure 2.6). The idea of the representation of the *delete* method is to allow only single deletion steps, i.e., after having deleted the actual cell no further step is possible. (This yields a *safer* model; deleting the whole list by pressing the delete button too long is prevented. Each deletion step has to be triggered explicitly by entering the delete model anew.) For that purpose the control states are enriched by *start* and *stop* flags; a *delete* step can only start in a *start* state and leads to a *stop* state. The control states of the *linked-list* transformation system $\mathbf{LL}^{del} = (TG^{del}_{LL}, ll^{del})$ modelling the deletion part are accordingly given by

- $CS^{del}_{LL} = (\{start, stop\} \times Env) \cup \{\Delta\} .$

The transitions are defined according to the four cases of the actual position (see Figure 2.7, showing the first three cases). This means $del \in T_{LL}^{del}(\langle s, e \rangle, \langle s', e' \rangle)$ iff the following conditions hold.

- $s = start$ and $s' = stop$.
- If $e(a) = e(f)$ and $e(n) \neq \oslash$ then

$$
\begin{aligned}
e'(f) &= e(n) \\
e'(a) &= e(n) \\
e'(n) &= right^{L[e]}(e(n)) \\
e'(x) &= e(x) \qquad \text{for all } x \in dom(e) - \{f, a, n\} \ .
\end{aligned}
$$

- If $e(a) \neq e(f)$ and $e(n) \neq \oslash$ then

$$
\begin{aligned}
e'(snd^{l[e]}(e(p))) &= e(n) \\
e'(a) &= e(n) \\
e'(n) &= right^{L[e]}(e(n)) \\
e'(x) &= e(x) \\
&\text{for all } x \in dom(e) - \{snd^{l[e]}(e(p)), a, n\} \ .
\end{aligned}
$$

- If $e(a) \neq e(f)$ and $e(n) = \oslash$ then

$$
\begin{aligned}
e'(snd^{l[e]}(e(p))) &= \oslash \\
e'(a) &= \oslash \\
e'(x) &= e(x) \ \text{ for all } x \in dom(e) - \{snd^{l[e]}(e(p)), a\} \ .
\end{aligned}
$$

- If $e(a) = e(f)$ and $e(n) = \oslash$ then

$$
e'(x) = \oslash \text{ for all } x \in dom(e) \ .
$$

The idle transitions are given by

- $idle \in T_{LL}^{del}(\langle s, e \rangle, \langle s, e \rangle)$

and the initialisations and finalisations are given by

- $enter \in T_{LL}^{del}(\Delta, \langle start, e \rangle)$
- $leave \in T_{LL}^{del}(\langle stop, e \rangle, \Delta)$

for all $e \in Env$.

The data states are defined as in the *move* model; the *start* and *stop* flags do not affect the data state, nor are they reflected in it. Also the actions and tracking relations are defined analogously.

- $ll^{del}(\langle s, e \rangle) = L[e]$
- $act_{del}^{ll^{del}} = \{delete\}$

$$
act_{idle}^{ll^{del}} = act_{enter}^{ll^{del}} = act_{leave}^{ll^{del}} = \emptyset
$$

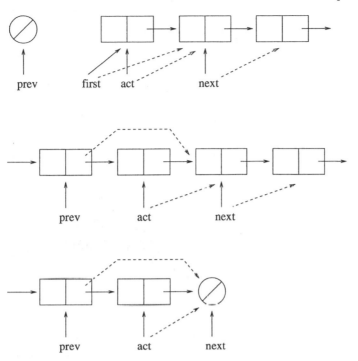

Fig. 2.7. The deletion of the actual cell

- $\sim_{del}^{\mathbf{ll^{del}}} = (id_D, id_P, id_{L[e]_{cell} \cup L[e']_{cell}})$

  $\sim_{idle}^{\mathbf{ll^{del}}} = (id_D, id_P, id_{L[e]_{cell}})$

  $\sim_{enter}^{\mathbf{ll^{del}}} = \sim_{leave}^{\mathbf{ll^{del}}} = \emptyset$

This completes the definition of the *delete* part $\mathbf{LL}^{del}$ of the model. The complete model $\mathbf{LL} = (TG_{\mathbf{LL}}, \mathbf{ll})$ is then given by the union of the transition graphs and label functions of $\mathbf{LL}^{move}$ and $\mathbf{LL}^{del}$ respectively.

(More powerful composition operations for transformation models are introduced in Example 4.29. The implementation of more complex list operations in terms of the basic ones defined here is discussed in Chapter 4.)

Example 2.13 (The CCS Sender Specification). The sender component of the alternating bit protocol accepts messages to send them safely via a faulty channel to a receiver at the other end of the channel (see Figure 2.8). For that purpose the message is coupled with a control bit and stored and sent repeatedly until its receipt is acknowledged by the receiver by sending back the control bit. The next message is then equipped with the toggled bit.

The behaviour of the sender can be formally described by specifying the temporal order of its basic actions, as in the following CCS specification of the sender agent S (cf. [Mil89], p. 144):

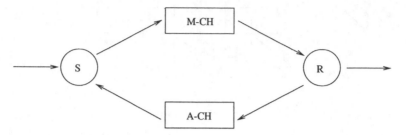

Fig. 2.8. The architecture of the alternating bit protocol

$$S \quad = S_{0,d_0}$$
$$S_{b,d} = \overline{send}(b,d).S'_{b,d}$$
$$S'_{b,d} = \tau.S_{b,d} + \ ack(b).accept(x).S_{\neg b,x} + \ ack(\neg b).S'_{b,d} \ .$$

The two indexed symbols $S_{b,d}$ and $S'_{b,d}$ denote the possible states of the sender, and are used in the CCS-equation system as recursion variables. The combinators $\_.\_$ (action prefix) and $\_+\_$ (choice) denote sequential composition and non-deterministic choice; τ is an internal action. The specification describes that in state $S_{b,d}$ the sender can send the pair (b, d) and then behave as in state $S'_{b,d}$, where it can either return to the preceding state (modelling a time-out) or read a bit from the acknowledgement channel. Depending on its value the sender either accepts the next message and toggles its bit, or it remains in the state, ignoring the bit because it must have been a false one. The sender starts with bit 0 and some given message d_0.

The process specification calculus CCS has two graphical descriptions of an agent or process. The first one shows its static structure, given by the ports of the agent through which it can communicate with the environment. Reading and writing at these ports, denoted by $port(x)$ and $\overline{port}(x)$ respectively, yields the agent's basic actions. The static structure of the sender for instance is shown in Figure 2.9.

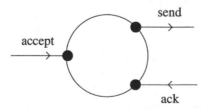

Fig. 2.9. The static structure of the sender

The behaviour of an agent is represented as an LTS whose transitions are labelled by the agent's actions. (The behaviour of the sender is shown in Figure 2.10.) These LTSs define the operational semantics of CCS, and are obtained via a deduction system for transitions (= labelled pairs) of process expressions.

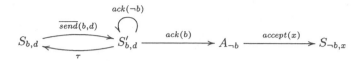

Fig. 2.10. The behaviour of the sender

In CCS the indexes of the state variables as well as the parameters of the actions are considered as abbreviations for sets of variables and actions (whose cardinality thus depends on the cardinality of the index and the parameter sets; usually these are therefore assumed to be finite). The formal semantics is defined only for non-parameterised agents and actions.

The basic idea of interpreting this sender specification as a transformation system $\mathbf{CCS}_S$ is to take the same transition system, but make the data states explicit. That means the indexes of the state variables are used to derive the data signature. In this case the messages are taken from an arbitrary set, whereas the control bits are boolean values with a toggle operation, i.e., negation.

In the action signature also the parameters of the actions are made explicit. The internal time-out action will be modelled by a transition with the empty set as action label. The data space signature $CCS\text{-}S$ is thus given by

CCS-S =
   sorts message, bool
   funs t, f: $\to$ bool
          $\neg$: bool $\to$ bool
          cbit: $\to$ bool
          msg: $\to$ message
   acts send: bool, message
         ack: bool
         accept: message

The sorts *message* and *bool*, and the boolean functions t, f, and $\neg$, yield the static subsignature $\Sigma^{static}_{CCS\text{-}S}$. The constants *cbit* and *msg* are mutable and yield the actual values of the control bit and the currently stored message. To formalise this let DB be a $\Sigma^{static}_{CCS\text{-}S}$-algebra with $DB_{message} = D$ for some set D, $DB_{bool} = I\!\!B = \{0,1\}$, and the usual interpretation of t,f, and $\neg$. For each $d \in D$ and $b \in I\!\!B$ the extensions $DB[b,d]$ and $DB[b]$ of DB to partial $\Sigma_{CCS\text{-}S}$-algebras are defined by

$$cbit^{DB[b,d]} = b , \quad msg^{DB[b,d]} = d , \quad \text{and} \quad cbit^{DB[b]} = b .$$

In the state $DB[b]$ the constant *msg* is not defined, i.e., there is currently no message stored.

As transition graph $TG_{\mathbf{CCS}_S}$ of the transformation system $\mathbf{CCS}_S = (TG_{\mathbf{CCS}_S}, \mathbf{ccs}_S)$ the underlying graph of the LTS given by the operational CCS-semantics of the specification above is taken, extended by idle transitions and an initialisation state Δ as in Example 2.12. That means the control states of $TG_{\mathbf{CCS}_S}$ are given by the set

$$
\begin{aligned}
CS_S = \quad & \{S_{b,d} \mid b \in \mathbb{B}, d \in D\} \\
\cup\, & \{S'_{b,d} \mid b \in \mathbb{B}, d \in D\} \\
\cup\, & \{A_b \mid b \in \mathbb{B}\} \\
\cup\, & \{\Delta\}
\end{aligned}
$$

(i.e., two copies of $\mathbb{B} \times D$, one copy of $\mathbb{B}$, and $\{\Delta\}$).

The data states are associated via

$$
\begin{aligned}
\mathbf{ccs}_S(S_{b,d}) = \mathbf{ccs}_S(S'_{b,d}) &= DB[b,d] \\
\mathbf{ccs}_S(A_b) &= DB[b] \\
\mathbf{ccs}_S(\Delta) &= \emptyset
\end{aligned}
$$

for all $b \in \mathbb{B}$ and $d \in D$. Note that the control states $S_{b,d}$ and $S'_{b,d}$ have the same underlying data states, but different communication/action capabilities as shown in the transition graph. This shows again how the separation of transition graph and data spaces saves encodings of the control flow information in the data states.

To define the transitions and their action labels the shorter notation $t : c \to d \mapsto act_t^{\mathbf{m}}$ is used. (That means, for example, for any $b \in \mathbb{B}$ and $d \in D$, $send_{b,d} : S_{b,d} \to S'_{b,d} \in T_{\mathbf{CCS}_S}$ and $act^{\mathbf{ccs}}_{send(b,d)} = \{send(b,d)\}$.)

$$
\begin{aligned}
send_{b,d} &: S_{b,d} \to S'_{b,d} &&\mapsto & \{send(b,d)\} \\
ack_b &: S'_{b,d} \to A_{\neg b} &&\mapsto & \{ack(b)\} \\
ack_b &: S'_{b,d} \to S'_{b,d} &&\mapsto & \{ack(b)\} \\
accept_d &: A_b \to S_{b,d} &&\mapsto & \{accept(d)\} \\
time\_out &: S'_{b,d} \to S_{b,d} &&\mapsto & \emptyset \\
init_{d_0} &: \Delta \to S_{0,d_0} &&\mapsto & \emptyset \\
idle &: x \to x &&\mapsto & \emptyset \quad (\text{for all } x \in CS_S)
\end{aligned}
$$

for each $b \in \mathbb{B}, d, d_0 \in D$. The tracking relations are the identities on the static data types $\mathbb{B}$ and D, and the empty relation for the $init$ transitions.

By definition the underlying LTS of $\mathbf{CCS}_S$ coincides (up to isomorphism and extension by the idle transitions) with its CCS-semantics, i.e., the transformation system semantics are a conservative extension.

As this example shows, infinite sets of control states are often due to infinitely many possible data values. In the *abstract object systems* introduced in [Web97, LW98] for example, finite state systems are used for the pure control and data states and actions are attached by taking the cartesian product to reflect this distinction. Since the number of data states is not restricted this may yield infinitely many states and transitions again, as in the example above. Using such pairs as control states and transitions (in the sense of transformation systems) and the projection to the data states and actions as label functions embeds these abstract object systems into the transformation system approach.

In Figure 2.11 the corresponding finite state system of the pure control and data parts are shown separately. Note, however, that the full cartesian product of the two systems contains states and transitions that are not allowed in the CCS-sender. This means an appropriate subsystem has to be taken that reflects the dependencies between the control and data states.

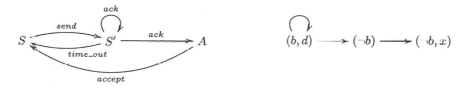

Fig. 2.11. Finite state control system and data states of the sender

2.3 Data Spaces from Other Specification Frameworks

Partial algebras have been used as data state models because of their adequacy and generality. Total algebras are obviously a special case of partial algebras, and first-order structures are subsumed because predicates can be considered as partial functions to a singleton set (see Appendix A). Beyond the partial functions that already occur in static data types, partiality in the context of dynamic systems with state also allows the separation of the *declaration* of an entity in the signature from its *initialisation* during runtime. In the states before its (semantic) initialisation the (syntactic) symbol remains undefined in the partial algebras representing these states. Defining it in some first state corresponds to its initialisation.

Nevertheless in some cases it might be useful to consider other data state models, incorporating for example order-sortedness, topological structures on the carrier sets, higher order types, or structures that represent collections of entities instead of single ones (cf. Section 2.4). To support such modifications transformation systems can be made generic w.r.t. the kind of data type models used. For that purpose the formalisation of the notion of a logical framework as *institution* as introduced in [BG77, GB84, GB92] is used.

An institution $I = (\mathbf{Sig}, Sen, Mod, \models)$ is given by

- a category **Sig** of *signatures*,
- a *sentence* functor $Sen : \mathbf{Sig} \to \mathbf{Set}$,

- a *model* functor $Mod : \mathbf{Sig} \to \mathbf{Cat}^{op}$, and
- a family of *satisfaction relations* $\models_\Sigma \subseteq |Mod(\Sigma)| \times Sen(\Sigma)$ that satisfies the *satisfaction condition*

$$M' \models_{\Sigma'} Sen(\sigma)(\varphi) \text{ iff } Mod(\sigma)(M') \models_\Sigma \varphi$$

for all $M' \in |Mod(\Sigma')|$, $\varphi \in Sen(\Sigma)$, and $\sigma : \Sigma \to \Sigma'$ in $\mathbf{Sig}$.

Usually the functors $Mod(\sigma)$ are called *forgetful functors* and are denoted by $Mod(\sigma) = V_\sigma$. Furthermore, signature morphisms σ and the corresponding sentence mappings $Sen(\sigma)$ are often identified notationally, i.e. $Sen(\sigma) = \sigma$. With this notation, the satisfaction condition looks as follows:

$$M' \models_{\Sigma'} \sigma(\varphi) \text{ iff } V_\sigma(M') \models_\Sigma \varphi .$$

To define actions and tracking relations for transformations of data state models in other data institutions the models cannot be entirely abstract, but must at least provide elements. Institutions whose models are based on carrier sets, like all the fragments and extensions of first- or higher order logic structures, are called *concrete institutions* (following [BT96]). As a technical precondition for their formal definition consider first sorted sets defined as follows. The functor $SSet : \mathbf{Set} \to \mathbf{Cat}^{op}$ is defined by mapping each set S to the category $SSet(S) = \mathbf{Set}^S$ of S-sorted sets and functions, and mapping each function $f : S \to S'$ to the forgetful functor

- $V_f : \mathbf{Set}^{S'} \to \mathbf{Set}^S$

given by

- $V_f((M'_{s'})_{s' \in S'}) = (M'_{f(s)})_{s \in S}$
  $V_f((h'_{s'})_{s' \in S'}) = (h'_{f(s)})_{s \in S} .$

A concrete institution $I = (\mathbf{Sig}, Sen, Mod, \models, sorts, |\_|)$ is given by an institution $(\mathbf{Sig}, Sen, Mod, \models)$ and

- a functor $sorts : \mathbf{Sig} \to \mathbf{Set}$, and
- a natural transformation $|\_| : Mod \Rightarrow SSet \circ sorts$, i.e., a family of functors $|\_|_\Sigma : Mod(\Sigma) \to \mathbf{Set}^{sorts(\Sigma)}$ such that

$$|\_|_\Sigma \circ V_\sigma = V_{sorts(\sigma)} \circ |\_|_{\Sigma'}$$

for all $\sigma : \Sigma \to \Sigma'$ in $\mathbf{Sig}$.

Concreteness means that each signature comes with a set of sort names, and each model is equipped with a corresponding family of sets, called the carrier sets of the model. Naturality of the carrier set assignment implies that the forgetful functors V_σ act on the carrier sets like the forgetful functors of sorted sets.

In an arbitrary concrete institution transformation signatures and actions can be defined as before, replacing algebraic signatures by signatures of the

institution and partial algebras by the corresponding models. A further useful
generalisation is obtained by replacing the construction of actions. For example, further components like boolean guards or a distinction between events
and actions could be added, or there could be algebraic operations on actions
like sequential composition. For the definition of a transformation system yet
no further properties of these constructions are required, except that they can
be expressed as functors.

Definition 2.14 (Specification Framework). *Let $Ins = (\mathbf{Sig}, Sen, Mod, \models$
$, sorts, |\_|)$ be a concrete institution.*

- *A* data space signature $D\Sigma = (\Sigma, A)$ *w.r.t. Ins is given by a signature*
  $\Sigma \in |\mathbf{Sig}|$ *and an $S^* \times S^*$-indexed set $A = (A_{w,w'})_{w,w' \in S^*}$, where $S = sorts(\Sigma)$.*
- *An* action structure AS *w.r.t. Ins is given by a family of functors*

$$AS_{D\Sigma} : \mathbf{Set}^S \times \mathbf{Set}^S \to \mathbf{Set}$$

  for each data space signature $D\Sigma = (\Sigma, A)$, where $S = sorts(\Sigma)$.

A specification framework for transformation systems $I\!F = (Ins, AS, I, \epsilon)$ *is
given by a concrete institution Ins, an action structure AS w.r.t. Ins, a family
I of designated Σ-models $I_\Sigma \in |Mod(\Sigma)|$ for each signature Σ, and a family
of designated actions $\epsilon_{D\Sigma,C} \in AS_{D\Sigma}(|C|, |C|)$ for each data space signature
$D\Sigma = (\Sigma, A)$ and each model $C \in |Mod(\Sigma)|$.*

In this general setting transformation systems in an arbitrary concrete
data institution can be defined as follows.

Definition 2.15 (Transformation System). *Let $I\!F = (Ins, AS, I, \epsilon)$ be a
specification framework for transformation systems and $D\Sigma = (\Sigma, A)$ a data
space signature w.r.t. $I\!F$.*

- *Given Σ-models C, D the set of* transformations $Tf^{\boldsymbol{F}}_{D\Sigma}(C, D)$ *is defined
  by*
$$Tf^{\boldsymbol{F}}_{D\Sigma}(C, D) = AS_{D\Sigma}(|C|, |D|) \times Rel^S(|C|, |D|) \ .$$

- *The* data space

$$I\!D^{\boldsymbol{F}}_{D\Sigma} = (|\mathbf{Mod}(\Sigma)|, Tf^{\boldsymbol{F}}_{D\Sigma}, I_\Sigma, (\epsilon_{D\Sigma}, \Delta))$$

  *is the large transition graph given by the class $|\mathbf{Mod}(\Sigma)|$ as the class of
  control states, the set $Tf^{\boldsymbol{F}}_{D\Sigma}(C, D)$ as the set of transitions from C to D, I_Σ
  as the initialisation state, and $\epsilon_{D\Sigma,C}$ and the identity relation (diagonal)
  Δ_C as the idle transition for each control state C.*
- *A $D\Sigma$-transformation system $\mathbf{M} = (TG_{\mathbf{M}}, \mathbf{m})$ w.r.t. $I\!F$ is given by a
  transition graph $TG_{\mathbf{M}}$ and a transition graph morphism $\mathbf{m} : TG_{\mathbf{M}} \to
  I\!D^{\boldsymbol{F}}_{D\Sigma}$.*

- *The category $\mathbf{TF}^{F}(D\Sigma)$ of $D\Sigma$-transformation systems w.r.t. F is the comma category $\mathbf{TG} \downarrow D^{F}_{D\Sigma}$, where $\mathbf{TG}$ is the category of transition graphs as defined in Section 2.1.*

The empty partial algebra has been chosen as the initialisation state in Definition 2.6 since this state is considered as lying outside the model, i.e., there is no data state information. Moreover, the empty algebra is a unit w.r.t. composition of data states by colimits, as discussed in Chapter 5, because it is the initial partial algebra. That means, when composing a local data state with the (empty) data state of a component in its initialisation states, the local data state remains unchanged. (Take the union of partial algebras as an example: $A \cup \emptyset = A$.) Thus if an institution has initial models in all its model categories these should be taken as the initialisation state of the data spaces $D^{F}_{D\Sigma}$. As long as only signatures are considered, this requirement is not overly restrictive.

When different specification frameworks are used for the data spaces these have to be related of course in order to compare the corresponding transformation systems. Formally morphisms of specification frameworks would be required for this purpose. However, the definition of morphisms for institutions leads to broad ramifications (see [AC92, Cer93, CM93] and [WM97, MW98, MW99, Mar99] for a survey and a discussion of their relations). Thus in this book a more pragmatic solution is used in that all transformation systems are assumed to be defined w.r.t. a *maximal* specification framework that subsumes the other ones as special cases. Whenever specification frameworks other than partial algebras and action sets are considered the corresponding embedding is given.

2.4 Objects and Object References

In Example 2.12 a linked list has been modelled as an object whose state is given by the definition of a set of pointers connecting the cells. Reinterpreting this example in a more object-oriented style the cells also could be considered as objects. Their first attribute is the data value they store, and the second one a reference to another cell object with dereferencing given by the partial function !. In this way not only single objects but also systems given by sets of linked objects can be represented by transformation systems. In fact, many of the formal approaches to model object systems (like [Gro91, Bre91, Pie94]) are based on this idea of introducing sets of identifiers and (partial) dereferencing functions. The disadvantage of this approach, however, is that a relevant part of the structure—the object references and the dereferencing—is encoded in the data state structure. In particular, there are no objects in this approach. There are identifiers and a representation of object systems, but the single objects are not directly represented.

The purpose of this section is to discuss an extension of transformation systems, using the extension mechanism of employing another specification framework, in such a way that data states are states of object systems, i.e., sets of linked objects, but also single objects are still included as algebra transformation systems. That means the states of a single object are modelled as partial algebras as before, and the states of the object system are modelled as sets of algebras plus the linking information. In this approach objects have an identity, given via the tracking relations, that is different from and independent of any internal concept of referencing objects by identifiers or whatever. The basic idea is to represent the reference to objects by functions from corresponding carrier sets of the algebras representing the object's states to the set of all algebras, i.e., the state of the object system. This also makes explicit the hierarchical difference between object references as elements of algebras and object states as algebras.

Consider as an example the following *cell*-signature.

cell =
    sorts data, cell
    funs value: $\to$ data
            next: $\to$ cell
    acts change_value: data
            change_next: cell

The constants *value* and *next* correspond to the data value attribute and the next cell attribute respectively, where the latter is a reference to a cell object. With the *change_value* and *change_next* methods the data attribute and the next object reference of a cell object can be updated.

The state of a single cell object is thus represented by a partial Σ_{cell}-algebra, where Σ_{cell} is the data signature of *cell*. Let for example the algebras $C_k \in |\mathbf{PAlg}(\Sigma_{cell})|$, $(k \in \mathbb{Z})$, be defined by

- $(C_k)_{data} = \mathbb{Z}$, $(C_k)_{cell} = \{r\}$, $value^{C_k} = k$, $value^{C_k} = r$.

The data items in these algebras are integers, there is only one reference r in each object, the value of the data attribute is k, and the next object reference is r.

A *system snapshot* (= state of an object system) is then given by a family $\mathcal{C} = (C_i)_{i \in I}$ of partial Σ_{cell}-algebras and, for each member C_i of the family $\mathcal{C}$, a partial function $ref_i : (C_i)_{cell} \to I$. The reference function ref_i states which member of the family $\mathcal{C}$ the object reference $r \in (C_i)_{cell}$ refers to. (Taking sets $\mathcal{A}$ of algebras instead of families $\mathcal{C}$ in a system snapshot would yield the more intuitive functionality $ref_i : (C_i)_{cell} \to \mathcal{A}$ for the reference function, i.e., a reference would refer directly to an algebra instead of its index in the family. However, different objects may have the same state, whence sets cannot be employed for system snapshots.) In Figure 2.12 for example there are five objects

- $\mathcal{C} = (C_k)_{k \in \{2,4,6,8,20\}}$

and the links are given by

- $ref_2(r) = 4$ (the reference r of C_2 points to C_4.)
  $ref_4(r) = 6$
  $ref_6(r) = 8$
  $ref_8(r) = 20$
  $ref_{20} \quad = \emptyset$

This defines the system snapshot $\mathcal{O} = (\mathcal{C}, ref)$, with $ref = (ref_k)_{k \in \{2,4,6,8,20\}}$.

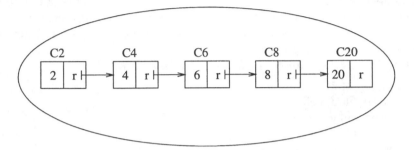

Fig. 2.12. A state of an object system with links given by object references

The general definition is given as follows.

Definition 2.16 (System Snapshot). *Let $D\Sigma = (\Sigma, A)$ with $\Sigma = (S, F)$ be a data space signature with designated set $CS \subseteq S$ of class sorts. A system snapshot $\mathcal{O} = (\mathcal{C}, ref)$ is given by a family $\mathcal{C} = (C_i)_{i \in I}$ of partial Σ-algebras C_i and a family $ref = (ref_{i,cs})_{i \in I, cs \in CS}$ of partial functions $ref_{i,cs} : (C_i)_{cs} \longrightarrow I$.*

System snapshots yield the institution of data states for *snapshot* transformation systems as models of object systems. The single object states can be obtained from a system snapshot by selecting the corresponding index $i \in I$, $\mathcal{O} \mapsto C_i$. Conversely, each algebra transformation system can be considered as a snapshot transformation system with a single object and without object references. (That means $CS = \emptyset$ and $I = \{i_0\}$ in each state.) The extension to snapshot systems thus comprises algebra transformation systems in the sense discussed above.

A step, i.e., a transformation of a system snapshot, is given as before by a pair of system snapshots $(\mathcal{O}, \mathcal{O}')$, a tracking relation, and a set of actions. The tracking relation is given here by a relation $\approx$ on the index sets I and I', and for each pair $i \approx i'$ of related indexes a tracking relation $\sim_{i,i'} \subseteq |C_i| \times |C'_{i'}|$ of the corresponding algebras as before. (This would be formalised by the underlying sorts $|\mathcal{O}|$ in the corresponding concrete institution.) The actions must be associated to one object of the system, because only objects can execute methods and it must be clear which one executes the method concerned. Consider for example the snapshot $\mathcal{O}' = (\mathcal{C}', ref')$ with $\mathcal{C}' = (C_k)_{k \in \{2,4,8,16\}}$ and the links

- $ref'_2(r) = 4$
  $ref'_4(r) = 8$
  $ref'_8(r) = 16$
  $ref'_{16} = \emptyset$

as shown in the lower part of Figure 2.13. The step from $\mathcal{O}$ to $\mathcal{O}'$ could model the deletion of C_6 in the state $\mathcal{O}$ and changing the value of C_{20} to 16. The former would be given by setting the link of C_4 to C_8 and removing C_6. This behaviour is expressed by the transformation $\mathcal{O} \Rightarrow \mathcal{O}'$ with tracking relation

- $\approx \; = \{\langle 2,2\rangle, \langle 4,4\rangle, \langle 8,8\rangle, \langle 20,16\rangle\} \subseteq I \times I'$
  $\sim \; = (id_{\mathbb{Z}}, id_{\{r\}}) \subseteq |C_k| \times |C_{k'}|$

and the action set

- $\{C_4.change\_next(8), C_{20}.change\_value(16)\}$.

The parameters of the actions are given—as for algebra transformation systems—by elements of the carrier sets that now also contain the index sets of the system snapshots.

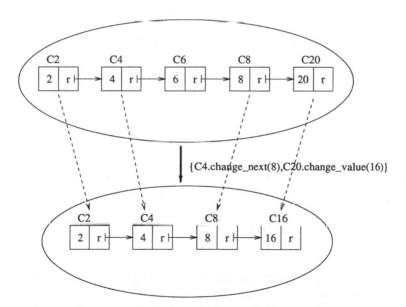

Fig. 2.13. A transformation of a system snapshot

The tracking relations on the index sets yield the object identities as equivalence classes, as in the D-oid approach [AZ93, AZ95]. These are clearly different from and independent of the object references, i.e., the elements of the class sorts. There may be objects that cannot be accessed (garbage), different objects may have different knowledge or views of the configuration, represented by their individual class sorts and reference functions, and objects might always have the same values without ever being the same.

System snapshots with links immediately yield an extension of the usual algebraic definition of terms (variables, constants, function applications) by a dot notation for object references. That means

- if $\quad o : cs \in Term \quad$ is a term of a class sort cs
  and $\quad t : s \in Term \quad$ is any term
  then $\quad o.t : s \in Term \quad$ is also a term.

The term $o.t$ denotes the element which is denoted by t in the algebra the object reference o points to. To evaluate $o.t$ in a system snapshot $\mathcal{O} = (\mathcal{C}, ref)$ w.r.t. an object (algebra) $C_i \in \mathcal{C}$ first o is evaluated in C_i. This yields a reference $o^{C_i} \in (C_i)_{cs}$, i.e., an element of one of the class sorts of C_i. This refers to an object/algebra $ref_i(o^{C_i})$, where the term t can be evaluated. If t is itself a dot term the first step is repeated, until finally an algebra and a dot-free term are reached.

This evaluation procedure is reflected in the following definition.

Definition 2.17 (Evaluation of Dot Terms). *Let $\mathcal{O} = (\mathcal{C}, ref)$ be a system snapshot and τ be a term according to the definition above. The evaluation $\tau^{\mathcal{O},i}$ of τ in $\mathcal{O}$ in the context of an object $C_i \in \mathcal{C}$ is defined by*

$$\tau^{\mathcal{O},i} = \tau^{C_i} \qquad \text{if } \tau \text{ is dot free,}$$
$$\tau^{\mathcal{O},i} = \bar{\tau}^{\mathcal{O},ref_i(o^{C_i})} \ \text{if } \tau = o.\bar{\tau} .$$

In the system snapshot $\mathcal{O}$ of the cell signature for example we have

- $(next.next.value)^{\mathcal{O},4} = 8$

because

- $next^{C_4} = r, ref_4(r) = 6, next^{C_6} = r, ref_6(r) = 8, value^{C_8} = 8 .$

This dot notation thus allows us to navigate along links in system snapshots. It may be used for example to express constraints on object systems like the data invariants of OCL [WK98], such as

- $next.value \leq 2 * value .$

(Constraints and specification means for transformation systems in general are introduced in the next chapter.)

Correspondingly, the parameter of the action $change\_next(8)$ in the transformation $\mathcal{O} \Rightarrow \mathcal{O}'$ in the context of C_4 above can be denoted by the term $next.next$, which yields the action term $4.change\_next(next.next)$ to denote this part of the transformation.

Without working out the details it should have become clear how object systems can be modelled formally in this way as transformation systems with an appropriate specification framework. A more complete presentation is developed in [Par01].

2.5 Discussion

The idea of the construction of transformation systems has been to use simple and well-investigated domains to model the different aspects of a system, and to integrate these domains appropriately to obtain one synthesised domain for integrated system models. The relevant aspects of a system are its static structure, i.e., the structure of its data states and its actions, and its dynamic behaviour. These are formally represented by partial algebras and action sets for the static part and transition systems for the dynamic part. Concerning the static part, data states and transformations can also be represented more generally by abstract data type models of another institution and other action structures than plain sets of actions. The appropriate integration of these two domains is given by labelling the states and transitions of the transition graph by data states and transformations. Methodologically, the control states may thereby be obtained as appropriate abstractions of the data states, containing only the information of the data states that is relevant for the control flow. The corresponding data states might then be reconstructed, for instance as free constructions w.r.t. the control state information. (Cf. Example 2.7 and the *move* part of the linked-list example 2.12.) But the control states may also contain further specific control flow information (as in the *delete* part of the linked-list example and the sender model in Example 2.13) that is not reflected in the data state. In this case different control states may have the same underlying data state. On the other hand, there must not be different data states associated to one control state, i.e., the (abstract) information in the latter must be sufficient to recover the data state by means of the label function. However, relations between (finite state) transition systems and (infinite) data states can also be realised in this framework by using pairs of pure control states in this sense and data states as control states in the sense of transformation systems. The labelling function is then given by the corresponding projection. (Cf. the discussion at the end of Section 2.2.)

Very often the definition of the data space and the transition graph are very closely related. It might happen for example that the set of control states is the same as the set of data states and the state labelling is given by the identical function. An embedding of the states-as-algebras approaches into the transformation system framework yields control states and data state labellings of this kind (the embedding is discussed below, on page 61). But also in this extreme case it is important to distinguish the two levels due to the different roles of the transition graphs on the one hand and the data spaces on the other hand. The former only state the existence of states and transitions that can be accessed but not inspected, whereas the latter show the internal structure. A partial algebra for example can be inspected by evaluating terms and equations. This difference becomes evident when morphisms of transformation systems are considered (in particular when development relations and composition operations are defined based on these morphisms, as in the following chapters). At the transition graph level states and transitions can be mapped to arbitrary states and transitions of the other graph, independently of how they are defined or constructed, as long as the graph structure is preserved. At the data space level, however, structure must be preserved. In the morphisms defined above (Definition 2.10) the underlying algebras must even coincide; in the generalisation in Definition 5.27 in Chapter 5 they must at least be related by homomorphisms, i.e., structure preserving mappings. To give an extreme example: suppose A and B are algebras that are used as control states in transformation systems $\mathbf{M}$ and $\mathbf{N}$ respectively. (This is at least not forbidden.) Then it is possible to map A to B if the data states $\mathbf{m}(A)$ and $\mathbf{n}(B)$ coincide, which does not depend on A and B but only on $\mathbf{m}$ and $\mathbf{n}$.

The integration of the two semantic domains of partial algebras with action sets and transition systems also yields the guidelines for the definition of the further structure of the domain of transformation systems. Specification means, development operations and relations, and composition operations for transformation systems are all defined by reusing corresponding constructions for partial algebras, structured sets, and transition systems, and integrating them appropriately.

A first comparison with related approaches can already be given here, although only the elements of the reference model, the transformation systems, have been introduced yet, and nothing of its structure. The principal idea of modelling dynamic systems by some form of labelled transition system is of course very common. Many specification formalisms have operational semantics explicitly or implicitly defined in terms of transition systems or extensions of them. *Process calculi* like CCS [Mil89], LOTOS [LOT87, vVD89], or process algebra [BW90] explicitly use LTS in the usual sense, i.e., labelled transitions but unlabelled states. Extended transition systems, where also the states are labelled with an internal structure, have also already been used, for instance for the definition of operational semantics for programming languages. Even finite models have already been considered to model programs abstractly, as in [Ste93a, SS98]. Internal data states given by assignments of values to some given state variables have been used for the extended transition systems introduced in [WC89]. Similar to the transformation system approach they are used there to compare the semantics of LOTOS and Z [Spi88, Spi92]. The LOTOS semantics is therefore rephrased by using the parameters of the agents as data states, analogous to the interpretation of the CCS-sender specification as the transformation system in Example 2.13. Also software specification techniques for dynamic behaviours like statecharts [Har87, HG95, HN95] and UML state machine, collaboration, and sequence diagrams use data types for the parameters of actions and data states for the evaluation of boolean guards, without treating these very precisely in the semantics. The operational semantics is always defined by LTSs (see [HPSS87, HN95]). The control states of a statechart are given by the configurations of the chart, and the transitions are defined and labelled by the sets of enabled parallel synchronous transitions and their effects on the configurations. The data states are implicit. Similarly, the control states of a sequence diagram are its cuts, i.e., maximal independent sets of locations on the life lines of the objects, and its transitions are given by the sending and receiving of messages and events [DH98, DH99]. Semantic issues like these are discussed in more detail in Chapter 6.

On the other hand, the implicit interpretation of the data and operation schemes of Z as dynamic systems [Spi92], as well as other rule-based specification formalisms, is also made explicit by considering them as transformation systems. The operational semantics of a Z schema is implicitly given by a transition system whose states are labelled by data states according to the data schemes, i.e., bindings of values to variables, and whose transitions are given by pairs of data states according to the pre- and postcondition of the operation schemes, labelled by the operation names and the parameters. This coincides exactly with the transformation system representation, except that the latter is more explicit w.r.t. the control states as discussed above. This interpretation of the operational semantics of specifications as transformation systems can be carried over easily to other formalisms. An example for the parallel programming language UNITY [CM88] is given in Chapter 4. Different kinds of graph grammars (see [Roz97]) and Petri nets (see [Rei85, PR91]) yield further examples, as discussed in the following.

Graph grammars

A graph grammar $\mathbf{G} = (N, \pi)$ is essentially given by a set N of rule names and a mapping π that associates a graph transformation rule to each rule name. Sometimes also an initial graph G_0 is given. The operational semantics of $\mathbf{G}$ is then given by the set of all graphs as states, with initial state G_0, and for each pair G, H of graphs a transition $G \to H$ with label n/m, if the rule $\pi(n)$ applied to G via the match m yields H. How the application of a rule and the result H are defined, whether H is completely determined by n, m, and G, what a match is, and which kinds of graphs are considered depend on the particular graph transformation approach. Considered as a transformation system $\mathbf{T}(\mathbf{G})$ the different roles that graphs, rule names, and matches play are made explicit. The corresponding data signature is given by a signature of graphs, as for instance

> **graph** =
> **sorts** nodes, edges
> **funs** source, target : edge $\to$ node

Other kinds of graphs (simple, attributed, typed, graph structure, etc.) can be specified correspondingly. The rule names of $\mathbf{G}$ yield the action names, whose parameters are given by all nodes and edges of the corresponding rules that can be matched when applying the rules. That means the action signature is given by

$$\mathbf{act} \quad n : \underbrace{\text{node}, \ldots, \text{node}}_{k}, \underbrace{\text{edge}, \ldots, \text{edge}}_{l}$$

for each rule name n such that $\pi(n)$ has k nodes and l edges that can be matched. (Suppose k and l are finite.) This defines the data space.

The transition graph of $\mathbf{T(G)}$ is defined like the transition system representing the operational semantics of $\mathbf{G}$ given above, where, however, the labels n/m are now the identities of the transitions, not their labels. Thus the set of control states coincides with the set of data states and the state labelling is given by the identical function. (The set of control states could also be restricted to the reachable graphs, whence the labelling becomes an inclusion.) Analogously, each transition $n/m : G \to H$ is now labelled by the singleton action set $\{n(m(\nu_1), \ldots, m(\nu_k), m(\epsilon_1), \ldots, m(\epsilon_l))\}$, where ν_i and ϵ_j are the nodes and edges of $\pi(n)$ that are matched in G via m. This means that $m(\nu_i)$ and $m(\epsilon_j)$ are indeed elements of G, as required in the action set definition of transformation systems. Parallel or amalgamated rule applications would be labelled by sets of actions with more than one element. (Note that the possibility to declare parameters of actions explicitly in the action signature immediately yields submatches as observable rule applications, as used in the graph transformation languages AGG [Tae00, ERT99] and PROGRES [Sch91, SWZ95], for example.) The definition of the tracking relation again depends on the particular graph transformation approach. In the DPO approach [CMR+97] it is given by a graph span, in the SPO approach [EHK+97] by a partial graph homomorphism, and in the algorithmic approaches [ER97] the nodes and edges have persistent identities.

Although the transition graph in this construction is almost the same as the data space the different roles of the two levels show up again when the morphisms are considered. Considered as LTSs the internal states, i.e. the graphs themselves, do not matter. For example, two systems that consist of exactly one step (with the same label) are isomorphic, i.e., have to be considered as being essentially the same, completely independent of the state of the graph at the initial and final states. As a transformation system the graph structure also must be preserved.

Petri nets

The interpretation of the operational semantics of Petri nets as transformation systems stresses the same fact: that the internal structure matters. Consider a place/transition net $PN = (P, T, pre, post : T \to P^{\oplus})$, given by sets P and T of places and transitions respectively, and functions pre and $post$ that associate to each transition the number of tokens it withdraws from and adds to the places in its pre- and post-domain respectively. The data states of the operational semantics of PN are its markings, i.e., the number of tokens on each place; the action names are given by the transitions. This yields the following data space signature, where the *nat*-parameter of a transition action indicates the multiplicity of its firing.

$$\text{marking(PN)} = \text{nat} +$$
$$\textbf{funs } p: \to \text{nat} \quad (p \in P)$$
$$\textbf{acts } t: \text{nat} \quad (t \in T)$$

The transition graph is given by the marking graph or the reachability graph of the net PN, with identity (or inclusion) as the state label function. A step (=transition) $M[\sum_{i=1}^{s} n_i t_i\rangle M'$, given by the parallel firing of the transitions t_i with multiplicities n_i, is labelled in the transformation system by the action set $\{t_1(n_1), \ldots, t_s(n_s)\}$. The tracking relation is given by the identity on $I\!N$. Other kinds of Petri nets like nets with capacities, coloured nets [Jen92, Jen94], or (algebraic) high-level nets [RV87, Vau87, Hum89] are interpreted analogously. The enriched notions of markings and tokens are captured by refined data signatures (or specifications); the firing conditions only refine the definitions of the transition graphs and the data state transformations.

States as Algebras

Using the same pattern other states-as-algebras approaches can be embedded into the transformation system model. Consider as a most general example D-oids as presented in [AZ93, AZ95]. Although this is more a general semantical framework than a specification formalism, it serves well to compare the states-as-algebras approaches due to its generality. The data states of a D-oid are given by a discrete subcategory of a generic category of static structures, as in the institution-independent version of transformation systems. Its transformations are given by constant dynamic operations, which are just initial data states, corresponding to the initialisations of transformation systems, and (non-constant) dynamic operations. The latter associate with each data state A and list of input parameters $\bar{a} \in A_w$ in their domain an output state B and a partial tracking map $|A| \to |B|$, possibly together with a return value $b \in B_s$. In terms of transformation systems this is a transformation $A \Rightarrow B$, with the dynamic operation together with the input parameters as the action label, and a tracking relation which happens to be a partial mapping. (Cf. Remark 2.8, where also the treatment of return values in transformation systems is discussed.) Morphisms of D-oids are more general than the morphisms of transformation systems as discussed in this chapter, but coincide (almost) with the extension given in Chapter 5. Basically, data states of related control states need not coincide, but may be connected via homomorphisms.

Abstract State Machines

The embedding of abstract state machines (ASMs,[1] formerly called evolving algebras, see [Gur91, Gur94]) into the transformation system framework could be inherited from their embedding into D-oids discussed in [AZ95]. The main difference here, however, is the purpose of the ASMs, which serve to define

---

[1] See http://www.eecs.umich.edu/gasm/.

precise and well-structured semantics for programming languages and proving compiler correctness ([BS91, BR92]). The general system modelling purpose of transformation systems is not addressed primarily, and not supported to the same extent. More technically speaking, ASMs are less flexible w.r.t. their definition of data states and large parts of the necessary structure (partiality, predicates, object identities, references, creation and deletion, composition, etc.) are encoded in the data states and not put into the logic. On the other hand, the control flow is handled explicitly by rules and rule composition operations, as opposed to the implicit control flow of D–oids. Finally, the definition of the semantics of the transformations in an ASM is rather pragmatic in order to avoid dealing with possible inconsistencies.

The discussions above show that all these different specification formalisms can be interpreted in the reference model, i.e., their operational semantics can be faithfully rephrased in terms of transformation systems. This common semantic interpretation yields the possibility of formal comparisons of heterogeneous specifications given in different languages even with different underlying paradigms. For instance, CCS uses synchronous message passing for communication, while the parallel programming language UNITY uses shared variables with asynchronous access (see the corresponding examples in Chapter 4); Petri nets, graph grammars, Z, and abstract state machines are rule-based state transformation approaches as opposed to the temporal ordering of atomic actions and non-inspectable states in process calculi. This possibility of a common semantic interpretation does not mean, however, that this is the only or fixed semantic level for all specification formalisms. As mentioned above, transformation systems represent an operational semantics that may be too concrete for certain contexts. In these cases abstractions are defined, like bisimulation or observation congruence [Par81, Mil89, Hen88], or event structures [Win88b], to obtain reduced and more adequate representations. If a formal comparison of heterogeneous specifications can be achieved at the operational semantics level this obviously already suffices, provided the abstraction preserves the comparison. The further investigation of abstraction equivalences for transformation systems that generalise the above-mentioned ones by also taking into account the data states, however, is a topic for further research.

3

Specification of Properties

Data space signatures have been used to specify the static structure of transformation systems, i.e., their data states and their actions. Beyond that it is important to have means for the specification of their semantic properties, such that the desired properties of the systems can be modelled. These properties can be classified according to the structure of transformation systems. Their data states are given by partial algebras, whose properties are described by equations, more precisely conditional existence equations (see [Rei87, CGW95] and Appendix A). A data state transformation $T : C \Rightarrow D$ is given by the commencing and the ending states C and D and a label $T = \langle act, \sim \rangle$ that consists of an action set and a tracking relation. The two data states can be specified by a pair of sets of equations, describing pre- and postconditions of the transformation. Together with a formal action expression for the specification of the action set act this yields a *transformation rule*. The relation of the elements of the data states C and D is given by the tracking relation $\sim$ that now allows the evaluation of the common variables of the two sets of equations of the transformation rule by identified (=related) elements in the two different algebras. In this way relations between the values of functions and constants before and after the execution of the actions of the transformation can be expressed. Note that this concept of transformation rules also allows the specification of dynamic properties w.r.t. mutable carrier sets, for instance in the case of creation and deletion of elements.

As opposed to the equations for partial algebras there is no canonical specification format for the transition graphs or control flow in general. Some specification formalisms describe behaviours uniquely, i.e., they are used to *construct* transition systems. That means, given a specification, one can ask for *the* model (operational semantics) of the specification. Process calculi specify the temporal ordering of atomic actions; their operational semantics is given via deduction rules that yield LTSs. Petri nets represent the causal dependencies of actions; their operational semantics can also be considered as transition systems, given by the marking graphs or the reachability graphs induced by the nets. In this case, however, the states carry relevant internal structure, given by the markings. The place invariants for instance refer to this structure. Logical formalisms, like modal, dynamic, and temporal logics [Eme90, Sti92], on the other hand, in general do not specify or construct single transition systems. Instead, a set of formulae *describes* a *set* of transition systems, the ones that satisfy the formulae. That means, given a model and a specification (a formula or a set of formulae), one can ask whether the model satisfies the specification. Due to this situation control flow specifications for transformation systems are treated generically here. An abstract definition of control flow logics is given, similar to institutions, that can be instantiated for example by the above-mentioned formalisms.

After the introduction of the specification means—equations and transformation rules for the data spaces (Section 3.1) and control flow specifications for the behaviour (Section 3.2)—the examples of the preceding chapter are discussed in detail again, i.e., their properties are specified with the different formalisms (Section 3.3). Then, in Section 3.4, it is shown that transformation rules can also be used as replacement or rewriting rules in the sense of rule-based specification. That means a rule can be applied to an algebra to transform it by constructing a new algebra representing the new state. As in the preceding chapter, in Section 3.5 the specification means for transformation systems w.r.t. other specification frameworks are introduced that allow for instance the use of arbitrary logical formulae in pre- and postconditions. The chapter ends with a discussion of the new concepts and a comparison with other approaches

3.1 Data Space Specification

Properties of data states and transformations can be specified in order to reduce the data space, i.e., to exclude certain states and transformations. The data state part of a data space specification comprises the specification of the static data types and the data invariants, i.e., the properties that must hold in each state. These comprise for instance consistency conditions and the definitions of derived mutable functions, whose definition (input/output relation) depends on the actual state, like the function *right* in Example 2.12. In the latter case, therefore, some parts (attributes) determine the actual state; the other ones are derived from it. Beyond these invariant properties, conditions on the initial and final states of the system can be stated, like initialisation values for variables or attributes in the initial states, or consistency conditions like completed garbage collection for the final states.

Since the data states are represented by partial algebras the categorical choice of the format of their specification is given by conditional existence equations.

Definition 3.1 (Data Specification). *A data specification $DS = (Ax, In, Fi)$ w.r.t. a given algebraic signature Σ is given by sets Ax, In, and Fi of*

conditional Σ-equations, called the data invariants, *the* initialisation, *and the* finalisation conditions *respectively. A $D\Sigma$-transformation system* $\mathbf{M} = (TG_{\mathbf{M}}, \mathbf{m})$ *with* $TG_{\mathbf{M}} = (CS, T, in, id)$ satisfies *the data specification DS, written* $\mathbf{M} \models DS$, *if*

- $\mathbf{m}(c) \models Ax$ *for each control state* $c \in CS - \{in\}$,
- $\mathbf{m}(c_0) \models In$ *for each initial state* $c_0 \in \{c \in CS - \{in\} \mid T(in, c) \neq \emptyset\}$,
- $\mathbf{m}(c_1) \models Fi$ *for each final state* $c_1 \in \{c \in CS - \{in\} \mid T(c, in) \neq \emptyset\}$.

Example 3.2 (Data Specification of the Program with Pointers). The *prog*-signature introduced in Example 2.3 can be enhanced by first adding axioms for the specification of the natural numbers as usual. Furthermore, the designated pointer p should always be defined, which can be specified by the invariant $p \downarrow$. (The downarrow $\downarrow$ denotes the definedness predicate for terms in equational specifications of partial algebras. An axiom $t \downarrow$ is satisfied in a partial algebra A if t can be evaluated in A, see Appendix A, p. 306).

Data state transformations are pairs of data states, the commencing and the ending states, labelled by an action set and a tracking relation. Accordingly, a specification of a data state transformation is given by two parts: a pair of sets of equations specifying the commencing and the ending state of the transformation, and a set of actions with formal parameters specifying the action set of the transformation. These transformation specifications are called *transformation rules*, covering both their descriptive and their constructive meaning. On the one hand, a transformation rule describes the class of transformation systems that satisfy the rule; on the other hand, a transformation rule can be applied to a given algebra to construct a new one, representing the new data state. The descriptive interpretation of transformation rules can also be generalised to other data institutions, whereas the constructive one is based on a property (existence of free models) that holds essentially for algebraic models. The tracking relation modelling the identity of elements at the semantical level is reflected at the syntactical level of transformation rules by using identical variable names in the specification of the commencing and the ending states of the transformation.

Definition 3.3 (Transformation Rule). *Let $D\Sigma = (\Sigma, A)$ be a data space signature with $\Sigma = (S, F)$. A $D\Sigma$-transformation rule $r = (\alpha \mathrel{\hat{=}} L \to R)$ is given by*

- *left and right hand sides $L = (X_l : E_l)$ and $R = (X_r : E_r)$, given by S-indexed sets of variables X_l and X_r and sets of equations $E_l \subseteq Eqns_{\Sigma}(X_l)$ and $E_r \subseteq Eqns_{\Sigma}(X_r)$,*
- *a set of formal actions $\alpha \subseteq Act_{D\Sigma}(X, Y)$, where $X \subseteq X_l$ and $Y \subseteq X_r$.*

If the action set α of a rule $r = (\alpha \mathrel{\hat{=}} L \to R)$ is empty the rule is called an anonymous rule, *and also denoted by $r = (L \to R)$. The class of all $D\Sigma$-transformation rules is denoted by $Rules_{D\Sigma}$.*

Example 3.4 (Pointer Incrementation Rule). (Cf. Example 2.3, 2.5, 3.2.) The incrementation of the contents of pointers by the action *inc* : *pointer*, *nat* is specified by the following rule:

$$inc(q, l) \triangleq$$
$$q \in pointer, x, l \in nat : !(q) = x$$
$$\longrightarrow$$
$$q \in pointer, x, l \in nat : !(q) = x + l .$$

The formal action parameter sets X and Y are given implicitly by $X_{pointer} = \{q\}$, $X_{nat} = \{l\}$, $Y_{pointer} = \emptyset$, and $Y_{nat} = \emptyset$.

In the sequel variables that occur on both sides of a rule will be listed only once, immediately after the action set. In the left and right hand sides of the rule in this notation then, only the variables that are only in the corresponding variable sets are listed. Using this notation the *inc* rule is given by

$$inc(q, l) \triangleq q \in pointer; x, l \in nat : \quad !(q) = x \rightarrow !(q) = x + l .$$

The auxiliary variable x : nat in the *inc* rule, that does not appear as a parameter of the method, is used to read the actual value of the pointer ($!(q) = x$ on the left hand side of the rule) and store it for the specification of the output state ($!(q) = x + k$ on the right hand side). The other variables are parameters of *inc* and indicate to which pointer it is applied and by which amount it is increased. (Note that the variable l : nat also belongs to the variable declaration of the left hand side, although it does not appear in the left equation. For the descriptive meaning this does not matter, but in the constructive interpretation it means that the value l already exists and need not be created by the rule.)

To check whether a transformation system $\mathbf{M} = (TG_{\mathbf{M}}, \mathbf{m})$ satisfies a rule $r = (\alpha \triangleq L \rightarrow R)$ each control state c and each outgoing transition $t : c \rightarrow d$ must be checked as follows. First the formal parameter sets X and Y of the actions in $\alpha \subseteq Act_{D\Sigma}(X, Y)$ are bound to elements of the data states $C = \mathbf{m}(c)$ and $D = \mathbf{m}(d)$ in such a way that the action set $act_t^{\mathbf{m}}$ of the transition t becomes an instance of α. (If this is not possible the chosen transition $t : c \rightarrow d$ satisfies the rule in that it is not concerned by it.) The binding is thus given by functions $\xi : X \rightarrow |C|$ and $\zeta : Y \rightarrow |D|$ that satisfy

$$act_t^{\mathbf{m}} = \alpha[\xi, \zeta] ,$$

where the instantiation $\alpha[\xi, \zeta]$ is given by the substitution of its formal parameters according to ξ and ζ, i.e.,

$$a(c_i, \ldots, c_n; d_1, \ldots, d_k) \in \alpha[\xi, \zeta]$$
iff
$$c_i = \xi(x_i) \text{ for } i = 1, \ldots, n \text{ and } d_i = \zeta(y_j) \text{ for } j = 1, \ldots, k .$$

Then the remaining variables of the left hand side are bound to elements of C in such a way that this yields a solution of L in C. That means mappings $\gamma : X_l \to |C|$ are considered with $\gamma|_X = \xi$ and $\gamma \in Sol(L, C)$. For each such γ there must be a binding of the variables in X_r to elements in D (i.e., a mapping $\delta : X_r \to |D|$) that

- extends the binding y of the formal action parameters: $\delta|_Y = \zeta$
- is a solution of R in D: $\delta \in Sol(R, D)$
- is compatible w.r.t. the tracking relation with the binding γ: $\delta(x) \sim_t^m \gamma(x)$ for all $x \in X_r \cap X_l$.

This is made precise in the following definition.

Definition 3.5 (Satisfaction of Transformation Rules). *Let $D\Sigma$ be a data space signature, $r = (\alpha \doteq L \to R)$ a $D\Sigma$-transformation rule with $L = (X_l : E_l)$, $R = (X_r : E_r)$, and $\alpha \subseteq Act_{D\Sigma}(X, Y)$. Furthermore let $\mathbf{M} = (TG_\mathbf{M}, \mathbf{m})$ be a $D\Sigma$-transformation system, $t : c \to d$ a transition in $TG_\mathbf{M}$, and $C = \mathbf{m}(c)$ and $D = \mathbf{m}(d)$ the associated data states.*

The system $\mathbf{M}$ satisfies the rule r at transition t, written $\mathbf{M}, t \models r$, if the following condition holds.

> *For all*　　$\xi : X \to |C|, \zeta : Y \to |D|$
> *if*　　　　$act_t^m = \alpha[\xi, \zeta]$
> *then for each* $\gamma \in Sol_\Sigma(L, C)$ *with* $\gamma|_X = \xi$
> *there is a*　$\delta \in Sol_\Sigma(R, D)$ *with* $\delta|_Y = \zeta$
> *such that*　$\gamma(x) \sim_t^m \delta(x)$
> *for all*　　$x \in X_l \cap X_r.$

The system $\mathbf{M}$ satisfies r, written $\mathbf{M} \models r$, if $\mathbf{M}, t \models r$ for each transition t in $TG_\mathbf{M}$.

Example 3.6 (Continuation of Example 3.4). Consider the rule of the *inc* method

$$inc \doteq q \leftarrow pointer, x, l \in nat \;:\; !(q) = x \to !(q) - x + l$$

and the *prog*-transformation system $\mathbf{X} = (TG_\mathbf{X}, \mathbf{x})$ defined in Example 2.7. The only transitions with non-empty action sets are the ones of the form $k : n \to n+k$, with $act_k^\mathbf{x} = \{inc(X, k)\}$, $\mathbf{x}(n) = X_n$, and $\mathbf{x}(n+k) = X_{n+k}$. The only possible bindings $\xi : \{q, l\} \to |X_n|$ and $\zeta : \emptyset \to |X_{n+k}|$ that instantiate $inc(q, l)$ to $inc(X, k)$ are given by $\xi(q) = X \in (X_n)_{pointer}$, $\xi(l) = k$ for some $k \in (X_n)_{nat}$, and $\zeta = \emptyset$.

Given this, the only solution $\gamma : \{q, l, x\} \to |X_n|$ of $!(q) = x$ in X_n that extends ξ is given by $\gamma(q) = \xi(q) = X$, $\gamma(l) = \xi(l) = k$, and $\gamma(x) = !^{X_n}(\gamma(q)) = !^{X_n}(X) = n$. For this solution γ there is now the binding $\delta : \{q, l, x\} \to |X_{n+k}|$ given by $\delta(q) = X \in (X_{n+k})_{pointer}$, $\delta(l) = k \in (X_{n+k})_{nat}$, and $\delta(x) = n \in (X_{n+k})_{nat}$ such that

- δ extends ζ, i.e., $\delta|_\emptyset = \emptyset$
- δ is a solution of $!(q) = x + l$ in X_{n+k}, i.e.,

$$!^{X_{n+k}}(\delta(q)) = !^{X_{n+k}}(X) = n + k = \delta(x) + \delta(l)$$

- δ is compatible with γ w.r.t. the tracking relation $\sim_k^x$, which is the identity here.

This means the system $\mathbf{X}$ satisfies the *inc*–rule.

Example 3.7 (Insertion and Deletion Rules for Lists). In the previous example the carrier sets of the input and output data states $C = \mathbf{m}(c)$ and $D = \mathbf{m}(d)$ of the considered transition $t : c \to d$ were identical, with the identity as the tracking relation. With transformation rules the creation of elements and their insertion into the algebras, as well as deletion, can be described. Consider for example the insertion of an element into a linear structure (a list) and its deletion. The structure is specified by

> **linear =**
>   **sorts** element
>   **funs** next: element $\to$ element
>   **acts** insert, delete: element

For example, *insert* should create a new element and insert it next to the one indicated by its parameter. (Insertion of an existing element given as a second parameter is discussed below.) *Delete* deletes the element next to its parameter and closes the gap (cf. also the specification of the delete method for linked lists in Example 3.13). This behaviour is specified by the following rules:

$$insert(e) \hateq e, e' \in element :$$
$$next(e) = e' \to n \in element : next(e) = n, next(n) = e'$$

$$delete(e) \hateq e, e' \in element :$$
$$next(next(e)) = e' \to next(e) = e' \ .$$

Let us check these rules against the data state transformations $In : C_{In} \Rightarrow D_{In}$ and $Del : C_{Del} \Rightarrow D_{Del}$ depicted in Figure 3.1 and formally defined in Table 3.1. The binding of the formal parameter e of the *insert* step is given

$$1 \to 2 \to 4 \qquad \xRightarrow{\;insert(2)\;} \qquad 1 \to 2 \to 3 \to 4$$

$$1 \to 2 \to 5 \to 3 \qquad \xRightarrow{\;delete(2)\;} \qquad 1 \to 2 \to 3$$

Fig. 3.1. Insertion and deletion of list elements

	C_{In}	D_{In}	C_{Del}	D_{Del}
element	$\{1,2,4\}$	$\{1,2,3,4\}$	$\{1,2,3,5\}$	$\{1,2,3\}$
next	$1 \mapsto 2$	$1 \mapsto 2$	$1 \mapsto 2$	$1 \mapsto 2$
	$2 \mapsto 4$	$2 \mapsto 3$	$2 \mapsto 5$	$2 \mapsto 3$
		$3 \mapsto 4$	$5 \mapsto 3$	
	In		*Del*	
act	$\{insert(2)\}$		$\{delete(2)\}$	
$\sim$	$1 \sim 1, 2 \sim 2, 4 \sim 4$		$1 \sim 1, 2 \sim 2, 3 \sim 3$	

Table 3.1. Insertion and deletion steps

by $\xi : \{e\} \to \{1,2,4\}$, $\xi(e) = 2$, $\zeta : \emptyset \to \{1,2,3,4,\}$. The only solution of $next(e) = e'$ in C_{In} that extends ξ is $\gamma : \{e, e'\} \to \{1,2,3,\}, \gamma(e) = 2, \gamma(e') = next^{C_{In}}(2) = 4$. This γ has an extension $\delta : \{e, e', n\} \to \{1,2,3,4\}, \delta|_{\{e,e'\}} = \gamma$, $\delta(n) = 3$ that extends ζ ($\delta|_\emptyset = \emptyset$), is a solution of the right hand side $next^{D_{In}}(\delta(e)) = next^{D_{In}}(2) - 3 = \delta(n)$, $next^{D_{In}}(\delta(n)) = next^{D_{In}}(3) = 4 = \delta(e')$, and is compatible with γ w.r.t. the tracking relation.

Note that the rule does not prescribe a name for the element that is inserted. It just happened in this system that a 3 has been chosen. Any other step that yields *the same structure* (like $1 \to 2 \to 124 \to 4$) also satisfies the rule. To specify names for newly created elements the creation parameters can be used. This is discussed in Example 3.21. Inserting a given element can be modelled with an action *insert : element, element* and a corresponding rule

$$insert(e, n) \mathrel{\hat{=}} e, e' \in element; n \in nat :$$
$$next(e) = e' \to next(e) = n, next(n) = e' \; .$$

That means the variable n is moved from the right hand side (expressing a creation) to the left hand side (expressing a precondition).

Also the deletion step $Del : C_{Del} \Rightarrow D_{Del}$ satisfies its rule. The only possible binding $\zeta : \{e\} \to \{1,2,3,5\}$ that matches the action is given by $\xi(e) = 2$. The only solution $\gamma : \{e, e'\} \to \{1,2,3,5\}$ of $next(next(e)) = e'$ in C_{Del} that extends ξ is given by $\gamma(e) = 2, \gamma(e') = 3$. This has an extension $\delta : \{e, e'\} \to \{1,2,3\}, \delta(e) = 2, \delta(e') = 3$ that is compatible with the tracking relation ($\delta(x) = \gamma(x)$ for all $x \in \{1,2,3\}$), extends $\zeta = \emptyset$, and is a solution of $next(e) = e'$ in D_{Del}:

$$next^{D_{Del}}(\delta(e)) = next^{D_{Del}}(2) = 3 = \delta(e')$$

q.e.d.

Note also that the deletion step without garbage collection

$$1 \to 2 \to 5 \to 3 \quad \xRightarrow{\;delete(2)\;} \quad 1 \longrightarrow 2 \quad 5 \quad 3$$

satisfies the rule. The deletion of the element 5 in the upper step is a minimal interpretation of the rule in the sense that each element that is bound to a variable on the left hand side of the rule that no longer occurs on its right hand side is deleted. These minimal interpretations of transformation rules are discussed in Section 3.4.

In a transformation rule the relation between the commencing and the ending state of a transformation is established by the identical variables of the two sets of equations that are instantiated by identical elements w.r.t. the tracking relation of the two algebras. An equation $t = x$ on the left side of a rule, for example, where t is a ground term (for instance, a constant) and x is a variable, serves to store the value of t in the commencing state. Then x can be used on the right hand side in an expression (term) $e(x)$ to update the value of t by $t = e(x)$.

In other approaches specific notation is used to refer to the values of syntactic entities before and after some action or transformation. This can be translated to transformation rules as discussed in the following.

Example 3.8 (Rules in Other Formalisms). In this example transformation rules are compared with other specification means for data state transformations.

1. In an assignment $X := expr(X)$ in a programming language the occurrence of X on the right side denotes its state before the execution of the assignment. The corresponding equivalent transformation rule is

$$(x \in type : X = x) \rightarrow (x \in type : X = expr(x))$$

   where $X :\rightarrow type$ is a constant in the data signature representing the program variable X and $expr(x)$ is a term of type *type* that may contain the (algebraic) variable x.

2. In the specification language Z new states of variables $V : type$ in an operation schema are identified by a dash, as in $V' = expr(V)$. The corresponding equivalent transformation rule is again

$$(v \in type : V = v) \rightarrow (v \in type : V = expr(v)) .$$

3. In the object constraint language OCL of UML the construct $t@pre$ can be used in the postcondition of an operation to denote the value of the expression t before the application of the operation, i.e., at the time of the evaluation of the precondition. Its translation to a transformation rule proceeds as in the examples above.

4. A *pointwise function update* $f(t_1, \ldots, t_n) := t$ of an ASM is translated into a transformation rule analogously:

$$(x \in s : t = x) \rightarrow (x \in s : f(t_1, \ldots, t_n) = x)$$

where s is the sort of t. The left hand side corresponds to evaluating t, which may contain the function name f with arbitrary parameters in the actual state and bind it to x. On the right hand side this value is then assigned as the new result to the function application $f(t_1, \ldots, t_n)$.

5. In [AZ96] dynamic terms are introduced that allow the denotation of elements of a future state that is reachable from the actual one via the application of dynamic operations dop (corresponding to methods or actions). Term constructors R and M are defined to denote elements in the ending state B of the step $dop : A \Rightarrow B$. The dynamic term R denotes the return value of dop in B; the dynamic term $M(t)$, where t is a normal static term, denotes the element of B that corresponds to the value of t in A under the tracking map.

The representation of return values in transformation systems has been discussed in Remark 2.8,2. The relation of elements through state changes is specified in a transformation rule as in the examples above: On the left hand side of the rule the value is bound to a variable ($x \in s : t = x$) that can then be used on the right hand side within terms then. That means the expression $M(t)$ of [AZ96] corresponds to the variable x used on the right hand side of a transformation rule. By definition of the satisfaction of transformation rules the evaluations of x in A and B are in the tracking relation, as in the M-notation of dynamic terms.

Sets of transformation rules together with data specifications finally yield data space specifications.

Definition 3.9 (Data Space Specification). *A data space specification $D\Gamma = (DS, R)$ w.r.t. a given data space signature $D\Sigma = (\Sigma, A)$ is given by a data specification DS w.r.t. Σ and a set R of $D\Sigma$-transformation rules.*

A $D\Sigma$-transformation system $\mathbf{M}$ satisfies $D\Gamma$ if $\mathbf{M} \models DS$ and $\mathbf{M} \models r$ for each $r \in R$.

Remark 3.10. As mentioned above, a data space specification $D\Gamma$ reduces the data space $I\!D_{D\Sigma}$ by excluding all data states and transformations that do not satisfy the axioms and rules. Accordingly, the data space $I\!D_{D\Gamma}$ can be defined as the subtransition graph of $I\!D_{D\Sigma}$ given by all partial (Σ, Ax)-algebras as states, all transformations from $Tf_{D\Sigma}$ that satisfy the transformation rules, and the initialisations and finalisations restricted to the ones that reach/leave states that satisfy the initialisation/finalisation conditions. The identities are the ones from $I\!D_{D\Sigma}$. Then a $D\Sigma$-transformation system $\mathbf{M} = (TG_{\mathbf{M}}, \mathbf{m})$ satisfies $D\Gamma$ if $\mathbf{m}$ factorises through the inclusion $I\!D_{D\Gamma} \subseteq I\!D_{D\Sigma}$.

3.2 Control Flow Specification

A transformation system composes its runs from the states and transformations of the data space. This is formally represented by the transition graph and its labelling in the data space. Accordingly, a specification of the properties of the system must provide the means to describe how the transformation steps are selected and composed. As opposed to the data specification, however, there is no categorical format for this control flow specification. For the specification of data states conditional equations can be used both to describe and to construct partial algebras. That means a set of equations can be validated in a given algebra, i.e., it can be asked whether the equations hold in the algebra, or the equations can be used to construct an algebra: the quotient term algebra. An analogous twofold interpretation is possible of transformation rules as mentioned above. They can be checked in models for their validity or they can be used to construct algebras by applying them to given ones. Concerning control flow or processes in general, however, different specification formats are used for the two tasks. To *construct* a process from a given set of actions a process term, built w.r.t. a process calculus or specification language like CCS, CSP, or LOTOS for example, can be used. It describes the temporal ordering of the actions, for instance as their sequential or parallel execution or their non-deterministic choice. On the other hand, there are logical formalisms, like temporal or modal logics or the modal μ-calculus, that *describe* processes (represented by LTSs) in the above-mentioned sense. That means, given a set of formulae and an LTS, it can be asked whether the formulae hold in the LTS. But in general there is no smallest or canonical model satisfying the set of formulae. Whether there exist such smallest models depends on the model structure considered. If these models themselves allow looseness, smallest models may well exist (see [LX91, LT91]). Then there is a third kind of process specification approach, based on the notion of causality— or its dual independence—instead of the temporal ordering of actions. (See [WN97] for a categorical survey and connections between these approaches.)

Due to this situation the control flow part of a transformation system's specification is treated as a generic component from the beginning, not just in the specification framework-independent version. The instantiation by different approaches like the ones mentioned above will be illustrated in the examples. Formally control flow specifications are treated as the sentences of an institution, whose signatures are obtained from the data space signatures and whose models are transformation systems. In order not to constrain the possibilities offered by transformation systems unnecessarily, control flow specifications are allowed to make use of the data states, too. For example, the capability of performing a certain action may depend on a condition of the actual data state. Since signature morphisms have not yet been used, only local sets of formulae, i.e., formulae of one signature, are required here. Translations of control flow formulae are considered in Chapter 4.

Definition 3.11 (Control Flow Logic). *A control flow logic* $CL = (CF,$ $\models^{CL})$ *is given by a function* CF *that assigns a set* $CF(D\Sigma)$ *to each transformation signature* $D\Sigma$*, called the set of* $D\Sigma$*-control flow formulae, and a family of* satisfaction relations

$$\models_{D\Sigma}^{CL} \; \subseteq \; |\mathbf{TF}(D\Sigma)| \times CF(D\Sigma)$$

between $D\Sigma$-transformation models and $D\Sigma$-control flow formulae.

In the following some presentations of control flow logics for the above-mentioned specification techniques are sketched. There is of course no unique way of how to present specification techniques for dynamic behaviour as control flow logics, since there are many different approaches and paradigms that cannot all be treated in the same way. Most of them come in different variants and extensions, whose roles would have to be taken into account in each case. Moreover, even a single formalism—like P/T-nets for example—can be used in different styles that have significant impact on their meaning when compared to other approaches (cf. the discussion in Section 1.2 and Example 3.14). Nevertheless, the presentations below yield some guidelines on how to obtain such reformulations of specification techniques as control flow logics.

As a first aspect to be considered in such a reformulation note that the structure of actions can be conceived in different ways. Usually in the basic calculi only finite sets of atomic actions are considered, without (or with little) internal structure. Mostly there are extensions that then allow the use of parameterised actions also. The CCS extensions in the concurrency workbench,[1] LOTOS and ELOTOS, the algebraic extensions of Petri nets, or the integration μSZ of Z and statecharts are examples of such data type extensions. Then, as mentioned above, data states are sometimes used implicitly, and actions are ordered in time or in causal relationship for example, which obviously requires different translations into control flow logics.

In the following paragraphs let $D\Sigma = (S, F, A)$ be a data space signature that is used to define the corresponding control flow logics $(CF(D\Sigma), \models_{D\Sigma})$.

CCS with Parameterised Actions

The basic idea of the translation of CCS into a control flow logic

$$CL_{CCS} = (CCS(D\Sigma), \models_{D\Sigma}^{CCS})$$

is to use CCS-process expressions as formulae, and the operational semantics of an expression as the only LTS that satisfies this expression.

To define the set of CCS-process expressions first a set $\mathcal{A}$ of atomic actions has to be fixed. The action signature A of $D\Sigma$ yields the actions $Act_{D\Sigma}(M, M)$ for some given S-sorted set M of actual parameters. Since there are no data states in CCS the set of actual parameters also cannot vary and no new elements can be created. In CCS communication of processes is based on the concept of complementary actions (read and write, or receive and send) that is realised by a (syntactic) operation $\bar{} : \mathcal{A} \to \mathcal{A}$, with $\bar{\bar{\alpha}} = \alpha$. The composition of transformation systems does not use such naming conventions or complementation operations, but arbitrary synchronisation relations between actions

---

[1] See http://www.dcs.ed.ac.uk/home/cwb/.

(see Chapter 5). To reconcile the two approaches let us assume for the sake of simplicity that $D\Sigma$ contains for each action a also an action $\bar{a}$ of the same arity, i.e., $\overline{Act}_{D\Sigma} = Act_{D\Sigma}$. Then we define

$$\mathcal{A}_{D\Sigma} = Act_{D\Sigma}(M, M) \cup \{\tau\} \, .$$

The CCS-operators $\_.\_$ (action prefix), $\_ + \_$ (non-deterministic choice), and $rec(X, \_)$ (recursion) then yield the set $P_{\mathcal{A}_{D\Sigma}}$ of CCS–process expressions. (Using the recursion operator allows the use of single expressions only, but could also be replaced by systems of equations with recursion variables. The latter are easier to read, since the recursion variables can often be understood as agents or states. For this reason they are also used in the examples.) We thus obtain the CCS-control flow formulae

$$CCS(D\Sigma) = P_{\mathcal{A}_{D\Sigma}} \, .$$

The deduction rules of CCS yield a set of transition expressions $e \xrightarrow{l} e'$, where e and e' are process expressions and $l \in \mathcal{A}_{D\Sigma}$ is an action. With these transitions $P_{\mathcal{A}_{D\Sigma}}$ becomes an LTS, and the operational semantics $\|e\|$ of an expression e can be understood as the sub-LTS of $P_{\mathcal{A}_{D\Sigma}}$ that is reachable from e.

A $D\Sigma$-transformation system $\mathbf{M}$ then satisfies a formula (= CCS-process expression) e, if the underlying LTS of $\mathbf{M}$ coincides with the CCS–semantics of e, up to the idle transitions, the renaming ρ of the labels given by $\rho(\{a(c; d)\}) = a(c; d)$ and $\rho(\emptyset) = \tau$, and isomorphism of the states. That means

$$\mathbf{M} \models_{D\Sigma}^{CCS} e \text{ if } LTS(\mathbf{M})[\rho] \cong \|e\|.$$

Note that, according to this definition, only sequential transformation systems can satisfy a CCS-specification. This corresponds to the interleaving semantics of CCS that excludes truly parallel actions. The latter are allowed in the extension to synchronous processes SCCS [Mil83], however.

Modal μ-Control Flow Logic

Formulae of the modal μ-calculus are evaluated in LTSs with a fixed set of actions $\mathcal{A}$ that also yields the modalities that are part of the formulae. Following [Sti92] the set $Mu(\mathcal{A})$ of modal μ-formulae Φ is defined by

$$\Phi ::= Z \mid true \mid false \mid \Phi_1 \wedge \Phi_2 \mid \Phi_1 \vee \Phi_2 \mid [K]\Phi \mid \langle K \rangle \Phi \mid \nu Z.\Phi \mid \mu Z.\Phi$$

where Z ranges over a given set of propositional variables $\mathcal{Z}$ and K ranges over subsets of $\mathcal{A}$. The modal formulae $[K]\Phi$ and $\langle K \rangle \Phi$ mean 'after any transition labelled by an $a \in K$ the formula Φ holds' (necessity) and 'there is a transition labelled by an $a \in K$ such that afterwards formula Φ holds' (possibility). The fixed point operators νZ and μZ yield the greatest and least fixed points respectively. The formal semantics $\|\Phi\|_{\mathcal{V}}$ of a formula Φ is defined in terms of solution sets in a given LTS $L = (S, \mathcal{A}, \rightarrow)$, i.e., $\|\Phi\|_{\mathcal{V}} \subseteq S$. These are defined relative to a valuation $\mathcal{V} : \mathcal{Z} \rightarrow S$ of the propositional variables as follows:

$$\|Z\|_{\mathcal{V}} \quad = \mathcal{V}(Z)$$
$$\|\Phi_1 \wedge \Phi_2\|_{\mathcal{V}} = \|\Phi_1\|_{\mathcal{V}} \cap \|\Phi_2\|_{\mathcal{V}}$$
$$\|\Phi_1 \vee \Phi_2\|_{\mathcal{V}} = \|\Phi_1\|_{\mathcal{V}} \cup \|\Phi_2\|_{\mathcal{V}}$$
$$\|[K]\Phi\|_{\mathcal{V}} \quad = \|[K]\| \, \|\Phi\|_{\mathcal{V}}$$
$$\|\langle K \rangle \Phi\|_{\mathcal{V}} \quad = \|\langle K \rangle\| \, \|\Phi\|_{\mathcal{V}}$$
$$\|\nu Z.\Phi\|_{\mathcal{V}} \quad = \bigcup \{E \subseteq S \,:\, E \subseteq \|\Phi\|_{\mathcal{V}[E/Z]}\}$$
$$\|\mu Z.\Phi\|_{\mathcal{V}} \quad = \bigcap \{E \subseteq S \,:\, \|\Phi\|_{\mathcal{V}[E/Z]} \subseteq E\}$$

where

$$\|[K]\|(X) = \{F \in S \,:\, F \xrightarrow{a} E \wedge a \in K \;\rightarrowtail\; E \in X\}$$
$$\|\langle K \rangle\|(X) = \{F \in S \,:\, \exists E \in X \exists a \in K.F \xrightarrow{a} E\}$$

for all $X \subseteq S$. An LTS L satisfies a formula Φ if $\|\Phi\|_{\mathcal{V}} = S$ for all valuations $\mathcal{V}$.

As above, the actions $Act_{D\Sigma}$ instantiated w.r.t. a fixed S-sorted set M of actual parameters yields the actions to define the control flow formulae

$$Mu(D\Sigma) = Mu(Act_{D\Sigma}(M,M))$$

and the satisfaction relation

$$\mathbf{M} \models^{Mu}_{D\Sigma} \Phi \;\; \text{if} \;\; LTS(\mathbf{M}) \models \Phi \,.$$

This defines the control flow logic $(Mu(D\Sigma), \models^{Mu}_{D\Sigma})$.

Algebraic High-Level Nets

Like a CCS-expression a Petri net describes a single behaviour which—in a first approximation—can be described as an LTS, given by the reachability graph of the net. As opposed to CCS-processes, however, the states of the marking graph, i.e., the markings of the net, express relevant semantic properties that can be considered as a kind of data state. (Cf. the discussion in Section 2.5.)

Petri nets have been extended in many ways to ease the representation of more complex applications, for instance by token colours to distinguish different types of tokens, transitions with special behaviours, or timing annotations, etc. Algebraic high-level nets (AHL nets), introduced in [Vau87, Hum89], offer very general structuring means for Petri nets, based on algebras of tokens and terms and equations for the specification of the behaviour of transitions. Due to this algebraic approach this version is a good candidate to explain a translation to a control flow logic for transformation systems. For the construction of a control flow logic a slightly adapted version is presented here.

An AHL net schema $N = (\Sigma, P, T, vars, pre, post, cond)$ is given by

- an algebraic signature $\Sigma = (S, F)$,
- sets P and T of places and transitions respectively,

- a function $vars : T \to S^*$ that assigns an anonymous variable declaration to each transition,
- functions $pre, post : T \times P \to \mathcal{M}(T_\Sigma)$ that assign to each transition and place a multiset of terms with (anonymous) variables, the pre- and post-domains, such that each term $r \in pre(t,p) \cup post(t,p)$ has the functionality $r : vars(t) \to v \in T_\Sigma$ for some $v \in S^*$,
- a function $cond : T \to Eqns_{\Sigma,vars(t)}$ that assigns a condition ($= \Sigma$-equation with anonymous variables declared by $vars(t)$) to each transition.

To play the token game a net schema N is instantiated by a partial Σ-algebra B, which yields an AHL net $N(B)$. A marking of $N(B)$ is a function $m : P \to \mathcal{M}(B)$ that assigns to each place a multiset of elements of B (the algebra B is identified with the disjoint union of its carrier sets here). Usually a net is given together with an initial marking m_0.

The class of all AHL nets yield the formulae $AHL(D\Sigma)$ of the control flow logic AHL for each data space signature $D\Sigma$. Note that the AHL-net signature Σ need not coincide with the data signature of the data space signature $D\Sigma$. The difference is discussed in the definition of the satisfaction relation $\models_{D\Sigma}^{AHL}$ below.

A transition $t \in T$ with $vars(t) = w$ is enabled (to fire) with a list of elements $b \in B_w$ by a marking m, if the following conditions hold:

- b satisfies $cond(t)$, i.e., b is a solution of $cond(t)$ in B, and
- there are enough elements in the pre-domain of t. That means, for each place $p \in P$ and each term $r \in pre(t,p)$, the element $r^B(b)$ is contained in $m(p)$ at least as often as r is contained in $pre(t,p)$. Formally

$$\forall p \in P, r \in pre(t,p) \; r^B(b) \leq m(p) .$$

The firing of t with b then yields the successor marking m' given by

$$m'(p) = (m(p) - pre(t,p)^B(b)) + post(p,t)^B(b)$$

where $M^B(b) = \{r^B(b) \mid r \in M\}$ for all multisets of terms $M \subseteq \mathcal{M}(T_\Sigma)$ with the same variable declaration. Such a firing is denoted by $m \, [t(b)\rangle \, m'$.

A multiset $\mathbf{t} = \sum_{i \in I} n_i t_i$ of net transitions t_i, where t_i occurs n_i times in $\mathbf{t}$, can be fired with a list $b = (b_1, \ldots, b_k)$ of lists of elements $b_i \in B_{w_i}$ if

- each b_i satisfies $cond(t_i)$, and
- there are enough tokens on each place to withdraw the instantiated pre-domains of all transitions n_i times.

The corresponding firing is denoted by $m \, [\mathbf{t}(b)\rangle \, m'$, where

$$m'(p) = (m(p) - \sum_{i \in I} pre(t_i,p)^B(b)) + \sum_{i \in I} post(p,t)^B(b) .$$

Let $Mark(N(B))$ be the transition graph given by all markings of $N(B)$ as states, plus an initialisation state Δ, all parallel firings $m \, [\mathbf{t}(b)\rangle \, m'$ as transitions, and an initialisation $init : \Delta \to m_0$, where m_0 is the initial marking of

$N(B)$. Furthermore let $Reach(N(B))$ be the reachable transition subgraph of $Mark(N(B))$, which is considered as the operational semantics of $N(B)$.

To compare $Reach(N(B))$ with a $D\Sigma$-transformation system a relationship with the data space $I\!D_{D\Sigma}$ has to be established. Usually the markings are not directly interpreted as data states, but an additional interpretation is used that allows markings to be correlated with data states. Since not all possible markings (i.e., all states of $Mark(N(B))$) might be meaningful under this interpretation, the correlation is expressed as a partial function. The latter is treated as a parameter in the comparison (satisfaction relation) of $D\Sigma$-transformation systems as models and the net $N(B)$ as specification.

For that purpose let $\nu\ :\ Mark(N(B))\ \leftrightarrow\ I\!D_{D\Sigma}$ be a partial transition graph morphism such that $dom(\nu)$ contains $Reach(N(B))$. The restriction of ν to $Reach(N(B))$ then yields a total transition graph morphism $\mathbf{n}\ :\ Reach(N(B))\ \rightarrow\ I\!D_{D\Sigma}$ that makes $(Reach(N(B)), \mathbf{n})$ a $D\Sigma$-transformation system.

The satisfaction relation can now be defined by saying that a $D\Sigma$-transformation system $\mathbf{M} = (TG_{\mathbf{M}}, \mathbf{m})$ satisfies the net $N(B)$ with respect to a data interpretation ν, if the two $D\Sigma$-transformation models $\mathbf{M}$ and $(Reach(N(B)), \mathbf{n})$ are isomorphic in $\mathbf{TF}(D\Sigma)$:

$$\mathbf{M} \models_{D\Sigma}^{AHL,\nu} N(B) \ \text{ if } \ \mathbf{M} \cong (Reach(N(B)), \mathbf{n})$$

That means there must be a transition graph isomorphism

$$\gamma : Reach(N(B)) \rightarrow TG_{\mathbf{M}}$$

such that $\mathbf{m} \circ \gamma = \mathbf{n}$.

Examples for the specification of a transformation system by AHL nets are given in the next section.

Each set of control flow formulae of a given signature $D\Sigma$ can be considered as a specification of the dynamic behaviour of $D\Sigma$-transformation systems, i.e., a control flow specification. Data space specifications and control flow specifications together then yield the transformation specifications.

Definition 3.12 (Transformation Specification). *A transformation specification $T\Gamma = (DS, R, C\Gamma)$ w.r.t. a data space signature $D\Sigma$ and a control flow logic $CL = (CF, \models^{CL})$ is given by*

- *a data specification $DS = (Ax, In, Fi)$ w.r.t. $D\Sigma$,*
- *a set R of $D\Sigma$-transformation rules, and*
- *a control flow specification $C\Gamma \subseteq CF(D\Sigma)$.*

A $D\Sigma$-transformation system $\mathbf{M} = (TG_{\mathbf{M}}, \mathbf{m})$ with $TG_{\mathbf{M}} = (CS, T, in, id)$ satisfies the transformation specification $T\Gamma = (D\Sigma, DS, R, C\Gamma)$, if

- $\mathbf{m}(c) \models Ax$ *for each control state $c \in CS - \{in\}$,*

- $\mathbf{m}(c_0) \models In$ *for each initial state* $c_0 \in \{c \in CS - \{in\} \mid T(in, c) \neq \emptyset\}$,
- $\mathbf{m}(c_1) \models Fi$ *for each final state* $c_1 \in \{c \in CS - \{in\} \mid T(c, in) \neq \emptyset\}$,
- $\mathbf{M} \models r$ *for each transformation rule* $r \in R$,
- $\mathbf{M} \models_{D\Sigma}^{CL} C\Gamma$.

The set of transformation specifications w.r.t. $D\Sigma$ *is denoted by* $TSpec(D\Sigma)$.

3.3 Examples

The examples from Section 2.2, the linked list and the CCS sender, are now specified with appropriate data specifications, transformation rules, and different control flow logics as introduced in Section 3.2.

Example 3.13 (Specification of Linked Lists). The different kinds of axioms of transformation specifications can be used to give more detailed (semantic) information about the linked-list model introduced in Example 2.12. The data invariants comprise the static data type axioms and the consistency conditions for the data states. Corresponding to the description on p. 40 these can be stated as conditional equations as follows.

The only data type invariants constraining the interpretation of the static data type signature Σ_{ll}^{static} are that the list pointers are always:

- *first* $\downarrow$, *prev* $\downarrow$, *act* $\downarrow$, *next* $\downarrow$

The consistency conditions for environments yield the following data state axioms.

- $!(first) \downarrow$, $!(prev) \downarrow$, $!(act) \downarrow$, $!(next) \downarrow$
  Note that these axioms imply the data type invariants above due to the strictness of partial functions. Nevertheless they have been stated in order to support the distinction between static data type and dynamic data state specification and thus enhance the documentation.
- $!(act) = !(first) \Leftrightarrow !(prev) = void$
- $!(snd(!(prev))) = !(act) \Leftrightarrow nonvoid(!(prev))$
- $nonvoid(!(act)) \Rightarrow !(snd(!(act))) = !(next)$
- $!(act) = void \wedge !(x) \downarrow \Rightarrow !(x) = void$

The last property of environments cannot be defined directly by conditional existence equations.

- The condition on the connection of the cells to a finite list ending in a void cell contains existential quantifications. To express it first-order logic is needed (unless the list of pointers is introduced as an auxiliary function, like a Skolem function). Also the requirement that the list pointers *first*, *prev*, *act*, and *next* are not contained in the list is not algebraic due to the negation. This condition could be expressed, however, by distinguishing a sort of list pointers from the cell pointers, both pointing to cells. (This would also support hiding of the internal pointers in an easier way, cf. Chapter 4.)

In each state, represented by an environment e, the *cell* part of the data state can be derived from e, as well as the *right* function (see p. 42). This can be specified by the remaining data state axioms.

- $\langle d, p \rangle \downarrow \; \Rightarrow \; fst(\langle d, p \rangle) = d \wedge snd(\langle d, p \rangle) = p \wedge nonvoid(\langle d, p \rangle)$
- $!(p) \downarrow \; \Rightarrow \; right(\langle d, p \rangle) =!(p)$

  (At this point the specification could be refined by requiring that each non-void cell also has a right neighbour, i.e., there are no dead end streets: $\langle d, p \rangle \downarrow \; \Rightarrow \; !(p) \downarrow .$)

Note that only the initial interpretation of these axioms yields the *cell* part as defined in the model. Thus a *data constraint* (cf. [EM90]) would be required in addition. The same holds for the data type axioms. Conditional equations alone cannot guarantee that they are interpreted by the same sets and constant elements in each state.

This concludes the definition of the data axioms. The initialisation and finalisation conditions are empty.

The transformation rules rephrase the definitions of the model directly (see p. 41). Note how the conditions of the steps are represented on the left hand sides of the rules and how the variable names are used to connect left and right hand sides.

- $move \; \hat{=} \; c_a, c_n \in cell :$
  $nonvoid(!(next)), !(act) = c_a, !(next) = c_n$
  $\rightarrow$
  $!(prev) = c_a, !(act) = c_n, !(next) = right(c_n)$
- $move \; \hat{=} \; c_f \in cell :$
  $!(next) = void, nonvoid(!(prev)), !(first) = c_f$
  $\rightarrow$
  $!(prev) = void, !(act) = c_f, !(next) = right(c_f)$
- $move \; \hat{=} \; q \in pointer, c \in cell :$
  $!(next) - void, !(prev) - void, !(q) - c$
  $\rightarrow$
  $!(q) = c$
- $move \; \hat{=} \; q \in pointer, c \in cell;$
  $!(act) = void, !(q) = c$
  $\rightarrow$
  $!(q) = c$

Analogous to the initial interpretation of the *cell* part that could be forced by a data constraint as mentioned above, only an initial (constructive) interpretation of the right hand sides of the rules would yield exactly the transformations of the model. Otherwise the states reached by a *move* action for example could also satisfy further unexpected equations. Using the construction of

Section 3.4 this least interpretation of the right hand sides of transformation rules is guaranteed. However, explicit information on the left hand side of the rules would be required concerning the removal of the function definitions $(!(prev) = c_p)$ in the input state. Moreover, this interpretation then implies that the environment is not changed for pointers that do not occur in the rule, corresponding to the 'else $e'(x) = e(x)$' branch of the definition.

The transformation rules for the *delete* part are obtained analogously to the *move* rules presented above. Note that the *start* and *stop* flags cannot be taken into account in these rules, because they are not part of the data signatures. This control flow aspect has to be specified with the control flow logic. In the second and third rule, moreover, inequality are used, corresponding to the description on p. 44. Although this is not covered by Definition 3.3 the semantics of these transformation rules can easily be reduced to the one given in Definition 3.5, because inequalities are semantically interpreted by solution sets, like equations. The formal definitions for this extension to other formulae than equations are given in Section 3.5.

- *delete* $\hat{=} c_n \in cell$:
  $!(act) = !(first), nonvoid(!(next)), !(next) = c_n$
  $\rightarrow$
  $!(first) = c_n, !(act) = c_n, !(next) = right(c_n)$
- *delete* $\hat{=} c_n \in cell$:
  $!(act) \neq !(first), nonvoid(!(next)), !(next) = c_n$
  $\rightarrow$
  $!(snd(!(prev))) = c_n, !(act) = c_n, !(next) = right(c_n)$
- *delete* $\hat{=}$
  $!(act) \neq !(first), !(next) = void$
  $\rightarrow$
  $!(snd(!(prev))) = void, !(act) = void$
- *delete* $\hat{=} c \in cell$:
  $!(act) = !(first), !(next) = void, !(c) \downarrow$
  $\rightarrow$
  $!(c) = void$

Let us check the validity of one of the transformation rules in **LL**, for example the first *move* rule. Take any transition $t : c \rightarrow d$, labelled with $act_t^{ll^{move}} = \{move\}$. Thus t must be of the form $move : e \rightarrow e'$ with environments e and e' satisfying the conditions stated on p. 41. Furthermore, there is at most one solution of the left hand side equations in $L[e]$, given by $\gamma(c_a) = e(a) \in L[e]_{cell}$ and $\gamma(c_n) = e(n) \in L[e]_{cell}$. Since $e(n) \neq \emptyset$ must also hold in $L[e]$, only the first case of the transition definition applies, whence $e'(p) = e(a) = \gamma(c_a)$, $e'(a) = e(n) = \gamma(c_n)$, and $e'(n) = e(\pi_2(e(n)))$. Then obviously $\delta = \gamma$ also satisfies the right hand side of the rule, and is in tracking relation with γ by definition. Thus, the rule is satisfied. The other rules can be checked analogously.

The control flow of **LL** can be specified in different ways, for example by a modal μ-formula or a by a CCS expression. Recall that in **LL** either the *move* action is executed arbitrarily often or the *delete* action is executed exactly once.

In CCS this behaviour can be expressed by

$$LL = move.M \ + \ delete.done$$
$$M \ = move.M \ + \ done$$

where *done* is a special action that reports successful termination of a process (see [Mil89], p. 172 ff.) and corresponds to the finalisations of transformation systems.

For the modal μ-specification the set of control states is divided into three parts:

Env	the control states that allow a *move* action, leading again to an *Env* state,
$\{\langle start, e \rangle \mid e \in Env\}$	the control states that only allow a *delete* action, leading to a $\langle stop, e' \rangle$ state,
$\{\langle stop, e \rangle \mid e \in Env\}$	the control states that only allow a finalisation.

Their union yields the set of all control states, except the initialisation state. It can be specified by the formula

$$(\nu X. \langle move \rangle X) \vee ([delete][delete, move]false) \vee ([delete, move]false) \ ,$$

and yields another control flow specification of **LL**.

Example 3.14 (Specification of the Sender). The static data type of the transformation system $\mathbf{CCS}_S$ defined in Example 2.13 is given by the set D of messages and the type $I\!B$ of boolean values $\{0, 1\}$ and the operations corresponding to t, f, and $\neg$, specified by the equations

- $\neg(t) = f, \ \neg(f) = t$.

The only data state axiom is

- $cbit \downarrow$

saying that the control bit is always defined. The initialisation condition is given by

- $cbit = f$.

The formulation of the second one, $msg = d_0$, would require a constant $d_0 :\to message$ in the signature. There are no finalisation conditions.

Transformation rules for the actions *ack* and *accept* are given by

- $ack(b) \hat{=} b \in bool$:
  $b = cbit, msg \downarrow \ \to \ cbit = \neg(b)$

- $ack(b) \triangleq b \in bool, d \in message$:

  $b = \neg(cbit), msg = d \rightarrow b = \neg(cbit), msg = d$
- $accept(d) \triangleq b \in bool, d \in message$:

  $cbit = b \rightarrow msg = d, cbit = b$

The second ack rule just checks whether $b = \neg(cbit)$ and msg is defined, and ensures that the data state is not changed. An analogous identity rule can be given for the $send$ action that also does not change the data state:

- $send(b, d) \triangleq b \in bool, d \in message$:

  $cbit = b, msg = d \rightarrow cbit = b, msg = d$

The information given by an identity rule like the last one is that whenever a $send$ action occurs at least the states of $cbit$ and msg do not change. In the minimal (initial) interpretation defined in Section 3.4 it is furthermore guaranteed that a $send$ action is performed if and only if both $cbit$ and msg are defined, and then nothing in the data state changes.

The difference between the control states $S_{b,d}$ and $S'_{b,d}$ that allow only $send$ or ack actions respectively can only be stated in the control flow specification. As in Example 3.13, different variants are presented here: a CCS specification, a specification with modal μ-formulae, and two AHL net specifications corresponding to a control flow view and a data flow view.

The CCS specification is simply the original one:

$$S \quad = S_{0,d_o}$$
$$S_{b,d} = \overline{send}(b,d).S'_{b,d}$$
$$S'_{b,d} = \tau.S_{b,d} + \ ack(b).accept(x).S_{\neg b,x} + \ ack(\neg b).S'_{b,d} \ .$$

A specification with modal μ-formulae is given by the set of mutually recursive formulae

$$\nu X_{b,d}.(\ \langle send(b,d) \rangle \langle send(b,d), ack(\neg b) \rangle X_{b,d}$$
$$\vee$$
$$\langle send(b,d) \rangle \langle ack(b) \rangle \langle accept(d') \rangle X_{\neg b,d'} \ ) \ .$$

The first AHL net $CF\_net_{CCS_S}$, depicted in Figure 3.2, represents the control flow of the sender and thus resembles the transition system representing the behaviour of the CCS expression (see Figure 2.10). Its four places correspond to the control states $S_{b,d}, S'_{b,d}, A_b, \Delta$, where the indexes are represented by the tokens that may reside on the places. Its transitions correspond to the actions, indicated by their labels, where the parameters of the actions are given by the variables of the net transitions that are also used in the labels. The signature of the net schema is accordingly given by the static subsignature $\Sigma^{static}_{CCS\text{-}S}$ that contains the signature of the booleans and a sort $message$.

The $\Sigma^{static}_{CCS\text{-}S}$-algebra DB from Example 2.13 then yields a net $N = CF\_net_{CCS_S}(DB)$, initially marked by one token $*$ of unit type λ on the initialisation place Δ.

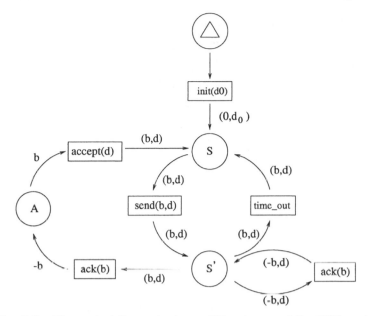

Fig. 3.2. The control flow net schema $CF\_net_{CCS_S}$ of the CCS sender

Now the data interpretation $\nu : Mark(N) \multimap\!\!\!\rightarrow I\!D_{CCS\text{-}S}$ has to be defined. Let $m : P \to \mathcal{M}(DB)$ be a marking of the places of N such that $m(p) = \{x\}$ for exactly one place $p \in \{S, S', A, \Delta\}$ and $m(p') = \emptyset$ for all other places, where $x = (b, d)$ if $p = S$ or $p = S'$, $x = b$ if $p = A$, and $x = *$ if $p = \Delta$. Then $\nu(m) = DB[x]$. For all other markings ν is not defined. On the transitions ν is defined by $\nu(t) = \{t\}$ if $t \in \{send(b, d), ack(b), accept(d)\}$ and $\nu(t) = \emptyset$ if $t \in \{init(d_0), time\_out\}$. Obviously ν is defined on the reachability graph $Reach(N)$. Furthermore the transition graph morphism $\gamma : Reach(N) \to TG_{CCS_S}$ given by

$$\gamma(m) = p_x \qquad \text{if } m(p) = \{x\}, \quad p \in \{S, S', A\}$$
$$\gamma(t) = label(t) \ \text{ on the net transitions}$$

is an isomorphism and compatible with the transition graph morphisms $\mathbf{n} : Reach(N) \multimap\!\!\!\rightarrow I\!D_{CCS\text{-}S}$ and $\mathbf{ccs}_S : TG_{CCS_S} \multimap\!\!\!\rightarrow I\!D_{CCS\text{-}S}$. Thus

$$\mathbf{CCS}_S \models_{D\Sigma}^{AHL,\nu} CF\_net_{CCS_S}(DB) \ .$$

The second AHL net description $N = DF\_net_{CCS_S}(DB)$ models the data flow in the sender instead of the control flow (see Figure 3.3), similar to the net specification given in [Rei98]. The *msg* and *cbit* places correspond to the constants *msg* and *cbit* of the data space signature; the other places are *open* places that represent the interface for communication with the other components. For the sake of brevity we assume that there are infinitely many tokens on the open places *accept* and *ack* in the initial marking that can be consumed by the sender. Furthermore let there be a 0 on the lowermost *cbit* place.

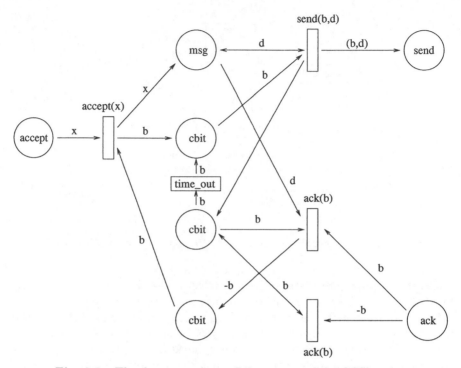

Fig. 3.3. The data net schema $DF\_net_{CCS_S}$ of the CCS sender

The data interpretation ν is defined for a marking of N if there is at most one token of type *message* on the place labelled *msg*, and exactly one token on a place labelled *cbit*. Then $\nu(m) = DB[b, d]$ if the token on the *msg* place is d and the token on a *cbit* place is b, and $\nu(m) = DB[b]$ if there is no token on the *msg* place and the token on a *cbit* place is b. The markings in the domain of ν are preserved by the firing of transitions of N, i.e., $Reach(N) \subseteq dom(\nu)$. Furthermore there is a transition graph isomorphism $\gamma : Reach(N) \to TG_{CCS_S}$, given by

$$\gamma(m) = \begin{cases} S_{b,d} & \text{if } m(msg) = d \text{ and } m(cbit) = b \text{ for the topmost } cbit \text{ place} \\ S'_{b,d} & \text{if } m(msg) = d \text{ and } m(cbit) = b \text{ for the central } cbit \text{ place} \\ A_b & \text{if } m(cbit) = b \text{ for the lowermost } cbit \text{ place} \end{cases}$$

and $\gamma(t) = label(t)$ for the transitions. Thus also

$$\mathbf{CCS}_S \models_{D\Sigma}^{AHL,\nu} DF\_net_{CCS_s}(DB) \ .$$

This discussion shows how a single specification formalism can be used in very different styles which yield specifications with different formal operational semantics. The interpretation as transformation systems, incorporating here the data interpretations, allow us to make explicit the intentions and assumptions comprised in a style. In this interpretation the two nets turn out to specify the same behaviour.

An analogous equivalence result would have been obtained by considering the event structures associated to the nets ([Win86]) that are an abstraction of the operational semantics. In the event structure semantics, however, the data states also are abstracted. That means nets with different data state properties (data invariants) cannot be distinguished. Transformation systems allow us to retain data states so long as their properties represent relevant properties of the modelled system.

3.4 Rewriting Algebras with Transformation Rules

In this section the rewriting of algebras by the application of transformation rules is introduced, i.e., the constructive interpretation of transformation rules. Rewriting an algebra means replacing some of its elements and redefining some of its functions. (That means its properties are rewritten.) For the rewriting algebras are presented by families of sets, whence simple set-theoretic operations like subtraction and union can be used to delete and add elements and properties. The technical means for this reduction of algebra rewriting to set rewriting are given by *presentations* and an adjunction of presentations and algebras. A presentation is thereby given by a set of generators and a set of relations between the generators, where the latter are given as equations.

Definition 3.15 (Presentation). *Let $\Sigma = (S, F)$ be an algebraic signature. A Σ-presentation $P = (P_S, P_E)$ is given by an S-indexed set $P_S = (P_s)_{s \in S}$, the generators, and a set $P_E \subseteq Eqns_\Sigma(P_S)$, the equations. A presentation is functional if P_E is a set of function entries over P_S, i.e.,*

$$P_E \subseteq \{f(a) = b \mid f : w \to v \in F, a \in P_w, b \in P_v\} \subseteq Eqns_\Sigma(P_S).$$

Given an S-indexed subset $Q_S \subseteq P_S$ the restriction $P|_{Q_S}$ is defined by

$$P|_{Q_S} = (Q_S, P_E \cap Eqns_\Sigma(Q_S)).$$

A morphism of Σ-presentations $p : (P_S, P_E) \to (P'_S, P'_E)$ is given by an S-indexed function $p = (p_s : P_s \to P'_s)_{s \in S}$ such that $P_E[p] \subseteq P'_E$, where _[p] denotes the substitution of generators in equations according to p. Σ-presentations and morphisms yield the category $\mathbf{Pres}(\Sigma)$.

Finally let $\mathbf{Pres}(\Gamma) = \mathbf{Pres}(\Sigma)$ for each partial equational specification $\Gamma = (\Sigma, CE)$ extending Σ.

Consider a partial equational specification Γ. To each Γ-presentation $P = (P_S, P_E)$ there is a *smallest* partial Γ-algebra A^P that contains the generators P_S and satisfies the equations P_E. This property is formally stated as the existence of a free functor from the category of Γ-presentations to the category of partial Γ-algebras, i.e., a left adjoint to the *presentation functor* that maps partial Γ-algebras to Γ-presentations. If P_E is *consistently functional* and CE is empty, then A^P is essentially the same as P (see Corollary 3.17).

Proposition 3.16. *Let $\Gamma = (\Sigma, CE)$ be a partial equational specification. The presentation functor $Pres_\Gamma : \mathbf{PAlg}(\Gamma) \to \mathbf{Pres}(\Gamma)$, given by*

$$Pres_\Gamma(A_S, A_{OP}) = (A_S, \{f(a) = b \mid f^A(a) = b\}) ,$$

and $Pres_\Gamma(h) = h$, has a left adjoint $PAlg_\Gamma : \mathbf{Pres}(\Gamma) \to \mathbf{PAlg}(\Gamma)$ satisfying $PAlg_\Gamma \circ Pres_\Gamma \cong Id_{\mathbf{PAlg}(\Gamma)}$.

Proof. The existence of free partial Γ-algebras $PAlg(P)$ for Γ-presentations P is shown in [Bur86, Rei87].

It remains to be shown that each partial Γ-algebra A is free over its presentation $P = Pres_\Gamma(A)$, because then the assignment $Pres_\Gamma(A) \mapsto A$ and $Q \mapsto PAlg_\Gamma(Q)$ for $Q \notin Pres_\Gamma(|\mathbf{PAlg}(\Gamma)|)$ yields a free functor F that satisfies $F \circ Pres_\Gamma = Id_{\mathbf{PAlg}(\Gamma)}$. Since F must be naturally isomorphic to $PAlg_\Gamma$ the assertion then follows.

Consider $id_P : P \to Pres_\Gamma(A)$ as unit, and an arbitrary $B \in |\mathbf{PAlg}(\Gamma)|$ and $p : P \to Pres_\Gamma(B)$ in $\mathbf{Pres}(\Gamma)$.

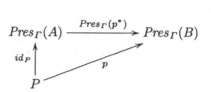

Define $p^* : A \to B$ by $p_s^* = p_s : A_s \to B_s$ ($s \in S$). For any $a \in dom(f^A)$ with $f^A(a) = b$ for some $f : w \to v \in F$ and $b \in A_v$, we have $(f(a) = b) \in Pres_\Gamma(A)$, whence $(f(a) = b)[p] = (f(p(a)) = p(b)) \in Pres_\Gamma(B)$. Thus $p(a) \in dom(f^B)$ and $f^B(p(a)) = p(b)$, i.e., p^* is a Γ-homomorphism. By definition of $Pres_\Gamma$ on morphisms p^* is obviously also the only Γ-homomorphism $A \to B$ that satisfies $Pres_\Gamma(p^*) \circ id_P = p$.

Given an algebraic signature Σ, the partial Σ-algebra generated by a functional Σ-presentation that does not contain inconsistent function entries $f(a) = b$ and $f(a) = b'$ with $b \neq b'$ is essentially the same as the presentation itself. If axioms also are considered, however, or if there are inconsistent function entries, further elements may be generated and some generators or generated elements may be identified.

Corollary 3.17. *Let Σ be an algebraic signature and $P = (P_S, P_E)$ be a Σ-presentation. If P is consistently functional, i.e., P is functional and satisfies*

$$(f(a) = b) \in P_E \wedge (f(a) = b') \in P_E \Rightarrow b = b'$$

for all $f : w \rightarrow v \in F, a \in P_w, b, b' \in P_v$, then

$$Pres_\Sigma(PAlg_\Sigma(P)) \cong P .$$

Proof. Define the partial Σ-algebra A^P as follows. Each carrier set $(A^P)_s$ for $s \in S$ is given by the set P_s, an element $a \in P_w$ is in the domain of a partial function $f^{A^P} : A_w^P \rightarrow\!\!\!\!\rightarrow A_v^P$ iff there is a function entry $f(a) = b$ in P_E, and in this case $f^{A^P}(a) = b$. Then $Pres_\Sigma(A^P) = P$ and A^P is obviously free over P, i.e., $A^P \cong PAlg_\Sigma(P)$.

The left and right hand sides $L = (X_l : E_l)$ and $R = (X_r : E_r)$ of a transformation rule $r = (\alpha \stackrel{\scriptstyle\triangle}{=} L \rightarrow R)$ are obviously also presentations. This is now used to define the application of a rule r to an algebra A via the presentation of A. For that purpose let the symmetric differences and intersections of r be given by

$$X_l^0 = X_l - X_r , \; X_c = X_l \cap X_r , \; X_r^0 = X_r - X_l ,$$
$$E_l^0 = E_l - E_r , \; E_c = E_l \cap E_r , \; E_r^0 = E_r - E_l .$$

The sets X_l^0 and X_r^0 represent elements that should be deleted and added respectively when applying the rule. The variables in X_c must be matched when the rule is applied, but are retained during the rewriting. They are used to fix the context of the rewriting that determines how the new parts— elements and equations—are inserted into the algebra. The same holds for the equation sets E_l^0, E_c, and E_r^0 that represent the properties that are to be deleted, retained, and added respectively.

For the description of the rewriting consider first a rule $r = (\alpha \stackrel{\scriptstyle\triangle}{=} L \rightarrow R)$ that does not create new elements, i.e., $X_r^0 = \emptyset$. Note that E_r^0 might be non-empty also in this case, using variables of X_c only.

To apply r to a partial algebra A the variables $X_l = X_l^0 \cup X_c$ of the left hand side L must be mapped to A in such a way that the equations E_l are respected. The rewriting of A is then obtained in three steps:

1. the *subtraction* of the image of (X_l^0, E_l^0) w.r.t. the matching in A,
2. the *addition* of the instantiated equations E_r^0, and
3. the *free construction* of the corresponding Γ-algebra.

The carrier sets B_S of the result of the rewriting are accordingly given by $B_S = (A_S - a(X_l^0))$, where a is the mapping $X_l \rightarrow A$. Its generating set of equations B_E consists of two components: the sets $A_E - E_l^0[a]$ and $E_r^0[a]$, corresponding to the subtraction and addition of the function entries E_l^0 and the equations E_r^0 respectively. Finally, all equations still containing variables from A_S that no longer belong to B_S must be removed in order to obtain a well-defined presentation again. Thus the deletion of an element $\tilde{a}$ of A has the side effect of removing all function entries containing $\tilde{a}$ in any position.

The action label of the rewrite step records the names of the actions that have been applied and the instantiations of their parameters in A. The tracking relation is given for the general case in Definition 3.22 below.

Definition 3.18 (Algebra Rewriting Without Creation).   *Let* $D\Gamma =$ (Ax, In, Fi, R) *be a data space specification w.r.t. a signature* $D\Sigma = (\Sigma, A)$, *and let the algebraic specification* Γ *be given by* $\Gamma = (\Sigma, Ax)$. *Furthermore let* $r = (\alpha \mathrel{\hat{=}} L \rightarrow R)$ *be a transformation rule with* $X_r^0 = \emptyset$ *and let* A *be a partial* Γ-*algebra with* $Pres_\Gamma(A) = (A_S, A_E)$.

1. *A* match a *for* r *in* A *is a* Γ-*presentation morphism* $a : L \rightarrow (A_S, A_E)$.
2. *The* rewrite step r/a *given by a match* a *for* r *in* A *is defined as the transformation*

$$r/a = (\alpha[a] : A \Rightarrow B)$$

where $\alpha[a]$ *is the instantiation of* $\alpha \subseteq Act_{D\Sigma}(X, Y)$ *w.r.t.* a *and the partial* Γ-*algebra* B *is constructed as follows:*

$$B_S = (A_S - a(X_l^0)),$$
$$B_E = ((A_E - E_l^0[a]) \cup E_r^0[a])|_{B_S},$$
$$B = PAlg_\Gamma(B_S, B_E).$$

Example 3.19 (Assignment). Consider a specification with pointers (similar to the one in Example 2.3) with an assignment action and the rule for an assignment similar to the ones in Examples 3.4 and 3.8,1.

prog =
    sorts pointer, value
    funs p: $\rightarrow$ pointer
         !: pointer $\rightarrow$ value
    acts assign: pointer, nat
    rules assign $\mathrel{\hat{=}}$ x $\in$ pointer, v, v' $\in$ value :
        !(x) = v' $\rightarrow$!(x) = v

The variable v' is used to delete the old function entry. It does not occur as a parameter of the *assign* method, but the instantiation of x and v induces a unique matching of the rule, since v' must be mapped to the actual value of x.

Given now a partial algebra A with $A_{value} = I\!N$, the set of natural numbers, $A_{prog-var} = \{X, Y, \ldots\}$, and $!^A(X) = n$ for some $n \in I\!N$ for example, the *assign* rule can be applied as follows.

The rewriting step $assign(X, k) : A \Rightarrow B$ for some $k \in I\!N$ yields a state B which differs from A only in that $!^B(X) = k$. More formally, the match is given by $a(x) = X$, $a(v') = n$, and $a(v) = k$. This is the only match with $a(x) = X$ and $a(v) = k$, since the left equation $!(x) = v'$ enforces $a(v') =!^A(a(x)) = n$. Then

$$B_S = A_S \quad \text{since } X_l^0 = \emptyset, \text{ and}$$
$$B_E = (A_E - \{!(X) = n\}) \cup \{!(X) = k\} \,.$$

Moreover, each term $t \in T_\Sigma(A_S)$ over the elements of A, such as $t = 2*!(X)$, also denotes an element of A; for example, $(2*!(X))^A = 2*!^A(X)$. Correspondingly, the step $assign(X, 2*!(X)) : A \Rightarrow B$ yields a state B which differs from A only in that $!^B(X) = 2*!^A(X)$. The match is given by $a(x) = X$, $a(v') =!^A(X) = n$, and $a(v) = 2*!^A(X) = 2*n$. Then $B_S = A_S$ and $B_E = (A_E - \{!(X) = n\}) \cup \{!(X) = 2*n\}$. Thus $assign(X, 2*!(X))$ models the usual assignment $X := 2 * X$.

Pointwise function updates as in Example 3.8 yield analogous algebra rewriting steps.

When a rule creates new elements, i.e., $X_r^0 \neq \emptyset$, the generators B_S of the result of the rewriting are given by $B_S = (A_S - a(X_l^0)) \uplus X_r^0$ instead of $B_S = A_S - a(X_l^0)$. That means the variables X_r^0 themselves are added as generators. For the sake of brevity it is assumed that $A_S - a(X_l^0)$ and X_r^0 are disjoint. Otherwise a coproduct $B_S = (A_S - a(X_l^0)) + X_r^0$ with explicit coproduct injections $\iota_1 : A_S - a(X_l^0) \to B_S$ and $\iota_2 : X_r^0 \to B_S$ would have to be used. Since the free construction of the resulting algebra B is defined only up to isomorphism anyway, this can be avoided by the assumption made above, or an appropriate renaming.

Now the creation parameters of the actions in α can be used to give names to the new elements, or to embed them into the structure of the new algebra. For that purpose terms are used. A constant c of the signature for example can be given to an action as a creation parameter. Then the corresponding new element in the output state B is bound to c and can be accessed via this name. (If c corresponds to a program variable for example this means that c is an output parameter.) In the following definition this binding is achieved by adding an equation $x = c$ to the presentation equations of B. Terms with variables can be used as actual creation parameters to state properties of new elements. For example, let $x_c \in X_c$ and $x_r \in X_r$ be variables in the rule, $f : s \to s$ a function symbol, and $act : s; s$ an action name. Then the application of $act(a; f(x_c))$ with actual parameter a for x_c and actual creation parameter $f(x_c)$ for x_r introduces an element x_r that satisfies $x_r = f(a)$. If the value $f(a)$ is already defined then x_r is identified with it, otherwise x_r is a new element.

These two aspects, creating new elements and making them available by inserting them into the algebraic structure via creation parameters, are made precise in the following definition.

Definition 3.20 (Algebra Rewriting). *Let $D\Gamma = (Ax, In, Fi, R)$ be a data space specification w.r.t. a signature $D\Sigma = (\Sigma, A)$, and let the algebraic* *specification Γ be given by $\Gamma = (\Sigma, Ax)$. Furthermore, let $r = (\alpha \doteq L \to R)$ be a transformation rule and let A be a partial Γ-algebra with $Pres_\Gamma(A) = (A_S, A_E)$.*

1. *A match $at = (a, t)$ for r in A is given by a Γ-presentation morphism $a : L \to (A_S, A_E)$ and an S-indexed function $t : X_r^0 \to Term_\Sigma(X_l \cup X_r)$.*
2. *The rewrite step r/at given by a match at for r in A is defined as the transformation*

$$r/at = (\alpha[at] : A \Rightarrow B)$$

where the substitution $[at]$ is given by

$$x_i \mapsto \begin{cases} a(x_i) & \text{if } x_i \in X_l \\ t(x_i)[a] & \text{if } x_i \in X_r^0 \end{cases}$$

with the mapping a extended to $X_l \cup X_r$ by $a(x) = x$ for all $x \in X_r^0$, and the partial Γ-algebra B is constructed as follows:

$$B_S = (A_S - a(X_l^0)) \uplus X_r^0 ,$$

$$B_E = ((A_E - E_l^0[a]) \cup E_r^0[a] \cup \{x = t(x) \mid x \in X_r^0\}[a]) |_{B_S} ,$$

$$B = PAlg_\Gamma(B_S, B_E) .$$

Example 3.21 (Deletion and Creation). The rule for the deletion of a single element is obvious; creation can be defined as its inverse rule.

> **acts**   delete: s
> create: λ ; s
> **rules** delete(x) $\doteq$ x $\in$ s : $\emptyset \to \emptyset$: $\emptyset$
> create(x) $\doteq$ $\emptyset$: $\emptyset \to$ x $\in$ s : $\emptyset$

Application of the *delete* rule to an element $\alpha \in A_s$ via the match $a(x) = \alpha$ yields a state B given by

> $B_s = A_s - \{\alpha\}$, and $B_{s'} = A_{s'}$ for all $s' \neq s$,
> $B_E = A_E|_{B_S}$,   i.e., all function entries containing α are removed.

The *create* rule can be used to create a new element and bind it to an identifier, given for instance by a ground term. Let $c :\to s$ be a constant symbol and A a partial algebra where c is not defined. Then the application of *create(c)* via the match $t(x) = c$ yields a state B given by $B_s = A_s \uplus \{x\}$, where x is an arbitrary new element not contained in A_s, $B_{s'} = A_{s'}$ for all $s' \neq s$, and $B_E = A_E \cup \{x = c\}$. That means x is the interpretation of c in B. Thus in B a new element is created that can be referenced by the name c. If c were already defined in A, then B would be isomorphic to A, because the equations $x = c$ and $c^A = c$ imply $x = c^A$.

Now, after the general definition of an algebra rewriting step, the tracking relation for a step is also defined. For this purpose the intermediate state and its embeddings into the commencing and ending states is considered.

Definition 3.22 (Intermediate State). *Let $r/a = (\alpha[a] : A \Rightarrow B)$ be a rewrite step. The intermediate state $C = PAlg_\Gamma(C_S, C_E)$ of r/a is given by the partial Γ-algebra induced by the Γ-presentation $C_S = A_S - a(X_l^0)$ and $C_E = (A_E - E_l^0[a])|_{C_S}$.*

The inclusions $\iota_l : (C_S, C_E) \to (A_S, A_E)$ and $\iota_r : (C_S, C_E) \to (B_S, B_E)$ yield Γ-homomorphisms $\tilde{i}_l = PAlg(\iota_l) : C \to PAlg(A_S, A_E) \cong A$ and $i_r = PAlg(\iota_l) : C \to PAlg(B_S, B_E) = B$. Let $i_l : C \to A$ be the composition of $\tilde{i}$ with the isomorphism $PAlg(A_S, A_E) \cong A$. Then the tracking relation $\sim_{r/a} \subseteq |A| \times |B|$ is given by the span $A \xleftarrow{i_l} C \xrightarrow{i_r} B$, i.e.,

$$(a, b) \in \sim_{r/a} \quad if \quad \exists c \in C \,.\, i_l(c) = a \wedge i_r(c) = b \,.$$

Example 3.23 (Graph Rewriting). Graphs can be considered as partial algebras of the specification

> **graph** =
>   **sorts** node, edge
>   **funs** s,t: edge $\to$ node
>   **ceqns** s(e)$\downarrow$, t(e)$\downarrow$

where $r \downarrow$ is the definedness predicate. That means s and t must be total functions. Consider now the following method *del* for the deletion of nodes.

> **acts** del: node
> **rules** del(n) $\hat{=}$ (n$\in$node : $\emptyset$) $\to$ ($\emptyset$: $\emptyset$)

The application of *del*(3) for instance is depicted in Figure 3.4. In the last step

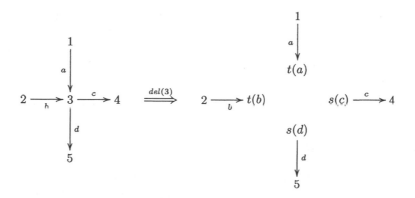

Fig. 3.4. The deletion of node 3, with active constraints

$(B_S, B_E) \mapsto PAlg(B_S, B_E)$ of the construction of the result of the rewriting, sources and targets are reconstructed for the dangling edges. These are enforced by the consistency axioms $s(e) \downarrow, t(e) \downarrow$ (totality of source and target)

in the specification. This means the axioms become *active constraints* that repair the inconsistencies arising from the deletion.

Edges may also be specified by labelled relations, as follows:

sorts node, label
funs edge: node, label, node

In this case they do not have their own identity, but are properties. Concerning the deletion of elements (nodes), this means that incident edges of deleted nodes are then deleted too as side effects (see Figure 3.5). In the formal definition this is expressed by the restriction $\_|_{B_S}$ of the equations to the elements B_S that are retained in the rewriting. Note that the set of labels in the example is not affected by the deletion of the edges. They are just no longer used as labels for these edges, since they no longer exist!

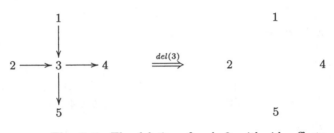

Fig. 3.5. The deletion of node 3, with side effects

Under certain conditions on the matching of a rule the corresponding rewrite step can be described semantically by commutative diagrams and pushouts in the category of partial algebras. The set of side effects of a rule application is defined for that purpose as the set of all function entries that are not directly deleted, but contain an element that is deleted. Compare also the definition of conflicts given in [Löw93, EHK$^+$97].

Definition 3.24. *Let $r/at = (\alpha[a] : A \Rightarrow B)$ be a rewrite step as in Definition 3.20.*

1. The set $Side(r/at)$ of side effects of r/at is defined by

$$Side(r/at) = \{\, e = (f(a_1, \ldots, a_n) = a_0) \in A_E \mid$$
$$e \notin E_l^0[a] \ \wedge\ \exists i \in \{0, \ldots, n\}\,.\, a_i \in a(X_l^0)\,\}\,.$$

2. The match $at = (a, t)$ is conflict free if

$$a(X_l^0) \cap a(X_c) = \emptyset\ \text{and}\ E_l^0[a] \cap E_c[a] = \emptyset\,.$$

Recall that (X_l^0, E_l^0) is the deletion part of a rule, and (X_c, E_c) contains the variables and function entries that should be preserved. Thus a match is conflict free if it does not require an entity to be deleted and retained. (Arbitrary matches are allowed in Definition 3.20. In the case of conflicts deletion is superior to preservation.)

Theorem 3.25. *Let $r/at = (\alpha[a] : A \Rightarrow B)$ be a rewrite step w.r.t. a rule $r = (\alpha \hat{=} L \to R)$ as in Definition 3.20.*

1. *If the match at is conflict free then there are Γ-homomorphisms α_l, α_c, α_r, p_l, p_r, i_l, i_r such that the following diagram in $\mathbf{PAlg}(\Gamma)$, where $P_C = (X_c, E_c)$, commutes.*

$$
\begin{array}{ccccc}
PAlg(L) & \xleftarrow{\ p_l\ } & PAlg(P_C) & \xrightarrow{\ p_r\ } & PAlg(R) \\
\alpha_l \downarrow & (1) & \alpha_c \downarrow & (2) & \downarrow \alpha_r \\
A & \xleftarrow{\ i_l\ } & C & \xrightarrow{\ i_r\ } & B
\end{array}
$$

2. *If at is conflict free and $l : X_r^0 \to T_\Sigma(X_l \uplus X_r)$ is the inclusion then diagram (2) is a pushout diagram.*
3. *If at is conflict free, $a|_{X_l^0} : X_l^0 \to A_S$ is injective, and $Side(r/at) = \emptyset$ then diagram (1) is a pushout diagram.*

Proof. Let $\epsilon_A : PAlg_\Gamma \circ Pres_\Gamma(A) \to A$ be the natural isomorphism given by Proposition 3.16.

1. The 'horizontal morphisms' p_l, p_r and i_r are the images under $PAlg_\Gamma$ of the inclusions $in_l : P_C \subseteq L$ and $in_r : P_C \subseteq R$ and $in_C : C_S \to B_S = C_S \uplus X_r^0$. The last one is a presentation morphism since

$$C_E = (A_E - E_l^0[a])|_{C_S} \subseteq (A_E - E_l^0[a])|_{B_S} \subseteq B_E .$$

The horizontal morphism i_l is given by the composition of the image of the inclusion $(C_S, C_E) \subseteq (A_S, A_E)$ under $PAlg_\Gamma$ and ϵ_A. Finally $\alpha_l = \epsilon_A \circ PAlg_\Gamma(a)$.

Since $a(X_l^0) \cap a(X_c) = \emptyset$, a restricts to $a_c = a|_{X_c} : X_c \to C_S$. Furthermore, by definition of $Side(r/at)$ and the restriction of presentations,

$$C_E = A_E - (E_l^0[a] \cup Side(r/at)) .$$

Moreover, $E_c[a] \cap Side(r/at) = \emptyset$, because

$$
\begin{aligned}
& f(x) = y \in E_c \\
\Rightarrow\ & x, y \in X_c \\
\Rightarrow\ & a(x), a(y) \notin x(X_l^0) \qquad \text{since } a(X_c) \cap a(X_l^0) = \emptyset \\
\Rightarrow\ & (f(x) = y)[a] \notin Side(r/at)
\end{aligned}
$$

By definition $E_c[a] \subseteq A_E$. Since $E_c[a] \cap E_l^0[a] = \emptyset$, and $E_c[a] \cap Side(r/at) = \emptyset$, thus $a_c : P_C \to (C_S, C_E)$ is a Γ-presentation morphism, which induces a Γ-homomorphism $\alpha_c = PAlg_\Gamma(a_c) : PAlg_\Gamma(P_C) \to C$.

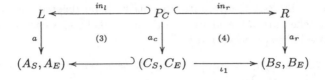

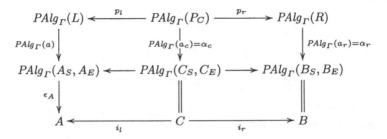

Fig. 3.6. Inclusions of presentations yield algebraic homomorphisms

By definition diagram (3) in Figure 3.6 commutes, and thus diagram (1) also commutes.

Since $a(X_c) \cap a(X_l^0) = \emptyset$, the restriction a_r of a to X_r factorises through $C_S \uplus X_r^0 \subseteq A_S \uplus X_r^0$, i.e., we obtain $a_r : X_r \to C_S \uplus X_r^0 = B_S$ with

$$a_r(x) = \begin{cases} a(x) & \text{if } x \in X_c \\ x & \text{if } x \in X_r^0 \ . \end{cases}$$

Furthermore, $E_c[a] \subseteq C_E = (A_E - E_l^0[a])|_{C_S}$ as shown above, so by the definition of a_r we have $E_c[a_r] \subseteq (A_E - E_l^0[a])|_{C_S}$. Since $C_S \subseteq B_S$ this implies $E_c[a_r] \subseteq (A_E - E_l^0[a])|_{B_S}$ and $E_c[a_r] \subseteq B_E$ by the definition of B_E. Furthermore, $a_r(X_r) \subseteq B_S$ implies $E_r^0[a_r]|_{B_S} = E_r^0[a_r]$, whence $E_r^0[a_r] \subseteq B_E$.

From $E_c[a_r] \subseteq B_E$ and $E_r^0[a_r] \subseteq B_E$ it follows that $a_r : P_r \to (B_S, B_E)$ is a Γ-presentation morphism, which induces a Γ-homomorphism $\alpha_r = PAlg_\Gamma(a_r) : PAlg_\Gamma(P_r) \to B$.

Due to the construction diagram (4) in Figure 3.6 commutes, and thus diagram (2) also commutes.

2. By definition the diagram

$$
\begin{array}{ccc}
X_c \hookrightarrow X_r & = X_c \uplus X_r^0 \\
a_c \downarrow \qquad \downarrow a_r & \\
C_S \xrightarrow{\iota_1} B_S & = C_S \uplus X_r^0
\end{array}
$$

is a pushout diagram in $\mathbf{Set}^S$. Under the condition $t(x) = x$ for all $x \in X_r^0$ we have $B \cong PAlg_\Gamma(B_S, C_E \cup E_r^0[a])$, since $(C_E \cup E_r^0[a])|_{B_s} = (C_E \cup E_r^0[a])$ as shown above, and the equations $x = x$ are always satisfied. Since

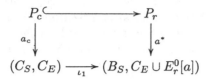

is a pushout diagram in $\mathbf{Pres}_\Gamma$ and $PAlg_\Gamma$ is a left adjoint, diagram (2) is also a pushout diagram.

3. $A_S = a(X_l^0) \uplus C_S$. Thus if $a|_{X_l^0}$ is injective

is a pushout diagram in $\mathbf{Set}^S$. Furthermore, if $Side(r/at) = \emptyset$ then $A_E = C_E \cup E_l^0[a] \cup Side(r/at) = C_E \cup E_l[a]$, whence

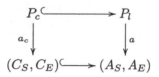

is a pushout diagram in $\mathbf{Pres}(\Gamma)$, and (1) is a pushout diagram in $\mathbf{PAlg}(\Gamma)$.

3.5 Specification with Other Formulae

Conditional equations might not be sufficient for the data space specification, as already noted in the examples. Very often negation and/or existential quantification is needed, i.e., first-order logic formulae. And if data state models from other institutions, like system snapshots as in Section 2.4 for example, are used, obviously also other kinds of formulae are required. In order to generalise the data space specification means to other specification frameworks, however, more structure than that offered by a general concrete institution is needed. This is due to the fact that the satisfaction of a transformation rule is defined in terms of solutions of its left and right hand sides. A concrete institution instead only supplies closed formulae (sentences). To define open formulae for institutions sorted sets of variables and their translation w.r.t. signature morphisms are used. The latter is based on the forgetful functor $V_f : \mathbf{Set}^{S'} \to \mathbf{Set}^S$ for a mapping $f : S \to S'$ introduced in Section 2.3, whose left adjoint $F_f : \mathbf{Set}^S \to \mathbf{Set}^{S'}$ is given by the families of disjoint unions

$$F_f((M_s)_{s \in S}) = (\sum_{s:f(s)=s'} M_s)_{s' \in S'} \; ,$$
$$F_f((h_s)_{s \in S}) \; = (\sum_{s:f(s)=s'} h_s)_{s' \in S'} \; .$$

Now a *concrete institution with formulae* $I = (\mathbf{Sig}, Form, Mod, Sol, sorts, |\_|)$ is defined like a concrete institution (see Section 2.3, p. 50), except that the sentence functor $Sen : \mathbf{Sig} \to \mathbf{Set}$ is replaced by a *formula* functor $Form$ and the satisfaction relation is replaced by solution sets Sol as follows.

- For each signature $\Sigma \in |\mathbf{Sig}|$ and each S-sorted set $X = (X_s)_{s \in S}$, where $S = sorts(\Sigma)$, there is a set $Form_\Sigma(X)$ of Σ-formulae with variables from X. Elements of $Form_\Sigma(X)$ are denoted by $(X : \varphi) \in Form_\Sigma$ or $\Phi \in Form_\Sigma(X)$.
- For each signature morphism $\sigma : \Sigma \to \Sigma'$ and each S-sorted set $X = (X_s)_{s \in S}$ there is a translation function

$$Form_{\sigma,X} : Form_\Sigma(X) \to Form_{\Sigma'}(F_s(X)) \; ,$$

  where $s = sorts(\sigma)$. Slightly abusing the notation, the function $Form_{\sigma,X}$ is often also denoted by σ, analogous to the abbreviation $Sen(\sigma) = \sigma$.
- For each formula $\Phi \in Form_\Sigma(X)$ and each model $M \in |Mod(\Sigma)|$ there is a solution set $Sol_\Sigma(\Phi, M) \subseteq |M|^X$, where $|M|^X$ denotes the set of S-indexed mappings from X to $|M|$, such that the bijection of the sets $|M'|^{F_s(X)} \cong V_s(|M'|)^X = |V_\sigma(M)|^X$ given by the adjunction $F_s \dashv V_s$ preserves the solution sets, i.e.,

$$Sol_{\Sigma'}(\sigma(\Phi), M') \cong Sol_\Sigma(\Phi, V_\sigma(M'))$$

  for all $M' \in |Mod(\Sigma')|$, $\Phi \in Form_\Sigma(X)$, and $\sigma : \Sigma \to \Sigma'$ in $\mathbf{Sig}$.

Satisfaction of open formulae can then be defined by implicit universal quantification, i.e.,

- $M \models_\Sigma (X : \varphi)$ iff $Sol((X : \varphi), M) = |M|^X$.

With this definition and

$$Sen(\Sigma) = \sum_{X \in |\mathbf{Set}^S|} Form_\Sigma(X) \; ,$$
$$Sen(\sigma) \; = \sum_{X \in |\mathbf{Set}^S|} Form_{\sigma,X} \; ,$$

the tuple

- $(\mathbf{Sig}, Sen, Mod, \models, sorts, |\_|)$

becomes a concrete institution again. (The union over all S-indexed sets X may cause a definition problem here. But obviously it suffices to consider subsets $X_s \subseteq I\!N$ for the variables. Compare the discussion on anonymous variables in Appendix A.) The satisfaction condition holds because

$$M' \models_{\Sigma'} \sigma(X : \varphi) \;\Leftrightarrow\; Sol_{\Sigma'}(\sigma(X : \varphi), M') = |M'|^{F_s(X)}$$
$$\Leftrightarrow\; Sol_\Sigma((X : \varphi), V_\sigma(M')) = |V_\sigma(M')|^X$$
$$\Leftrightarrow\; V_\sigma(M') \models_\Sigma (X : \varphi) \; .$$

In the following transformation specifications w.r.t. arbitrary specification framework $I\!F = (Ins, AS, I, \epsilon)$ are defined. For that purpose it is required now that Ins be a concrete institution with formulae. Its induced satisfaction relation will be denoted by $\models^{Ins}$ in the remainder of this section to distinguish it from the other satisfaction relations.

In the first component of a transformation specification, the data specification, only closed formulae are used.

Definition 3.26 (Data Specification). *Let $I\!F = (Ins, AS, I, \epsilon)$ be a specification framework with a concrete institution with formulae Ins and let $\Sigma \in |\mathbf{Sig}|$ be a signature of Ins. A Σ-data specification $DS = (Ax, In, Fi)$ w.r.t. $I\!F$ is given by sets $Ax, In, Fi \subseteq Sen(\Sigma)$ of Σ-sentences (closed Σ-formulae), called the* data invariants, *the* initialisation, *and the* finalisation conditions *respectively. A $D\Sigma$-transformation system $\mathbf{M} = (TG_{\mathbf{M}}, \mathbf{m}) \in |\mathbf{TF}^{\mathbf{F}}(D\Sigma)|$ with $TG_{\mathbf{M}} = (CS, T, in, id)$ satisfies the data specification DS, written $\mathbf{M} \models DS$, if*

- $\mathbf{m}(c) \models_{\Sigma}^{Ins} Ax$ *for each control state $c \in CS - \{in\}$,*
- $\mathbf{m}(c_0) \models_{\Sigma}^{Ins} In$ *for each initial state $c_0 \in \{c \in CS - \{in\} \mid T(in, c) \neq \emptyset\}$,*
- $\mathbf{m}(c_1) \models_{\Sigma}^{Ins} Fi$ *for each final state $c_1 \in \{c \in CS - \{in\} \mid T(c, in) \neq \emptyset\}$.*

Transformation rules are given as above by pairs of sets of open formulae to specify the input and the output states of transformations, and action structures with formal parameters (variables) that specify the steps to which the rules apply.

Definition 3.27 (Transformation Rule). *Let $I\!F = (Ins, AS, I, \epsilon)$ be a specification framework with a concrete institution with formulae Ins and let $D\Sigma = (\Sigma, A)$ be a data space signature w.r.t. Ins, with $sorts(\Sigma) = S$ (see Definition 2.14). A $D\Sigma$-transformation rule $r = (\alpha \triangleq L \to R)$ w.r.t. $I\!F$ is given by*

- *left and right hand sides $L = (X_l : \Phi_l)$ and $R = (X_r : \Phi_r)$ given by S-indexed sets of variables $X_l, X_r \in |\mathbf{Set}^S|$ and sets of formulae $\Phi_l \subseteq Form_{\Sigma}(X_l)$ and $\Phi_r \subseteq Form_{\Sigma}(X_r)$,*
- *a formal action structure $\alpha \in AS_{D\Sigma}(X, Y)$, where $X \subseteq X_l$ and $Y \subseteq X_r$.*

If the action structure α of a rule $r = (\alpha \triangleq L \to R)$ is the empty structure ϵ the rule is called an anonymous rule, *and also denoted by $r = (L \to R)$. The class of all $D\Sigma$-transformation rules w.r.t. $I\!F$ is denoted by $Rules_{D\Sigma}^{\mathbf{F}}$.*

Definition 3.28 (Satisfaction of Transformation Rules). *Let $D\Sigma = (\Sigma, A)$ be a data space signature w.r.t. Ins and $r = (\alpha \triangleq L \to R)$ a $D\Sigma$-transformation rule w.r.t. $I\!F$ with $L = (X_l : \Phi_l)$, $R = (X_r : \Phi_r)$, and $\alpha \in AS_{D\Sigma}(X, Y)$. Furthermore, let $\mathbf{M} = (TG_{\mathbf{M}}, \mathbf{m})$ be a $D\Sigma$-transformation system w.r.t. $I\!F$, $t : c \to d$ a transition in $TG_{\mathbf{M}}$, and $C = \mathbf{m}(c)$ and $D = \mathbf{m}(d)$ the associated data states.*

The system $\mathbf{M}$ satisfies the rule r at transition t, written $(\mathbf{M}, t) \models_{D\Sigma}^{Rule} r$, if the following condition holds.

> *For all* $x : X \to |C|, y : Y \to |D|$
> *if* $act_t^m = AS_{D\Sigma}(x, y)(\alpha)$
> *then for each* $\gamma \in Sol_\Sigma(L, C)$ *with* $\gamma|_X = x$
> *there is a* $\delta \in Sol_\Sigma(R, D)$ *with* $\delta|_Y = y$
> *such that* $\gamma(x) \sim_t^m \delta(x)$
> *for all* $x \in X_l \cap X_r$.

The system $\mathbf{M}$ *satisfies* r, *written* $\mathbf{M} \models_{D\Sigma}^{Rule} r$, *if* $\mathbf{M}, t \models_{D\Sigma}^{Rule} r$ *for each transition* t *in* $TG_\mathbf{M}$.

Finally a control flow logic is added. It is defined generically as above, where the satisfaction relation must now be defined for transformation systems w.r.t. the given specification framework IF.

Definition 3.29 (Control Flow Logic). *Let* $\mathit{IF} = (Ins, AS, I, \epsilon)$ *be a specification framework with a concrete institution with formulae Ins. A control flow logic* $CL = (CF, \models^{CL})$ *w.r.t.* IF *is given by a function* CF *that assigns a set* $CF(D\Sigma)$ *to each transformation signature* $D\Sigma$ *w.r.t. Ins, called the set of* $D\Sigma$-*control flow formulae, and a satisfaction relation* $\models_{D\Sigma}^{CL} \subseteq |\mathbf{TF}^F(D\Sigma)| \times CF(D\Sigma)$ *between* $D\Sigma$-*transformation systems and* $D\Sigma$-*control flow formulae for each signature* $D\Sigma$.

Further structural properties of control flow logics (functoriality, satisfaction condition) are only considered in the next chapter. Data specifications, transformation rules, and control flow specifications yield transformation specifications.

Definition 3.30 (Transformation Specification). *Let* $\mathit{IF} = (Ins, AS, I, \epsilon)$ *be a specification framework with a concrete institution with formulae Ins and let* $CL = (CF, \models^{CL})$ *be a control flow logic w.r.t.* IF. *Furthermore, let* $D\Sigma = (\Sigma, A)$ *be a data space signature w.r.t. Ins.*

A $D\Sigma$-*transformation specification* $T\Gamma = (DS, R, C\Gamma)$ *w.r.t.* IF *and* CL *is given by*

- *a* $D\Sigma$-*data specification* $DS = (Ax, In, Fi)$ *w.r.t.* IF,
- *a set* R *of* $D\Sigma$-*transformation rules w.r.t.* IF, *and*
- *a control flow specification* $C\Gamma \subseteq CF(D\Sigma)$ *w.r.t.* CL.

A $D\Sigma$-*transformation system* $\mathbf{M} = (TG_\mathbf{M}, m)$ *with* $TG_\mathbf{M} = (CS, T, in, id)$ *satisfies the transformation specification* $T\Gamma = (DS, R, C\Gamma)$, *if*

- $m(c) \models_\Sigma^{Ins} Ax$ *for each control state* $c \in CS - \{in\}$,
- $m(c_0) \models_\Sigma^{Ins} In$ *for each initial state* $c_0 \in \{c \in CS - \{in\} \mid T(in, c) \neq \emptyset\}$,
- $m(c_1) \models_\Sigma^{Ins} Fi$ *for each final state* $c_1 \in \{c \in CS - \{in\} \mid T(c, in) \neq \emptyset\}$,
- $\mathbf{M} \models_{D\Sigma}^{Rule} r$ *for each transformation rule* $r \in R$,
- $\mathbf{M} \models_{D\Sigma}^{CL} C\Gamma$.

3.6 Discussion

In this chapter abstract syntactic means for the specification of properties of transformation systems have been introduced. Thus the properties are classified according to the structure of transformation systems, given by the data states, transformations, and the overall control flow represented by the transition graph and its labelling in the data space. Data states are thereby considered to comprise static data types as well as the mutable data parts. This classification yields corresponding formulae/equations for the specification of data invariants and transformation rules for the specification of the state changes (i.e., the side effects of the actions). The latter also cover the local transformational aspect of pre- and postconditions. The control flow specification has been treated generically; its models are the whole transformation systems because data space information may be affected by the control flow specification, too.

In other approaches different means for these specification tasks are used, where the individual specification formalisms usually only address a specific task.

The specification of static data types, that comprises the data invariants for the case when algebras or other static data type models are used as states, has found its most general formulation in the form of institutions. Therefore the specification means for data states could be taken over directly, given by conditional equations for partial algebras, or the sentences defined for an arbitrary concrete institution.

State transformations are specified by some kind of rules in many approaches, with a left and a right hand side corresponding to the commencing and ending state respectively. This comprises the graph grammar rules of graph transformation approaches [Roz97], the function updates of the abstract state machines, and also programming language like approaches such as the parallel programming language UNITY [CM88]. Analogously the pre- and post-domains of Petri nets describe states before and after a state change. The representation of these specification means by transformation rules as introduced here has been given in the examples of this section (see Example 3.8). The main problem in the definition of transformation rules in general has been to provide a mechanism to refer to mutable elements in different states within one rule. Obviously, this is related to the tracking of the identity of elements through state changes. Usually this problem is avoided in that constant carrier sets are assumed. That means the structure (function definitions) may change, but the elements never change. Of course, this excludes creation and deletion of elements. Therefore creation and deletion are often encoded, for instance via a universe of elements that can be moved into the sets of defined elements (creation) or vice versa (deletion) by updating their typing predicates, as in the ASM approach. Analogously, logical approaches (temporal, dynamic, and modal logics) either assume fixed carrier sets or use similar encodings. But also the different values of entities with identities in different states must be taken into account. Some approaches introduce specific syntactic means to denote the values of constants in the commencing and ending state of a transformation, like the dashed variables of Z and the @*pre* construct of the OCL.

In the transformation system approach no such encodings or restrictions are necessary. Using tracking relations on the data states, arbitrarily changing algebras can be considered. The evaluation of variables in different states is then supported by the tracking relation at the semantic level.

In the basic specification framework with partial algebras as data states even a constructive semantics of transformation rules has been given that allows the rewriting of partial algebras. As a special case, with restrictions concerning the algebraic structure of states and the possibility to match rules and delete elements, this comprises for instance DPO graph rewriting [CMR+97], see Example 3.23 and Theorem 3.25.

The specification means for data states and transformations are distinguished in an analogous way in the Reference Model of Open Distributed Processing RM-ODP ([ODP]). As a requirement on specification languages for the information viewpoint it is stated that they must provide static, invariant, and dynamic schemes. Static schemes are used to describe single states, and the initial and final states of a system. This corresponds to the initialisation and finalisation conditions In and Fi of a data space specification $D\Gamma$. An invariant schema defines properties that must hold in each state, corresponding to the data invariants Ax. Finally dynamic schemata specify the state transformations, like the transformation rules.

Control flow specifications have been treated generically. In Chapter 4 they will also be extended to institutions by also taking into account signature morphisms. The presentation of particular specification means as control flow logic has been given for CCS, modal μ-calculus, and AHL nets in the examples in Section 3.2. In [FC95] other institutions of process and behaviour specifications are investigated, which can be used to embed them into the transformation system approach, too.

The hierarchical definition of transformation specifications for arbitrary specification frameworks in Section 3.5 states the dependencies of specification means in general. This can be used as a conceptual basis for the integration of specification languages, beyond the integration of individual specifications considered so far. The basis of the specification hierarchy is given by an institution for the data states. The only constraint is that the institution must be concrete, i.e., it must have a notion of carrier sets. Its sentences yield the specification means for the data states. Then action structures can be defined, where the carrier sets of the data state models yield the parameters of the actions. This dependency of action structures on data state specification formalisms is expressed in the definition of specification frameworks. Transformation rules for the specification of the single steps can then be defined uniformly on top of the specification framework. For the overall behaviour a control flow logic is required, whose structure also depends on that of the specification framework.

Using this hierarchy for the integration of specification languages it has to be checked which parts of the specification hierarchy are affected by the languages. If common points in the specification hierarchy are addressed by several languages they have to be made consistent there. For example, if two languages contain means for the specification of action structures, one for the specification of single steps and the other one for the composition of steps to processes, then these parts of the two languages have to be unified. An integration of Z and a process calculus would be an example of this situation. Z allows the specification of operations as actions for the transformation of states; process calculi use actions as elements of processes. In this case the unification is simple, since the actions of the process calculus are unstructured elements, which can be defined as the operation applications of the Z specifications. In this example, however, Z operation specifications also address a part of the control flow in that preconditions for operations can be specified. To solve this conflict that is encountered at the level of the control flow specification other means are required. The opposite case of language integration tasks is that common points in the hierarchy are missing; these then have to be added at some place in order to obtain an integrated language.

4

Development of Transformation Systems

The construction of models of software systems is a process, that proceeds from more abstract and conceptual descriptions to more concrete and technical ones. To support this process a modelling technique must provide operations for the construction of new models from given ones, and relations that allow the comparison of given models. According to the semantical focus of the transformation system approach, only semantically compatible development relations are considered here. This means that if a more concrete model is a development of a more abstract one, then the structure and the behaviour specified by the abstract model should in a certain sense be preserved or reflected by the more concrete one. There are different possibilities to formulate this property. The overall approach pursued here is again to combine development relations from abstract data type specification and behaviour specification techniques. According to the structure of transformation systems, these are reflected as mappings at the behaviour (transition graph) and structure (data space) levels. Thus the two mappings may have the same or opposite directions.

It should be mentioned that only a very general schema of development relations is considered here, which is based on total mappings on the two layers of transformation systems. From the categorical point of view the development relations obtained in this way are the natural candidates, and thus serve best to study the relationships of development relations with specifications, i.e., the *preservation of properties* by developments, and with the composition of models, i.e., the *compositionality* of developments. Especially in the context of process specifications, however, more elaborate relations might be required. Corresponding extensions of the notions introduced here are discussed at the end of the chapter. The general categorical approach has been chosen because it stresses very clearly the structural relationships of development, composition (Chapter 5), and properties (Chapter 3) from the very beginning. As in [WN97], where a categorical analysis of LTSs is given, these results are then used to state general compositionality results, as in Section 4.6 and Section 5.6. Concrete development operations and relations from other languages can be reduced to the categorical constructions, showing their specific properties. (See also [WN97], where the operations of the process specification language CCS are analysed categorically and their properties are reduced to the categorical ones.)

Like the relations, the development operations are also inherited from the corresponding techniques in behaviour and data type specification, where in this case the relationship between known operations like restriction and hiding and the categorical constructions presented here is closer than for the development relations. Since transformation systems are defined as transition graph morphisms (from the transition graph of a model to its data space) operations can directly be defined by composing these morphisms with other ones that represent the passage to another transition graph (behaviour) and/or another data space (structure).

The chapter is organised as follows. In the first section the development operations for transformation systems are introduced: *restriction* to a subbehaviour and *view* of a subdata structure, and the complementary operations *exclusion* of certain behaviours and *hiding* of a part of the data structure. Furthermore, renaming of actions is introduced. Then in Section 4.2 the development relations extension and reduction are introduced, and it is shown that the development operations are semantically compatible with the development relations. Then an example for a development relation is presented, given by two specifications of the channel component of the alternating bit protocol in two different languages, CCS and UNITY. The latter is a parallel programming language whose operational semantics is based on the non-deterministic execution of parallel assignments. As opposed to the temporal ordering of actions in CCS specifications, UNITY follows a rule-based approach. Moreover, its communication mechanism is asynchronous, based on shared variables, in contrast with the synchronisation of actions in CCS. This example shows very concretely the comparison of heterogeneous specifications.

After this introduction the categorical structure of the development relations is investigated (Section 4.3). It is based on the relation of development relations with the morphisms that are obtained by gluing the categories of transformation system of given signatures to one global category of all transformation systems. This analysis yields a clue to the compositionality results for developments w.r.t. properties and composition of systems. In Section 4.4 the development relations introduced in Section 4.2 are generalised by allowing the refinement of single steps in the abstract system by sequential and parallel compositions of steps in the concrete system. Formally these are based on closure operations on transformation systems that add all sequential and parallel compositions of steps to a system. Two variants of developments are considered. *Refinements* allow the replacement of an abstract model by a more concrete one, whereas *implementations* add more concrete information of abstract models, whereby the latter are retained, however, to serve as semantic interfaces for the (concrete) implementation models. As in the previous chapters, two larger examples of refinement and implementation are then discussed, again using the linked-list example and the different specifications of the alternating bit protocol. The relationship of developments with the specification of properties as introduced in Chapter 3 is discussed in Section 4.6, where it is shown which kinds of properties are preserved by the operations and relations. As a theoretical summary the institutional properties of transformation systems are then investigated in Section 4.7. In fact, transformation systems are *almost* an institution: the satisfaction condition only holds for injective signature morphisms. In Section 4.8 the generalisation of the development operations and relations for transformation systems with other specification frameworks are introduced. Moreover, sufficient criteria are given that guarantee that transformation systems w.r.t. a given specification framework have the properties discussed in this chapter. The chapter ends with a discussion of related works and further questions that should be investigated, for instance to close the gap between the development relations presented here and the ones proposed in other areas of formal specification.

4.1 Development Operations

The first two operations to be introduced are the restriction of the behaviour to a given subtransition graph, and the restriction of the visibility of the data states and actions w.r.t. a given *view*. Note that the behaviour restriction is defined as restriction *to* a certain sub-behaviour, as opposed to the restriction (= exclusion) *of* certain steps. The complementary operations, excluding steps and hiding parts of the data space, are introduced below. In the general semantic definition the restriction and view operations are introduced w.r.t. arbitrary morphisms of transition graphs and data spaces respectively. The more intuitive special cases of subtransition graph inclusion and the syntactically representable restriction to a subset of actions and view by restriction to a subdata space signature are discussed afterwards.

Definition 4.1 (Restriction and View). *Let* $\mathbf{M} = (TG_{\mathbf{M}}, \mathbf{m})$ *be a* $D\Sigma$-*transformation system.*

1. *Given a transition graph* TG' *and a transition graph morphism* $g : TG' \to TG_{\mathbf{M}}$ *the restriction of* $\mathbf{M}$ *by* g *is defined as the* $D\Sigma$-*transformation system* $res(\mathbf{M}, g)$ *given by*

$$res(\mathbf{M}, g) = (TG', \mathbf{m} \circ g) .$$

2. *Given another data space signature* $D\Sigma_0$ *and a transition graph morphism* $s : I\!D_{D\Sigma} \to I\!D_{D\Sigma_0}$ *the view* s *of* $\mathbf{M}$ *is defined as the* $D\Sigma_0$-*transformation system* $view(s, \mathbf{M})$ *given by*

$$view(s, \mathbf{M}) = (TG_{\mathbf{M}}, s \circ \mathbf{m}) .$$

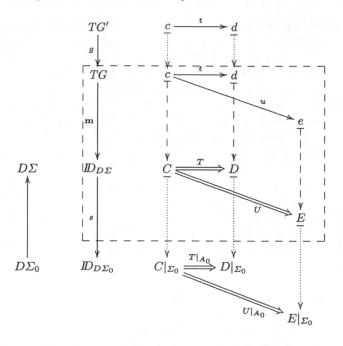

Fig. 4.1. Restriction to t and view $D\Sigma_0$ of a transformation system

Usually restriction and view are represented syntactically by restricting to a subset of allowed actions, and showing only those actions and those parts of the data states that correspond to a given data space subsignature. These inclusions (or, more generally, arbitrary morphisms) of data space signatures induce subtransition graphs and data spaces related by transition graph morphisms to the transition graph and data space of the model respectively. The latter is given by the *forgetful functor* of partial algebras corresponding to a signature inclusion $\Sigma_0 \subseteq \Sigma$ (or morphism $\Sigma_0 \rightarrow \Sigma$) that restricts a partial Σ-algebra to those sorts and functions respectively that are in Σ_0 (see Figure 4.1, where the forgetful functor is denoted by $C|_{\Sigma_0}$). This means that, for example, if Σ_0 contains the public attributes of a model, and $\Sigma \supseteq \Sigma_0$ contains the public and the private attributes, then the view corresponding to Σ_0 of a model with data signature Σ only shows the public attributes in each state, and hides the private ones. In the same way private actions can be hidden.

Of course, not all restrictions and views can be represented by sub-signatures or signature morphisms. The ones that have such a syntactic representation will be called *uniform* restrictions and views respectively. Before their definition is stated data space signature morphisms are formally defined, extending algebraic signature morphisms to action signatures straightforwardly.

Definition 4.2 (Signature Morphism). *Let $D\Sigma = (\Sigma, A)$ and $D\Sigma' = (\Sigma', A')$ be data space signatures with $\Sigma = (S, F)$. A (data space) signature morphism $\sigma = (\sigma_\Sigma, \sigma_A) : D\Sigma \to D\Sigma'$ is given by an algebraic signature morphism $\sigma_\Sigma : \Sigma \to \Sigma'$ and a family of mappings $\sigma_A = (\sigma_{A,w,w'} : A_{w,w'} \to A'_{\sigma_\Sigma(w),\sigma_\Sigma(w')})_{w,w' \in S^*}$.*

Subsignatures obviously correspond to signature morphisms whose components are inclusions.

The algebraic signature part $\sigma_\Sigma : \Sigma \to \Sigma'$ of a data space signature morphism σ induces a forgetful functor $V_{\sigma_\Sigma} : \mathbf{PAlg}(\Sigma') \to \mathbf{PAlg}(\Sigma)$ (see Appendix A). This can be extended to a transition graph morphism $I\!D_\sigma : I\!D_{D\Sigma'} \to I\!D_{D\Sigma}$ of the corresponding data spaces, which yields the uniform restriction and view.

Definition and Fact 4.3 (Uniform Restriction and View). *Let $D\Sigma = (\Sigma, A)$ be a data space signature with $\Sigma = (S, F)$ and $\mathbf{M} = (TG_\mathbf{M}, \mathbf{m})$ be a $D\Sigma$-transformation system with $TG_\mathbf{M} = (CS, T, in, id)$.*

1. Each $S^* \times S^*$-sorted subset $A_0 \subseteq A$ induces a transition graph $TG_{A_0} = (CS, T_{A_0}, in, id_{A_0})$ with the same control states and initialisation state as $TG_\mathbf{M}$, and transitions

$$T_{A_0}(c, d) = \{t \in T(c, d) \mid act_t^\mathbf{m} \subseteq Act_{(\Sigma, A_0)}(|\mathbf{m}(c)|, |\mathbf{m}(d)|)\}$$

   for all $c, d \in CS$. The idle transitions are given as in $TG_\mathbf{M}$, i.e., $id_{A_0}(c) = id(c)$.

   The restriction of $\mathbf{M}$ to A_0, denoted by $res(\mathbf{M}, A_0)$, is then defined by $res(\mathbf{M}, A_0) = res(\mathbf{M}, g_{A_0})$, where $g_{A_0} : TG_{A_0} \to TG_\mathbf{M}$ is the inclusion morphism.

2. Each data space signature morphism $\sigma = (\sigma_\Sigma, \sigma_A) : D\Sigma_0 \to D\Sigma$, with $D\Sigma_0 = (\Sigma_0, A_0)$, induces a transition graph morphism $I\!D_\sigma : I\!D_{D\Sigma} \to I\!D_{D\Sigma_0}$ by

$$I\!D_\sigma(C) \quad = V_{\sigma_\Sigma}(C) \qquad \text{(for all } C \in |\mathbf{PAlg}(\Sigma)| \text{)}$$
$$I\!D_\sigma(\alpha, \sim) = (\sigma_A^{-1}(\alpha), V_{\sigma_\Sigma}(\sim)) \quad \text{(for all } (\alpha, \sim) \in Tf_{D\Sigma} \text{)},$$

   where

$$\sigma_A^{-1}(\alpha) \quad = \{a_0(c; d) \mid a_0 \in A_0, \sigma_A(a_0)(c; d) \in \alpha\}$$
$$(V_{\sigma_\Sigma}(\sim))_{s_0} = \sim_{\sigma_\Sigma(s_0)} \quad (s_0 \in S_0).$$

   The *view σ of* $\mathbf{M}$, denoted by $view(\sigma, \mathbf{M})$, is then defined by $view(\sigma, \mathbf{M}) = view(I\!D_\sigma, \mathbf{M})$.

   For a subsignature inclusion $\sigma : D\Sigma_0 \subseteq D\Sigma$ the view $view(\sigma, \mathbf{M})$ is also denoted by $view(D\Sigma_0, \mathbf{M})$.

A restriction is called *uniform* (or A_0-uniform) if it is a restriction $res(\mathbf{M}, A_0)$ induced by an action subsignature $A_0 \subseteq A$. Correspondingly a view is called uniform (σ-uniform, $D\Sigma_0$-uniform) if it is a view induced by a signature morphism σ or a subsignature $D\Sigma_0$.

Proof. 1.　Since idle transitions are labelled by empty action sets, i.e., $act^{\mathrm{m}}_{id_c} = \emptyset$, the transition graph TG_{A_0} is well defined, and obviously a subtransition graph of $TG_{\mathbf{M}}$.

2.　The only thing to be shown is that $I\!\!D_\sigma$ is a transition graph morphism, i.e., it preserves the source and target of transitions, the initialisation state, and idle transitions.

Let $(\alpha, \sim) \in Tf_{D\Sigma}(C, D) = \mathcal{P}(Act_{D\Sigma}(|C|, |D|)) \times Rel^S(|C|, |D|)$, and let $\sigma_A(a_0)(c; d) \in \alpha$ for some $a_0 \in (A_0)_{v,v'}$. Since $\sigma_A(a_0) \in A_{\sigma_\Sigma(v), \sigma_\Sigma(v')}$ the elements c and d must be $c \in C_{\sigma_\Sigma(v)} = V_{\sigma_\Sigma}(C)_v$ and $d \in D_{\sigma_\Sigma(v')} = V_{\sigma_\Sigma}(D)_{v'}$. Thus $a_0(c; d) \in Act_{D\Sigma_0}(|V_{\sigma_\Sigma}(C)|, |V_{\sigma_\Sigma}(D)|)$.

Furthermore, $V_{\sigma_\Sigma}(\sim)$ is an S_0-sorted relation on $|V_{\sigma_\Sigma}(C)|$ and $|V_{\sigma_\Sigma}(D)|$ by definition. Thus $I\!\!D_\sigma(\alpha, \sim) \in Tf_{D\Sigma_0}(V_{\sigma_\Sigma}(C), V_{\sigma_\Sigma}(D))$, i.e., $I\!\!D_\sigma$ preserves the source and target of transitions.

The preservation of empty algebras, empty action sets, and identity relations is obviously satisfied.

Example 4.4 (Public Attributes and Methods). Consider a transformation system $\mathbf{O} = (TG_{\mathbf{O}}, \mathbf{o})$ modelling the behaviour of an object that has two attributes a_1 and a_2 and two methods m_1 and m_2. Its structure is represented by the data space signature $D\Sigma_{complete}$ given below. Suppose the attribute a_1 and the method m_1 are public, whereas a_2 and m_2 are private. The distinction of private and public parts can be represented by a subsignature $D\Sigma_{private}$ as shown below, which contains only the public parts.

$$
\begin{array}{ll}
D\Sigma_{complete} = & D\Sigma_{public} = \\
\quad \textbf{sorts } s_1, s_2 & \quad \textbf{sorts } s_1 \\
\quad \textbf{funs } a_1 \colon \to s_1 & \quad \textbf{funs } a_1 \colon \to s_1 \\
\qquad\quad a_2 \colon \to s_2 & \\
\quad \textbf{acts } m_1 \colon & \quad \textbf{acts } m_1 \colon \\
\qquad\quad m_2 \colon &
\end{array}
$$

The inclusion $D\Sigma_{public} \subseteq D\Sigma_{complete}$ induces a uniform view $\mathbf{O}'$ of the $D\Sigma_{complete}$-transformation system $\mathbf{O}$, given by $\mathbf{O}' = view(D\Sigma_{public}, \mathbf{O})$, that represents the same internal behaviour as $\mathbf{O}$, but in each state only the public attribute a_1 of sort s_1 is visible, and in each step only the public method m_1 can be observed. Transitions corresponding to the application of the private method m_2 in $\mathbf{O}$ are still in $\mathbf{O}'$, but now they are internal steps, labelled by the empty set.

Note that $D\Sigma_{public}$ must be a signature as well, i.e., since the attribute a_1 is in $D\Sigma_{public}$ the sort s_1 must also be in $D\Sigma_{public}$. This does not mean that a whole type (s_1) is exported, because, according to the principles of abstract data types, elements of types can only be accessed via the functions of the type. So in this example, in a given state, only the element of s_1 that is the actual value of the attribute a_1 can be accessed. In another state this might be another element.

On the other hand, arbitrary subsets of functions (attributes) and actions (methods) can be made visible, even if other attributes or methods of the same sort are hidden.

The complementary operations of restriction and view are the *exclusion* of some actions, i.e., prohibition of their execution, and *hiding* some actions and some parts of the data states. These operations are (and can only be) defined directly via their syntactic presentation. Hiding parts corresponding to a subsignature must thereby satisfy conditions complementary to the subsignature condition discussed in the previous example.

Definition 4.5 (Exclusion and Hiding). *Let* $\mathbf{M} = (TG_\mathbf{M}, \mathbf{m})$ *be a* $D\Sigma$-*transformation system, with* $D\Sigma = (S, F, A)$.

1. *For any subset* $A^0 \subseteq A$ *the exclusion of* A^0 *in* $\mathbf{M}$ *is given by the* $D\Sigma$-*transformation system* $exc(\mathbf{M}, A^0)$ *defined by*

$$exc(\mathbf{M}, A^0) = res(\mathbf{M}, A - A^0) .$$

2. *Let* $D\Sigma^0 = (S^0, F^0, A^0)$ *be given by subsets* $S^0 \subseteq S, F^0 \subseteq F, A^0 \subseteq A$, *such that whenever* $f \in F_{w,v}$ *with* $wv \notin (S - S^0)^*$ *then* $f \in F^0$, *and whenever* $a \in A_{w,w'}$ *with* $ww' \notin (S - S^0)^*$ *then* $a \in A^0$. *Then the* hiding *of* $D\Sigma^0$ *in* $\mathbf{M}$ *is defined as the* $(D\Sigma - D\Sigma^0)$-*transformation system* $hide(D\Sigma^0, \mathbf{M})$ *given by*

$$hide(D\Sigma^0, \mathbf{M}) = view(D\Sigma - D\Sigma^0, \mathbf{M}) .$$

The conditions on the subsets S^0, F^0, and A^0 can be explained as follows. If a function $f : s_1 \ldots s_n \to s_1' \ldots s_k'$ contains in its signature a sort $\tilde{s}$ that is hidden, then f must also be hidden. (The condition $s_1 \ldots s_n s_1' \ldots s_k' \notin (S - S^0)^*$ is equivalent to the condition that there is an index i such that $\tilde{s} := s_i \in S^0$ or $\tilde{s} := s_i' \in S^0$.) The same holds for actions: if any parameter is of a hidden sort the action is hidden, too. These conditions guarantee that $D\Sigma - D\Sigma^0$ is a signature and that $hide(D\Sigma^0, \mathbf{M})$ is well defined.

Note that an action can be excluded or hidden. In the first case the corresponding steps are removed, in the second case they are still there, but no longer observable (see Figure 4.2).

Remark 4.6. Exclusion and hiding correspond to the restriction and hiding operations in process calculi like CCS, LOTOS, and CSP. For an LTS $L = (S, A, \to)$ with $\to \subseteq S \times A \times S$ the restriction $L \backslash A^0$ for some subset $A^0 \subseteq A$ is defined by

$$L \backslash A^0 = (S, A^0, \to_0) \text{ with } s \xrightarrow{a}_0 s' \text{ iff } s \xrightarrow{a} s' \text{ and } a \notin A^0 .$$

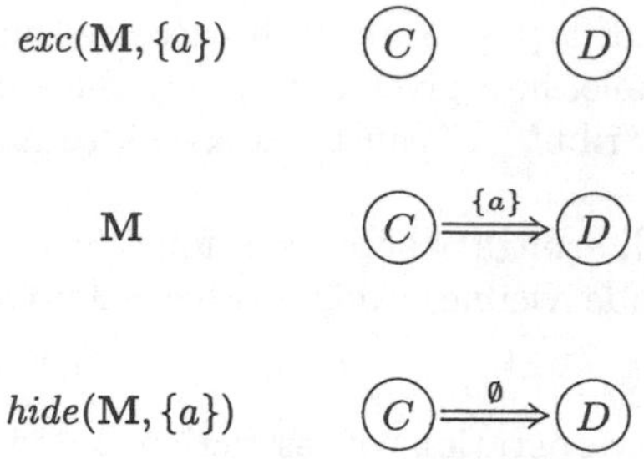

$$exc(\mathbf{M}, \{a\}) \qquad \textcircled{C} \qquad \textcircled{D}$$

$$\mathbf{M} \qquad \textcircled{C} \xrightarrow{\{a\}} \textcircled{D}$$

$$hide(\mathbf{M}, \{a\}) \qquad \textcircled{C} \xRightarrow{\emptyset} \textcircled{D}$$

Fig. 4.2. Exclusion and hiding of an action

The underlying LTS of a transformation system $\mathbf{M}$ (see Definition 2.9) then satisfies

$$LTS(\mathbf{M})\backslash A^0 = LTS(exc(\mathbf{M}, A^0)) .$$

Analogously the hiding $L[A_1]$ of actions $a \in A_1 \subseteq A$ is defined by

$$L[A_1] = (S, (A - A_1), \rightarrow_1)$$

with $s \xrightarrow{\alpha}_1 s'$ iff $s \xrightarrow{\alpha} s'$ and $\alpha \in (A - A_1)$, or $s \xrightarrow{a} s'$ and $a \in A_1$ and $\alpha = \tau$.

We then have

$$LTS(\mathbf{M})[A_1] = LTS(hide((\Sigma, A_1), \mathbf{M}) ,$$

where again τ corresponds to the empty action label.

The last operation to be introduced is *renaming* of action symbols. Note that renaming the data signatures would not make sense for transformation systems, because the class of partial Σ-algebras only depends on the structure of Σ, not on the chosen names. (In Chapter 5 a free functor is introduced that allows the translation of $D\Sigma$-transformation systems to $D\Sigma'$-transformation systems along a signature morphism $\sigma : D\Sigma \rightarrow D\Sigma'$. This is a translation of structure, however, not a translation of names.) Renaming of the data signature is implicitly covered by the signature morphisms used in the other operations that also allow the mapping of sorts, functions, and actions independently of their names, provided their arities and parameter types respectively are preserved.

Definition 4.7 (Renaming). *Given data space signatures $D\Sigma = (\Sigma, A)$ and $D\Sigma' = (\Sigma, A')$ with the same data signature Σ and a family of functions $r = (r_{w,w'} : A_{w,w'} \rightarrow A'_{w,w'})_{w,w' \in S^*}$, the renaming of a $D\Sigma$-transformation system $\mathbf{M} = (TG_{\mathbf{M}}, \mathbf{m})$ by r is given by the $D\Sigma'$-transformation system $ren(r, \mathbf{M})$ defined by $ren(r, \mathbf{M}) = (TG_{\mathbf{M}}, \mathbf{m}')$ with*

$$\mathbf{m}'(c) = \mathbf{m}(c) \qquad\qquad\qquad (c \in CS)$$
$$act_t^{\mathbf{m}'} = r(act_t^{\mathbf{m}}) = \{r(a)(c; d) \mid a(c; d) \in act_t^{\mathbf{m}}\} \; (t \in T)$$
$$\sim_t^{\mathbf{m}'} = \sim_t^{\mathbf{m}} \qquad\qquad\qquad (t \in T)$$

Note that if each $r_{w,w'}$ is an inclusion renaming does not change the transformation system itself, but allows us to consider a (Σ, A)-system as a (Σ, A')-system, in which the actions from $A' - A$ do not occur.

To conclude this section some basic properties of the operations are shown, stated as *algebraic laws* as in [Mil89, Hoa85] for CCS and CSP. Further ones can be derived easily. All development operations are depicted in Figure 4.3.

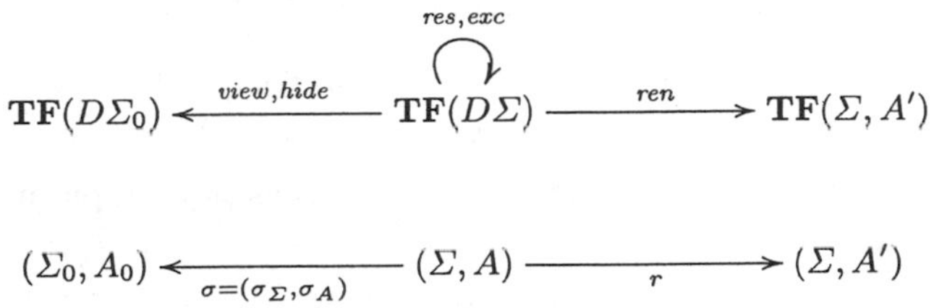

$$\mathbf{TF}(D\Sigma_0) \xleftarrow{\quad view,hide \quad} \mathbf{TF}(D\Sigma) \xrightarrow{\overset{res,exc}{\curvearrowright} \quad ren \quad} \mathbf{TF}(\Sigma, A')$$

$$(\Sigma_0, A_0) \xleftarrow{\quad \sigma=(\sigma_\Sigma, \sigma_A) \quad} (\Sigma, A) \xrightarrow{\qquad r \qquad} (\Sigma, A')$$

Fig. 4.3. The development operations

Proposition 4.8 (Algebraic Laws). *Let* $\mathbf{M}$ *be a* $D\Sigma$-*transformation system, with* $D\Sigma = (\Sigma, A)$.

1. *Let* $A_0' \subseteq A_0 \subseteq A$. *Then*

$$res(\mathbf{M}, A_0') = res(res(\mathbf{M}, A_0), A_0') .$$

2. *For all signature morphisms* $\sigma : D\Sigma_0 \to D\Sigma$ *and* $\sigma' : D\Sigma_0' \to D\Sigma_0$

$$view(\sigma \circ \sigma', \mathbf{M}) = view(\sigma', view(\sigma, \mathbf{M})) .$$

If σ *and* σ' *are inclusions*

$$view(D\Sigma_0', \mathbf{M}) = view(D\Sigma_0', view(D\Sigma_0, \mathbf{M})) .$$

3. *Let* $A_2 \subseteq A_1 \subseteq A$. *Then*

$$res(view(A_1, \mathbf{M}), A_2) = view(A_1, res(\mathbf{M}, A_2)) .$$

4. *Let* $A_0, A_0' \subseteq A$. *Then*

$$exc(\mathbf{M}, A_0 \cup A_0') = exc(exc(\mathbf{M}, A_0), A_0' - A_0)$$
$$= exc(exc(\mathbf{M}, A_0'), A_0 - A_0') .$$

Proof. 1.   Let $g_{A_0} : TG_{A_0} \to TG_{\mathbf{M}}$ and $g_{A_0'} : TG_{A_0'} \to TG_{A_0}$ be the transition graph morphisms induced by the inclusions $A_0 \subseteq A$ and $A_0' \subseteq A_0$. Then

$$res(\mathbf{M}, A_0') = res(\mathbf{M}, g_{A_0} \circ g_{A_0'})$$
$$\overset{*}{=} res(res(\mathbf{M}, g_{A_0}), g_{A_0'})$$
$$= res(res(\mathbf{M}, A_0), A_0')$$

where $\overset{*}{=}$ holds because $\mathbf{m} \circ (g_{A_0} \circ g_{A_0'}) = (\mathbf{m} \circ g_{A_0}) \circ g_{A_0'}$.

2.   Since $V_{\sigma \circ \sigma'} = V_{\sigma'} \circ V_{\sigma}$ and $(V_{\sigma'} \circ V_{\sigma}) \circ \mathbf{m} = V_{\sigma'} \circ (V_{\sigma} \circ \mathbf{m})$

$$\begin{aligned} view(\sigma \circ \sigma', \mathbf{M}) &= view(V_{\sigma \circ \sigma'}, \mathbf{M}) \\ &= view(V_{\sigma'} \circ V_{\sigma}, \mathbf{M}) \\ &= view(\sigma', view(\sigma, \mathbf{M})) . \end{aligned}$$

3.   Let $in_{A_1} : (\Sigma, A_1) \subseteq (\Sigma, A)$ be the inclusion, and $g_2 : TG_{A_2} \to TG_{\mathbf{M}}$ be the transition graph inclusion induced by $A_2 \subseteq A_1$. Then

$$\begin{aligned} res(view(A_1, \mathbf{M}), A_2) &= res(TG_{\mathbf{M}}, V_{in_{A_1}} \circ \mathbf{m}), A_2) \\ &= (TG_{A_2}, (V_{in_{A_1}} \circ \mathbf{m}) \circ g_2) . \end{aligned}$$

Since the inclusion $A_2 \subseteq A$ induces the same transition graph inclusion $g_2 :$
$TG_{A_2} \to TG_{\mathbf{M}}$

$$\begin{aligned} view(A_1, res(\mathbf{M}, A_2)) &= view(A_1, (TG_{A_2}, \mathbf{m} \circ g_2)) \\ &= (TG_{A_2}, V_{in_{A_1}} \circ (\mathbf{m} \circ g_2)) \end{aligned}$$

which proves the assertion.

4.   The assertion follows immediately from the commutativity of the inclusions $A - (A_0 \cup A_0') \subseteq A - (A_0 - A_0') \subseteq A$ and $A - (A_0 \cup A_0') \subseteq A - (A_0' - A_0) \subseteq A$.

4.2 Extension and Reduction

Beyond the development operations introduced above, development relations are needed that allow the comparison of already given models. For example, a model of an existing implementation as a transformation system might have already been developed, and now another transformation system modelling a required functionality should be mapped to the implementation model to realise the functionality in the given implementation. In this case an appropriate notion of development relation should be provided that allows us to consider the implementation as a development of the requirements model.

Development relations of transformation systems are defined by mappings of their transition graphs and data spaces, that may have the same or opposite directions.

Definition 4.9 (Extension and Reduction). *Let* $\mathbf{M} = (TG_{\mathbf{M}}, \mathbf{m})$ *be a* $D\Sigma$-*transformation system and* $\mathbf{M}' = (TG_{\mathbf{M}'}, \mathbf{m}')$ *be a* $D\Sigma'$-*transformation system.*

1. *A pair* $(g, s) : \mathbf{M} \to \mathbf{M}'$, *given by transition graph morphisms* $g : TG_{\mathbf{M}} \to TG_{\mathbf{M}'}$ *and* $s : \mathbb{D}_{D\Sigma'} \to \mathbb{D}_{D\Sigma}$, *is an* extension *(*$\mathbf{M}'$ *extends* $\mathbf{M}$ *via* (g, s)*)* *if* $s \circ \mathbf{m}' \circ g = \mathbf{m}$.

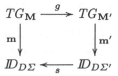

2. *A pair $(g, s) : \mathbf{M} \to \mathbf{M}'$, given by transition graph morphisms $g : TG_{\mathbf{M}'} \to TG_{\mathbf{M}}$ and $s : \mathbb{D}_{D\Sigma'} \to \mathbb{D}_{D\Sigma}$, is a reduction ($\mathbf{M}'$ reduces $\mathbf{M}$ via (g, s)) if $\mathbf{m} \circ g = s \circ \mathbf{m}'$.*

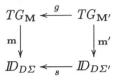

Suppose g is an inclusion. Then in an extension $(g, s) : \mathbf{M} \to \mathbf{M}'$ the system $\mathbf{M}'$ includes the behaviour of $\mathbf{M}$ but may also extend it by further steps. In this most general form extension does not always represent a desired development, since $\mathbf{M}'$ may also do things not foreseen in $\mathbf{M}$. However, if all the new steps correspond to internal actions of $\mathbf{M}'$, i.e., actions that are not in the signature of $\mathbf{M}$, extension corresponds to inheritance, where the behaviour of $\mathbf{M}$ is preserved conformly, and new functionality may be added. (Cf. the discussion in [FW99].)

Reduction via an inclusion g can be used to represent reduction of non-determinism, but also removal of arbitrary steps. By further conditions corresponding to the ones above, reduction of non-determinism can be singled out.

Both for extension and reduction the direction of the data space morphism is $s : \mathbb{D}_{D\Sigma'} \to \mathbb{D}_{D\Sigma}$. In the case of a *uniform* extension or reduction, where $s = \mathbb{D}_\sigma$ for a signature morphism $\sigma : D\Sigma \to D\Sigma'$, this means that $\mathbf{M}'$ has a finer or larger signature, introducing new (private) structure in the concrete model.

Due to the compositionality of commutative diagrams the following proposition obviously holds.

Proposition 4.10. *Extension and reduction are transitive and reflexive.*

Proof. Let $(g, s) : \mathbf{M} \to \mathbf{M}'$ and $(g', s') : \mathbf{M}' \to \mathbf{M}''$ be extensions. Then $(g' \circ g, s \circ s') : \mathbf{M} \to \mathbf{M}''$ is an extension, too, since $s' \circ s \circ \mathbf{m}'' \circ g' \circ g = s' \circ \mathbf{m}' \circ g = \mathbf{m}$. The pair $(id_{TG_{\mathbf{M}}}, V_{id_{D\Sigma}})$ is obviously an extension $\mathbf{M} \to \mathbf{M}$. The proofs for reductions are analogous.

The development operations introduced in Section 4.1 yield the following development relations.

Proposition 4.11. *Let $\mathbf{M}$ be a $D\Sigma$-transformation system.*

1. *$\mathbf{M}$ extends $res(\mathbf{M}, g)$ via $(g, id_{\mathbf{D}_{D\Sigma}})$.*
2. *$res(\mathbf{M}, g)$ reduces $\mathbf{M}$ via $(g, id_{\mathbf{D}_{D\Sigma}})$.*
3. *$\mathbf{M}$ extends and reduces $view(s, \mathbf{M})$ via $(id_{TG_{\mathbf{M}}}, s)$.*
4. *$\mathbf{M}$ extends $exc(\mathbf{M}, A_0)$ and $exc(\mathbf{M}, A_0)$ reduces $\mathbf{M}$.*
5. *$\mathbf{M}$ extends and reduces $hide(D\Sigma_0, \mathbf{M})$.*
6. *$\mathbf{M}$ extends and reduces $ren(r, \mathbf{M})$.*

Proof. The assertions follow immediately from the definitions, as indicated in the following diagrams for restriction, view, and renaming.

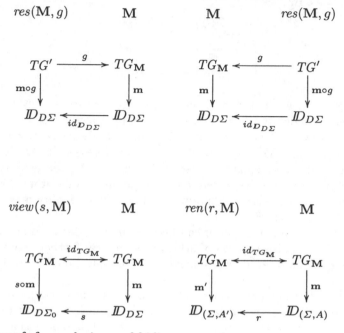

The proofs for exclusion and hiding are analogous.

As an example of a reduction relation between transformation systems, two different specifications of the faulty channel of the alternating bit protocol are now considered. The first system (Example 4.12) is a model of the corresponding CCS specification from [Mil89], analogous to the interpretation of the CCS sender specification as a transformation system in Example 2.13. For the second one (Example 4.13) another specification of the same faulty channel is used, from the book [CM88]. It is given in the parallel programming language UNITY that is introduced in this book. As opposed to the paradigm of CCS, given by synchronous message passing and temporal ordering of actions, this one is based on asynchronous access to shared variables and rule-based non-deterministic execution of parallel assignments changing the data states. Nevertheless, due to the interpretation of both specifications as transformation systems it can be shown formally that the UNITY model is a reduction of the CCS model.

Example 4.12 (The CCS Faulty Channel Specification). The faulty channel the alternating bit protocol is designed for transmits the messages, or loses or duplicates them. It is modelled in CCS by an agent CH, parameterised by a queue of items that indicates the actual internal state of the channel (see [Mil89], p. 144).

$$CH_\lambda = in(x).CH_x$$
$$CH_{x_n \ldots x_1} = in(x_{n+1}).CH_{x_{n+1} \ldots x_1}$$
$$+ \overline{out}(x_1).CH_{x_n \ldots x_2}$$
$$+ \sum_{i=1}^n \tau.CH_{x_n \ldots x_{i+1} x_{i-1} \ldots x_1}$$
$$+ \sum_{i=1}^n \tau.CH_{x_n \ldots x_i x_i \ldots x_1} \ .$$

In its initial state the channel accepts an input value that it appends to the end of its internal queue, then it may accept a further input, output the first element of the queue, or lose or duplicate some element.

Analogous to the construction of the sender model $\mathbf{CCS}_S$ in Example 2.13 the index $x_n \ldots x_1$ of CH indicates the data state signature, and the actions yield the action signature. The internal τ-actions, representing the faulty behaviours of the channel, are modelled again by transitions labelled by the empty action set.

For the definition of the data states consider first a parameterised data type specification $queue(item)$ that contains additional functions $lose, dup :$ $int, queue \to queue$ to model the loss and duplication of data items at a given position, and a function $\bullet : queue, queue \to queue$ for the concatenation of queues ($x_n \ldots x_1 \bullet y_k \ldots y_1 = x_n \ldots x_1 y_k \ldots y_1$). The latter is needed for the comparison of the transformation systems in Example 4.14.

queue(item) = **int** +
    sorts item, queue
    funs empty: $\to$ queue
            enq: item, queue $\to$ queue
            deq: queue $\to$ queue
            fst: queue $\to$ item
            lose, dup: int, queue $\to$ queue
            $\_ \bullet \_$: queue, queue $\to$ queue

The data space signature $CCS\text{-}CH$ is then given by the $queue(item)$ signature, extended by a constant $chan :\to queue(item)$ which is bound to the actual value of the queue of items in the channel in each state, and actions in and out.

CCS-CH = **queue(item)** +
    funs chan: $\to$ queue(item)
    acts in, out: item

Now let Q be a partial $queue(item)$-algebra with a generic set $M = Q_{item}$ as the set of items, $Q_{queue} = M^*$, the set of words over M, and the queue operations. Furthermore let $Q[w]$ be the extension of Q to the data signature of CCS-CH by $chan^{Q[w]} = w$ for each $w \in M^*$, i.e., $Q[x_n, \ldots, x_1]$ is the state in which the elements $x_n, \ldots, x_1$ are in the channel. Then the transformation system $\mathbf{CCS}_{CH}$ is given as follows. Its set of control states CS_{CH} is given by

$$CS_{CH} = M^* \uplus \{\Delta\} \ ,$$

and the data states are associated by

$$\mathbf{ccs}_{CH}(w) = Q[w] \text{ and } \mathbf{ccs}_{CH}(\Delta) = \emptyset \,.$$

The transitions $t \in T_{CH}(c,d)$ and their action labels, presented in the form $t : c \to d \mapsto \mathbf{ccs}_{CH}(t)$ as in the previous examples, are given by

$$
\begin{array}{rlccl}
T_{CH} : & init : & \Delta \;\to\; & \lambda & \mapsto & \emptyset \\[4pt]
& in_x : & w \;\to\; & xw & \mapsto & \{in(x)\} \\
& out_x : & wx \;\to\; & w & \mapsto & \{out(x)\} \\
& lose_i : & uxv \;\to\; & uv & \mapsto & \emptyset \\
& dup_i : & uxv \;\to\; & uxxv & \mapsto & \emptyset \\[4pt]
& idle : & \omega \;\to\; & \omega & \mapsto & \emptyset
\end{array}
$$

for all $w, u, v \in M^*, x \in M, i \in I\!N$ with $length(u) = i - 1$ and $\omega \in M^* \uplus \{\Delta\}$. The tracking relations are given by the identity on the static data type Q for each transition.

The restriction of $\mathbf{CCS}_{CH}$ to an LTS by the functor given in Definition 2.9 obviously yields the CCS-semantics of CH, with τ-actions given by the empty set as label.

In the following example the channel component of the alternating bit protocol is specified using the parallel programming language UNITY.

Example 4.13 (The UNITY Faulty Channel Specification). A UNITY program consists of three parts, the *declare*, *initially*, and *assign* parts. In the *declare* part the program variables are declared, and in the *initially* part the initial values of the variables are defined. The *assign* part consists of a set of conditional parallel assignments, assignments for short, separated by []. An assignment is of the form

$$x_1 := exp_1 || \dots || x_n := exp_n \text{ if } cond \,,$$

where $x_1, \dots, x_n$ are program variables, $exp_1, \dots, exp_n$ are expressions, and *cond* is a condition. The computational model is given as follows. An assignment is chosen non-deterministically, the expressions are evaluated, and then their values are assigned to the corresponding variables, provided the condition of the assignment is true. Otherwise another assignment is chosen. This computation proceeds (fairly) until all variables are stable, i.e., none of the enabled assignments can no longer alter the value of any variable.

Consider now the UNITY program of the channels (cf. [CM88], p. 411, and Figure 4.4), where only the part of the program is given that manipulates the channel variables.

Program CHANNEL **is**
    declare in, out: queue(item)
    initially in = out = empty
    assign   in:= deq(in) || out:= enq(first(in),out) **if** in ≠ empty

          [] in:= deq(in)   **if** in ≠ empty

          [] out:= enq(first(in),out)   **if** in ≠ empty

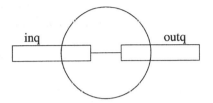

Fig. 4.4. Structure of the UNITY channel

The first assignment specifies the expected behaviour of a channel; transmitting an element from the input to the output queue. the other ones specify loss and duplication as faults in the transmission. An important difference between the UNITY specification and the CCS specification can be noticed immediately. Initially all conditions of the UNITY specification are false, i.e., as a standalone component the sender does not do anything, as opposed to the CCS sender, whose control flow graph is not void. This difference is due to the different interpretation of actions in the two specification techniques. The actions of a CCS agent are input and output actions, i.e., actions that the agent performs actively as well as actions the agent would engage in if the environment offered them. A UNITY program only specifies the active actions of a component, whose performance, however, depends on the actual state. The component becomes active as soon as the environment has changed some of the program's variables in such a way that at least one of the conditions becomes true. (This 'lack of behaviour' of the UNITY sender as a standalone component is of course due to its separation from the enclosing program of the complete protocol.)

To model composition semantically later on the possible data state transformations in the component that are induced by the environment must be included in the behaviour of the component. (That means the prerequisite for semantical composition is an *open semantics* of the component, see [HEET99].) In the UNITY channel program these passive actions can be rephrased by assignments that specify the allowed actions of the environment, i.e., the ones that may alter its input and output queues as follows:

   assign [] in:= enq(x,in)

          [] out:= deq(out) **if** out ≠ empty

The semantics of the program $CHANNEL$ is now reconstructed as a transformation system $\mathbf{U}_{CH} = (TG_{\mathbf{U}_{CH}}, \mathbf{u}_{CH})$. The declaration part of the UNITY program immediately yields the data part of the corresponding data space signature. Furthermore appropriate action names in and out are introduced, and the input and output queues are renamed to inq and $outq$ in order to distinguish them from the actions.

> **U-CH** = **queue(item)** +
> **funs** inq, outq: $\to$ queue(item)
> **acts** in, out : item

For the following constructions a partial $queue(item)$-algebra Q is assumed as in Example 4.12, with $Q_{item} = M$ and $Q_{queue} = M^*$. Like the CCS model $\mathbf{CCS}_{CH}$ the UNITY–channel model $\mathbf{U}_{CH}$ is defined generically w.r.t. the set M of items it transports.

The control states of $TG_{\mathbf{U}_{CH}}$ are given by pairs $(u, v) \in M^* \times M^*$ representing the actual values of the input and output queue, plus an initialisation state Δ.

$$CS_{\mathbf{U}_{CH}} = (M^* \times M^*) \uplus \{\Delta\}.$$

The data states are defined analogous to the system $\mathbf{CCS}_{CH}$ by

$$\mathbf{u}_{CH}(u,v) = Q[u,v] \text{ and } \mathbf{u}_{CH}(\Delta) = \emptyset,$$

where $Q[u, v]$ is the extension of Q to the U-CH data signature by $inq^{Q[u,v]} = u$ and $outq^{Q[u,v]} = v$. The transitions and action labels are given by

$$
\begin{array}{rrccl}
T_{\mathbf{U}_{CH}}: & init: & \Delta \to (\lambda, \lambda) & \mapsto & \emptyset \\[4pt]
& transmit_x: (ux, v) \to (u, xv) & & \mapsto & \emptyset \\
& lose_i: (ux, v) \to (u, v) & & \mapsto & \emptyset \\
& dup_i: (ux, v) \to (ux, xv) & & \mapsto & \emptyset \\[4pt]
& in_x: (u, v) \to (xu, v) & & \mapsto & \{in(x)\} \\
& out_x: (u, vx) \to (u, v) & & \mapsto & \{out(x)\} \\[4pt]
& idle: \quad \omega \quad \to \quad \omega & & \mapsto & \emptyset
\end{array}
$$

for all $\omega \in CS_{\mathbf{U}_{CH}}, u, v \in M^*, x \in M, i \in I\!\!N$ with $length(u) = i - 1$, corresponding to the assignments of the extended program.

Example 4.14. Now the two transformation systems can be compared by a uniform reduction $\mathbf{ch} = (\sigma_{ch}, ch): \mathbf{CCS}_{CH} \to \mathbf{U}_{CH}$ according to Definition 4.9 (see also Figure 4.6, left) as follows. The signature morphism σ_{ch}:CCS-CH $\to$ U-CH is given by the identity on $queue(item)$ and the identity on the action signatures $\{in, out : item\}$. The constant $chan :\to queue(item)$ is mapped to the term $inq \bullet outq$. According to the definition of the forgetful functor of partial algebras, this means that the value of $chan$ in a $\mathbf{CCS}_{CH}$-data state $V_{\sigma_{ch}}(Q[u, v])$ is given by the concatenation $(inq \bullet outq)^{Q[u,v]}$ of $inq^{Q[u,v]}$ and

$outq^{Q[u,v]}$ in the $\mathbf{U}_{CH}$-data state $Q[u,v]$. This means that the value of *chan* is uv.

The transition graph morphism $ch : CG_{\mathbf{U}_{CH}} \to CG_{\mathbf{CCS}_{CH}}$ is given by $ch(\Delta) = \Delta$ and $ch(u,v) = uv \in M^*$ for all control states $(u,v) \in M^* \times M^*$. Furthermore, ch is defined on the transitions by

$$
\begin{array}{rcll}
init : & \Delta & \to & (\lambda, \lambda) \\
\end{array}
$$

$$
\begin{array}{rcl@{\quad}c@{\quad}rcl}
init : & \Delta & \to & (\lambda,\lambda) & \mapsto & init : \Delta \to \lambda \\[4pt]
transmit_x : & (ux,v) & \to & (u,xv) & \mapsto & idle : uxv \to uxv \\
lose_i : & (ux,v) & \to & (u,v) & \mapsto & lose_i : uxv \to uv \\
dup_i : & (ux,v) & \to & (ux,xv) & \mapsto & dup_i : uxv \to uxxv \\[4pt]
in_x : & (u,v) & \to & (xu,v) & \mapsto & in_x : uv \to xuv \\
out_x : & (u,vx) & \to & (u,v) & \mapsto & out_x : uvx \to uv \\[4pt]
idle : & (u,v) & \to & (u,v) & \mapsto & idle : uv \to uv \\
idle : & \Delta & \to & \Delta & \mapsto & idle : \Delta \to \Delta \\
\end{array}
$$

for all $x \in M, u, v \in M^*$, and $i \in I\!N$ with $length(u) = i-1$. As in the previous example the tracking relations are given by the identity on Q.

It can be easily checked that this morphism is well defined, i.e., all data states and action sets are preserved by the forgetful functor. Thus $\mathbf{ch} = (\sigma_{ch}, ch) : \mathbf{CCS}_{CH} \to \mathbf{U}_{CH}$ is indeed a uniform reduction.

Beyond the existence of the reduction $\mathbf{ch} : \mathbf{CCS}_{CH} \to \mathbf{U}_{CH}$, some further statements about the relation between $\mathbf{U}_{CH}$ and $\mathbf{CCS}_{CH}$ can be made. First, note that the existence of the reduction $\mathbf{ch}$ implies that the set of traces $Tr(\mathbf{U}_{CH})$ is contained in $Tr(\mathbf{CCS}_{CH})$, since σ_{ch} is the identity on the action signatures. Moreover, the transition graph morphism ch is surjective, but it does not have an inverse. In fact, there is no reduction $\mathbf{U}_{CH} \to \mathbf{CCS}_{CH}$ at all. This is due to the fact that the states of $\mathbf{U}_{CH}$ carry more information relevant for the behaviour than the $\mathbf{CCS}_{CH}$ states. In the state (u,v) all elements of v have already been transmitted safely to the output port and can no longer be lost or duplicated. Moreover, elements can only be lost or duplicated in the order in which they occur in the channel. In the CCS specification this decision is not represented. In any state w any element in the queue can be lost or duplicated, and this may happen in any order. That means the non-determinism of the CCS specification is reduced in the UNITY specification, but not vice versa. The difference w.r.t. the decision points also indicates that the two models are not weakly bisimilar. They are testing equivalent, however, because choice points are not relevant for testing equivalence.

4.3 Categorical Structure

At this point it is convenient to exhibit the categorical structure of the development relations and compare it with the categories of transformation systems introduced in Chapter 2, Definition 2.10. In the latter only transformation systems of the same signature are compared, whereas the development relations compare systems of different signatures. In order to lift morphisms to this more general setting the flattening construction for indexed categories is used (see [TBG91, Pho92]). As a precondition for this construction, the category of data space signatures and forgetful functors are first introduced that allow the representation of the model functor as an indexed category.

Definition 4.15 (Category of Data Space Signatures). *The category* **DSig** *is given by data space signatures and data space signature morphisms. Composition and identities are inherited from the category of algebraic signatures* **Sig** *and families of mappings. That means, if* $\sigma = (\sigma_\Sigma, \sigma_A) : D\Sigma \to D\Sigma'$ *and* $\sigma' = (\sigma'_\Sigma, \sigma'_A) : D\Sigma' \to D\Sigma''$ *are data space signature morphisms, their composition* $\sigma' \circ \sigma : D\Sigma \to D\Sigma''$ *is given by*

$$(\sigma' \circ \sigma)_\Sigma = \sigma'_\Sigma \circ \sigma_\Sigma : \Sigma \to \Sigma' \to \Sigma''$$

$$(\sigma' \circ \sigma)_{A,w,w'} = (\sigma'_{A,\sigma^*_\Sigma(w),\sigma^*_\Sigma(w')}) \circ \sigma_{A,w,w'} :$$
$$A_{w,w'} \to A'_{\sigma^*_\Sigma(w),\sigma^*_\Sigma(w')} \to A''_{(\sigma'\circ\sigma)^*_\Sigma(w),(\sigma'\circ\sigma)^*_\Sigma(w')} .$$

In Definition 4.3 the *uniform view* of a $D\Sigma'$-transformation system w.r.t. a signature morphism $\sigma : D\Sigma \to D\Sigma'$ has already been defined. It is based on the transition graph morphism $\mathbb{D}_\sigma : \mathbb{D}_{D\Sigma'} \to \mathbb{D}_{D\Sigma}$ on the corresponding data spaces that is induced by σ. For the sake of reference its definition is repeated here.

Definition and Fact 4.16 (Data Space Functor). Let $D\Sigma = (\Sigma, A)$ and $D\Sigma' = (\Sigma', A')$ be data space signatures with $\Sigma = (S, F)$ and $\Sigma' = (S', F')$, and let $\sigma = (\sigma_\Sigma, \sigma_A) : D\Sigma \to D\Sigma'$ be a signature morphism.

1. The induced transition graph morphism $\mathbb{D}_\sigma : \mathbb{D}_{D\Sigma'} \to \mathbb{D}_{D\Sigma}$ is defined by

$$\mathbb{D}_\sigma(C') \quad = V_{\sigma_\Sigma}(C') \qquad \text{(for all } C' \in |\mathbf{PAlg}(\Sigma')| \text{)}$$
$$\mathbb{D}_\sigma(\alpha', \sim') = (\sigma_A^{-1}(\alpha'), V_{\sigma_\Sigma}(\sim')) \quad \text{(for all } (\alpha', \sim') \in Tf_{D\Sigma'}) ,$$

where

$$\sigma_A^{-1}(\alpha') \quad = \{a(c;d) \mid a \in A, \sigma_A(a)(c;d) \in \alpha'\}$$
$$(V_{\sigma_\Sigma}(\sim'))_s = \sim'_{\sigma_\Sigma(s)} \quad (s \in S) .$$

2. The data space functor $\mathbb{D} : \mathbf{DSig} \to \mathbf{Cat}^{op}$ is defined by $\mathbb{D}(D\Sigma) = \mathbb{D}_{D\Sigma}$ and $\mathbb{D}(\sigma) = \mathbb{D}_\sigma$.

Proof. 1. $\mathbb{D}_\sigma$ is well defined as shown in the proof of 4.3.
2. The functoriality properties of $\mathbb{D}$ follow immediately from the functoriality properties of the forgetful functors for partial algebras and the properties of the inverse image, $\sigma_{id_A}^{-1} = id_{Act_{D\Sigma}}$ and $(\sigma'_A \circ \sigma_A)^{-1} = \sigma_A^{-1} \circ (\sigma'_A)^{-1}$.

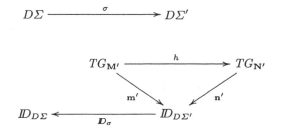

Fig. 4.5. Construction of the forgetful functor $V_\sigma = \_\circ I\!D_\sigma : \mathbf{TF}(D\Sigma') \to \mathbf{TF}(D\Sigma)$

The morphism $I\!D_\sigma$ induced by a signature morphism $\sigma : D\Sigma \to D\Sigma'$ relates the data spaces w.r.t. different signatures. Its composition with a transition graph morphism $\mathbf{m} : TG_\mathbf{M} \to I\!D_{D\Sigma}$ thus maps a $D\Sigma'$-transformation system to a $D\Sigma$-transformation system (see Figure 4.5) and thus it yields a forgetful functor. Note that by definition the forgetful functor of transformation systems does not change the behaviour of systems, but just reduces the visibility.

Definition and Fact 4.17 (Forgetful Functor). Given a data space signature morphism $\sigma : D\Sigma \to D\Sigma'$ the *forgetful functor* $V_\sigma : \mathbf{TF}(D\Sigma') \to \mathbf{TF}(D\Sigma)$ is defined by

$$V_\sigma(\mathbf{M}') = view(\sigma, \mathbf{M}) = (TG_{\mathbf{M}'}, I\!D_\sigma \circ \mathbf{m}')$$
$$V_\sigma(h') = h' .$$

Proof. The functor is well defined since for morphisms $h' : \mathbf{M}' \to \mathbf{N}'$ in $\mathbf{TF}(D\Sigma')$

$$(I\!D_\sigma \circ \mathbf{n}') \circ h' = I\!D_\sigma \circ \mathbf{m}' ,$$

i.e., $V_\sigma(h') : V_\sigma(\mathbf{M}') \to V_\sigma(\mathbf{N}')$ is a morphism in $\mathbf{TF}(D\Sigma)$. The functoriality properties obviously hold.

The association of a category of models (transformation systems) to each signature, and a contravariant forgetful functor to each signature morphism, yields a model functor. (In categorical terms it is thus an indexed category.)

Definition 4.18 (Model Functor). *The mapping* $TS : \mathbf{DSig} \to \mathbf{Cat}^{op}$, *defined by*

$$TS(D\Sigma) = \mathbf{TF}(D\Sigma)$$

for each data space signature $D\Sigma$, *and*

$$TS(\sigma : D\Sigma \to D\Sigma') = V_\sigma : \mathbf{TF}(D\Sigma') \to \mathbf{TF}(D\Sigma)$$

for each signature morphism σ, *is a functor.*

The local categories $\mathbf{TF}(D\Sigma)$ can now be glued together by considering the signatures as parts of the models, and transporting models along signature morphisms via the forgetful functors to relate them within the category corresponding to the smaller signature.

Definition and Fact 4.19 (Global Category). The *global category of transformation systems* $\mathbf{TF}$ is defined as follows.

- Its objects are pairs $(D\Sigma, \mathbf{M})$, where $D\Sigma$ is a data space signature and $\mathbf{M}$ is a $D\Sigma$-transformation system.
- Its morphisms $\mathbf{h} : (D\Sigma, \mathbf{M}) \to (D\Sigma', \mathbf{M}')$ are pairs $\mathbf{h} = (\sigma, h)$, where $\sigma : D\Sigma' \to D\Sigma$ is a data space signature morphism (in the reverse direction) and $h : V_\sigma(\mathbf{M}) \to \mathbf{M}'$ is a $D\Sigma'$-transformation system morphism. That means $h : TG_\mathbf{M} \to TG_{\mathbf{M}'}$ is a transition graph morphism that satisfies $\mathbb{D}_\sigma \circ \mathbf{m} = \mathbf{m}' \circ h$.
- Composition of morphisms $(\sigma, h) : (D\Sigma, \mathbf{M}) \to (D\Sigma', \mathbf{M}')$ and $(\sigma', h') : (D\Sigma', \mathbf{M}') \to (D\Sigma'', \mathbf{M}'')$ is given by

$$(\sigma', h') \circ (\sigma, h) = (\sigma \circ \sigma', h' \circ h) .$$

- The identities are given by $id_{(D\Sigma, \mathbf{M})} = (id_{D\Sigma}, id_{TG_\mathbf{M}})$.

Proof. This is the usual flattening construction of an indexed category $TS : \mathbf{DSig} \to \mathbf{Cat}^{op}$, given by the model functor TS of transformation systems $TS(D\Sigma) = \mathbf{TF}(D\Sigma)$, $TS(\sigma) = V_\sigma$, see [TBG91, Her94].

Note that the morphisms $(\sigma, h) : (D\Sigma, \mathbf{M}) \to (D\Sigma', \mathbf{M}')$ in $\mathbf{TF}$ coincide with the uniform reductions $(h, \mathbb{D}_\sigma) : \mathbf{M}' \to \mathbf{M}$. The uniform extensions can also be reconstructed as morphisms in a global category by starting with the opposite of the local category of transformation systems $\mathbf{TF}(D\Sigma)^{op}$. These relationships between global morphisms, reductions, and extensions of transformation systems are summarised in Figure 4.6.

4.4 Refinement and Implementation

In an extension of transformation systems the steps of the abstract system are mapped to steps of the concrete system, preserving the visible part of the associated data states, tracking relations, and action sets. This relationship can be generalised by allowing the mapping of steps to sequences or other compositions of steps, with the same preservation property as above. To formalise this, first composition operations on steps are defined that yield closure operations on transition graphs and transformation systems. We will first consider *sequential* refinements and implementations, where the steps of the concrete system can be composed *in time* to refine/implement an abstract step. Thereafter other closure operations are defined that admit the composition of (concrete) steps *in space*. Such *parallel closures* can be defined in different

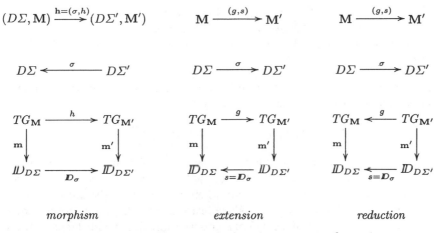

morphism   extension   reduction

Fig. 4.6. Summary of the global relationships between transformation systems

ways. In the simplest one new parallel transitions are introduced for all pairs of consecutive transitions that are independent of each other, which means that they can be executed in any order always leading to the same result. The more complex parallel closure operations also introduce new states that are obtained as unions or pushouts of their data parts. In these *multithreaded* versions of parallel closures the original system is considered to be able to be in different states simultaneously, which are then formally combined, to one state. All parallel closures allow the refinement of abstract steps by parallel threads in the concrete system. Sequential and parallel closure operations can be combined, which yields more complex patterns of refinement in time and space.

The sequential closure operation corresponds to constructing the path graph of a transition graph, i.e., its transitive closure. In the following an inductive definition of the transitive closure is given in an algebraic style. That means equations representing the associativity of sequential composition and the idle transitions as neutral elements are taken into the definition immediately. Thus formally a transition in the path graph is an equivalence class of expressions. Due to the associativity, however, these can be represented as usual by expressions $t_1; \ldots; t_n$, where the t_i's are transitions from the given transition graph.

Definition 4.20 (Path Graph). *Given a transition graph $TG = (CS, T, in, it)$ its path graph $TG^* = (CS^*, T^*, in^*, id^*)$ is defined by*

- $CS^* = CS, in^* = in, id^* = id$

and the sets $T^*(c, d)$ of transitions are given by the following inductive definition:

- $T(c, d) \subseteq T^*(c, d)$ *for all $c, d \in CS$*

- $t \in T^*(c,d) \wedge t' \in T^*(d,e) \Rightarrow t; t' \in T^*(c,e)$
- $t; id(d) = id(c); t = t$ for all $t \in T^*(c,d), c, d \in CS$
- $(t_1; t_2); t_3 = t_1; (t_2; t_3)$ for all $t_1 \in T^*(c,d), t_2 \in T^*(d,e), t_3 \in T^*(e,g)$, and $c, d, e, g \in CS$

The construction of the path graph induces also an associative sequential composition operation on paths, given by

$$(t_1; \ldots; t_n); (t'_1; \ldots; t'_k) = t_1; \ldots; t_n; t'_1; \ldots; t'_k \, .$$

The idle transitions are then the neutral elements for this composition. This yields the algebraic structure that is needed to extend the sequential closure to transformation systems. Note that when constructing the path graph of a data state space $I\!D_{D\Sigma}$ new actions are introduced, which are formal sequential compositions of action sets. This construction thus yields transformation systems w.r.t. a specification framework that coincides with the one used so far, except that the powerset functor $\mathcal{P}$ used for the construction of action sets is replaced by formal strings of action sets as action structures.

According to Definition 2.15, this yields categories $\mathbf{TF}^*(D\Sigma)$ of $D\Sigma$-transformation systems with action sequences via

$$Tf^*_{D\Sigma}(C, D) = (\mathcal{P}(Act_{D\Sigma}(|C|, |D|)))^* \, .$$

With the homomorphic extension $I\!D^*_\sigma : I\!D^*_{D\Sigma'} \to I\!D^*_{D\Sigma}$ of $I\!D_\sigma$ for each signature morphism $\sigma : D\Sigma \to D\Sigma'$ this also yields a global category $\mathbf{TF}^*$ of sequentially closed transformation systems. Now let $\eta_{D\Sigma} : I\!D_{D\Sigma} \to I\!D^*_{D\Sigma}$ be the embedding of $I\!D_{D\Sigma}$ into its sequential closure, for each data space signature $D\Sigma$. This yields an embedding functor $\mathbf{TF} \to \mathbf{TF}^*$, given by

$$\begin{aligned}(D\Sigma, (TG_\mathbf{M}, \mathbf{m})) &\mapsto (D\Sigma, (TG_\mathbf{M}, \eta_{D\Sigma} \circ \mathbf{m})) \\ (\sigma, h) &\mapsto (\sigma, h)\end{aligned}$$

that allows us to consider each transformation system (as defined so far) as a transformation system with action sequences.

Definition 4.21 (Sequential Closure). *Given a $D\Sigma$-transformation system* $\mathbf{M} = (TG_\mathbf{M}, \mathbf{m})$ *its sequential closure* $\mathbf{M}^* = (TG_{\mathbf{M}^*}, \mathbf{m}^*)$ *is given by* $TG_{\mathbf{M}^*} = (TG_\mathbf{M})^*$ *and the unique homomorphic extension* $\mathbf{m}^*$ *of* $\mathbf{m} : TG_\mathbf{M} \to I\!D_{D\Sigma}$ *to* $TG^*_\mathbf{M} \to I\!D^*_{D\Sigma}$, *i.e.,*

- $\mathbf{m}^*(c) = \mathbf{m}(c)$ $(c \in CS^* = CS)$
- $\mathbf{m}^*(t) = \mathbf{m}(t)$ $(t \in T)$ *(that means* $act^{\mathbf{m}^*}_t = act^\mathbf{m}_t$ *and* $\sim^{\mathbf{m}^*}_t = \sim^\mathbf{m}_t$*)*
- $\mathbf{m}^*(t; t') = (act^{\mathbf{m}^*}_{t;t'}, \sim^{\mathbf{m}^*}_{t;t'})$, *where*

$$\begin{aligned}act^{\mathbf{m}^*}_{t;t'} &= act^{\mathbf{m}^*}_t ; act^{\mathbf{m}^*}_{t'} &\in \mathcal{P}(Act_{D\Sigma})^* \\ \sim^{\mathbf{m}^*}_{t;t'} &= \sim^{\mathbf{m}^*}_{t'} \circ \sim^{\mathbf{m}^*}_t &\in Rel^S\end{aligned}$$

The sequential composition of steps is used in the following definition of *refinements* and *implementations*, both of which allow the mapping of single steps of one system to composed steps of another one. The difference of refinement and implementation is that the first one must preserve the visible parts of the data states and the action labels, whereas an implementation may ignore the action labels. Thus in the first case the action labels are considered as representing the interaction capacity and therefore must be preserved. An implementation on the other hand just implements one action by a composition of internal actions, independently of their names. In this case the first system serves as an interface for the second one through which the second one can be accessed, whereas in a refinement the second system can completely replace the first one.

Definition 4.22 (Sequential Refinement and Implementation). *Let* $\mathbf{M}$ *and* $\mathbf{M}'$ *be* $D\Sigma$- *and* $D\Sigma'$-*transformation systems respectively.*

1. A sequential refinement $\mathbf{r} = (r_{TG}, r_D) : \mathbf{M} \to \mathbf{M}'$ *is an extension*

$$\mathbf{r} = (r_{TG}, r_D) : \mathbf{M} \to (\mathbf{M}')^* \ in \ \mathbf{TF}^* .$$

2. A sequential implementation $\mathbf{r} = (r_{TG}, r_D) : \mathbf{M} \to \mathbf{M}'$ *is an extension*

$$\mathbf{r} = (r_{TG}, r_D) : view((\Sigma, \emptyset), \mathbf{M}) \to view((\Sigma', \emptyset), (\mathbf{M}')^*) \ in \ \mathbf{TF}^*.$$

The models $\mathbf{M}$ and $(\mathbf{M}')^*$ of an implementation $\mathbf{r} : \mathbf{M} \to \mathbf{M}'$ are also called the *interface* and the *body* of the implementation. A refinement or implementation $\mathbf{r} : \mathbf{M} \to \mathbf{M}'$ is called *uniform* if $r_D : I\!D^*_{D\Sigma'} \to I\!D_{D\Sigma}$ (resp. $r_D : I\!D^*_{(\Sigma', \emptyset)} \to I\!D_{(\Sigma, \emptyset)}$) is the data space morphism $I\!D_\rho$ induced by a signature morphism $\rho : D\Sigma \to D\Sigma'$ (resp. $\rho : (\Sigma, \emptyset) \to (\Sigma', \emptyset)$). Such a refinement or implementation will often be denoted by $\mathbf{r} = (r, \rho)$.

In order to define a refinement or implementation $\mathbf{r} : \mathbf{M} \to \mathbf{M}'$ it is not necessary to construct the whole closure $(\mathbf{M}')^*$. In such a relation it suffices to construct the compositions of steps that are actually needed to refine (implement) single abstract steps. The condition to be checked is then that the visible parts of the initial and final states of the composition coincide with the input and output states of the abstract step respectively (see Example 4.30).

Proposition 4.23 (Transitivity). *Sequential refinements and implementations are reflexive and transitive.*

Proof. Refinement is reflexive, because $(\eta_{\mathbf{M}}, id_{\mathbf{D}_{D\Sigma}}) : (D\Sigma, \mathbf{M}) \to (D\Sigma, \mathbf{M})$ is a refinement, as shown in the diagram in Figure 4.7. The equation $\mathbf{m}^* \circ \eta_{\mathbf{M}} = \eta_{D\Sigma} \circ \mathbf{m}$ holds by definition of homomorphic extensions.

Transitivity follows from the uniqueness of the homomorphic extension of morphisms, as shown in Figure 4.8. It has to be shown that the outer diagram in Figure 4.8 commutes. The following equations and implications prove this claim.

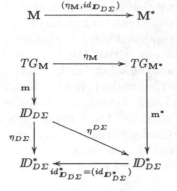

Fig. 4.7. Reflexivity of refinements

$$s_1^* \circ s_2^* \circ \mathbf{m}_3^* \circ r_{TG_2}^* \circ \eta_{\mathbf{M}_2}$$
$$= s_1^* \circ s_2^* \circ \mathbf{m}_3^* \circ r_{TG_2}$$
$$= s_1^* \circ \eta_{D\Sigma_2} \circ \mathbf{m}_2$$
$$= s_1^* \circ \mathbf{m}_2^* \circ \eta_{\mathbf{M}_2}$$
$$\Rightarrow s_1^* \circ s_2^* \circ \mathbf{m}_3^* \circ r_{TG_2}^* = s_1^* \circ \mathbf{m}_2^*$$
$$\Rightarrow s_1^* \circ s_2^* \circ \mathbf{m}_3^* \circ r_{TG_2}^* \circ r_{TG_1}$$
$$= s_1^* \circ \mathbf{m}_2^* \circ r_{TG_1}$$
$$= \eta_{D\Sigma_1} \circ \mathbf{m}_1 .$$

The assertion for implementations follows analogously, replacing $I\!\!D_{D\Sigma_i}$ by $I\!\!D_{(\Sigma_i,\emptyset)}$.

Parallel composition represents composition of steps in time, complementing the composition in space given by the sequential closure. The parallel closure operation adds transitions to a transformation system that are com-

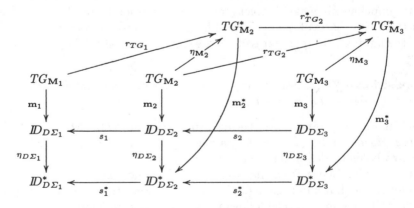

Fig. 4.8. Reflexivity of refinements

positions of sequentially independent transitions. This means that whenever two consecutive transformations can be executed in any order with the same effect, then they are combined to one parallel transformation with this effect. The property of having the same effect is thereby defined in terms of the action labels attached to the transitions. The situation is depicted in Figure 4.9: the consecutive transitions $t_1; t_2$ and $t_3; t_4$ both lead from state c_1 to state c_4 and execute the transformations A and B in different orders. Since they have the same effect they can be applied in parallel, represented by the transition $t_1 \| t_3$ with $\mathbf{m}(t_1 \| t_3) = A \cup B$.

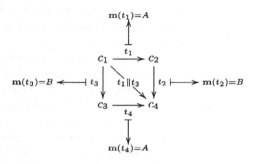

Fig. 4.9. Parallel transition for sequentially independent transitions

Definition 4.24 (Parallel Closure). *Given a $D\Sigma$-transformation system* $\mathbf{M} = (TG_{\mathbf{M}}, \mathbf{m})$ *with* $TG_{\mathbf{M}} = (CS, T, in, id)$ *its parallel closure* $\mathbf{M}^{\|} = (TG_{\mathbf{M}^{\|}}, \mathbf{m}^{\|})$ *with* $TG_{\mathbf{M}^{\|}} = (CS^{\|}, T^{\|}, in^{\|}, id^{\|})$ *is given as follows:*

$$CS^{\|} = CS$$
$$in^{\|} = in$$
$$id^{\|} = id$$
$$T(c, d) \subseteq T^{\|}(c, d) \quad (c, d \in CS^{\|})$$
$$\mathbf{m}^{\|}(t) = \mathbf{m}(t) \quad (t \in T)$$
$$\textit{if} \quad t_1 : c_1 \to c_2, t_2 : c_2 \to c_4,$$
$$t_3 : c_1 \to c_3, t_4 : c_3 \to c_3 \in T^{\|}$$
$$\textit{and} \quad \mathbf{m}^{\|}(t_1) = \mathbf{m}^{\|}(t_4)$$
$$\textit{and} \quad \mathbf{m}^{\|}(t_1) = \mathbf{m}^{\|}(t_4)$$
$$\textit{then} \quad t_1 \| t_3 : c_1 \to c_4 \in T^{\|}$$
$$\textit{and} \quad \mathbf{m}^{\|}(t_1 \| t_3) = \mathbf{m}^{\|}(t_1) \cup \mathbf{m}^{\|}(t_3)$$

The operation $\|$ is commutative, has $id(c)$ and $id(c)$ as neutral elements for $t : c \to d$, and $t_1 \| t_3 = t_4 \| t_2$ for all $t_1 : c_1 \to c_2, t_2 : c_2 \to c_4, t_3 : c_1 \to c_3, t_4 : c_3 \to c_3 \in T^{\|}$.

As opposed to the parallel closure, the following multithreaded closure operations also add new states. These are unions or superpositions of states that represent situations where the original system is considered to be in two states simultaneously. As above, the multithreaded versions of parallel closure are defined as closure operations on transition graphs, the algebraic structure of which induces the extension to transformation systems. The multithreaded parallel closures remains within the category **TF**, like the parallel closure, because the action label of a parallel step is given by the union of the action labels of the components. In this way the informal interpretation of an action set as the label of a transition in a simple transformation system as the parallel execution of all elements of the action set is covered by a formal definition. The tracking relation of a parallel step is accordingly defined as the union of the tracking relations of the components.

To make the union on the data state and transformation level precise the underlying data states have to be considered more closely. The idea is to represent unions of the local data states—in a first approximation—by the *coproduct* of partial Σ-algebras. Basically this is a symmetric superposition that identifies the common term-generated parts of partial algebras and takes the disjoint union of the remainders. To explain this in more detail consider first partial Σ-algebras A_1 and A_2 that are compatible in the following sense.

- A_1 and A_2 coincide on the common term-generated parts:
  If a ground term $t : \lambda \to w \in T_\Sigma$ can be evaluated in both A_1 and A_2, then $t^{A_1} = t^{A_2}$.
- A_1 and A_2 are disjoint on the remainder:
  Whenever an element $a_1 \in A_1$ is not the value of any ground term $t : \lambda \to w \in T_\Sigma$ that can also be evaluated in A_2, then $a_1 \notin A_2$, and vice versa.

Note that the second condition implies that

- the functions of A_1 and A_2 are consistent:
  For each $f : w \to v \in F$ and each $a \in dom(f^{A_1}) \cap dom(f^{A_2})$ we have $f^{A_1}(a) = f^{A_2}(a)$.

Under these conditions a coproduct $A_1 + A_2$ of A_1 and A_2 is given by their union, i.e.,

$$
\begin{aligned}
(A_1 + A_2)_s &= (A_1)_s \cup (A_2)_s & (s \in S) \\
dom(f^{A_1+A_2}) &= dom(f^{A_1}) \cup dom(f^{A_2}) & (f \in F) \\
f^{A_1+A_2}(a) &= \begin{cases} f^{A_1}(a) & \text{if } a \in dom(f^{A_1}) \\ f^{A_2}(a) & \text{if } a \in dom(f^{A_2}) . \end{cases} &
\end{aligned}
$$

Due to the consistency of the functions, the functions of $A_1 + A_2$ are also well-defined. Note that if the functions of A_1 and A_2 are consistent up to isomorphism the compatibility conditions can always be achieved by appropriate renamings. Otherwise the coproduct construction leads to identifications of the elements $f^{A_1}(a)$ and $f^{A_2}(a)$, which may then lead to further identifications.

The algebras A_1 and A_2 are subalgebras of the construction $A_1 + A_2$ above. If renamings are required these can still be traced by injective Σ-homomorphisms (embeddings) $\iota_i : A_i \to A_1 + A_2$ $(i = 1, 2)$. Finally note that a coproduct $A_1 + A_2$ with Σ-homomorphisms $\iota_i : A_i \to A_1 + A_2$ $(i = 1, 2)$ exists for all partial Σ-algebras A_1 and A_2, but in general ι_1 and ι_2 need not be injective.

Definition 4.25 (Mutlithreaded Parallel Closure). *The multithreaded parallel closure $\mathbf{M}^\varnothing = (TG_{\mathbf{M}^\varnothing}, \mathbf{m}^\varnothing)$ with $TG_{\mathbf{M}^\varnothing} = (CS^\varnothing, T^\varnothing, in^\varnothing, id^\varnothing)$ of a $D\Sigma$-transformation system $\mathbf{M} = (TG_{\mathbf{M}}, \mathbf{m})$ is given by the following inductive definition:*

- $CS \subseteq CS^\varnothing$
- $c, c' \in CS^\varnothing \Rightarrow c + c' \in CS^\varnothing$

- $in^\varnothing = in$

- $\mathbf{m}^\varnothing(c) = \mathbf{m}(c) \quad (c \in CS)$
- $\mathbf{m}^\varnothing(c + c') = \mathbf{m}^\varnothing(c) + \mathbf{m}^\varnothing(c')$
  where $+$ on the right hand side denotes a designated coproduct of partial Σ-algebras, with corresponding designated coproduct injections $\iota_1^{c,c'}$ and $\iota_2^{c,c'}$

- $T(c, d) \subseteq T^\varnothing(c, d) \quad (c, d \in CS)$
- $t \in T^\varnothing(c, d) \wedge t' \in T^\varnothing(c', d') \Rightarrow t + t' \in T^\varnothing(c + c', d + d')$

- $id^\varnothing(c) = id(c) \quad (c \in CS)$
- $id^\varnothing(c + d) = id^\varnothing(c) + id^\varnothing(d)$

- $\mathbf{m}^\varnothing(t) = \mathbf{m}(t) \quad (t \in T)$
- $\mathbf{m}^\varnothing(t + t') - (\iota_1^{c,c'} \times \iota_1^{d,d'})(\mathbf{m}^\varnothing(t)) \sqcup (\iota_2^{c,c'} \times \iota_2^{d,d'})(\mathbf{m}^\varnothing(t'))$, *i.e.,*

$$act_{t+t'}^{\mathbf{m}^\varnothing} = (\iota_1^{c,c'} \times \iota_1^{d,d'})(act_t^{\mathbf{m}^\varnothing}) \cup (\iota_2^{c,c'} \times \iota_2^{d,d'})(act_{t'}^{\mathbf{m}^\varnothing})$$

$$\sim_{t+t'}^{\mathbf{m}^\varnothing} = (\iota_1^{c,c'} \times \iota_1^{d,d'})(\sim_t^{\mathbf{m}^\varnothing}) \cup (\iota_2^{c,c'} \times \iota_2^{d,d'})(\sim_{t'}^{\mathbf{m}^\varnothing})$$

It can easily be checked that $\mathbf{M}^\varnothing$ is a well-defined $D\Sigma$-transformation system.

The identification of the common term-generated parts of A_1 and A_2 in the coproduct $A_1 + A_2$ cannot be avoided, because there must be at most one value of a term in $A_1 + A_2$. If a further overlapping of A_1 and A_2 is required for the superposition (for instance, if there are no or too few ground terms), this can be expressed by defining explicitly a shared part as a Σ-algebra A_0 with embeddings (or arbitrary Σ-homomorphisms) $h_i : A_0 \to A_i$ $(i = 1, 2)$.

Then in the *pushout* of $h_1 : A_0 \rightarrow A_1$ and $h_2 : A_0 \rightarrow A_2$ elements $a_1 \in A_1$ and $a_2 \in A_2$ are identified if there is an element $a_0 \in A_0$ with $h_1(a_0) = a_1$ and $h_2(a_0) = a_2$, or both are evaluations of one ground term. As above, there may be further identifications as side effects due to inconsistencies in the functions of A_1 and A_2 w.r.t. the shared part A_0. Thus A_0, with the homomorphisms h_1 and h_2, extends the role of the common term-generated part in the coproduct in the pushout construction. Finally, for any partial Σ-algebra A_0 and Σ-homomorphisms $h_i : A_0 \rightarrow A_i$ $(i = 1, 2)$ a pushout $A_1 +_{\langle h_1, h_2 \rangle} A_2$ exists, including the Σ–homomorphisms $\bar{h}_i : A_i \rightarrow A_1 +_{\langle h_1, h_2 \rangle} A_2$ $(i = 1, 2)$ that relate the components with their superposition.

Definition 4.26 (Amalgamated parallel closure). *The* amalgamated parallel closure $\mathbf{M}^\oplus = (TG_{\mathbf{M}^\oplus}, \mathbf{m}^\oplus)$ *of a $D\Sigma$-transformation system* $\mathbf{M} = (TG_{\mathbf{M}}, \mathbf{m})$ *is given by the following inductive definition:*

- $CS \subseteq CS^\oplus$
- *If* $c, c' \in CS^\oplus$

  and $f : A \rightarrow \mathbf{m}^\oplus(c), f' : A \rightarrow \mathbf{m}^\oplus(c')$ *in* $\mathbf{PAlg}(\Sigma)$

  then $c +_{\langle f, f' \rangle} c' \in CS^\oplus$

- $in^\oplus = in$

- $\mathbf{m}^\oplus(c) = \mathbf{m}(c)$ $(c \in CS)$
- $\mathbf{m}^\oplus(c +_{\langle f, f' \rangle} c') = \mathbf{m}^\oplus(c) +_{\langle f, f' \rangle} \mathbf{m}^\oplus(c')$

  where the right hand side denotes a designated pushout object of the given span $\langle f, f' \rangle$ in $\mathbf{PAlg}(\Sigma)$*, with corresponding designated injections* $\bar{f} : \mathbf{m}^\oplus(c) \rightarrow \mathbf{m}^\oplus(c +_{\langle f, f' \rangle} c')$ *and* $\bar{f}' : \mathbf{m}^\oplus(c') \rightarrow \mathbf{m}^\oplus(c +_{\langle f, f' \rangle} c')$

- $T(c, d) \subseteq T^\oplus(c, d)$ $(c, d \in CS)$
- *If* $t \in T^\oplus(c, d), t' \in T^\oplus(c', d')$

  and $f : A \rightarrow \mathbf{m}^\oplus(c), f' : A \rightarrow \mathbf{m}^\oplus(c')$ *in* $\mathbf{PAlg}(\Sigma)$

  and $g : B \rightarrow \mathbf{m}^\oplus(d), g' : B \rightarrow \mathbf{m}^\oplus(d')$ *in* $\mathbf{PAlg}(\Sigma)$

  then $t +_{\langle f, f', g, g' \rangle} t' \in T^\oplus(c +_{\langle f, f' \rangle} c', d +_{\langle g, g' \rangle} d')$

- $id^\oplus(c +_{\langle f, f' \rangle} c') = id^\oplus(c) +_{\langle f, f', f, f' \rangle} id^\oplus(c')$

- $\mathbf{m}^\oplus(t) = \mathbf{m}(t)$ $(t \in T)$
- $\mathbf{m}^\oplus(t +_{\langle f, f', g, g' \rangle} t') = (\bar{f} \times \bar{g})(\mathbf{m}^\oplus(t)) \cup (\bar{f}' \times \bar{g}')(\mathbf{m}^\oplus(t'))$, *i.e.,*

$$act^{\mathbf{m}^\oplus}_{t +_{\langle f, f', g, g' \rangle} t'} = (\bar{f} \times \bar{g})(act^{\mathbf{m}^\oplus}_t) \cup (\bar{f}' \times \bar{g}')(act^{\mathbf{m}^\oplus}_{t'})$$

$$\sim^{\mathbf{m}^\oplus}_{t + t'} = (\bar{f} \times \bar{g})(\sim^{\mathbf{m}^\oplus}_t) \cup (\bar{f}' \times \bar{g}')(\sim^{\mathbf{m}^\oplus}_{t'})$$

The well-definedness of the $D\Sigma$-transformation system $\mathbf{M}^\oplus$ *is again easy to check.*

Note that $\mathbf{M}^{\oplus}$ contains $\mathbf{M}^{\oslash}$ because a coproduct $A_1 + A_2$ is a pushout w.r.t. the initial algebra $\mathbf{1}$ and the morphisms $A_1 \leftarrow \mathbf{1} \rightarrow A_2$.

Sequential and parallel compositions can be combined recursively (by taking the unions of their definitions) and yield the full closure in time and space of a transformation system. In the following definition of general refinement and implementation we use an arbitrary closure operation $\overline{\mathbf{M}}$. Therefore it is assumed that the category $\mathbf{TF}$ can be embedded into the corresponding generalised category of transformation systems, as for the sequential and parallel closures.

Definition 4.27 (Refinement and Implementation). *Let* $\mathbf{M}$ *and* $\mathbf{M}'$ *be* $D\Sigma$- *and* $D\Sigma'$-*transformation systems respectively.*

1. *A refinement* $\mathbf{r} = (r_{TG}, r_D) : \mathbf{M} \rightarrow \mathbf{M}'$ *is an extension* $\mathbf{r} = (r_{TG}, r_D) :$ $\mathbf{M} \rightarrow \overline{\mathbf{M}'}$.
2. *An implementation* $\mathbf{r} = (r_{TG}, r_D) : \mathbf{M} \rightarrow \mathbf{M}'$ *is an extension* $\mathbf{r} =$ $(r_{TG}, r_D) : view((\Sigma, \emptyset), \mathbf{M}) \rightarrow view((\Sigma', \emptyset), \overline{\mathbf{M}'})$.

In Figure 4.10 an example for an implementation of some abstract step t is shown, where after a first concrete step r the data state is divided into two possibly overlapping parts (specified by the morphisms f and g), then two local threads are started, the final data states are glued together again (w.r.t. the transformed morphisms f' and g'), and then a last concrete step q leads to the final state. The decomposition into local states and the parallel threads are represented by parallel transitions as defined in 4.25 and 4.26. Note that inner states of the two threads may be inconsistent with each other; they are never compared, nor are the steps sequentialised in any order.

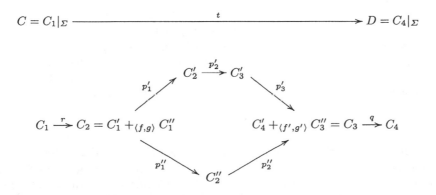

Fig. 4.10. Implementation in time and space $t \mapsto r; ((p_1'; p_2'; p_3') +_{\langle f, f', g, g' \rangle} (p_1''; p_2'')); q$

Proposition 4.28. *Refinement and implementation are reflexive and transitive.*

Proof. Since the proof of Proposition 4.23 only uses the general properties of closure operations it proves this more general assertion, too.

4.5 Examples

In this section two larger examples are presented. First an implementation of a *delete* method for linked lists is defined, based on the basic linked-list operations presented in Example 2.12. Then a specification of the sender of the alternating bit protocol in UNITY is defined and it is shown that it is a refinement of the sender specification in CCS presented in Example 2.13.

Example 4.29 (Implementation of a Delete-Method). In Example 2.12 basic methods for a class of linked lists have been defined for moving a list cursor continuously through a list from left to right, and to delete the actual cell of the list. Now these basic operations will be used to implement a method that deletes a cell at a specific position, which is given to the method as a parameter. The idea of the implementation is to move the cursor first to the desired position, then to delete the cell, and then to move the cursor back to its initial position.

Since implementation is defined as relation here, first transformation systems have to be constructed that model the visible behaviour of the parameterised *delete* method (the semantic interface) and the implementation body. Then the implementation relation between the two models has to be established.

The implementation body $\mathbf{B}$ is given by a combination of the models $\mathbf{LL}^{move}$ and $\mathbf{LL}^{del}$ from Example 2.12 that contain the basic *move* and (non-parameterised) *delete* actions. Since the parameterised *delete* method has a parameter of type *nat*, this type must also be provided by the implementation. For that purpose each data state is extended by the type $I\!N$, which is preserved identically by the tracking relations $\Delta_{I\!N} = \{(n,n) \,|\, n \in I\!N\}$ in each transition. Correspondingly, the data signature Σ_B of $\mathbf{B}$ is given by the linked-list data signature Σ_{ll} extended by the signature Σ_{nat} of natural numbers.

$$\Sigma_B = \Sigma_{ll} + \Sigma_{nat}$$

Since furthermore the execution order of the actions will be induced by the implementation relation (more precisely, by the transition graph morphism) there is no need to have specific control flow information in the body. This means that the *start* and *stop* flags of the *delete* method are removed. The union of these two models then yields the body $\mathbf{B} = (TG_{\mathbf{B}}, \mathbf{b})$ given explicitly in the following description (compare also Example 5.14):

control states

$$CS_{\mathbf{B}} = Env \cup \{\Delta\} = CS_{\mathbf{LL}}^{move}, \text{ with initialisation state } \Delta$$

transitions

$$T_\mathbf{B} = T_\mathbf{LL}^{move} \cup T_\mathbf{LL}^{del}, \text{ with idle transitions as in } \mathbf{LL}^{move}$$

data states

$$\mathbf{b}(e) = (L[e], I\!N)$$
$$\mathbf{b}(\Delta) = \emptyset$$

actions

$$act_t^\mathbf{b} = \begin{cases} act_t^{\mathbf{ll}^{move}} & t \in \{move, enter, leave, idle\} \\ act_t^{\mathbf{ll}^{del}} & t = del \end{cases}$$

tracking relations

$$\sim_t^\mathbf{b} = \sim_t^{\mathbf{ll}^{move}} \cup \Delta_{I\!N} = \sim_t^{\mathbf{ll}^{del}} \cup \Delta_{I\!N}$$

The interface model $\mathbf{D} = (TG_\mathbf{D}, \mathbf{d})$ modelling the parameterised *delete* method is defined analogously. Its data signature coincides with the one of $\mathbf{B}$, i.e., $\Sigma_D = \Sigma_B$, and its action signature contains only the *delete* action, i.e.,

delete $= \Sigma_B +$
    acts delete: nat

Also its control and data states coincide with the ones of $\mathbf{B}$:

- $CS_\mathbf{D} = CS_\mathbf{B}$
- $\mathbf{d}(e) = \mathbf{b}(e)$ $(\forall e \in CS_\mathbf{D})$

To define the transitions of $\mathbf{D}$ some auxiliary functions on the data states are defined first that yield the position of a cell, the position of the cursor, the length of the list, and the cell at the i-th position of the list. They are introduced as derived functions by the following extension Σ_H of Σ_D.

$\Sigma_H - \Sigma_D$ |
    funs pos: cell $\to$ nat
            pos, length: $\to$ nat
            cell: nat $\to$ cell
    axms for all c $\in$ cell, n $\in$ nat :
            c = !(first) $\Rightarrow$ pos(c) = 1
            pos(c) = n $\wedge$ right(c) = c' $\Rightarrow$ pos(c') = n+1
            pos(!(act))$\downarrow$ $\Rightarrow$ pos = pos(!(act))
            right(c) = void $\wedge$ pos(c) = n $\Rightarrow$ length = n
            cell(1) = !(first)
            right(cell(n))$\downarrow$ $\Rightarrow$ cell(n+1) = right(cell(n))

Then the transitions are defined as follows. There is a transition $delete(i) \in T_{\mathbf{D}}(e, e')$ for some $i \in I\!N$ with $i \leq length^{L[e]}$ if the environments e and e' satisfy the conditions stated below, $T_{\mathbf{D}}(\Delta, e) = \{enter\}$ and $T_{\mathbf{D}}(e, \Delta) = \{leave\}$ for each environment $e \in Env$, $idle \in T_{\mathbf{D}}(c, c)$ for each control state c, and $T_{\mathbf{D}}(e, e') = \emptyset$ for all other cases. The conditions formalising the behaviour of the *delete* method are the following (cf. Figure 4.11; for the sake of brevity the special cases for lists of length 1 are omitted).

- If $i \in \{2, \ldots, length^{L[e]}\}$ and $i \notin \{pos^{L[e]} - 1, pos^{L[e]}, pos^{L[e]} + 1\}$ then

$$
\begin{aligned}
e'(snd^{L[e]}(cell^{L[e]}(i-1))) &= cell^{L[e]}(i+1) \\
e'(x) &= e(x) \\
&\qquad \text{for all } x \neq snd^{L[e]}(cell^{L[e]}(i-1))
\end{aligned}
$$

- If $i = 1$ and $pos^{L[e]} = 1$ then

$$
\begin{aligned}
e'(f) &= e(n) \\
e'(a) &= e(n) \\
e'(n) &= right^{L[e]}(e(n)) \\
c'(x) &= e(x) \qquad \text{for all } x \notin \{f, a, n\}
\end{aligned}
$$

- If $i = 1$ and $pos^{L[e]} = 2$ then

$$
\begin{aligned}
e'(f) &= e(a) \\
e'(p) &= \oslash \\
e'(x) &= e(x) \text{ for all } x \notin \{f, p\}
\end{aligned}
$$

- If $1 < i = pos^{L[e]} - 1$ then

$$
\begin{aligned}
e'(p) &= cell^{L[e]}(i-1) \\
e'(snd^{L[e]}(cell^{L[e]}(i-1))) &= e(a) \\
e'(x) &= e(x) \\
&\qquad \text{for all } x \notin \{p, snd^{L[e]}(cell^{L[e]}(i-1))\}
\end{aligned}
$$

- If $1 < i = pos^{L[e]}$ then

$$
\begin{aligned}
e'(snd^{L[e]}(e(p))) &= e(n) \\
e'(a) &= e(n) \\
e'(n) &= right^{L[e]}(e(n)) \\
e'(x) &= e(x) \qquad \text{for all } x \notin \{snd^{L[e]}(e(p)), a, n\}
\end{aligned}
$$

- If $1 < i = pos^{L[e]} + 1$ then

$$
\begin{aligned}
e'(snd^{L[e]}(e(a))) &= right^{L[e]}(e(n)) \\
e'(n) &= right^{L[e]}(e(n)) \\
e'(x) &= e(x) \qquad \text{for all } x \notin \{snd^{L[e]}(e(a)), n\}
\end{aligned}
$$

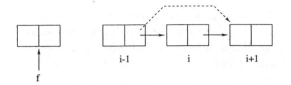

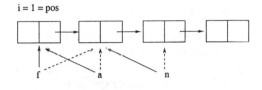

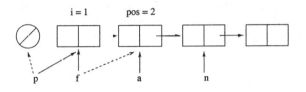

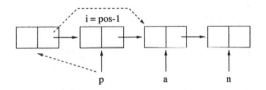

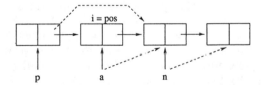

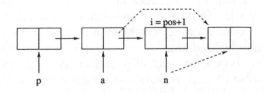

Fig. 4.11. Deletion of the i-th cell

The action label of a *delete(i)* transition is $\{delete(i)\}$, the other ones are empty; the tracking relations are the (partial) identities as in Example 2.12.

This formal definition reflects the following design decisions that were left open in the informal presentation of the *delete* method in the beginning.

1. Whenever the parameter i is outside the scope of the list, i.e., $i > length^{L[e]}$, the model blocks. There is no transition that supports this action.
2. If the actual cell is deleted the cursor is moved to its right neighbour.

Finally the uniform sequential implementation $(r, id_{\Sigma_D}) : \mathbf{D} \rightarrow \mathbf{B}$ is given by the identical data signature morphism $id_{\Sigma_D} : \Sigma_D \rightarrow \Sigma_D = \Sigma_B$, the action names need not be mapped—and in this case cannot be mapped—by definition of an implementation, and the transition graph morphism $r : TG_{\mathbf{D}} \rightarrow TG_{\mathbf{B}}^*$ is defined as follows. The control states are mapped identically, i.e., $g(c) = c$ for each $c \in CS_{\mathbf{D}} = CS_{\mathbf{B}}$. A transition $delete(i) : e \rightarrow e'$ is mapped to the sequence of actions moving the cursor to the right position, deleting the cell, and moving the cursor back:

$$g(delete(i)) = \underbrace{move; \ldots; move}_{n}; del; \underbrace{move; \ldots; move}_{k}$$

where

$$n = \begin{cases} i - pos^{L[e]} & \text{if } i \geq pos^{L[e]} \\ (length^{L[e]} - pos^{L[e]}) + i & \text{if } i < pos^{L[e]} \end{cases}$$

$$k = \begin{cases} 0 & \text{if } i = pos^{L[e]} \\ length^{L[e]} - (n+1) & \text{if } i \neq pos^{L[e]} . \end{cases}$$

The reader is invited to check that this indeed defines an implementation, i.e., that each path $move^n; del; move^k$ implementing a $delete(i) : e \rightarrow e'$ step leads from e to e', thus preserving the data states.

A brief discussion on the *relational* approach is in order here. It might seem awkward to define an implementation of the parameterised *delete* method, if a complete formal model of this method had to be given before already specifying its behaviour completely. One of the reasons for this is the duality between implementation models and implementations in (programming language) code. An implementation model (= implementation body in the implementation relation of transformation systems) should be considered as a formal model of an implementation in code, whose adequacy or correctness has already been shown, or as a model that is sufficiently close to such an implementation. Of course, since code implementations are not formal models (in the sense of transformation systems) a formal relationship between code and implementation model cannot be achieved. Nevertheless, it should somehow be possible to state that a model is an adequate representation of a code implementation or that the implementation is correct w.r.t. the model. This is altogether the precondition for the model-based approach. If such relationships cannot be provided, there is no use in modelling at all.

For more abstract models this relationship with a code implementation might be less obvious. The implementation relation (on models) is then used to connect abstract with concrete models, where concreteness means to be close to a code implementation. Then, on the one hand, the implementation mapping shows how the abstract steps are realised by more concrete (program) steps. The implementation condition states that this implementation is correct, i.e., the visible part of the state transformation obtained by executing the concrete steps of the implementation coincides with the state transformation as specified in the interface model. On the other hand, the abstract model represents the more complex behaviour directly and can be used for further constructions, without reference to its implementation. That means the implementation can be hidden completely and at the same time a full (semantical) definition of the relevant behaviour of the method is given.

From another point of view, the implementation relation can also be used to *define* interfaces of given models, similar to the restriction operation introduced in Section 4.1. Having defined the implementation body **B** for instance, the interface **D** could be defined by having the same control and data states as **B**, and a transition $delete(i) : e \rightarrow e'$ if and only if there is a path $move^n; del; move^k$ with n and k as specified above. This—perhaps more intuitive—construction of an interface, however, does not explicitly show the state transforming input/output behaviour of $delete(i)$. It has to be computed from the stepwise behaviour of the **B**-actions.

Such an interface definition could then be provided with a specification that beyond the pure signature information also states semantic properties via data invariants (axioms), pre- and postconditions (transformation rules), and control flow properties. (A further discussion on refinements as software development steps as in the Catalysis approach [DW98] for example is given in Section 4.9.)

In the following example a UNITY specification of the sender of the alternating bit protocol is discussed and it is shown that its transformation system semantics is a refinement of the corresponding CCS specification given in Example 2.13.

Example 4.30 (The UNITY Sender Specification). Consider the UNITY specification of the sender component of the alternating bit protocol given in Table 4.1. (cf. [CM88], p. 411, and Figure 4.12).

As for the channel in Example 4.13 it is already extended by assignments that update the *send* queue, the *ack* queue, and the *accept* queue that are used for communication with the environment. The meaning of this program is now rephrased as a transformation system $\mathbf{U}_S = (TG_{\mathbf{U}_S}, \mathbf{u}_S)$. The declaration part of the SENDER program immediately yields the data signature of the corresponding data space signature, where the queues are called *sendq*, *ackq*,

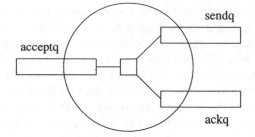

Fig. 4.12. Structure of the UNITY sender

and *acceptq* to distinguish them from the corresponding actions representing
the observable state changes of these queues.

**U-S = queue(message) + queue(bool) + queue(bool,message)
+**

    funs   S: → bool

            acceptq: → queue(message)

            sendq: → queue(bool,message)

            ackq: → queue(bool)

    acts   send: bool, message

            ack: bool

            accept: message

Let $\Sigma_{U\text{-}S}$ be the data signature of U-S and $\Sigma_{U\text{-}S}^{static}$ be its subsignature given
by the three queue types. Furthermore, let QDB be a partial $\Sigma_{U\text{-}S}^{static}$-algebra
of queues of messages, booleans, and pairs of booleans and messages, with set
of messages D and booleans $\mathbb{B} = \{0,1\}$.

Program SENDER **is**

    declare   S:bool

               accept: queue(data)

               send: queue(bool, data)

               ack: queue(bool)

    initially   S = 0, send = ack = empty

    assign   send:= enq(($\langle$S,first(accept)$\rangle$),send)   **if** accept ≠ empty

           [] S:= ¬ S || ack:= deq(ack) || accept:= deq(accept)

               if S=first(ack), accept ≠ empty

           [] ack:= deq(ack)   **if** S≠first(ack), ack ≠ empty

           [] send:= deq(send)   **if** send ≠ empty

           [] ack:= enq(b,ack)

           [] accept:= enq(x,accept)

Table 4.1. The UNITY specification of the sender component

The control states of $\mathbf{U}_S$ are given by the tuples $\langle b, a, s, c \rangle \in \mathbb{B} \times D^* \times (\mathbb{B} \times D)^* \times \mathbb{B}^*$, representing the actual values of S, $acceptq$, $sendq$, and $ackq$ respectively, and the initialisation state Δ.

$$CS_{\mathbf{U}_S} = (\mathbb{B} \times D^* \times (\mathbb{B} \times D)^* \times \mathbb{B}^*) \uplus \{\Delta\} \ .$$

The data states are defined correspondingly by

$$\mathbf{u}_S(\Delta) = \emptyset \text{ and } \mathbf{u}_S(b, a, s, c) = QDB[b, a, s, c]$$

where the extensions $QDB[b, a, s, c]$ of the algebra QDB are defined by

$$S^{QDB[b,a,s,c]} = b \ , \quad sendq^{QDB[b,a,s,c]} = s \ ,$$
$$acceptq^{QDB[b,a,s,c]} = a \ , \quad ackq^{QDB[b,a,s,c]} = c \ .$$

The transitions and action labels are given by

$$
\begin{array}{llll}
T_{\mathbf{U}_S}: \ offer_{b,d}: & \langle b, ad, s, c \rangle & \rightarrow \langle b, ad, \langle b, d \rangle s, c \rangle & \mapsto \emptyset \\
\quad\quad switch: & \langle b, ad, s, cb \rangle & \rightarrow \langle \neg b, a, s, c \rangle & \mapsto \emptyset \\
\quad\quad ig\_ack: & \langle b, a, s, c \neg b \rangle & \rightarrow \langle b, a, s, c \rangle & \mapsto \emptyset \\
\\
send_{b,d}: & \langle b', a, s\langle b, d \rangle, c \rangle \rightarrow & \langle b', a, s, c \rangle & \mapsto \{send(b, d)\} \\
\quad\quad ack_b: & \langle b', a, s, c \rangle & \rightarrow \langle b', a, s, bc \rangle & \mapsto \{ack(b)\} \\
\quad\quad accept_d: & \langle b, a, s, c \rangle & \rightarrow \langle b, da, s, c \rangle & \mapsto \{accept(d)\} \\
\\
\quad\quad idle: & \omega & \rightarrow \omega & \mapsto \emptyset \quad (\omega \in CS_{\mathbf{U}_S}) \\
\quad\quad init_{d_0}: & \Delta & \rightarrow \langle 0, d_0, \lambda, \lambda \rangle & \mapsto \emptyset
\end{array}
$$

corresponding to the assignments of the program, the extension to the environment actions, and the initialisation and idle transitions. The tracking relations are given by the identity on the static data type QDB. Note that all assignments of the original program are modelled as internal actions. Communication with other programs is restricted to using the shared variables $sendq$, $acceptq$, and $ackq$ via the environment actions.

Now a uniform sequential refinement $r_S = (r_S, \sigma_S) : \mathbf{CCS}_S \rightarrow \mathbf{U}_S$ can be given as follows. The signature morphism $\sigma_S : \text{CCS-S} \rightarrow \text{U-S}$ is given by the inclusion of the data type signatures $message + bool \subseteq queue(message) + queue(bool) + queue(bool, message)$, the identity of the action signatures $\{send, ack, accept\}$, and $\sigma_S(cbit) = S$ and $\sigma_S(msg) = first(acceptq)$. The transition graph morphism $r_S : TG_{\mathbf{CCS}_S} \rightarrow TG_{\mathbf{U}_S}$ is given by

$$
\begin{array}{ll}
\text{control states} & \text{transitions} \\
\\
\begin{array}{lll}
S_{b,d} & \mapsto & \langle b, d, \lambda, \lambda \rangle \\
S'_{b,d} & \mapsto & \langle b, d, \lambda, \lambda \rangle \\
A_b & \mapsto & \langle b, \lambda, \lambda, \lambda \rangle \\
\Delta & \mapsto & \Delta
\end{array}
&
\begin{array}{lll}
send_{b,d} & \mapsto & offer_{b,d}; send_{b,d} \\
time\_out & \mapsto & idle \\
ack_b & \mapsto & ack_b; switch \\
ack_{\neg b} & \mapsto & ack_{\neg b}; ig\_ack \\
accept_d & \mapsto & accept_d \\
init_{d_0} & \mapsto & init_{d_0} \\
idle & \mapsto & idle
\end{array}
\end{array}
$$

for all $b \in I\!B, d, d_0 \in D$. It is easy to check that the refinement conditions are satisfied, i.e., input and output data states and observable actions are preserved.

Without being synchronised with its intended environment, however, the UNITY sender could also perform visible actions that are not possible in the CCS sender. For example, it can send in any state, provided the send queue is not empty, whereas the CCS sender only sends in its S-state. That means, in particular, there is no refinement $\mathbf{U}_S \to \mathbf{CCS}_S$ of the sender components.

4.6 Preservation of Properties

As discussed in Chapter 3, properties of transformation systems can be stated in transformation specifications. These comprise properties of the data states (data invariants), the transformations (local pre- and postconditions), and the control flow. Each specification determines a subcategory of those transformation systems that satisfy the specification. Obviously, the development relations can then be defined in the same way on these subcategories, simply by replacing $D\Sigma$-transformation systems by $T\Gamma$-transformation systems, where $T\Gamma$ is the transformation specification concerned.

When development operations or relations of transformation systems are considered it is important to know whether (already proved) properties of one model also hold in the other one. This preservation of properties obviously does not hold in general for all properties and all relations. Moreover, due to the generic treatment of control flow logics, no general statements can be made for these. But concerning data invariants, for example, the preservation of properties corresponds to the *satisfaction condition* for partial algebras, which states that satisfaction of (conditional existence) equations is invariant under translation w.r.t. signature morphisms. An algebra of a larger signature satisfies (the translation of) an equation of a smaller signature if and only if the reduction of the algebra to the smaller signature satisfies the original equation (see Appendix A). This satisfaction condition holds not only for partial algebras and conditional equations, but also for arbitrary institutions, since it is an axiom of institutions (see Section 2.3). A corresponding result concerning their preservation by development relations can be shown for transformation rules specifying the data state transformations. Again, it corresponds to a satisfaction condition in the sense of institutions.

These kinds of preservation of properties are discussed first at the categorical level again for morphisms of transformation systems, and then carried over to the development relations and operations. First data invariants and initialisation and finalisation conditions are discussed. According to Definition 3.9, they are given by conditional Σ-equations. A data invariant holds in a transformation system if it holds in each state, except the initialisation state (see Definition 3.1). As shown in the following lemma, the satisfaction condition for partial algebras implies that data invariants are reflected by global morphisms of transformation systems. Since the signature morphisms in extensions and reductions have the opposite direction this yields the preservation of data invariants property of the development relations discussed above. Concerning initialisation and finalisation conditions furthermore, surjectivity of the transition graph morphism, at least on the initialisations and finalisations, is required (see Proposition 4.32).

Lemma 4.31 (Reflection of Data Invariants). *Let* $h = (\sigma, h) : (D\Sigma, \mathbf{M}) \rightarrow (D\Sigma', \mathbf{M}')$ *be a morphism in the global category* **TF** *and* $ce' \in CEqns_{\Sigma'}(X)$ *be a conditional* Σ'-*equation. Then*

$$\mathbf{M}' \models cc' \ \ implies \ \ \mathbf{M} \models \sigma_\Sigma(ce') \ .$$

If furthermore $h : TG_\mathbf{M} \rightarrow TG_{\mathbf{M}'}$ *is surjective on the control states, then also*

$$\mathbf{M} \models \sigma_\Sigma(ce') \ \ implies \ \ \mathbf{M}' \models ce' \ .$$

Proof. Let $c \in CS_\mathbf{M}$.

$$\mathbf{m}(c) \models \sigma_\Sigma(ce')$$
$$\Leftrightarrow V_{\sigma_\Sigma}(\mathbf{m}(c)) \models ce' \ \ \text{satisfaction condition for partial algebras}$$
$$\Leftrightarrow \mathbf{m}'(h(c)) \models ce' \ \ \text{definition of global morphisms.}$$

Since $\mathbf{M}' \models ce'$ the first assertion holds. The second assertion follows immediately.

In the following proposition the corresponding preservation and reflection results for the data state properties are given. For uniform extensions, refinements, and implementations these hold for single states (like initial and final states), whereas for data invariants the transition graph morphism is required to be surjective on the control states.

Proposition 4.32. *Let* $\mathbf{M}$ *and* $\mathbf{M}'$ *be* $D\Sigma$- *and* $D\Sigma'$-*transformation systems respectively,* $\sigma = (\sigma_\Sigma, \sigma_A) : D\Sigma \rightarrow D\Sigma'$ *a data space signature morphism, and* $ce \in CEqns_\Sigma(X)$ *be a conditional* Σ-*equation.*

1. *Let* $(g, s) : \mathbf{M} \rightarrow \mathbf{M}'$ *be a* σ-*uniform extension, refinement, or implementation, and* $c \in CS_\mathbf{M}$. *Then*

$$(\mathbf{M}, c) \models ce \ \ if \ and \ only \ if \ \ (\mathbf{M}', g(c)) \models \sigma_\Sigma(ce) \ .$$

If $g : TG_\mathbf{M} \rightarrow TG_{\mathbf{M}'}$ *is furthermore surjective on the control states then*

$$\mathbf{M} \models ce \ \ if \ and \ only \ if \ \ \mathbf{M}' \models \sigma_\Sigma(ce) \ .$$

2. *Let* $(g, s) : \mathbf{M} \rightarrow \mathbf{M}'$ *be a* σ-*uniform reduction, then*

$$\mathbf{M} \models ce \ \ implies \ \mathbf{M}' \models \sigma_\Sigma(ce) \ .$$

If $g : TG_{\mathbf{M}'} \rightarrow TG_\mathbf{M}$ *is furthermore surjective on the control states then also*

$$\mathbf{M}' \models \sigma_\Sigma(ce) \ \ implies \ \mathbf{M} \models ce \ .$$

Proof. The assertions are shown as in Lemma 4.31.

The results show in particular that uniform developments with surjective transition graph morphisms preserve the satisfaction of data specifications (see Definition 3.1).

Corollary 4.33. *Let* $\mathbf{M}$ *be a* $D\Sigma$*-transformation system that satisfies a data specification* DS *w.r.t.* $D\Sigma$ *and* $\mathbf{M}'$ *be a* $D\Sigma'$*-transformation system such that there is a* σ*-uniform development relation (reduction, extension, refinement, implementation) w.r.t. a signature morphism* $\sigma = (\sigma_\Sigma, \sigma_A) : D\Sigma \to D\Sigma'$.

If the transition graph morphism of the development relation is surjective, then $\mathbf{M}'$ *satisfies* $\sigma_\Sigma(DS)$.

Corresponding preservation and reflection results can be shown for transformation rules, at least for anonymous ones. For rules with names the signature morphism is required to be injective, and only steps in the image of the transition graph morphism can be checked.

Lemma 4.34 (Reflection of Transformation Rules). *Let* $\mathbf{h} = (\sigma, h)$: $(D\Sigma, \mathbf{M}) \to (D\Sigma', \mathbf{M}')$ *be a* **TF***-morphism,* $r_0' = (L \to R)$ *an anonymous* $D\Sigma'$*-transformation rule, and* $r' = (\alpha \hat{=} L \to R)$ *a* $D\Sigma'$*-transformation rule.*

1. *If* $\mathbf{M}' \models r_0'$ *then* $\mathbf{M} \models \sigma_\Sigma(r_0')$.
   If $h : TG_\mathbf{M} \to TG_{\mathbf{M}'}$ *is surjective then also* $\mathbf{M} \models \sigma_\Sigma(r_0')$ *implies* $\mathbf{M}' \models r_0'$.
2. *If* $\mathbf{M}' \models r'$ *and* σ *is injective, then* $\mathbf{M} \models \sigma(r')$.
   If σ *is injective and* h *is surjective then also* $\mathbf{M} \models \sigma(r')$ *implies* $\mathbf{M}' \models r'$.

Proof. 1.   Let $t : c \to d$ be a transition in $TG_\mathbf{M}$. The translation of r_0' to Σ is given by $\sigma_\Sigma(r_0') = (\sigma_\Sigma(L) \to \sigma_\Sigma(R))$. According to the invariance of solution sets under translation (see Appendix A) and the definition of global morphisms we have

$$Sol_\Sigma(\sigma_\Sigma(L), \mathbf{m}(c)) = Sol_{\Sigma'}(L, V_{\sigma_\Sigma}(\mathbf{m}(c))) = Sol_{\Sigma'}(L, \mathbf{m}'(h(c)))$$

and

$$Sol_\Sigma(\sigma_\Sigma(R), \mathbf{m}(d)) = Sol_{\Sigma'}(R, V_{\sigma_\Sigma}(\mathbf{m}(d))) = Sol_{\Sigma'}(R, \mathbf{m}'(h(d))) .$$

Since, moreover, $|\mathbf{m}(c)|_{\sigma_\Sigma(s')} = |\mathbf{m}'(h(c))|_{s'}$ for all $s' \in S'$ we obtain by Definition 3.5 with $X = Y = \emptyset$ and $\alpha = \emptyset$

$$(\mathbf{M}, t) \models \sigma_\Sigma(r_0') \quad \Leftrightarrow \quad (\mathbf{M}', h(t)) \models r_0' ,$$

which proves the assertion.

2.   According to Definition 3.5 it remains to be shown that $act_t^\mathbf{m}$ is an instance of $\sigma_A(\alpha)$ w.r.t. some solutions $\gamma \in Sol_\Sigma(\sigma_\Sigma(L), \mathbf{m}(c))$ and $\delta \in Sol_\Sigma(\sigma_\Sigma(R), \mathbf{m}(d))$ iff $act_{h(t)}^{\mathbf{m}'}$ is an instance of α w.r.t. γ and δ. Due to the injectivity of σ, however,

$$act_t^\mathbf{m} = \sigma_A(\alpha[\gamma, \delta]) \quad \Leftrightarrow \quad act_{h(t)}^{\mathbf{m}'} = \alpha[\gamma, \delta]$$

since $act_{h(t)}^{\mathbf{m}'} = \sigma_A^{-1}(act_t^\mathbf{m})$.

Analogous to the preservation of data properties the preservation of transformation rules by the development relations follows immediately from their reflection by global morphisms.

Proposition 4.35. *Let* $\mathbf{M}$ *and* $\mathbf{M}'$ *be* $D\Sigma$*- and* $D\Sigma'$*-transformation systems respectively, and* $r = (\alpha \mathrel{\hat{=}} L \to R)$ *a* $D\Sigma$*–rule.*

1. *Let* $(g, s) : \mathbf{M} \to \mathbf{M}'$ *be a* σ*-uniform refinement or implementation with injective signature morphism* σ*. Then*

$$(\mathbf{M}, t) \models r \text{ iff } (\mathbf{M}', g(t)) \models \sigma(r)$$

   for each transition t *in* $TG_\mathbf{M}$*. Furthermore, each transition* t' *of* $\mathbf{M}'$ *whose action label contains action names from* $A' - \sigma_A(A)$ *satisfies* $\sigma(r)$*.*
2. *Let* $\mathbf{r} = (r, \sigma) : \mathbf{M} \to \mathbf{M}'$ *be a* σ*-uniform refinement or implementation and* $r_0 = (L \to R)$ *be an anonymous* $D\Sigma$*-transformation rule. Then*

$$(\mathbf{M}, t) \models r_0 \text{ iff } (\mathbf{M}', r(t)) \models \sigma_\Sigma(r_0) .$$

3. *Let* $(g, s) : \mathbf{M} \to \mathbf{M}'$ *be a* σ*-uniform reduction, such that* σ *is injective. Then*
$$\mathbf{M} \models r \text{ implies } \mathbf{M}' \models \sigma(r) .$$

Proof. The assertions are shown as in Lemma 4.34.

Furthermore, if $act_{t'}^{\mathbf{m}'}$ contains an action name from $A' - \sigma_A(A)$ it cannot be an instance of $\sigma_A(\alpha)$, and thus satisfies $\sigma(r)$ by definition.

Since the development operations induce development relations the preservation results can be carried over directly to the operations.

Proposition 4.36. *Let* $\mathbf{M}$ *be a* $D\Sigma$*-transformation system,* $ce \in CEqns_\Sigma(X)$*, and* $r = (\alpha \mathrel{\hat{=}} L \to R) \in Rules_{D\Sigma}$ *such that* $\mathbf{M} \models ce$ *and* $\mathbf{M} \models r$*. Furthermore, let* $g : TG' \to TG_\mathbf{M}$ *be a transition graph morphism and* $\sigma : D\Sigma' \to D\Sigma$ *a signature morphism. Then the following assertions hold.*

1. $res(\mathbf{M}, g) \models ce$ *and* $res(\mathbf{M}, g) \models r$*.*
2. $view(\sigma, \mathbf{M}) \models \sigma_\Sigma(ce)$ *and* $view(\sigma, \mathbf{M}) \models \sigma(r)$*.*
3. $exc(\mathbf{M}, A_0) \models ce$ *and* $exc(\mathbf{M}, A_0) \models r$*.*
4. $hide(D\Sigma_0, \mathbf{M}) \models ce$ *and* $hide(D\Sigma_0, \mathbf{M}) \models r$
   provided $ce \in CEqns_{\Sigma - \Sigma_0}(X)$ *and* $r = (\alpha \mathrel{\hat{=}} L \to R) \in Rules_{D\Sigma - D\Sigma_0}$*.*
5. $ren(r, \mathbf{M}) \models ce$ *and* $ren(r, \mathbf{M}) \models (r(\alpha) : L \to R)$*.*

Proof. The assertions follow from Propositions 4.11, 4.32, and 4.35.

4.7 The Institution of Transformation Systems

All the preservation properties discussed above are based on the invariance of satisfaction under translation along signature morphisms. This has been used for the state properties, i.e., conditional equations that are evaluated in partial algebras, and behavioural properties, given by transformation rules that are tested against single steps of transformation systems. Probably due to its fundamental role this invariance—the *satisfaction condition*—has also become an axiom of institutions as general logical and model-theoretic frameworks.

The aim of this section is to complete the investigations of the institutional properties of transformation systems and to formulate the additional conditions that yield an institution of transformation systems. In the next section this will be generalised to show how institutions of transformation systems can be constructed from arbitrary specification frameworks for the data spaces and arbitrary control flow logics for the behaviour specification.

The category **DSig** of (data space) signatures was introduced in Definition 4.15, and the model functor $TS : \mathbf{DSig} \to \mathbf{Cat}^{op}$ in Proposition 4.18. The different kinds of sentences for the specification of transformation systems were defined in Chapter 3. The data specification $DS = (Ax, In, Fi)$ w.r.t. a data space signature $D\Sigma = (\Sigma, A)$ is given by three sets of conditional Σ-equations for the data invariants, initialisation, and finalisation conditions respectively. Furthermore, the transformations are specified by a set R of $D\Sigma$-transformation rules and the overall behaviour by a control flow specification $C\Gamma \subseteq CF(D\Sigma)$. Accordingly, the set of sentences $TSen(D\Sigma)$ can be defined by

$$TSen(D\Sigma) = CEqns_\Sigma + CEqns_\Sigma + CEqns_\Sigma + Rules_{D\Sigma} + CF(D\Sigma)\,,$$

i.e., a sentence is a data invariant (first component), or an initialisation or finalisation condition (second and third components), or a transformation rule or a control flow formula.

To extend $TSen$ to a functor the translation of sentences $TSen(\sigma) : TSen(D\Sigma) \to TSen(D\Sigma')$ w.r.t. a signature morphism $\sigma = (\sigma_\Sigma, \sigma_A) : D\Sigma \to D\Sigma'$ has to be defined. The translation of terms, equations, and conditional equation—always denoted by σ—is defined in Appendix A and has already been used in the previous section. For a rule $r = (\alpha \hat{=} L \to R)$ the translation $\sigma(r)$ is defined by $\sigma(r) = (\sigma_A(\alpha)\hat{=}\sigma_\Sigma(L) \to \sigma_\Sigma(R))$, which has also already been used in Section 4.6.

Now the translation of control flow formulae w.r.t. data space signature morphisms also has to be defined. This means the function that assigns the control flow formulae to signatures has to be extended to a functor. Moreover, compatibility of satisfaction and translation is required to obtain the satisfaction condition globally for all sentences for transformation systems.

Definition 4.37 (Functorial Control Flow Logic). *A functorial control flow logic $CL = (CF, \models^{CL})$ is given by a functor $CF : \mathbf{DSig} \to \mathbf{Set}$ and a* *family* $(\models_{D\Sigma}^{CL})_{D\Sigma \in |\mathbf{DSig}|}$ *of relations* $\models_{D\Sigma}^{CL} \subseteq |\mathbf{TF}(D\Sigma)| \times CF(D\Sigma)$, *such that for each signature morphism* $\sigma : D\Sigma \rightarrow D\Sigma'$ *in* $\mathbf{DSig}$, *each transformation system* $\mathbf{M}' \in |\mathbf{TF}(D\Sigma')|$, *and each control flow formula* $cf \in CF(D\Sigma)$

$$\mathbf{M}' \models_{D\Sigma'}^{CL} CF(\sigma)(cf) \Leftrightarrow V_\sigma(\mathbf{M}') \models_{D\Sigma} cf .$$

Obviously, a functorial control flow logic comprises a control flow logic as introduced in Definition 3.11 and extends it by translation mappings $CF(\sigma)$: $CF(D\Sigma) \rightarrow CF(D\Sigma')$ for each signature morphism $\sigma : D\Sigma \rightarrow D\Sigma'$. In the control flow logics given by CCS and the modal μ-calculus for example (see Section 3.2) the translations of sentences are basically given by a renaming of the actions. In addition, general algebraic signature morphisms can be used to relate the implicit data types used within the actions and agents. In [SNW93, FC95] this satisfaction condition is shown for different kinds of temporal logics and LTSs; thus they can be used as control flow logics for transformation systems.

By construction, functorial control flow logics are themselves institutions, given by the category $\mathbf{DSig}$ of data space signatures, the functor CF : $\mathbf{DSig} \rightarrow \mathbf{Set}$ as the sentence functor, the model functor $TF : \mathbf{DSig} \rightarrow \mathbf{Cat}^{op}$, and the satisfaction relation $\models^{CL}$. This property will be used below to exhibit the modular structure of the envisaged institution of transformation systems, basically given by a data institution with action structures and a control flow institution that are combined via transformation systems.

All translation mappings together complete the definition of the sentence functor as the corresponding coproduct of the translations of conditional equations, transformation rules, and control flow formulae.

The satisfaction condition holds for conditional equations and partial algebras as shown in Appendix A, p. 308, and for functorial control flow logics by definition. As shown next, it also holds for transformation rules. In fact, it is a consequence of the reflection property stated in Lemma 4.34, but it only holds for anonymous rules, or for injective signature morphisms.

Proposition 4.38 (Satisfaction Condition for Transformation Rules).
Let $\sigma = (\sigma_\Sigma, \sigma_A) : D\Sigma \rightarrow D\Sigma'$ *be a data space signature morphism and* $\mathbf{M}'$ *a* $D\Sigma'$-*transformation system. For each anonymous* $D\Sigma$-*transformation rule* $r_0 = (L \rightarrow R)$

$$\mathbf{M}' \models \sigma_\Sigma(r_0) \quad \textit{iff} \quad V_\sigma(\mathbf{M}') \models r_0 .$$

Furthermore, for each $D\Sigma$-*transformation rule (with names)* $r = (\alpha \hat{=} L \rightarrow R)$, *if* σ *is injective then*

$$\mathbf{M}' \models \sigma(r) \quad \textit{iff} \quad V_\sigma(\mathbf{M}') \models r .$$

Proof. Since $(\sigma, id_{TG_\mathbf{M}}) : \mathbf{M}' \rightarrow V_\sigma(\mathbf{M}')$ is a $\mathbf{TF}$-morphism with bijective transition graph component the assertions follow from Lemma 4.34.

The discussion of this section is summarised by the following theorem stating that transformation systems yield an institution. According to Proposition 4.38, however, either only transformation rules without action names or only injective signature morphisms can be used. The first option would exclude the binding of rules to the actions that are specified by these rules, which is not acceptable. Thus the second option is chosen. That means signature morphisms are restricted to renamings and inclusions.

Theorem 4.39 (Institution of Transformation Systems). *Let CL be a functorial control flow logic and* $\mathbf{DSig}^i$ *the subcategory of* $\mathbf{DSig}$ *given by the injective data space signature morphisms. Then* $\mathbf{DSig}^i$, *the restriction of the model functor*

$$TF : \mathbf{DSig}^i \to \mathbf{Cat}^{op} \quad (Definition \ 4.18),$$

the restriction of the sentence functor

$$TSen : \mathbf{DSig}^i \to \mathbf{Set} \quad (as \ defined \ above),$$

and the satisfaction relation $\models$ *given by the satisfaction relations of conditional equations and partial algebras, transformation rules and transformation systems, and the one of the control flow logic, constitute an institution. That means the satisfaction condition*

$$\mathbf{M}' \models_{D\Sigma'} TSen(\sigma)(\Phi) \iff V_\sigma(\mathbf{M}') \models_{D\Sigma} \Phi$$

holds for all models $\mathbf{M}' \in |\mathbf{TF}(D\Sigma')|$, *sentences* $\Phi \in TSen(D\Sigma)$, *and signature morphisms* $\sigma : D\Sigma \to D\Sigma'$ *in* $\mathbf{DSig}^i$.

Proof. The required functoriality properties were presented in Proposition 4.17 and in the discussion above. The satisfaction condition holds for partial algebras (Appendix A, p. 308), transformation rules (Proposition 4.38), and for control flow specifications by definition.

4.8 Development w.r.t. Other Specification Frameworks

To carry over the development concepts to transformation systems based on other specification frameworks it is easier to start with their categorical properties. That means signature morphisms and forgetful functors are defined as in Section 4.3 for the general case, which then yields the global category of transformation systems w.r.t. arbitrary specification frameworks and control flow logics.

Definition 4.40 (Signature Morphism). *Let* $D\Sigma = (\Sigma, A)$ *and* $D\Sigma' = (\Sigma', A')$ *be data space signatures w.r.t. a concrete institution with formulae* $Ins = (\mathbf{Sig}, Form, Mod, Sol, sorts, |\text{-}|)$. *A (data space) signature morphism*

$\sigma = (\sigma_\Sigma, \sigma_A) : D\Sigma \to D\Sigma'$ *is given by a signature morphism* $\sigma_\Sigma : \Sigma \to \Sigma'$ *in* **Sig** *and a family of mappings* $\sigma_A = (\sigma_{A,w,w'} : A_{w,w'} \to A'_{\sigma_S^*(w), \sigma_S^*(w')})_{w,w' \in S^*}$, *where* $S = sorts(\Sigma)$ *and* $\sigma_S = sorts(\sigma)$.

Data space signatures and morphisms with component-wise identities and composition define the category $\mathbf{DSig}^{Ins}$.

In order to generalise the pre-image of action sets used by the forgetful functor of transformation systems to action structures, appropriate natural transformations AS_σ associated to signature morphisms σ have to be introduced. That means the assignment of action structures to signatures becomes functorial.

Definition 4.41 (Functorial Action Structure). *A functorial action structure* AS *w.r.t. a concrete institution* Ins *is given by an action structure (family of functors)*

$$AS_{D\Sigma} : \mathbf{Set}^S \times \mathbf{Set}^S \to \mathbf{Set}$$

for each $D\Sigma = (\Sigma, A) \in |\mathbf{DSig}^{Ins}|$ *with* $S = sorts(\Sigma)$, *as in Definition 2.14, and a natural transformation*

$$AS_\sigma : AS_{D\Sigma'} \Rightarrow AS_{D\Sigma} \circ (V_{\sigma_S} \times V_{\sigma_S}) : \mathbf{Set}^{S'} \times \mathbf{Set}^{S'} \to \mathbf{Set}$$

for each $\sigma : D\Sigma \to D\Sigma'$ *in* $\mathbf{DSig}^{Ins}$, *such that*

$$AS_{id_{D\Sigma}} = id_{AS_{D\Sigma}} \text{ and } AS_{\sigma' \circ \sigma} = AS_\sigma \circ AS_{\sigma'}$$

for all $D\Sigma \in |\mathbf{DSig}^{Ins}|$ *and* $\sigma : D\Sigma \to D\Sigma'$ *and* $\sigma' : D\Sigma' \to D\Sigma''$ *in* $\mathbf{DSig}^{Ins}$.

The naturality condition on AS_σ means that for each pair of parameter sets $M', N' \in |\mathbf{Set}^{S'}|$ there must be mappings $AS_{\sigma,M'N'}$ in **Set** that make the diagrams

$$
\begin{array}{ccc}
AS_{D\Sigma'}(M', N') & \xrightarrow{\;AS_{\sigma,M',N'}\;} & AS_{D\Sigma}(V_{\sigma_S}(M'), V_{\sigma_S}(N')) \\
{\scriptstyle AS_{D\Sigma'}(f',g')} \downarrow & & \downarrow {\scriptstyle AS_{D\Sigma}(V_{\sigma_S}(f'), V_{\sigma_S}(g'))} \\
AS_{D\Sigma'}(M'', N'') & \xrightarrow[\;AS_{\sigma,M'',N''}\;]{} & AS_{D\Sigma}(V_{\sigma_S}(M''), V_{\sigma_S}(N''))
\end{array}
$$

commute for all $f' : M' \to M'', g' : N' \to N''$ in $\mathbf{Set}^{S'}$.

In the following let $\mathbb{F} = (Ins, AS, I, \epsilon)$ be a specification framework (see Definition 2.14) with a concrete institution with formulae Ins and a functorial action structure AS. The data spaces $\mathbb{D}_{D\Sigma}^{\mathbf{F}}$ and the categories $\mathbf{TF}^{\mathbf{F}}(D\Sigma)$ of transformation systems w.r.t. $\mathbb{F}$ are then given as in Definition 2.15. As in Section 4.3, Definitions 4.16, 4.17, and 4.18, the data space, forgetful, and model functors are defined. The first one is based on the forgetful functors V_{σ_Σ} of Ins and the action structure transformations AS_σ.

Definition and Fact 4.42 (Data Space, Forgetful, and Model Functor).

1. For each signature morphism $\sigma : D\Sigma \to D\Sigma'$ in $\mathbf{DSig}^{Ins}$ let the transition graph morphism $I\!D_\sigma^F : I\!D_{D\Sigma'}^F \to I\!D_{D\Sigma}^F$ be defined by

$$I\!D_\sigma^F(C') \;\;= V_{\sigma\Sigma}(C') \qquad\qquad\qquad (C' \in |\mathbf{Mod}(\Sigma')|)\,,$$

$$I\!D_\sigma^F(\alpha',\sim') = (AS_{\sigma,|C'|,|D'|}(\alpha'), V_{\sigma s}(\sim')) \quad (\alpha' \in AS_{D\Sigma'}(|C'|,|D'|),$$
$$\sim' \in Rel^{S'}(|C'|,|D'|))\,.$$

Together with $I\!D^F(D\Sigma) = I\!D_{D\Sigma}^F$ this yields a functor

$$I\!D^F : \mathbf{DSig}^{Ins} \to \mathbf{TG}^{op}\,,\; D\Sigma \mapsto I\!D_{D\Sigma}^F,\; \sigma \mapsto I\!D_\sigma^F\,.$$

2. Given a data space signature morphism $\sigma : D\Sigma \to D\Sigma'$ in $\mathbf{DSig}^{Ins}$ the *forgetful functor* $V_\sigma^F : \mathbf{TF}^F(D\Sigma') \to \mathbf{TF}(D\Sigma)$ is defined by

$$V_\sigma^F(\mathbf{M}') = (TG_{\mathbf{M}'}, I\!D_\sigma^F \circ \mathbf{m}')\,,$$
$$V_\sigma^F(h') \;\;= h'\,.$$

3. The *model functor* $TF^F : \mathbf{DSig}^{Ins} \to \mathbf{Cat}^{op}$ is defined by

$$TF^F(D\Sigma) = \mathbf{TF}^F(D\Sigma)$$

for each data space signature $D\Sigma \in \mathbf{DSig}^{Ins}$, and

$$TF^F(\sigma : D\Sigma \to D\Sigma') = V_\sigma^F : \mathbf{TF}^F(D\Sigma') \to \mathbf{TF}^F(D\Sigma)$$

for each signature morphism σ in $\mathbf{DSig}^{Ins}$.

Proof. 1. The well-definedness of $I\!D_\sigma^F$ follows from the definition of the forgetful functors in *Ins* and their compatibility with the *sorts* (see page 50) as well as the definition of the action structure mappings AS_σ. These allow the extension of the proof of Fact 4.3 to the general case.

The functoriality properties of $I\!D_\sigma^F$ also follow from the ones of the forgetful functors in *Ins* and the functoriality of the action structure mappings.
2. Composition with a morphism preserves identities and composition, i.e., V_σ^F is a functor.
3. Follows immediately from 1 and 2.

Categories of local transformation systems and signature morphisms yield the following global category.

Definition 4.43 (Global Category of Transformation Systems). *For each specification framework* $I\!F = (Ins, AS, I, \epsilon)$ *the global category of transformation systems* $\mathbf{TF}^F$ *is defined as follows.*

- *Its objects are pairs $(D\Sigma, \mathbf{M})$, where $D\Sigma$ is a data space signature in* $\mathbf{DSig}^{Ins}$ *and $\mathbf{M}$ is a $D\Sigma$-transformation system in* $\mathbf{TF}^{F}(D\Sigma)$.
- *Its morphisms $\mathbf{h} : (D\Sigma, \mathbf{M}) \to (D\Sigma', \mathbf{M}')$ are pairs $\mathbf{h} = (\sigma, h)$, where $\sigma :$ $D\Sigma' \to D\Sigma$ is a data space signature morphism (in the reverse direction) in* $\mathbf{DSig}^{Ins}$ *and $h : V_\sigma(\mathbf{M}) \to \mathbf{M}'$ is a transformation system morphism in* $\mathbf{TF}^{F}(D\Sigma')$. *That means $h : TG_{\mathbf{M}} \to TG_{\mathbf{M}'}$ is a transition graph morphism that satisfies $\mathbb{D}^{F}_\sigma \circ \mathbf{m} = \mathbf{m}' \circ h$ (see Figure 4.13).*
- *Composition of morphisms $(\sigma, h) : (D\Sigma, \mathbf{M}) \to (D\Sigma', \mathbf{M}')$ and $(\sigma', h') :$ $(D\Sigma', \mathbf{M}') \to (D\Sigma'', \mathbf{M}'')$ is given by*

$$(\sigma', h') \circ (\sigma, h) = (\sigma \circ \sigma', h' \circ h) \, .$$

- *The identities are given by $id_{(D\Sigma, \mathbf{M})} = (id_{D\Sigma}, id_{TG_{\mathbf{M}}})$.*

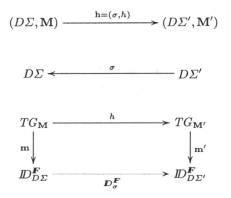

Fig. 4.13. Global morphisms of transformation systems w.r.t. F

Based on this categorical structure the development operations and relations can be defined. Only the uniform versions are considered here, and only the positive versions *restriction* and *view* of the operations. Their duals, *exclusion* and *hide*, can be reconstructed analogously, as well as the non-uniform versions. Renaming is defined below (Definition 4.51), since first renamings of action structures have to be introduced, which is done in the context of translation of specifications. Furthermore, the corresponding algebraic laws that have already been stated at a general level in Proposition 4.8 and also hold in general are not rephrased here.

Definition 4.44 (Development Operations). *Let $\mathbf{M} = (TG_{\mathbf{M}}, \mathbf{m})$ be a $D\Sigma$-transformation system w.r.t. F.*

1. *The restriction $res(\mathbf{M}, g)$ of $\mathbf{M}$ w.r.t. a transition graph morphism $g :$ $TG' \to TG_{\mathbf{M}}$ is defined by $res(\mathbf{M}, g) = (TG', \mathbf{m} \circ g)$.*

   (The transition graph morphism g might be induced by a subset of actions, see Definition 4.3.)

2. *The* view $view(\sigma, \mathbf{M})$ *of* $\mathbf{M}$ *via a signature morphism* $\sigma : D\Sigma_0 \to D\Sigma$ *is defined by* $view(\sigma, \mathbf{M}) = (TG_{\mathbf{M}}, \mathbb{D}^F_\sigma \circ \mathbf{m})$.

The development relations are given by the direct generalisations of the notions introduced in Definition 4.9.

Definition 4.45 (Reduction and Extension). *Let* $(D\Sigma, \mathbf{M})$ *and* $(D\Sigma', \mathbf{M}')$ *be transformation systems w.r.t.* $\mathbb{F}$, *with* $\mathbf{M} = (TG_{\mathbf{M}}, \mathbf{m})$ *and* $\mathbf{M}' = (TG_{\mathbf{M}'}, \mathbf{m}')$.

1. *A reduction* $r = (g, \sigma) : (D\Sigma, \mathbf{M}) \to (D\Sigma', \mathbf{M}')$ *is given by a transition graph morphism* $g : TG_{\mathbf{M}'} \to TG_{\mathbf{M}}$ *and a signature morphism* $\sigma : D\Sigma \to D\Sigma'$ *such that* $\mathbb{D}^F_\sigma \circ \mathbf{m}' = \mathbf{m} \circ g$. *That means* $(\sigma, g) : (D\Sigma', \mathbf{M}') \to (D\Sigma, \mathbf{M})$ *is a morphism in* $\mathbf{TF}^F$.
2. *An extension* $e = (g, \sigma) : (D\Sigma, \mathbf{M}) \to (D\Sigma', \mathbf{M}')$ *is given by a transition graph morphism* $g : TG_{\mathbf{M}} \to TG_{\mathbf{M}'}$ *and a signature morphism* $\sigma : D\Sigma \to D\Sigma'$ *such that* $\mathbb{D}^F_\sigma \circ \mathbf{m}' \circ g = \mathbf{m}$.

For the definition of refinements and implementations closure operations are needed, i.e., monads $\bar{\ } : \mathbf{TF}^F(D\Sigma) \to \mathbf{TF}^F(D\Sigma)$ with units $\eta_{\mathbf{M}} = (\eta_{TG_{\mathbf{M}}}, \eta_{D\Sigma}) : \mathbf{M} \to \overline{\mathbf{M}}$ that are compatible with the data space functor; that is, the following diagrams must commute.

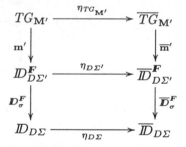

These might be defined for a larger specification framework containing the given one, as in Section 4.4.

Definition 4.46 (Refinement and Implementation). *Let* $(D\Sigma, \mathbf{M})$ *and* $(D\Sigma', \mathbf{M}')$ *be transformation systems with* $\mathbf{M} = (TG_{\mathbf{M}}, \mathbf{m})$ *and* $\mathbf{M}' = (TG_{\mathbf{M}'}, \mathbf{m}')$.

1. *A refinement* $\mathbf{r} = (r, \sigma) : (D\Sigma, \mathbf{M}) \to (D\Sigma', \mathbf{M}')$ *is given by a transition graph morphism* $r : TG_{\mathbf{M}} \to \overline{TG}_{\mathbf{M}'}$ *and a signature morphism* $\sigma : D\Sigma \to D\Sigma'$ *such that* $\overline{\mathbb{D}}^F_\sigma \circ \overline{\mathbf{m}}' \circ r = \eta_{D\Sigma} \circ \mathbf{m}$, *where* $\eta_{D\Sigma} : \mathbb{D}^F_{D\Sigma} \to \overline{\mathbb{D}}^F_{D\Sigma}$ *is the data space part of the unit of the closure operation (see Figure 4.14).*
2. *An implementation* $\mathbf{i} = (i, \sigma) : (D\Sigma, \mathbf{M}) \to (D\Sigma', \mathbf{M}')$ *with* $\sigma = (\sigma_\Sigma, \sigma_A)$ *is a refinement*

$$\mathbf{i} = (i, (\sigma_\Sigma, \emptyset)) : view((\Sigma, \emptyset), \mathbf{M}) \to view((\Sigma', \emptyset), \mathbf{M}').$$

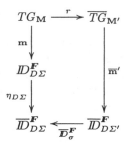

Fig. 4.14. Refinement w.r.t. an arbitrary closure operation

Proposition 4.47. *The development relations are reflexive and transitive.*

Proof. See the proofs of Proposition 4.10 and 4.28.

The preservation properties of development relations w.r.t. data state properties can be stated immediately. They only depend on the satisfaction condition of the data state institution *Ins* (see Lemma 4.31 and Proposition 4.32).

Proposition 4.48 (Reflection of Data Invariants). *Let* $h = (\sigma, h)$:
$(D\Sigma, \mathbf{M}) \rightarrow (D\Sigma', \mathbf{M}')$ *be a morphism in the global category* $\mathbf{TF}^{F}$ *and* $\Phi' \in Form_{\Sigma'}(X)$ *be a* Σ'-*formula. Then*

$$\mathbf{M}' \models_{D\Sigma'} \Phi' \ \ implies \ \ \mathbf{M} \models_{D\Sigma} \sigma_{\Sigma}(\Phi') .$$

If furthermore $h : TG_{\mathbf{M}} \rightarrow TG_{\mathbf{M}'}$ *is surjective on the control states, then also*

$$\mathbf{M} \models \sigma_{\Sigma}(\Phi') \ \ implies \ \ \mathbf{M}' \models \Phi' .$$

Proof. See Lemma 4.31.

Corollary 4.49. *Let* $\mathbf{M}$ *and* $\mathbf{M}'$ *be* $D\Sigma$- *and* $D\Sigma'$-*transformation systems respectively,* $\sigma = (\sigma_{\Sigma}, \sigma_{A}) : D\Sigma \rightarrow D\Sigma'$ *a data space signature morphism, and* $\Phi \in Form_{\Sigma}(X)$ *be a* Σ-*formula.*

1. *Let* $(g, s) : \mathbf{M} \rightarrow \mathbf{M}'$ *be a* σ *uniform extension, refinement, or implementation, and* $c \in CS_{\mathbf{M}}$ *be a control state of* $\mathbf{M}$. *Then*

$$(\mathbf{M}, c) \models_{D\Sigma} \Phi \ \ if \ and \ only \ if \ \ (\mathbf{M}', g(c)) \models_{D\Sigma'} \sigma_{\Sigma}(\Phi) .$$

If g *is furthermore surjective on the control states then*

$$\mathbf{M} \models_{D\Sigma} \Phi \ \ if \ and \ only \ if \ \ \mathbf{M}' \models_{D\Sigma'} \sigma_{\Sigma}(\Phi) .$$

2. *Let* $(g, s) : \mathbf{M} \rightarrow \mathbf{M}'$ *be a* σ-*uniform reduction, then*

$$\mathbf{M} \models_{D\Sigma} \Phi \ \ implies \ \ \mathbf{M}' \models_{D\Sigma'} \sigma_{\Sigma}(\Phi) .$$

If $g : TG_{\mathbf{M}'} \rightarrow TG_{\mathbf{M}}$ *is furthermore surjective on the control states then also*

$$\mathbf{M}' \models_{D\Sigma} \sigma_{\Sigma}(\Phi) \ \ implies \ \ \mathbf{M} \models_{D\Sigma'} \Phi .$$

Proof. See Lemma 4.31 and Proposition 4.32.

Another consequence of this corollary is that developments with surjective transition graph morphisms preserve data specifications (cf. Corollary 4.33).

As mentioned above, for the translation of transformation rules along signature morphisms corresponding translations of action structures in the same direction are needed. These are based on the left adjoints $F_f : \mathbf{Set}^S \to \mathbf{Set}^{S'}$ of the forgetful functors $V_f : \mathbf{Set}^{S'} \to \mathbf{Set}^S$ for functions $f : S \to S'$ (see Section 2.3, p. 50). They are defined by

$$F_f(M)_{s'} = \sum_{s \in S: f(s) = s'} M_s \; ,$$
$$F_f(h)_{s'} = \sum_{s \in S: f(s) = s'} h_s \; .$$

The units $\eta_M : M \to V_f \circ F_f(M)$ are given by the coproduct injections $M_s \to \sum_{\tilde{s} \in S: f(\tilde{s}) = f(s)} M_s$.

Definition 4.50 (Translation of Actions). *Given a functorial action structure AS w.r.t. IF a translation of action structures $AS^\sharp$ is given by a natural transformation*

$$AS_\sigma^\sharp : AS_{D\Sigma} \to AS_{D\Sigma'} \circ (F_{\sigma_S} \times F_{\sigma_S}) \quad \text{for each } \sigma : D\Sigma \to D\Sigma' \text{ in } \mathbf{DSig}^F \; ,$$

where $\sigma_S = sorts(\sigma)$, that satisfies

$$AS_{id_{D\Sigma}}^\sharp = id_{AS_{D\Sigma}} \text{ and } AS_{\sigma' \circ \sigma}^\sharp = AS_\sigma^\sharp \circ AS_{\sigma'}^\sharp$$

and

$$AS_{\sigma, F_{\sigma_S}(M), F_{\sigma_S}(N)} \circ AS_{\sigma, M, N}^\sharp = AS_{D\Sigma}(\eta_M, \eta_N)$$

for all $M, N \in |\mathbf{Set}^S|$ (see Figure 4.15, where pairs like $(F_{\sigma_S}(M), F_{\sigma_S}(N))$ are denoted for short by $F_{\sigma_S}(M, N)$, slightly abusing the notation).

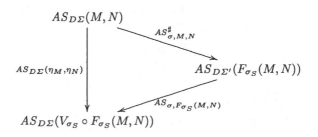

Fig. 4.15. Compatibility of action structure translation and inverse mapping

With the translation of action structures, transformation rules also can be translated along signature morphisms $\sigma : D\Sigma' \to D\Sigma$. Let $r' = (\alpha' \hat{=} L' \to$

R') $\in$ $Rules^{\textbf{F}}_{D\Sigma'}$ with $\alpha' \in AS_{D\Sigma'}(X',Y')$, $L \subseteq Form_{D\Sigma'}(X'_l)$, and $R \subseteq Form_{D\Sigma'}(X'_r)$. Then

$$\sigma(r') = (AS^{\sharp}_{\sigma,X',Y'}(\alpha') \doteq Form_{\sigma,X'_l}(L') \rightarrow Form_{\sigma,X'_r}(R')) \in Rules^{\textbf{F}}_{D\Sigma}.$$

With action translation along signature morphisms, the definition of the renaming operation can also be given.

Definition 4.51 (Renaming). *Let* $D\Sigma = (\Sigma, A)$ *and* $D\Sigma' = (\Sigma, A')$ *be data space signatures with the same data signature* Σ, *and* $r = (id_{\Sigma}, r_A)$: $D\Sigma \rightarrow D\Sigma'$ *be a signature morphism. For each* $D\Sigma$-*transformation system* $\textbf{M} = (TG_{\textbf{M}}, \textbf{m})$ *w.r.t.* $\textbf{IF}$ *the renaming* $ren(r, \textbf{M})$ *is given by the* $D\Sigma'$-*transformation system* $ren(r, \textbf{M}) = (TG_{\textbf{M}}, \textbf{m}')$ *with*

$$\textbf{m}'(c) = \textbf{m}(c) \qquad (c \in CS)$$
$$act^{\textbf{m}'}_t = AS^{\sharp}_r(act^{\textbf{m}}_t)$$
$$\sim^{\textbf{m}'}_t = \sim^{\textbf{m}}_t \qquad (t \in T).$$

Now Lemma 4.34 also can be generalised as follows.

Proposition 4.52 (Reflection of Transformation Rules). *Let* $h = (\sigma, h)$: $(D\Sigma, \textbf{M}) \rightarrow (D\Sigma', \textbf{M}')$ *be a* $\textbf{TF}^{\textbf{F}}$-*morphism,* $r'_0 = (L' \rightarrow R')$ *an anonymous* $D\Sigma'$-*transformation rule, and* $r' = (\alpha' \doteq L' \rightarrow R')$ *a* $D\Sigma'$-*transformation rule (with action names).*

1. *If* $\textbf{M}' \models r'_0$ *then* $\textbf{M} \models \sigma_{\Sigma}(r'_0)$.
   If $h : TG_{\textbf{M}} \rightarrow TG_{\textbf{M}'}$ *is surjective then also* $\textbf{M} \models \sigma_{\Sigma}(r'_0)$ *implies* $\textbf{M}' \models r'_0$.
2. *If* $\textbf{M}' \models r'$ *and* $AS^{\sharp}_{\sigma}$ *and* AS_{σ} *are isomorphisms, then* $\textbf{M} \models \sigma(r')$.
   If furthermore h *is surjective then also* $\textbf{M} \models \sigma(r')$ *implies* $\textbf{M}' \models r'$.

Proof. The first assertion is shown as in Lemma 4.34. The proof can be generalised, since in each concrete institution with formulae solution sets are invariant under translations.

To prove the second assertion it suffices to show that an action structure $act^{\textbf{m}'}_{h(t)} \in AS_{D\Sigma'}(|V_{\sigma_{\Sigma}}(C)|, |V_{\sigma_{\Sigma}}(D)|)$ is an instance of a formal action structure $\alpha' \in AS_{D\Sigma'}(X', Y')$ w.r.t. mappings $\xi' : X' \rightarrow |V_{\sigma_{\Sigma}}(C)|$ and $\zeta' : Y' \rightarrow |V_{\sigma_{\Sigma}}(D)|$ if and only if the corresponding action structure $act^{\textbf{m}}_t \in AS_{D\Sigma'}(|C|, |D|)$ is an instance of the translation $\alpha := AS^{\sharp}_{\sigma,X',Y'}(\alpha')$ of α' w.r.t. the free extensions $\xi^* : F_{\sigma_S}(X') \rightarrow |C|$ and $\zeta^* : F_{\sigma_S}(Y') \rightarrow |D|$. The first implication

$$act^{\textbf{m}}_t = AS_{D\Sigma}(\xi^*, \zeta^*)(\alpha) \Rightarrow act^{\textbf{m}'}_{h(t)} = AS_{D\Sigma'}(\xi', \zeta')(\alpha')$$

follows from the commutativity of the diagrams in Figure 4.16. The other direction follows with the additional condition that $AS^{\sharp}_{\sigma}$ and AS_{σ} are isomorphisms.

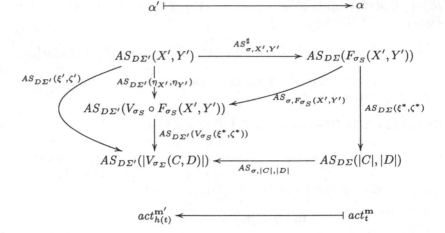

Fig. 4.16. Invariance of action instantiations under translation

The injectivity condition in Proposition 4.35 that guarantees that action structures are invariant under translation and pre-images has to be replaced in the general case by the explicit requirement that $AS_\sigma^\sharp$ and AS_σ be isomorphisms. Then the preservation of transformation rules can be shown.

Proposition 4.53. *Let* **M** *and* **M'** *be* $D\Sigma$*- and* $D\Sigma'$*-transformation systems w.r.t.* $I\!\!F$ *respectively, and* $r = (\alpha \mathrel{\hat=} L \to R)$ *a* $D\Sigma$*-rule.*

1. *Let* $(g, s) : (D\Sigma, \mathbf{M}) \to (D\Sigma', \mathbf{M}')$ *be a* σ*-uniform extension such that* $AS_\sigma^\sharp$ *and* AS_σ *are isomorphisms. Then*

$$(\mathbf{M}, t) \models r \text{ iff } (\mathbf{M}', g(t)) \models \sigma(r)$$

   for each transition t *in* $TG_\mathbf{M}$.
2. *Let* $\mathbf{r} = (r, s) : \mathbf{M} \to \mathbf{M}'$ *be a* σ*-uniform refinement or implementation and* $r_0 = (L \overset{\leftrightarrow}{\longrightarrow} R)$ *be an anonymous* $D\Sigma$*-transformation rule. Then*

$$(\mathbf{M}, t) \models r_0 \text{ iff } (\mathbf{M}', r(t)) \models \sigma_\Sigma(r_0) .$$

3. *Let* $(g, s) : \mathbf{M} \to \mathbf{M}'$ *be a* σ*-uniform reduction, such that* $AS_\sigma^\sharp$ *and* AS_σ *are isomorphisms. Then*

$$\mathbf{M} \models r \text{ implies } \mathbf{M}' \models \sigma(r) .$$

Proof. See Proposition 4.35 and Lemma 4.34.

In the same way as in Proposition 4.11 development operations can be reduced to development relations. Thus the preservation properties also can be carried over to the development operations.

As in Section 4.7 the institution of transformation systems w.r.t. a given specification framework $I\!F = (Ins, AS, I, \epsilon)$ and a control flow logic $CL = (CF, \models^{CL})$ can now be defined. This yields the general modular construction of transformation system mentioned in the previous section. First an institution Ins for the data state models is chosen, which must have carrier sets and open formulae to support tracking relations and the specification of transformation steps by transformation rules. That means Ins must be a concrete institution with formulae. Then action structures are defined to model the desired parallelism (by sets), encapsulation of sequences (by strings), or other structures that are to be considered as single steps. These are defined for arbitrary families of sets, which allows the use of the elements of the data state models as actual parameters. Data states and action structures yield the data spaces, whose properties are specified by the formulae of the institution and the transformation rules derived from them. Transition graphs with data space labels then yield transformation systems. To specify their global properties yet another control flow logic can be chosen. This may refer to the data space structures to different extents, using either the transition labels or, in addition, the data state properties. This construction clearly identifies the interfaces of data state institution, action structures, and control flow logics and shows how corresponding instances can be integrated (see Figure 4.17).

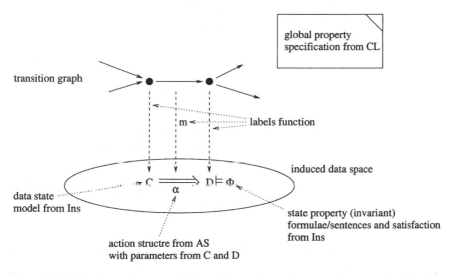

Fig. 4.17. The integration model for data state, action structure, and control flow specification techniques

The formal preconditions for the construction of the institution of transformation systems are thus:

- $Ins = (\mathbf{Sig}, Form, Mod, Sol, sorts, |\_|)$ is a concrete institution with formulae (see Section 3.5, p. 96).
- AS is a functorial action structure with translation of actions (see Definitions 4.41 and 4.50).
- $CL = (CF, \models^{CL})$ is a functorial control flow logic (see Definition 4.37).

Then the signatures, sentences, models, and satisfaction are given as follows.

Signatures

The category $\mathbf{DSig}^{Ins}$ was introduced in Definition 4.40. As in Theorem 4.39 it might be necessary to restrict the class of signature morphisms. Therefore a subcategory $\mathbf{DSig}_i^{Ins} \subseteq \mathbf{DSig}^{Ins}$ is introduced whose properties are stated in Theorem 4.54.

Sentences

Transformation specifications $T\Gamma = (DS, R, C\Gamma)$ w.r.t. data space signatures $D\Sigma = (\Sigma, A) \in |\mathbf{DSig}^{Ins}|$ were introduced in Definition 3.30. Their components are

- a data specification $DS = (Ax, In, Fi)$ whose components are subsets of $Sen(\Sigma)$, where Sen is the sentence functor of Ins,
- a set of transformation rules $R \subseteq Rules_{D\Sigma}^{\mathbf{F}}$, and
- a control flow specification $C\Gamma \subseteq CF(D\Sigma)$.

This yields the set of sentences

$$TSen^{\mathbf{F}}(D\Sigma) = Sen(\Sigma) + Sen(\Sigma) + Sen(\Sigma) + Rules_{D\Sigma}^{\mathbf{F}} + CF(D\Sigma)$$

for each signature $D\Sigma \in |\mathbf{DSig}^{Ins}|$.

Let $\sigma = (\sigma_\Sigma, \sigma_A) : D\Sigma \to D\Sigma'$ be a signature morphism in $\mathbf{DSig}^{Ins}$. It induces a translation of sentences $\sigma^{\sharp} := TSen^{\mathbf{F}}(\sigma)$ as follows.

- $\sigma^{\sharp}(\varphi) = Sen(\varphi)$ for each $\varphi \in Sen(\Sigma)$.
- For each transformation rule $r = (\alpha \,\hat{=}\, L \to R) \in Rules_{D\Sigma}^{\mathbf{F}}$ with $\alpha \in AS_{D\Sigma}(X, Y)$, $L \subseteq Form_\Sigma(X_l)$, $R \subseteq Form_\Sigma(X_r)$, the translation $\sigma^{\sharp}(r)$ is defined by

$$\sigma^{\sharp}(r) = (AS_{\sigma,X,Y}^{\sharp}(\alpha) \,\hat{=}\, Form_{\sigma_\Sigma, X_l}(L) \to Form_{\sigma_\Sigma, X_r}(R)) \ .$$

- $\sigma^{\sharp}(cf) = CF(\sigma)(cf)$ for each control flow formula $cf \in CF(D\Sigma)$.

Models

The model functor $TF^{\mathbf{F}} : \mathbf{DSig}^{Ins} \to \mathbf{Cat}^{op}$ was introduced in Definition 4.42. Its restriction to $\mathbf{DSig}_i^{Ins}$ yields the model functor of the institution. It is also denoted by $TF^{\mathbf{F}}$.

Satisfaction

The satisfaction relation $\models^{\boldsymbol{F}}$ is given by the satisfaction relations $\models^{Ins}$, $\models^{Rule}$, and $\models^{CF}$ that were defined in Section 3.5 (see Definitions 3.26, 3.28, and 3.29).

With these ingredients the institution of transformation systems can finally be constructed as follows.

Theorem 4.54 (Institution of Transformation Systems). *Let*

1. *$\boldsymbol{F} = (Ins, AS, I, \epsilon)$ be a specification framework with*
   - *a concrete institution with formulae Ins,*
   - *a functorial action structure AS with translation of actions $AS^{\sharp}$, and*
   - *initialisation models I and empty action structure ϵ (see Definition 2.14),*
2. *$\mathbf{DSig}_i^{Ins}$ be a subcategory of the data space signature category $\mathbf{DSig}^{Ins}$ induced by Ins (see Definition 4.40),*
3. *$CL = (CF, \models^{CL})$ be a functorial control flow logic*

such that $AS_{\sigma}^{\sharp}$ and AS_{σ} are isomorphisms for each signature morphism σ in $\mathbf{DSig}_i^{\boldsymbol{F}}$.

Then the satisfaction condition for transformation rules holds, i.e., for all $\sigma : D\Sigma \to D\Sigma'$ in $\mathbf{DSig}_i^{\boldsymbol{F}}$, $\mathbf{M'} \in |\mathbf{TF}^{\boldsymbol{F}}(D\Sigma')|$, and $r \in Rules_{D\Sigma}^{\boldsymbol{F}}$

$$\mathbf{M'} \models_{D\Sigma'}^{Ru} \sigma^{\sharp}(r) \quad \Leftrightarrow \quad V_{\sigma}(\mathbf{M'}) \models_{D\Sigma}^{Ru} r \;.$$

Moreover, $(\mathbf{DSig}^{Ins}, TSen^{\boldsymbol{F}}, TF^{\boldsymbol{F}}, \models^{\boldsymbol{F}})$ as defined above is an institution.

Proof. The satisfaction condition for transformation rules follows from Proposition 4.52,2 as in Proposition 4.38.

4.9 Discussion

Development operations and relations have been introduced for transformation systems, according to their structure given by the control flow and the data space levels respectively. For both levels relatively simple relations have been used: transition graph homomorphisms just preserve source and target states of transitions, as well as initialisation states and idle transitions. The latter have been used, as in [WN97], to mimic partial mappings on transitions. Data spaces have been related by forgetful functors that are induced by signature inclusions or signature morphisms. In the former case, the more intuitive one, the parts of the data states and action sets of the larger signature that are not also contained in the smaller one are *forgotten*. That means the corresponding parts are hidden (cf. Definition 4.3 and Example 4.4). Using more general signature morphisms more complex correspondences on the data space level can be expressed, as for instance in Example 4.14 where a constant is mapped to a derived value.

The combinations of these two kinds of mappings, transition graph morphisms and forgetful functors, yield a variety of relations that can be interpreted in the different application contexts and compared to development relations and operations in specification languages. Exclusion, hiding, and renaming for example are standard operations on labelled transition systems that are—accordingly—supported in most process specification languages (cf. 4.6).

Furthermore, closure operations have been introduced that allow the refinement of steps not only w.r.t. the structure, but also in time and space. In a refinement relation the more concrete system is supposed to replace the more abstract one, which imposes strict conditions on its observable behaviour. In contrast with that, implementations have been introduced as a relation between an interface and an implementation body, where the latter can only be accessed via the interface. Thus it is not directly observable; only the effects of the interface actions on the data states can be inspected and must coincide with the specified ones.

This combination of mappings and closure operations immediately yields the basic properties expected of development relations: *transitivity*, i.e., two consecutive development steps of the same kind yield a development of this same kind again, and *reflexivity*, i.e., each model is trivially a development of itself. The use of forgetful functors on the data space level, moreover, yields the invariance of data space properties under development relations. Basically it means that any property that can be formulated in the language of a model holds in the development of the model if and only if it holds in the restriction of the development to the smaller signature. The details of this invariance property, and which properties are preserved by which development relations, have been worked out in Section 4.6.

Concerning behavioural properties, no such general statements could be made, since the control flow specification is treated generically here. Besides, such preservation properties cannot be expected in general, since the global behaviour of the further developed system may deviate in many different ways from the behaviour of the original one. This generic treatment allows the incorporation of very different specification means—descriptive ones like the different logics as well as constructive ones like the different process calculi and Petri nets—as required for a reference model. On the other hand, only schemes of development relations have been treated at this general level here, and corresponding conditions like the satisfaction condition for control flow logics have been given. For concrete examples—like the comparison of the different alternating bit protocol models—this is sufficient and allows the derivation of the desired results. However, to map specification languages with their given refinement relations to the transformation system reference model refined notions of development relations have to be given and investigated.

Many refinement relations for labelled transition systems are based on *traces*, i.e., inclusion of the trace sets is required as one condition. Since transformation systems are not restricted to a particular shape of the transition graphs, this requirement can be covered by the extension relation, for example. That means trace sets, glued at the initialisation state, can be taken immediately as transition graphs of the considered models instead of arbitrary labelled transition systems. Then transition graph inclusion (monomorphism) with the corresponding condition on the data space labels (actions) amounts to the trace set inclusion condition. Alternatively, this condition can be obtained as in Example 4.14 via an appropriate condition on the signature morphism.

Extending this condition the other conditions, preservation of branching, failures, etc., would have to be added to the enhanced notions of refinement. A complete investigation of these concrete relations is out of scope here; further research is required. A survey of development relations for labelled transition systems, especially LOTOS development relations, can be found in [BSBD99]. A summary and survey of data refinements as used in program transformation has been given in [RE98]. Due to its full formal investigation and classification it can be used as a reference for data refinement in general. Refinements of algebraic specifications that are used here for the relations of the data states are discussed in [EM85] and in the more general context of specification frameworks or institutions in [EG94].

Composition of Transformation Systems

Orthogonal to the *vertical* development of more concrete models from more abstract ones—or vice versa, the development of abstractions—composition operations are needed that support the *horizontal* decomposition of the modelling task within one development stage. That means a system is modelled by specifying its components and their composition. In the transformation system reference model composition is supported by corresponding composition operations on the semantic system models.

The definition of a composition operation for transformation systems thereby comprises two tasks. First it has to be defined how transformation systems can be *connected*, i.e., how correspondences of their structures and behaviours can be defined. For that purpose relations on their signatures and on their transition graphs have to be given that express which parts of the structure are shared and which steps are compatible with each other, in the sense that they may be executed synchronously, i.e., within one global step. Composing several components these relations define the *architecture* of a system by stating how many components there are and how they are connected and synchronised.

The second task is to define the result of the application of the composition operation. This means a transformation system has to be defined that represents a global view of the overall structure and behaviour of the composed system, abstracting from its internal architecture. This second part of the definition of composition operations yields *compositionality* in the sense of *structural transparency*, since it is possible to consider a composed system as a single one again, with a single data space and transition graph.

The basic idea of the definition of composition operations is to follow the two-level structure of transformation systems again and integrate the appropriate composition operations for transition graphs (transition systems) and partial algebras. At the behaviour level, cartesian products or their appropriate subsystems yield a representation of synchronisation in the sense mentioned above. This reconstruction of composition operations for transition systems and process specification languages by categorical constructions was introduced in [WN97]. It is integrated here for the behaviour part of the composition operations for transformation systems. Concerning the structure level, algebras of different signatures can be composed by amalgamation (see [EM85]), which means to superpose them according to a given combination of their signatures.

After the elementary introduction of binary composition operations in Section 5.1 their categorical structure is derived in Section 5.2 in order to obtain compositions of arbitrary numbers of components and interconnections. From this more general point of view composition is given by diagrams of transformation systems and their limits, presented in Section 5.3. The categorical characterisation then also allows the derivation of further compositionality properties. In Section 5.4 it is shown that the semantics is compositional w.r.t. the syntax. That means the composition of signatures by colimits (pushouts, unions) induces an amalgamation operation on transformation systems that combines transformation systems of the local signatures and yields a global transformation system of the composed global signature. (In categorical terms this means that the model functor is continuous, respectively, that the amalgamation condition holds.) In Section 5.5 it is shown which properties are compositional, i.e., which properties of the local systems are preserved when embedding them into the global system representing the global view of the composed system. In general one can say that static, structural properties behave well w.r.t. composition, whereas control flow properties are usually not compositional. The compositionality of developments is investigate in Section 5.6, where it is shown that each compatible family of local development steps induces a development step of the composed global transformation system, which is of the same kind as the local ones and includes the local steps.

The composition operations combine data states and transformations by amalgamation. This is well defined if those parts of the data states and transformations in the local components that correspond to the shared signature coincide. An alternative approach also allows the superposition of data states and transformations that do not coincide on the shared parts. In this case an appropriate union of the local data sets and functions is taken to obtain the global view. In this more general approach interconnections of systems of the same signature can also be considered, where each one contributes a subset to the global system. To model this kind of composition a generalised definition of morphisms of transformation systems is introduced in Section 5.7. Diagrams and limits in the corresponding categories then represent the composition of components where data of one sort is distributed over several components.

In Section 5.8 it is then shown that the two approaches can be unified by considering the global category with the more general morphisms. This global category has all limits, i.e., composition is well defined, and these yield the two special cases discussed earlier.

In the remaining sections of this chapter more specific topics are discussed. In Section 5.9 sequential composition is discussed, which can be represented either by dualisation of the parallel synchronous composition, or—more appropriately—by reducing it to parallel composition. As in the other chapters, the definitions and results for the composition of transformation systems with other specification frameworks are then given (Section 5.10). Finally in Section 5.11 composition as defined here is discussed and compared with other approaches and other applications of the composition operations are sketched.

5.1 Binary Composition via Connection Relations

The architectural part of a composition of transformation systems—their interconnection—is given by an *identification relation* on their data space signatures and a *synchronisation relation* on their transition graphs. With the first one the sharing of common static data types such as booleans and strings, shared variables, or shared attributes can be expressed. Also commonly executed actions are identified with the identification relation. This is used for instance in process calculi, where complementary input and output actions of processes are synchronised. Analogously, method calls are synchronised with the corresponding method executions in the objects offering the methods, as in object-oriented statecharts (see [HG95]) and UML state machines. In the global view of the composed system, i.e., the result of the composition operation, these parts will be then identified and occur only once. In contrast with this, non-identified parts of the local components will appear in the global view as disjoint copies.

With the synchronisation relation the temporal compatibility of states and transitions can be expressed. The states and transitions in the global view are then given by tuples of states and transitions respectively of the local systems that are synchronous in this sense. In order to model also independent execution of actions in the components a transition can be declared to be synchronous with an idle transition of a state of another component. In the corresponding global step then, the first component performs a step, whereas the second one remains idle. Since a transition may be in relation with many transitions of another component, the synchronisation relation expresses that transitions *may be* synchronised, i.e., executed together in one global step. But if a transition is in relation with exactly one transition of another component these two *must be* synchronised, because the global view contains just tuples of steps. Accordingly, a transition that is not in relation with any state or transition of another component cannot be entered or executed in the composed system at all. Thus also the exclusion of a local behaviour by the environment can be modelled.

Synchronisation and identification relations have to be consistent with each other in the following sense. First they must be compatible with the structure of transition graphs and data space signatures. If $t : c \to d$ is synchronous (in synchronisation relation) with $t' : c' \to d'$ then also c and c' and d and d' respectively must be synchronous. Analogously, identified function and action names must have correspondingly identified signatures. Second, the synchronisation relation must be consistent with the identification relation w.r.t. the underlying data states and action sets. Consider control states c and c' in two transformation systems with associated data states C and C' respectively. If c and c' are synchronous then for each pair of identified sorts s and s' of the signatures of the two systems the carrier sets C_s and $C'_{s'}$ of the data states must coincide, and for each pair of identified function names f and f' the partial functions f^C and $f'^{C'}$ must coincide. Analogously, whenever two transitions t and t' are synchronous, then an action a identified with an action a' may occur in the action set of t if and only if a' occurs in the action set of t'. Furthermore, the tracking relations on identified sorts must coincide.

A synchronisation and an identification relation that are consistent with each other together define a *connection* of two systems. In this section only binary connections and compositions are considered. The general case is defined in the categorical setting introduced in Section 5.2.

Definition 5.1 (Connection Relations). *Let $D\Sigma_i = (S_i, F_i, A_i)$ for $i = 1, 2$ be data space signatures and $\mathbf{M}_i = (TG_{\mathbf{M}_i}, \mathbf{m}_i)$ be $D\Sigma_i$-transformation systems, with $TG_{\mathbf{M}_i} = (CS_i, T_i, in_i, id_i)$.*

1. *An* identification relation $\mathrm{id} = (\mathrm{id}_S, \mathrm{id}_F, \mathrm{id}_A)$ *on $D\Sigma_1$ and $D\Sigma_2$ is given by relations $\mathrm{id}_S \subseteq S_1 \times S_2$, $\mathrm{id}_F \subseteq F_1 \times F_2$, and $\mathrm{id}_A \subseteq A_1 \times A_2$ such that*
   - id_F *and* id_A *are compatible with* id_S, *i.e.,*

$$\text{if} \quad (f_1 : s_1 \ldots s_n \to \bar{s}_1 \ldots \bar{s}_m) \;\mathrm{id}_F\; (f_2 : s'_1 \ldots s'_k \to \bar{s}'_1 \ldots \bar{s}'_l)$$
$$\text{then} \quad n = k, m = l, \; s_i \;\mathrm{id}_S\; s'_i \text{ for each } i \in \{1, \ldots, n\},$$
$$\text{and } \bar{s}_j \;\mathrm{id}_S\; \bar{s}'_j \text{ for each } j \in \{1, \ldots, m\},$$

$$\text{if} \quad (a_1 : s_1 \ldots s_n) \;\mathrm{id}_A\; (a_2 : s'_1 \ldots s'_k)$$
$$\text{then} \quad n = k \text{ and } s_i \;\mathrm{id}_S\; s'_i \text{ for each } i \in \{1, \ldots, n\}.$$

   - id_X *is one-to-one for each* $X \in \{S, F, A\}$, *i.e.,*

$$x_1 \;\mathrm{id}_X\; x_2 \;\wedge\; x_1 \;\mathrm{id}_X\; x'_2 \;\Rightarrow\; x_2 = x'_2,$$
$$x_1 \;\mathrm{id}_X\; x_2 \;\wedge\; x'_1 \;\mathrm{id}_X\; x_2 \;\Rightarrow\; x_1 = x'_1.$$

2. *A* synchronisation relation $\mathsf{s} = (\mathsf{s}_{CS}, \mathsf{s}_T)$ *on $TG_{\mathbf{M}_1}$ and $TG_{\mathbf{M}_2}$ is given by relations $\mathsf{s}_{CS} \subseteq CS_1 \times CS_2$ and $\mathsf{s}_T \subseteq T_1 \times T_2$ such that*
   - $in_1 \;\mathsf{s}_{CS}\; in_2$,
   - $c_1 \;\mathsf{s}_{CS}\; c_2 \;\Rightarrow\; id(c_1) \;\mathsf{s}_T\; id(c_2)$,
   - $(t_1 : c_1 \to d_1) \;\mathsf{s}_T\; (t_2 : c_2 \to d_2) \;\Rightarrow\; c_1 \;\mathsf{s}_{CS}\; c_2 \;\wedge\; d_1 \;\mathsf{s}_{CS}\; d_2$.
3. *A synchronisation relation* s *on $TG_{\mathbf{M}_1}$ and $TG_{\mathbf{M}_2}$ is consistent with an identification relation* id *on $D\Sigma_1$ and $D\Sigma_2$ if the following conditions hold.*
   - *If* $c_1 \;\mathsf{s}_{CS}\; c_2$ *for* $c_1 \in CS_1, c_2 \in CS_2$
     then for all $s_1 \in S_1, s_2 \in S_2, f_1 \in F_1, f_2 \in F_2$

$$s_1 \;\mathrm{id}_S\; s_2 \quad \Rightarrow \quad \mathbf{m}_1(c_1)_{s_1} = \mathbf{m}_2(c_2)_{s_2},$$
$$f_1 \;\mathrm{id}_F\; f_2 \quad \Rightarrow \quad f_1^{\mathbf{m}_1(c_1)} = f_2^{\mathbf{m}_2(c_2)}.$$

- *If $t_1 \ s_T \ t_2$ for $t_1 : c_1 \to d_1 \in T_1, t_2 : c_2 \to d_2 \in T_2$*
  - *then for all $a_1 : s_1 \ldots s_n \in A_1, a_2 : s_1' \ldots s_k' \in A_2$ with $a_1 \ id_A \ a_2$*

$$a_1(p_1, \ldots, p_n) \in act_{t_1}^{\mathbf{m_1}} \Leftrightarrow a_2(p_1, \ldots, p_n) \in act_{t_2}^{\mathbf{m_2}}$$

  for all $p_i \in \mathbf{m_1}(c_1)_{s_i} (= \mathbf{m_2}(c_2)_{s_i'})$ and $i \in \{1, \ldots, n\} (= \{1, \ldots, k\})$
  - *and for all $s_1 \in S_1, s_2 \in S_2$ with $s_1 \ id \ s_2$*

$$(\sim_{t_1}^{\mathbf{m_1}})_{s_1} = (\sim_{t_2}^{\mathbf{m_2}})_{s_2} \ .$$

4. *A connection $((D\Sigma_1, \mathbf{M_1}), con, (D\Sigma_2, \mathbf{M_2}))$ with $con = (id, s)$ is given by transformation systems $(D\Sigma_1, \mathbf{M_1})$ and $(D\Sigma_2, \mathbf{M_2})$, an identification relation id on $D\Sigma_1$ and $D\Sigma_2$, and a synchronisation relation s on $TG_{\mathbf{M_1}}$ and $TG_{\mathbf{M_2}}$ that is consistent with id.*

In the following examples the connections of the sender and the channel models of the CCS and the UNITY specifications respectively are given, which reconstruct the compositions of the specifications at the semantic level. The CCS connection models the synchronisation of complementary input and output actions, whereas in the UNITY connection the state variables are shared (see Figure 5.1).

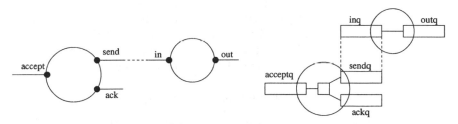

Fig. 5.1. Connections of the sender and the channel models in CCS and UNITY

Example 5.2 (CCS Sender and Channel Connection). In order to connect the sender and the channel models $\mathbf{CCS}_S$ and $\mathbf{CCS}_{CH}$ given in Examples 2.13 and 4.12, first the parameterised *queue(item)*–signature used in the CCS channel signature has to be instantiated by pairs of booleans and messages. This yields

CCS-CH = **queue(bool,message)** +
funs chan: $\to$ queue(bool,message)
acts in, out: bool, message

It is assumed that the instantiated signature *queue(bool,message)* contains the signatures *bool* and *message* as subsignatures.

Correspondingly, the generic set M in the definition of the partial *CCS-CH*-algebra Q has to be instantiated by $M = \mathbb{B} \times D$, where D is the set of messages as in Example 2.13. Then the parameters x of the *in* and *out* actions of $\mathbf{CCS}_S$ are given by pairs $x = (b, d)$ with $b \in I\!B$ and $d \in D$.

Now the identification relation can be defined. The static data types *bool* and *message* are shared, thus

$$
\begin{array}{llll}
bool & \mathrm{id}_S & bool & \quad message \; \mathrm{id}_S \; message \\
true & \mathrm{id}_F & true \\
\vdots & \mathrm{id}_F & \vdots
\end{array}
$$

i.e., the identification relation on the static sorts and functions is given by the identical relation. Note that if this identification is not stated the messages and boolean values of the two agents would have to be considered as different, and could not be communicated.

Since the mutable parts of the data states of the sender and the channel agent are completely encapsulated there is no identification on the constants *chan*, *cbit*, and *msg* representing them. Finally, the *send* action of the sender should correspond to the *in* action of the channel, which is expressed by the relation

$$send \; \mathrm{id} \; in \; .$$

This is compatible with their parameter declarations.

The synchronisation relation on the two transition graphs $TG_{\mathbf{CCS}_S}$ and $TG_{\mathbf{CCS}_{CH}}$ has to be defined in such a way that each action $send(b, d)$ of the sender must be synchronised with an $in(b, d)$ action of the channel and vice versa, whereas all other actions may be executed independently. This synchronisation is achieved as follows. First all control states are synchronous, i.e.,

$$c_S \; \mathsf{s} \; c_{CH} \quad (\text{whence also } id(c_S) \; \mathsf{s} \; id(c_{CH}))$$

for all $c_S \in CS_{\mathbf{CCS}_S}, c_{CH} \in CS_{\mathbf{CCS}_{CH}}$. This corresponds to the fact that the data states are encapsulated, i.e., the states of *cbit* and *msg* in the sender and *chan* in the channel are independent of each other and their values may accordingly occur in arbitrary combinations.

Then the $send_{b,d}$ and $in_{b,d}$ transitions are synchronised by

$$(send_{b,d} : S_{b,d} \rightarrow S'_{b,d}) \; \mathsf{s} \; (in_{b,d} : w \rightarrow \langle b, d \rangle w)$$

for all $b \in I\!B, d \in D, w \in (I\!B \times D)^*$. The initialisations are synchronised by

$$init_{d_0} \; \mathsf{s} \; init$$

for all possible initialisation values $d_0 \in D$. Finally

$$t_S \; \mathsf{s} \; t_{CH}$$

for all transitions $t_S \in T_S - \{send_{b,d}, init_{d_0} \mid b \in I\!B, d, d_0 \in D\}$ and $t_{CH} \in T_{CH} - \{in_{b,d}, init \mid b \in I\!B, d \in D\}$.

The compatibility condition in Definition 5.1,2 is satisfied by all pairs of transitions because all control states are synchronous. Furthermore, the synchronisation relation is consistent with the identification relation according to Definition 5.1,3 as shown in the following.

- The shared static data types *bool* and *message* are identical in all data states $\mathbf{ccs}_S(c_S)$ and $\mathbf{ccs}_{CH}(c_{CH})$.
- There are no shared mutable data parts.
- The identified action instances $send(b,d)$ and $in(b,d)$ only occur simultaneously, i.e., in synchronised transitions $send_{b,d}$ and $in_{b,d}$.
- The tracking relations are identical in all transitions.

This completes the definition of the connection con $= (\mathrm{id}, \mathsf{s})$ of the CCS sender and channel models.

The main difference in the following connection of the UNITY sender and channel models is that in this case also parts of the mutable data states are shared, given by the shared variables *sendq* and *inq* of the sender and the channel respectively that realise the communication in this model (see Figure 5.1).

Example 5.3 (UNITY Sender and Channel Connection). Following the pattern of the previous example the connection of the transformation systems $\mathbf{U}_S$ and $\mathbf{U}_{CH}$ can be defined as follows.

The instantiated channel signature for pairs of booleans and messages is given by

U-CH = **queue(bool,message)** +
 funs inq, outq: $\rightarrow$ queue(bool,message)
 acts in, out: bool, message

and the set M in the definition of the data states is again instantiated by $M = I\!\!B \times D$.

The identification relation is given by

- the identity on the sort and functions names of the shared static data types *bool*, *message*, and *queue(bool,message)*:

bool	id	bool
message	id	message
queue(bool, message)	id	queue(bool, message)

- and the identification of the *sendq* and the *inq*,

$$sendq \ \mathrm{id}_F \ inq \ .$$

There is no action identification because no pairs of observable actions are shared. As discussed in Example 4.13, the original assignments of each of the components are internal (active) actions. Only the possible actions of the environment that update the components variables are visible, i.e., labelled with actions. In the composition of two components an environment action is always synchronised with an internal action.

The synchronisation relation is now defined in such a way that two control states c_S of the sender and c_{CH} of the channel are synchronous if and only if the state of the shared variable is the same in the two underlying data states. Correspondingly, transitions are in the synchronisation relation if they manipulate the shared variable in the same way, or do not touch it at all. That means

$$\langle b, a, s, c \rangle \; \mathsf{s} \; \langle u, v \rangle \text{ iff } s = u$$

for all $\langle b, a, s, c \rangle \in CS_{\mathbf{U}_S}$, and all $\langle u, v \rangle \in CS_{\mathbf{U}_{CH}}$, and as usual $\Delta \; \mathsf{s} \; \Delta$ and $id(c_S) \; \mathsf{s} \; id(c_{CH})$ for all synchronous states $c_S \; \mathsf{s} \; c_{CH}$. By the definition of $\mathbf{u}_S$ and $\mathbf{u}_{CH}$ this is consistent with the identification relation. In particular

$$sendq^{\mathbf{u}_S(b,a,s,c)} = s = u = inq^{\mathbf{u}_{CH}(u,v)} \ .$$

On the transitions the synchronisation relation is defined by

$$
\begin{array}{lllll}
 & (\mathit{offer}_{b,d} : & \langle b, ad, s, c \rangle & \to & \langle b, ad, \langle b, d \rangle s, c \rangle) \\
\mathsf{s} & (\mathit{in}_{b,d} : & \langle s, v \rangle & \to & \langle \langle b, d \rangle s, v \rangle) \\[4pt]
 & (\mathit{send}_{b,d} : & \langle b', a, s\langle b, d \rangle, c \rangle \to & & \langle b', a, s, c \rangle) \\
\mathsf{s} & (\mathit{transmit}_{b,d} : & \langle s\langle b, d \rangle, v \rangle & \to & \langle s, \langle b, d \rangle v \rangle) \\[4pt]
 & (\mathit{send}_{b,d} : & \langle b', a, s\langle b, d \rangle, c \rangle \to & & \langle b', a, s, c \rangle) \\
\mathsf{s} & (\mathit{lose}_i : & \langle s\langle b, d \rangle, v \rangle & \to & \langle s, \langle b, d \rangle v \rangle) \\[4pt]
 & (\mathit{init}_{d_0} : & \Delta & \to & \langle 0, d_0, \lambda, \lambda \rangle) \\
\mathsf{s} & (\mathit{init} : & \Delta & \to & \langle \lambda, \lambda \rangle)
\end{array}
$$

for all $b \in I\!\!B, d, d_0 \in D, i = \mathit{length}(s) + 1$, and

$$
\begin{array}{llll}
(t_S : c_S \to d_S) \; \mathsf{s} \; (t_{CH} : c_{CH} \to d_{CH}) & \text{if} & c_S \; \mathsf{s} \; c_{CH} \text{ and } d_S \; \mathsf{s} \; d_{CH} \\
(t_S : c_S \to d_S) \; \mathsf{s} & id(c_{CH}) & \text{if} & c_S \; \mathsf{s} \; c_{CH} \text{ and } d_S \; \mathsf{s} \; c_{CH} \\
id(c_S) & \mathsf{s} \; (t_{CH} : c_{CH} \to d_{CH}) & \text{if} & c_S \; \mathsf{s} \; c_{CH} \text{ and } c_S \; \mathsf{s} \; d_{CH}
\end{array}
$$

for all $t_S \in \{\mathit{switch}, \mathit{ig\_ack}, \mathit{ack}_b, \mathit{accept}_d \mid b \in I\!\!B, d \in M\}$ and $t_{CH} \in \{\mathit{dup}_i, \mathit{out}_{b,d} \mid i \in I\!\!N, b \in I\!\!B, d \in D\}$.

Since there are no identified actions and the tracking relations are always the same, the transition part of the synchronisation relation is also consistent with the identification relation.

Having defined the connection of transformation systems by identification and synchronisation relations, now the result of the composition has to be defined, i.e., the global view of the composed systems as a single one. For that purpose the local data space signatures, the transition graphs, and the label mappings associating the data states, action sets, and tracking relations to the control states and transitions respectively have to be composed appropriately.

The global signature is basically given by the union of the local ones, where the explicit sharing (and 'keeping apart by default') via the identification relation has to be taken into account. This can be achieved by appropriate renamings that give equal names to identified items and distinct names to non-identified items. The concrete choice of renamings therefore does not matter.

Definition 5.4 (Global Signature). *Let $D\Sigma_i$ for $i = 1, 2$ be data space signatures and* id $= (\mathrm{id}_S, \mathrm{id}_F, \mathrm{id}_A)$ *be an identification relation on $D\Sigma_1$ and $D\Sigma_2$. A* global data space signature $D\Sigma$ *of the connection $(D\Sigma_1, \mathrm{id}, D\Sigma_2)$ is a union of renamings $\rho_1(D\Sigma_1)$ and $\rho_2(D\Sigma_2)$, i.e.,*

$$D\Sigma = \rho_1(D\Sigma_1) \cup \rho_2(D\Sigma_2)$$

where the renamings ρ_1 and ρ_2 have to satisfy

$$\rho_1(x_1) = \rho_2(x_2) \text{ if and only if } x_1 \text{ id } x_2$$

for all items x_i of $D\Sigma_i$.

According to the compatibility property of identification relations (Definition 5.1,1) the component-wise union is well defined and yields a data space signature. Furthermore, the renamings ρ_1 and ρ_2 yield data space signature morphisms $\rho_i : D\Sigma_i \to D\Sigma$ for $i = 1, 2$.

The global transition graph of the composition contains all pairs of synchronous states and transitions respectively. In order also to obtain the compositionality of developments and properties (see Sections 5.5 and 5.6) the pairs in the transitive closure have to be taken up, too. That means there may be induced synchronisations.

Definition 5.5 (Global Transition Graph). *Let $TG_i = (CS_i, T_i, in_i, id_i)$ for $i = 1, 2$ be transition graphs and let* s $= (s_{CS}, s_T)$ *be a synchronisation relation on TG_1 and TG_2. Furthermore let*

$$\bar{s}_X = \bigcup_{n \in \mathbb{N}} s_X \circ (s_X^{-1} \circ s_X)^n \subseteq X_1 \times X_2$$

for $X = CS, T$ be the transitive closures of s_{CS} and s_T respectively. The global transition graph $TG = (CS, T, in, id)$ *of the connection (TG_1, s, TG_2) is given by*

$$CS = \{(c_1, c_2) \in CS_1 \times CS_2 \mid c_1 \; \bar{s}_{CS} \; c_2\}$$
$$T((c_1, c_2), (d_1, d_2)) = \{(t_1, t_2) \in T_1(c_1, d_1) \times T_2(c_2, d_2) \mid t_1 \; \bar{s}_T \; t_2\}$$
$$in = (in_1, in_2)$$
$$id(c_1, c_2) = (id_1(c_1), id_2(c_2)) \;.$$

Due to the compatibility condition 5.1,2 TG is well defined.

The space of all possible data states and transformations of the global view is determined by the global data space signature defined above. The composition of the local label mappings now yields the ones that are actually entered by the global system. According to the definition, each global control state is given by a pair of synchronous local control states. Its underlying data state is then given by a superposition (amalgamation) of the local data states, where each carrier set and each function corresponding to the global signature are taken from the component that provides them. Shared data parts are identical in synchronous states due to the consistency conditions of synchronisation and identification relations, whence they can be chosen from either component. The global action sets are analogously given by the unions of the local ones, renamed according to the signature morphisms realising the identification relation. The tracking relations are inherited from the components like the carrier sets.

Definition 5.6 (Global Transformation System). *Let $(D\Sigma_i, \mathbf{M}_i)$ for $i = 1, 2$ be transformation systems, with $D\Sigma_i = (S_i, F_i, A_i)$ and $\mathbf{M}_i = (TG_{\mathbf{M}_i}, \mathbf{m}_i)$, and let $\mathrm{con} = (\mathrm{id}, \mathsf{s})$ be a connection of $(D\Sigma_1, \mathbf{M}_1)$ and $(D\Sigma_2, \mathbf{M}_2)$.*

The global transformation system $(D\Sigma, \mathbf{M})$, with $\mathbf{M} = (TG_{\mathbf{M}}, \mathbf{m})$, of the connection $((D\Sigma_1, \mathbf{M}_1), \mathrm{con}, (D\Sigma_2, \mathbf{M}_2))$ is given by the global signature $D\Sigma = (S, F, A)$ of the connection $(D\Sigma_1, \mathrm{id}, D\Sigma_2)$ with renamings ρ_1 and ρ_2, the global transition graph $TG = (CS, T, in, id)$ of the connection (TG_1, s, TG_2), and the transition graph morphism $\mathbf{m} : TG \to \mathbb{D}_{D\Sigma}$ defined as follows:

$$\mathbf{m}(c)_s = \begin{cases} \mathbf{m}_1(c_1)_{s_1} & \text{if } \rho_1(s_1) = s \\ \mathbf{m}_2(c_2)_{s_2} & \text{if } \rho_2(s_2) = s \end{cases}$$

$$f^{\mathbf{m}(c)} = \begin{cases} f_1^{\mathbf{m}_1(c_1)} & \text{if } \rho_1(f_1) = f \\ f_2^{\mathbf{m}_2(c_2)} & \text{if } \rho_2(f_2) = f \end{cases}$$

for all $s \in S, f \in F$, and $c = (c_1, c_2) \in CS$, and $\mathbf{m}(t) = (act_t^{\mathbf{m}}, \sim_t^{\mathbf{m}})$ with

$$act_t^{\mathbf{m}} = \rho_A^1(act_{t_1}^{\mathbf{m}_1}) \cup \rho_A^2(act_{t_2}^{\mathbf{m}_2})$$

$$(\sim_t^{\mathbf{m}})_s = \begin{cases} (\sim_{t_1}^{\mathbf{m}_1})_{s_1} & \text{if } \rho_S^1(s_1) = s \\ (\sim_{t_2}^{\mathbf{m}_2})_{s_2} & \text{if } \rho_S^2(s_2) = s \end{cases}$$

for all $t = (t_1, t_2) \in T$.

The following theorem shows that the global view is well defined and that there are projections to the local systems, i.e., it contains the local systems as parts.

Theorem 5.7 (Compositionality). *Each connection of transformation systems $((D\Sigma_1, \mathbf{M}_1), \mathrm{con}, (D\Sigma_2, \mathbf{M}_2))$ induces a global transformation system $(D\Sigma, \mathbf{M})$ and morphisms $\mathbf{p}_1 : (D\Sigma, \mathbf{M}) \to (D\Sigma_1, \mathbf{M}_1)$ and $\mathbf{p}_2 : (D\Sigma, \mathbf{M}) \to (D\Sigma_1, \mathbf{M}_2)$ in the category $\mathbf{TF}$.*

Proof. According to the consistency conditions of identification and synchronisation relations, the mapping $\mathbf{m} : TG \to I\!D_{D\Sigma}$ of the global transformation system defined above is a transition graph morphism. That means

- $\mathbf{m}(c)$ is a partial $D\Sigma$-algebra for each control state $c \in CS$, due to condition 5.1,3,
- $\mathbf{m}(t) \in Tf_{D\Sigma}(\mathbf{m}(c), \mathbf{m}(d))$ for each transition $t : c \to d \in T$,
- $\mathbf{m}(in) = \emptyset$.

To define the morphisms $\mathbf{p_1}$ and $\mathbf{p_2}$ let the transition graph morphisms $\pi^i_{TG} : TG \to TG_i$ $(i = 1, 2)$ be given by the projections

$$\pi_1(c_1, c_2) = c_1 , \; \pi_2(c_1, c_2) = c_2 \quad ((c_1, c_2) \in CS)$$
$$\pi_1(t_1, t_2) = t_1 , \; \pi_2(t_1, t_2) = t_2 \quad ((t_1, t_2) \in T) .$$

Due to condition 5.1,2 these are well defined. Since id is one-to-one (condition 5.1,1) the action parts of ρ_1 and ρ_2 are injective. Furthermore, for all $a_1 \in A_1, a_2 \in A_2$ we have $\rho^1_A(a_1) = \rho^2_A(a_2)$ only if $a_1 \; id_A \; a_2$, whence a_1 occurs in $act^{\mathbf{m_1}}_{t_1}$ if and only if a_2 occurs in $act^{\mathbf{m_2}}_{t_1}$, for all $t_1 \; s_T \; t_2$. Thus

$$(\rho^i_A)^{-1}(act^{\mathbf{m}}_t) = act^{\mathbf{m_i}}_{t_i} \quad (i = 1, 2)$$

for all $t = (t_1, t_2) \in T$. Furthermore

$$V_{\rho^i_\Sigma}(\mathbf{m}(c)) = \mathbf{m}_i(c_i) \quad (i = 1, 2)$$

for all $c = (c_1, c_2) \in CS$ by definition, and

$$V_{\rho^i_\Sigma}(\sim^{\mathbf{m}}_t) = \sim^{\mathbf{m_i}}_{t_i} \quad (i = 1, 2)$$

due to condition 5.1,3.

Thus $\mathbf{m}_i \circ \pi^i_{TG} = I\!D_{\rho_i} \circ \mathbf{m}$ $(i = 1, 2)$, which means that the morphisms $\mathbf{p}_i = (\rho_i, \pi^i_{TG})$ for $i = 1, 2$ are well defined.

Example 5.8 (Global View of the CCS Composition). To conclude the example of the CCS sender and channel specifications as transformation systems the global view $\mathbf{CCS}_{S/CH}$ of their connection is now given. Then also its relation with the corresponding composition of the CCS agents with the parallel composition $(S[send/in]\|CH)\backslash\{send, in\}$ in CCS can be discussed.

The global signature is given by

CCS-S/CH = queue(bool,message) +
    funs cbit: $\to$ bool
          msg: $\to$ message
          chan: $\to$ queue(bool,message)
    acts send_in: bool, message
          ack: bool
          accept: message
          out: bool, message

It represents the identification of the *send* and the *in* action by a shared action $send\_in$. The renamings $\rho_S : CCS\text{-}S \to CCS\text{-}S/CH$ and $\rho_{CH} : CCS\text{-}CH \to CCS\text{-}S/CH$ are inclusions, except that $\rho_S(send) = send\_in$ and $\rho_{CH}(in) = send\_in$.

Since all states are synchronous the set of global control states is the full cartesian product of the local ones, i.e.,

$$CS_{S/CH} = CS_S \times CS_{CH} ,$$

with initialisation state (Δ, Δ).

The data states are given by the superpositions $Q[b, d, w] = DB[b, d] + Q[w]$ and $Q[b, w] = DB[b] + Q[w]$ of the algebras $DB[b, d]$ and $DB[b]$ for the sender part and $Q[w]$ for the channel part. These are defined as extensions of the *queue(bool,message)*-algebra Q to the data part of $CCS\text{-}S/CH$ by

$$cbit^{Q[b,d,w]} = b, \; msg^{Q[b,d,w]} = d, \; chan^{Q[b,d,w]} = w ,$$
$$cbit^{Q[b,w]} = b, \qquad\qquad\qquad chan^{Q[b,w]} = w .$$

They are attached to the control states by

$$\mathbf{ccs}_{S/CH}(S_{b,d}, w) = \mathbf{ccs}_{S/CH}(S'_{b,d}, w) = Q[b, d, w]$$
$$\mathbf{ccs}_{S/CH}(A_b, w) = Q[b, w] .$$

Furthermore $\mathbf{ccs}_{S/CH}(\Delta, \Delta) = \emptyset$.

In the transition sets the synchronised actions appear in one step:

$$(init_{d_0}, init) : \quad (\Delta, \Delta) \quad \to \quad (S_{0,d_0}, \lambda) \quad (d_0 \in D)$$
$$(send_{b,d}, in_{b,d}) : (S_{b,d}, w) \to (S'_{b,d}, \langle b, d \rangle w) \; (b \in \mathbb{B}, d \in D)$$
$$(t_S, t_{CH}) : (c_S, c_{CH}) \to \quad (d_S, d_{CH})$$

for all $t_S : c_S \to d_S$ in TG_S with $t_S \notin \{init_{d_0}, send_{b,d} \mid b \in \mathbb{B}, d_0, d \in D\}$ and all $t_{CH} : c_{CH} \to d_{CH}$ in TG_{CH} with $t_S \notin \{init, in_{b,d} \mid b \in \mathbb{B}, d \in D\}$. This yields the following action sets:

$$\mathbf{ccs}_{S/CH}(init_{d_0}, init) = \emptyset$$
$$\mathbf{ccs}_{S/CH}(send_{b,d}, in_{b,d}) = \{send\_in(b, d)\}$$
$$\mathbf{ccs}_{S/CH}(t_S, t_{CH}) = \mathbf{ccs}_S(t_S) \cup \mathbf{ccs}_{CH}(t_{CH})$$
$$(t_S \neq send_{b,d}, t_{CH} \neq in_{b,d})$$

The tracking relations are the identities on the static data types, as in the components.

The underlying LTS of $\mathbf{CCS}_{S/CH}$ is still different from the CCS-semantics of the parallel composition $S[send/in] \| CH$. CCS does not admit truly parallel actions (as opposed to SCCS, see [Mil83]). Instead, independent actions have to be sequentialised. Since the transformation system composition contains both synchronisations of true actions and synchronisations with idle transitions the global view has to be restricted to the latter. For that purpose the restriction operation of transformation systems $res(\mathbf{CCS}_{S/CH}, seq)$ can be used, where seq denotes the inclusion of the subtransition graph given by the (sequential) synchronisations with idle transitions. (Note that this restriction is not uniform, i.e., it is not induced by a sub-signature.)

Finally, in order to reconstruct the CCS semantics of

$$(S[send/in]\| CH)\backslash\{send, in\},$$

where the synchronised actions are internalised, they have to be hidden in the global view. That means the view w.r.t. the subsignature that does not contain the $send\_in$ action has to be taken. The underlying LTS of the system $hide(send\_in, res(\mathbf{CCS}_{S/CH}, seq))$ then coincides with the CCS semantics again, as for the local components. That means the CCS-semantics of composition is also reconstructed conservatively.

Example 5.9 (Global View of the UNITY Composition). The global view of the composed UNITY sender and channel models is presented without further discussion here, following the pattern of the previous example.

$$\mathbf{U\text{-}S/CH} = \mathbf{queue(message)} + \mathbf{queue(bool)} +$$
$$+ \mathbf{queue(bool,message)} +$$

funs S: $\to$ bool
    acceptq: $\to$ queue(message)
    sendq_inq: $\to$ queue(bool,message)
    ackq: $\to$ queue(bool)
    outq: $\to$ queue(bool,message)

acts send, in, out: bool, message
    ack: bool
    accept: message

- $CS_{\mathbf{U}_{S/CH}} = (\mathbb{B} \times D^* \times (\mathbb{B} \times D)^* \times \mathbb{B}^* \times (\mathbb{B} \times D)^*) \uplus \{\Delta\}$.
- $\mathbf{u}_S(b,a,s,c,v) = QDB[b,a,s,c,v]$, the extension of QDB to $U\text{-}S/CH$ by the constants b,a,s,c, and V.
- $\mathbf{u}_S(\Delta) = \emptyset$.
- $T_{\mathbf{U}_{S/CH}}$ is given by the pairs of synchronous transitions defined in Example 5.3.
- $act^{\mathbf{u}_{S/CH}}_{(t_S,t_{CH})} = act^{\mathbf{u}_S}_{t_S} \cup act^{\mathbf{u}_{CH}}_{t_{CH}}$.

The tracking relations are the identities on the static data types, as in the components.

Note that the environment steps *send* and *in* that have been added to the sender and channel programs respectively (to compare them with the CCS specifications) are now identified with internal steps (*offer* and *transmit, lose*) corresponding to assignments of the original programs. The global steps, given by the pairs $(offer_{b,d}, in_{b,d})$, $(send_{b,d}, transmit_{b,d})$, and $(send_{b,d}, lose_i)$ inherit their initial and final states from the components. In this way one system may be constrained by the other one (i.e. by the environment). The

$offer_{b,d}$ transition for example can only be executed when there is a message d in the accept queue. Thus the $in_{b,d}$ transition also only occurs in the composed system in this case, whereas it has not been constrained in the channel model alone. (In parallel program design this effect is called *superposition* or *superimposition*, see [FF90, FR92, FM97, WLF00]. In [FM92, FM97] it has been reconstructed categorically via pushouts of temporal logic theories. Since a dual—semantic—approach is pursued here, superposition on the transformation system level appears as pullback, see Section 4.3.)

Connecting all components of the alternating bit protocol (and hiding the action names) the added environment actions will thus disappear. The global transformation system then corresponds directly to the whole program presented in [CM88] in that its transitions are in one-to-one correspondence with the parallel assignments. That means the compositional transformation system semantics is a conservative extension of the UNITY semantics for unstructured programs.

This example also shows how a composition operation defined at the semantic level of transformation systems can be reflected to a particular language. First the components of a UNITY program have been separated and extended by environment actions. Then the components are composed by identifying these environment actions with internal actions of the other components, whence they disappear again.

5.2 Categorical Structure

In this section the constructions used in the previous one to connect and compose transformation systems are rephrased in categorical terms. This allows the generalisation of binary composition to arbitrary diagrams of components, and the derivation of the further compositionality results in the following sections. First it is shown that each identification relation id on data space signatures $D\Sigma_1$ and $D\Sigma_2$ yields a span of data space signature morphisms $D\Sigma_1 \leftarrow D\Sigma_{id} \rightarrow D\Sigma_2$, and that each synchronisation relation s on transition graphs TG_1 and TG_2 yields a cospan of transition graph morphisms $TG_1 \rightarrow TG_s \leftarrow TG_2$. Putting this together, it is shown then that a connection con $= (id, s)$ of transformation systems $(D\Sigma_1, \mathbf{M}_1)$ and $(D\Sigma_2, \mathbf{M}_2)$ finally yields a cospan of transformation system morphisms $(D\Sigma_1, \mathbf{M}_1) \rightarrow (D\Sigma_{id}, \mathbf{M}_{con}) \leftarrow (D\Sigma_2, \mathbf{M}_2)$. The global signature, transition graph, and transformation system of a connection can then be reconstructed as pushouts and pullbacks of these (co)spans.

Identification Relations

According to the compatibility conditions of identification relations (Definition 5.1,1) each identification relation id yields a data space signature $D\Sigma_{id}$, with sets of sort, function, and action names given by id_S, id_F, and

id_A respectively. The signature of a function name $(f_1, f_2) \in \text{id}_F$ with $f_1 : s_1 \ldots s_n \to \bar{s}_1 \ldots \bar{s}_m \in F_1$ and $f_2 : s_1' \ldots s_k' \to \bar{s}_1' \ldots \bar{s}_l' \in F_2$ is given by $(s_1, s_1') \ldots (s_n, s_n') \to (\bar{s}_1, \bar{s}_1') \ldots (\bar{s}_n, \bar{s}_n') \in \text{id}_S^* \times \text{id}_S^*$. Analogously, the signature of an action name $(a_1, a_2) \in \text{id}_A$ with $a_1 : s_1 \ldots s_n \in A_1$ and $a_2 : s_1' \ldots s_k' \in A_2$ is given by $(s_1, s_1') \ldots (s_n, s_n') \in \text{id}_S^*$. In both cases $k = n$ (and $l = m$).

The projection mappings $\kappa_S^i : \text{id}_S \to S_i$, $\kappa_F^i : \text{id}_F \to F_i$, $\kappa_A^i : \text{id}_A \to A_i$, with $\kappa_i(x_1, x_2) = x_i$ ($i = 1, 2$), then yield signature morphisms $\kappa_i = (\kappa_\Sigma^i, \kappa_A^i) : D\Sigma_{\text{id}} \to D\Sigma_i$ with $\kappa_\Sigma^i = (\kappa_S^i, \kappa_F^i)$. Due to the condition on the renamings the diagram

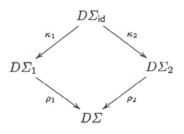

is a pushout in **DSig**.

Synchronisation Relations

Each synchronisation relation $s = (s_{CS}, s_T)$ with components $s_{CS} \subseteq CS_1 \times CS_2$ and $s_T \subseteq T_1 \times T_2$ can be translated into a transition graph $TG_s = (CS_s, T_s, \text{in}_s, \text{id}_s)$ and transition graph morphisms $f_i : TG_i \to TG_s$ ($i = 1, 2$) as follows. The control states and transitions of TG_s are given by the equivalence classes of s in $CS_1 \uplus CS_2$ and $T_1 \uplus T_2$ respectively.

$$CS_s \qquad = \{ [c]_s \mid c \in CS_1 \uplus CS_2 \}$$
$$T_s([c]_s, [d]_s) = \{ [t]_s \mid \exists c' \in [c]_s, d' \in [d]_s . t \in T_1(c', d') \cup T_2(c', d') \}$$
$$\text{in}_s \qquad = [\text{in}_1]_s = [\text{in}_2]_s$$
$$\text{id}_s([c]_s) \qquad = \begin{cases} [\text{id}_1(c)]_s & \text{if } c \in CS_1 \\ [\text{id}_2(c)]_s & \text{if } c \in CS_2 . \end{cases}$$

The transition graph morphisms $k_i : TG_i \to TG_s$ ($i = 1, 2$) are given by the projections to the equivalence classes.

$$k_i(c_i) = [c_i]_s \ (c_i \in CS_i)$$
$$k_i(t_i) = [t_i]_s \ (t_i \in T_i) .$$

Then straightforward computations show that

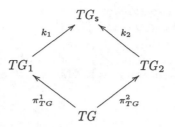

is a pullback in **TG**, where the projections $\pi_{TG}^i : TG \to TG_i$ $(i = 1, 2)$ are given by $\pi_{TG}^i(x_1, x_2) = x_i$ as usual.

Connections

Consider a connection $((D\Sigma_1, \mathbf{M}_1), (\mathsf{id}, \mathsf{s}), (D\Sigma_2, \mathbf{M}_2))$. Since the synchronisation relation s is consistent with the identification relation id the transition graph morphism $\mathbf{m}_{\mathsf{con}} : TG_{\mathsf{s}} \to I\!D_{D\Sigma_{\mathsf{id}}}$, given by

$$\mathbf{m}_{\mathsf{con}}([c]_{\mathsf{s}}) = V_{\kappa_{\Sigma}^i}(\mathbf{m}_i(c)) \quad \text{if } c \in CS_i$$

$$act_{[t]_{\mathsf{s}}}^{\mathbf{m}_{\mathsf{con}}} = (\kappa_A^i)^{-1}(act_t^{\mathbf{m}_i}) \text{ if } t \in T_i$$

$$\sim_{[t]_{\mathsf{s}}}^{\mathbf{m}_{\mathsf{con}}} = V_{\kappa_A^i}(\sim_t^{\mathbf{m}_i}) \quad \text{if } t \in T_i .$$

is well defined and satisfies the equations

$$\mathbf{m}_{\mathsf{con}} \circ k_i = I\!D_{\kappa_i} \circ \mathbf{m}_i : TG_i \to I\!D_{D\Sigma_{\mathsf{id}}} \quad (i = 1, 2) .$$

That means $\mathbf{k}_i = (\kappa_i, k_i) : (D\Sigma_i, \mathbf{M}_i) \to (D\Sigma_{\mathsf{id}}, \mathbf{M}_{\mathsf{con}})$, where $\mathbf{M}_{\mathsf{con}} = (TG_{\mathsf{s}}, \mathbf{m}_{\mathsf{con}})$, for $i = 1, 2$ is a transformation system morphism.

The relation between connections and cospans can be summarised as follows.

Proposition 5.10. *Each connection of transformation systems*

$$((D\Sigma_1, \mathbf{M}_1), \mathsf{con}, (D\Sigma_2, \mathbf{M}_2))$$

with $\mathsf{con} = (\mathsf{id}, \mathsf{s})$ *yields a cospan of transformation system morphisms*

$$(D\Sigma_1, \mathbf{M}_1) \xrightarrow{\mathbf{k}_1 = (\kappa_1, k_1)} (D\Sigma_{\mathsf{id}}, \mathbf{M}_{\mathsf{con}}) \xleftarrow{\mathbf{k}_2 = (\kappa_2, k_2)} (D\Sigma_2, \mathbf{M}_2) .$$

Conversely, each cospan

$$(D\Sigma_1, \mathbf{M}_1) \xrightarrow{\mathbf{h}_1 = (\vartheta_1, h_1)} (D\Sigma_0, \mathbf{M}_0) \xleftarrow{\mathbf{k}_2 = (\vartheta_2, h_2)} (D\Sigma_2, \mathbf{M}_2)$$

with injective signature morphisms ϑ_i *yields a connection*

$$((D\Sigma_1, \mathbf{M}_1), (\mathsf{id}, \mathsf{s}), (D\Sigma_2, \mathbf{M}_2))$$

via

$$s_1 \; \mathrm{id}_S \; s_2 \quad \textit{if} \quad \exists s_0 \in S_0 \; s_1 = \vartheta^1_S(s_0) \; \wedge \; s_2 = \vartheta^2_S(s_0)$$
$$f_1 \; \mathrm{id}_F \; f_2 \quad \textit{if} \quad \exists f_0 \in F_0 \; f_1 = \vartheta^1_F(f_0) \; \wedge \; f_2 = \vartheta^2_F(f_0)$$
$$a_1 \; \mathrm{id}_A \; a_2 \quad \textit{if} \quad \exists a_0 \in F_0 \; a_1 = \vartheta^1_A(a_0) \; \wedge \; a_2 = \vartheta^2_A(a_0)$$

$$c_1 \; \mathsf{s}_{CS} \; c_2 \quad \textit{if} \quad h_1(s_1) = h_2(s_2)$$
$$t_1 \; \mathsf{s}_T \; t_2 \quad \textit{if} \quad h_1(t_1) = h_2(t_2) \; .$$

Proof. The first part has been shown above; the well-definedness of the constructed connection is also easy to check.

The global signature and transition graph of a connection of transformation systems have already been reconstructed as pushouts and pullbacks respectively of the induced (co)spans. The global transformation system is a pullback in the category of transformation systems, too.

Theorem 5.11. *The global transformation system* $(D\Sigma, \mathbf{M})$ *of a connection* $((D\Sigma_1, \mathbf{M}_1), \mathrm{con}, (D\Sigma_2, \mathbf{M}_2))$ *together with the morphisms* $\mathbf{p}_i = (\rho_i, \pi^i_{TG})$: $(D\Sigma, \mathbf{M}) \rightarrow (D\Sigma_i, \mathbf{M}_i)$ $(i - 1, 2)$ *defined in the proof of Theorem 5.7 is a pullback of the induced cospan*

$$(D\Sigma_1, \mathbf{M}_1) \xrightarrow{\; \mathbf{k}_1 = (\kappa_1, k_1) \;} (D\Sigma_{\mathsf{Id}}, \mathbf{M}_{\mathrm{con}}) \xleftarrow{\; \mathbf{k}_2 = (\kappa_2, k_2) \;} (D\Sigma_2, \mathbf{M}_2) \; .$$

in the category **TF**.

Proof. A construction of the limits of more general diagrams of transformation systems is given in the proof of Theorem 5.18. It is easy to check that the corresponding labelling function (transition graph morphism) $\mathbf{m} : TG_{\mathbf{M}} \rightarrow I\!D_{D\Sigma}$ given there coincides with the definition of the global transformation system given in Definition 5.6.

The connection relations in Section 5.1 have been introduced to obtain cospans of transformation systems, whose pullbacks yield the global views of the connections. Whereas the identification relations are defined immediately at the syntactic level and these apply uniformly to all transformation systems of a given signature, the synchronisation relations can only be defined on the individual transition graphs of the local systems. In the remainder of this section syntactic means for the presentation of synchronisation relations are given, which allow an analogous uniform definition of synchronisation relations at the syntactic level. The basic idea is to use relations on terms for the synchronisation of states and relations on formal actions for the synchronisation of transitions. The definition is restricted to the elementary case of synchronising single actions, which is the only case that occurs in the examples. It can be immediately generalised to sets of actions in synchronisation relations. Then two control states are synchronous iff the evaluation of the related terms in their underlying data states coincide. Analogously, two transitions are synchronous iff their action sets are instances of related formal actions.

Definition 5.12 (Syntactic Synchronization Relation). *Let* $D\Sigma_i = (\Sigma_i, A_i)$ *for* $i = 1, 2$ *be data space signatures and* id *be an identification relation on* $D\Sigma_1$ *and* $D\Sigma_2$. *Furthermore, let* X_i, Y_i *for* $i = 1, 2$ *be* S_i-*indexed sets of variables such that* $(X_1)_{s_1} = (X_2)_{s_2}$ *and* $(Y_1)_{s_1} = (Y_2)_{s_2}$ *whenever* s_1 id s_2.

A syntactic synchronisation relation ss $= (\text{ss}_{CS}, \text{ss}_T)$ *on* $D\Sigma_1$ *and* $D\Sigma_2$ *w.r.t.* id *is given by relations*

$$\text{ss}_{CS} \subseteq \textit{Term}_{\Sigma_1} \times \textit{Term}_{\Sigma_2}$$

and

$$\text{ss}_T \subseteq \textit{Act}_{D\Sigma_1}(X_1, Y_1) \times \textit{Act}_{D\Sigma_2}(X_2, Y_2)$$

that satisfy the following conditions.

- *For all* $r_1 : s_{1,1} \ldots s_{1,n_1} \to s'_{1,1} \ldots s'_{1,k_1} \in \textit{Term}_{\Sigma_1}$
  and $\quad r_2 : s_{2,1} \ldots s_{2,n_2} \to s'_{2,1} \ldots s'_{2,k_2} \in \textit{Term}_{\Sigma_2}$

  if $\quad r_1 \;\; \text{ss}_{CS} \;\; r_2$
  then $\quad n_1 = n_2, \; k_1 = k_2$
  and $\quad s_{1,i} \; \text{id}_S \; s_{2,i} \quad (i = 1, \ldots, n_1)$
  and $\quad s'_{1,j} \; \text{id}_S \; s'_{2,j} \quad (j = 1, \ldots, k_1)$.

- *For all* $a_1 : w_1; w'_1 \in A_1, \; a_2 : w_2; w'_2 \in A_2$

  if $\quad a_1(\bar{x}_1; \bar{y}_1) \; \text{ss}_T \; a_2(\bar{x}_2; \bar{y}_2)$
  then $\quad a_1 \; \text{id}_A \; a_2$
  or $\quad \nexists a'_2 \in A_2 \; a_1 \; \text{id}_A \; a'_2 \; \text{ and } \; \nexists a'_1 \in A_1 \; a'_1 \; \text{id}_A \; a_2$.

A syntactic synchronisation relation on terms and formal action sets induces a synchronisation relation on transition graphs according to Definition 5.1 as follows.

Proposition 5.13. *Let* $(D\Sigma_i, \mathbf{M}_i)$ *for* $i = 1, 2$ *be* $D\Sigma_i$-*transformation systems, with* $\mathbf{M}_i = (TG_i, \mathbf{m}_i)$. *Furthermore, let* id *be an identification relation on* $D\Sigma_1$ *and* $D\Sigma_2$ *and* $D\Sigma_1 \xleftarrow{\kappa_1} D\Sigma_{\text{id}} \xrightarrow{\kappa_2} D\Sigma_2$ *its induced cospan.*

Each syntactic synchronisation relation ss $= (\text{ss}_{CS}, \text{ss}_T)$ *w.r.t.* id *induces a synchronisation relation* s $= (\text{s}_{CS}, \text{s}_T)$ *on* TG_1 *and* TG_2 *that is consistent with* id *as follows.*

- $c_1 \; \text{s}_{CS} \; c_2$ *if*
  - $V_{\kappa_1}(\mathbf{m}_1(c_1)) = V_{\kappa_2}(\mathbf{m}_2(c_2))$
  - *and* $r_1^{\mathbf{m}_1(c_1)} = r_2^{\mathbf{m}_2(c_2)}$

  for all $r_1 \in \textit{Term}_{\Sigma_1}$ *and* $r_2 \in \textit{Term}_{\Sigma_2}$ *with* $r_1 \; \text{ss}_{CS} \; r_2$.
- $(t_1 : c_1 \to d_1) \; \text{s}_T \; (t_2 : c_2 \to d_2)$ *if*
  - $c_1 \; \text{s}_{CS} \; c_2$ *and* $d_1 \; \text{s}_{CS} \; d_2$
  - *and* $t_1 = id_{c_1}$ *and* $t_2 = id_{c_2}$

– *or there are formal actions $a_1 \in Act_{D\Sigma_1}(X_1, Y_1)$, $a_2 \in Act_{D\Sigma_2}(X_2, Y_2)$, and variable evaluations (S_i-indexed mappings)*

$$\gamma_1 : X_1 \rightarrow \mathbf{m}_1(c_1) \; \delta_1 : Y_1 \rightarrow \mathbf{m}_i(d_1)$$
$$\gamma_2 : X_2 \rightarrow \mathbf{m}_2(c_1) \; \delta_1 : Y_2 \rightarrow \mathbf{m}_2(d_1)$$

that are compatible with the tracking relations, i.e.,

$$\forall z_1 \in X_1 \cap Y_1 \; \gamma_1(z_1) \sim^{\mathbf{m}_1}_{t_1} \delta_1(z_1)$$
$$\forall z_2 \in X_2 \cap Y_2 \; \gamma_2(z_2) \sim^{\mathbf{m}_2}_{t_2} \delta_2(z_2)$$

such that

$$act^{\mathbf{m}_1}_{t_1} = \{a_1(\gamma_1(\bar{x}_1), \delta_1(\bar{y}_1))\}$$
$$act^{\mathbf{m}_2}_{t_2} = \{a_2(\gamma_2(\bar{x}_2), \delta_2(\bar{y}_2))\} \, .$$

Proof. The conditions of Definition 5.1, parts 2 and 3, have to be shown.

part 2:

- $in_1 \; \mathsf{s}_{CS} \; in_2$ since $\mathbf{m}_1(in_1) = \emptyset$ and $\mathbf{m}_2(in_2) = \emptyset$,
- $c_1 \; \mathsf{s}_{CS} \; c_2 \Rightarrow id(c_1) \; \mathsf{s}_T \; id(c_2)$ and $(t_1 : c_1 \rightarrow d_1) \; \mathsf{s}_T \; (t_2 : c_2 \rightarrow d_2) \Rightarrow c_1 \; \mathsf{s}_{CS} \; c_2 \wedge d_1 \; \mathsf{s}_{CS} \; d_2$ hold by definition of s_T.

part 3:

- The first condition holds because $V_{\kappa_1}(\mathbf{m}_1(c_1)) = V_{\kappa_2}(\mathbf{m}_2(c_2))$.
- If $t_1 : c_1 \rightarrow d_1 \; \mathsf{s}_T \; (t_2 : c_2 \rightarrow d_2)$ then either both are identities and empty action sets, or they are instances of formal actions that must satisfy the second condition of Definition 5.12. Thus either they have identified action names or for both there are no identified action names in the complementary action signatures. In both cases the condition on the occurrence of action in $act^{\mathbf{m}_1}_{t_1}$ and $act^{\mathbf{m}_2}_{t_2}$ is satisfied.

The coincidence of the tracking relations on identified sorts follows again from $V_{\kappa_1}(\mathbf{m}_1(c_1)) = V_{\kappa_2}(\mathbf{m}_2(c_2))$ and $V_{\kappa_1}(\mathbf{m}_1(d_1)) = V_{\kappa_2}(\mathbf{m}_2(d_2))$.

Example 5.14 (Union of the Linked-List Subsystems). In Example 2.12 a transformation system **LL** as a formal model of linked lists has been constructed as a union of two subsystems. The latter, $\mathbf{LL}^{move} = (TG_{\mathbf{LL}^{move}}, \mathsf{ll}^{move})$ and $\mathbf{LL}^{del} = (TG_{\mathbf{LL}^{del}}, \mathsf{ll}^{del})$, represent the behaviours of the basic methods *move* and *del* respectively. With the connection relations now introduced for the composition of transformation systems this union can be made precise.

The intended meaning of the union is that both subsystems are transformation systems of the same signature, i.e., their labelling functions both have the functionality

$$\mathsf{ll}^{move} : TG_{\mathbf{LL}^{move}} \rightarrow I\!D_{linked\_list}$$
$$\mathsf{ll}^{del} \quad : TG_{\mathbf{LL}^{del}} \rightarrow I\!D_{linked\_list}$$

and their transition graphs are united disjointly. That means

$$\mathbf{LL} = (\ TG_{\mathbf{LL}^{move}} \uplus TG_{\mathbf{LL}^{del}}, \mathrm{ll}^{move} \cup \mathrm{ll}^{del}) \ .$$

The underlying identification relation of this composition is thus given by the identity on the whole signature *linked_list*.

The synchronisation relation is empty, representing the disjoint union of the subsystems. Note that this cannot be presented by a syntactic synchronisation relation, because the underlying data states on non-synchronous states are identical, whence they cannot be distinguished by terms of the data signatures.

In Example 4.29 where the implementation of a parameterised *delete* method w.r.t. the basic methods has been defined, another combination of the systems $\mathbf{LL}^{move}$ and $\mathbf{LL}^{del}$ was needed. In this case, where the *start* and *stop* flags are removed from the control states of $TG_{\mathbf{LL}^{del}}$, all control states from the two systems with identical data states are synchronous and transitions are never synchronous. The identification relation is again given by the identity on the data space signatures. Concerning the synchronisation, no further information is required to obtain the desired union. With the empty syntactic state synchronisation relation $\mathrm{ss}_{CS} = \emptyset$ two states are synchronous if they have the same underlying data states. The empty syntactic transition synchronisation relation $\mathrm{ss}_T = \emptyset$ ensures that transitions (except the idle ones) are never executed in one step.

Example 5.15 (Presentation of the Sender and Channel Synchronization). As a further example of a syntactic synchronisation relation consider the connection of the sender and channel models again (Examples 5.2 and 5.3). Note that with a syntactic relation only transitions with visible actions can be synchronised. Thus we assume for this example that all transitions are labelled with a single action, where the names of the transitions are chosen for those that were internal ones.

The syntactic synchronisation relations are given in Table 5.1.

5.3 Composition-by-Limits

In the previous sections the composition of two transformation systems has been discussed, using pullbacks of transition graphs for a description of the synchronisation and amalgamation of partial algebras, tracking relations, and action sets for the composition of the data spaces. This can be generalised to arbitrary numbers of components (transformation systems), arbitrarily connected by transformation system morphisms. In categorical terms this means that the global category of transformation systems has limits. A formal restriction has to be made here, however, due to the strict preservation properties of transformation system morphisms: all connection morphisms of a diagram whose limit is to be constructed must have injective signature morphisms, and the diagram must be a partial order, i.e., no parallel connection morphisms

Syntactic synchronisation relations for the CCS models:

$$\text{ss}_{SC} = \emptyset$$
$$\text{ss}_T = \{(send(b,d), in(b,d)) \mid b \in I\!B, d \in D\}$$
$$\cup \{(init(d), init) \mid d \in D\}$$
$$\cup \{ack(b), time\_out, accept(x) \mid b \in I\!B, d \in D\}$$
$$\times \{out(b',d), lose(i), dup(i) \mid b' \in I\!B, d \in D, i \in I\!N\} \ .$$

Syntactic synchronisation relations the UNITY models:

$$\text{ss}_{SC} = \{(sendq, inq)\}$$
$$\text{ss}_T - \{(offer(b,d), in(b,d)) \mid b \subset I\!B, d \in M\}$$
$$\cup \{(send(b,d), transmit(b,d)) \mid b \in I\!B, d \in D\}$$
$$\cup \{(send(b,d), lose(i)) \mid b \in I\!B, d \in D, i \in I\!N\}$$
$$\cup \{(init(d_0), init) \mid d_0 \in D, i \in I\!N\}$$
$$\cup \{switch, ig\_ack, ack(b), accept(d) \mid b \in I\!B, d \in M\}$$
$$\times \{dup(i), out(b,d) \mid i \in I\!N, b \in I\!B, d \in D\} \ .$$

Table 5.1. Syntactic synchronisation relations for the CCS and UNITY models

are allowed. That means two systems cannot be connected in two different ways (within one composition) and there must not be implicit identifications within one system within one composition. (So the restrictions are not too strict.) Note that in Section 5.7 a more general definition of morphisms is given and in Section 5.8 it is shown that w.r.t. these morphisms all limits exist without these constraints.

Analogous to the construction of the global transformation system in the previous sections a limit of a diagram of transformation systems is given by a colimit of signatures and amalgamations of the data states and transformations. Thus, first, colimits of signatures are needed.

Proposition 5.16. *The category* **DSig** *is cocomplete.*

Proof. **DSig** is equivalent to the comma category $(Id_{\mathbf{Set}} \downarrow (sorts^* \times sorts^*))$, where *sorts* is the functor that maps a signature $\Sigma = (S, F)$ to S and a signature morphism $\sigma = (\sigma_S, \sigma_F)$ to σ_S. Since **Set** and **Sig** are cocomplete and $Id_{\mathbf{Set}}$ preserves colimits the assertion holds.

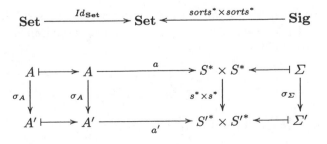

In the following lemma it is shown that the construction of data spaces of given data space signatures is co-continuous w.r.t. the composition of data space signatures. This means that under the conditions on diagrams mentioned above, the data space associated to a colimit of data space signatures is the limit of the local data spaces, considered in the category of transition graphs. Technically this property is a combination of the amalgamation of partial algebras, action sets, and tracking relations.

Lemma 5.17 (Data Space Amalgamation). *Let I be a partial order and $D : I \to \mathbf{DSig}$ be a diagram of data space signatures such that $D(k)$ is injective for each $k : i \to j$ in I. Furthermore, let $(D\Sigma, (\kappa_i)_{i \in |I|})$ be a colimit of D. Then $(\mathbb{D}_{D\Sigma}, (\mathbb{D}_{\kappa_i})_{i \in |I|})$ is a limit of the diagram $((\mathbb{D}_{D(i)})_{i \in |I|}, (\mathbb{D}_{D(k)})_{k:i \to j \in I})$ in the category $\mathbf{TG}$ of transition graphs.*

Proof. (Throughout the proof let $D(i) =: D\Sigma_i$ for $i \in |I|$ and $D(k) =: \sigma_k$ for $k : i \to j$ in I.)

The basic idea of the proof is to extend the amalgamation property of partial algebras to action sets and tracking relations. This shows that these are limits in **Set**, just like $(\mathbf{PAlg}(\Sigma), (V_{\kappa^i_\Sigma})_{i \in |I|})$ is a limit in **Cat**.

To show these amalgamation properties consider first partial Σ-algebras C and D, representing the input and output data states of a transformation $T : C \Rightarrow D$ in $\mathbb{D}_{D\Sigma}$. Due to the amalgamation property of partial algebras C and D are amalgamations of families $(C_i)_{i \in |I|}$ and $(D_i)_{i \in |I|}$ of partial Σ_i-algebras with $V_{\sigma_k}(C_j) = C_i$ and $V_{\sigma_k}(D_j) = D_i$ for all $k : i \to j$ in I. It is to be shown then that $T = (\alpha, \sim)$ is an amalgamation, too.

For that purpose consider first the tracking relation. Let $(\sim^i)_{i \in |I|}$ with $\sim^i \in Rel^{S_i}(|C_i|, |D_i|)$ be a family of relations with $V_{\sigma^k_\Sigma}(\sim^j) = \sim^i$ for each $k : i \to j$ in I. Its amalgamation $\sim = \sum_I \sim^i$ is defined similar to the amalgamation of algebras by

$$\sim_s = \sim^i_{s_i} \quad \text{if } \kappa^i_\Sigma(s_i) = s .$$

Well-definedness of $\sim$ and uniqueness w.r.t. the property $V_{\kappa^i_\Sigma}(\sim) = \sim^i$ for each $i \in |I|$ are shown as for partial algebras. This implies then that $(Rel^S(|C|, |D|), (V_{\kappa^i_\Sigma})_{i \in |I|})$ is a limit of the diagram

$$((Rel^{S_i}(|C_i|, |D_i|))_{i \in |I|}, (V_{\sigma^k_\Sigma})_{k:i \to j \in I}))$$

in **Set**.

Now let $(\alpha_i)_{i \in |I|}$ be a family of action sets $\alpha_i \subseteq Act_{D\Sigma_i}(|C_i|, |D_i|)$ with $(\sigma^k_A)^{-1}(\alpha_j) = \alpha_i$ for each $k : i \to j$ in I. Its amalgamation $\alpha = \sum_I \alpha_i \in Act_{D\Sigma}(|C|, |D|)$ is defined by

$$\alpha = \bigcup_{i \in |I|} \kappa^i_A(\alpha_i) ,$$

where $\kappa^i_A(\alpha_i) = \{\kappa^i_A(a_i)(\gamma, \delta) \mid a_i(\gamma, \delta) \in \alpha_i\}$.

Since $(C_i)_s = C_{\kappa^i_S(s)}$ and $(D_i)_s = D_{\kappa^i_S(s)}$ for each $i \in |I|, s \in S_i$, this means

$$a(\gamma, \delta) \in \alpha \ \text{if} \ \exists i \in |I|, a_i \in A_i \ . \ a = \kappa^i_A(a_i) \ \wedge \ a_i(\gamma, \delta) \in \alpha_i \ .$$

To prove the amalgamation property it has to be shown that

1. $(\kappa^i_A)^{-1}(\alpha) = \alpha_i$ for each $i \in |I|$.
2. $(\forall i \in |I| \ (\kappa^i_A)^{-1}(\beta) = \alpha_i) \Rightarrow \beta = \alpha$ for each $\beta \in Act_{D\Sigma}(|C|, |D|)$.

Part 1:

'$\supseteq$': $a_i(\gamma, \delta) \in \alpha_i \Rightarrow \kappa^i_A(a_i)(\gamma, \delta) \in \alpha \Rightarrow a_i(\gamma, \delta) \in (\kappa^i_A)^{-1}(\alpha)$.

'$\subseteq$': Let $a_i(\gamma, \delta) \in Act_{D\Sigma_i}(|C_i|, |D_i|)$. If $\kappa^i_A(a_i)(\gamma, \delta) \in \alpha$ then there are $j \in |I|$ and $a_j \in A_j$ such that $\kappa^j_A(a_j) = \kappa^i_A(a_i)$ and $a_j(\gamma, \delta) \in \alpha_j$. Suppose $j = i$. Since I is a partial order and each σ_k is injective also the injections κ_i are injective, whence $a_j = a_i$ and $a_i(\gamma, \delta) \in \alpha_i$. If $j \neq i$, then w.l.o.g. there is a $k : i \to j$ in I such that $\sigma^k_A(a_i) = a_j$, whence $a_i(\gamma, \delta) \in (\sigma^k_A)^{-1}(\alpha_j) = \alpha_i$.

Part 2:

'$\supseteq$': Let $a(\gamma, \delta) \in \alpha$. Then there are $i \in |I|$ and $a_i(\gamma, \delta) \subset Act_{D\Sigma_i}(|C_i|, |D_i|)$ such that $a = \kappa^i_A(a_i)$ and $a_i(\gamma, \delta) \in \alpha_i$. Since $\alpha_i = (\kappa^i_A)^{-1}(\beta)$ the latter is equivalent to $a(\gamma, \delta) = \kappa^i_A(a_i)(\gamma, \delta) \in \beta$.

'$\subseteq$': Let $a(\gamma, \delta) \in \beta$. Since $(D\Sigma, (\kappa_i)_{i \in |I|})$ is a colimit and C and D are amalgamations there are $i \in |I|$ and $a_i(\gamma, \delta) \in Act_{D\Sigma_i}(|C_i|, |D_i|)$ such that $a = \kappa^i_A(a_i)$. Now $\kappa^i_A(a_i)(\gamma, \delta) \in \beta$ implies $a_i(\gamma, \delta) \in \alpha_i$, whence by definition $a(\gamma, \delta) = \kappa^i_A(a_i)(\gamma, \delta) \in \alpha$.

These two properties imply that $(Act_{D\Sigma}(|C|, |D|), ((\kappa^i_A)^{-1})_{i \in |I|})$ is a limit of the diagram

$$((Act_{D\Sigma_i}(|C_i|, |D_i|))_{i \in |I|}, ((\sigma^k_A)^{-1})_{k \in I})$$

in **Set**.

To conclude the proof of the limit property of $(I\!\!D_{D\Sigma}, (I\!\!D_{\kappa_i})_{i \in |I|})$ let $TG = (CS, T, in, id)$ be a transition graph and $(h_i : TG \to I\!\!D_{D\Sigma_i})_{i \in |I|}$ be a family of transition graph morphisms with $I\!\!D_{\sigma_k} \circ h_j = h_i$ for each $k : i \to j$ in I.

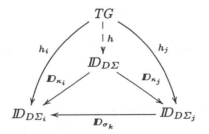

Due to the amalgamation properties of partial algebras, action sets, and tracking relations the mediating morphism $h : TG \to I\!\!D_{D\Sigma}$ given by

$$h(c) = \sum_I h_i(c)$$

$$h(t) = \left(\sum_I act^{m_i}_{h_i(t)}, \sum_I \sim^{m_i}_{h_i(t)}\right)$$

is well defined. Its existence and uniqueness w.r.t. the property $\mathbb{D}_{\kappa_i} \circ h = h_i$ for all $i \in |I|$ imply the desired limit property.

Theorem 5.18 (Limits of Transformation Systems). *Each diagram D : $I \to \mathbf{TF}$ of transformation systems whose schema I is a partial order and whose signature morphism components are injective has a limit in $\mathbf{TF}$.*

Proof. Let $D(i) =: (D\Sigma_i, \mathbf{M}_i)$ for $i \in |I|$ and $D(k) =: \mathbf{h}_k = (\sigma_k, h_k)$ for $k : i \to j$ in I. Furthermore, let $(D\Sigma, (\kappa_i)_{i\in|I|})$ be a colimit of the diagram $((D\Sigma_i)_{i\in|I|}, (\sigma_k)_{k:i\to j\in I})$ of data space signatures, and let $(TG_{\mathbf{M}}, (\pi^i_{TG})_{i\in|I|})$ be a limit of the diagram $((TG_{\mathbf{M}_i})_{i\in|I|}, (h_k)_{k:i\to j\in I})$ of transition graphs.

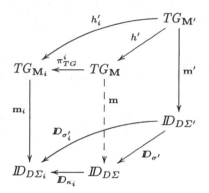

According to Lemma 5.17, the family $(\mathbf{m}_i \circ \pi^i_{TG} : TG_{\mathbf{M}} \to \mathbb{D}_{D\Sigma_i})_{i\in|I|}$ uniquely determines a transition graph morphism $\mathbf{m} : TG_{\mathbf{M}} \to \mathbb{D}_{D\Sigma}$ with $\mathbb{D}_{\kappa_i} \circ \mathbf{m} = \mathbf{m}_i \circ \pi^i_{TG}$ for all $i \in |I|$, since $\mathbb{D}_{\sigma_k} \circ \mathbf{m}_i \circ \pi^i_{TG} = \mathbf{m}_j \circ \pi^j_{TG}$ for all $k : i \to j$ in I.

Let $(D\Sigma', \mathbf{M}')$ be a transformation system and $(\mathbf{h}'_i)_{i\in|I|}$ be a family of transformation system morphisms $\mathbf{h}'_i = (\sigma'_i, h'_i) : (D\Sigma', \mathbf{M}') \to (D\Sigma_i, \mathbf{M}_i)$ with $\mathbf{h}_k \circ \mathbf{h}'_i = \mathbf{h}'_j$ for all $k : i \to j$ in I, i.e., $h_k \circ h'_i = h'_j$ and $\mathbb{D}_{\sigma_k} \circ \mathbb{D}_{\sigma'_j} = \mathbb{D}_{\sigma'_i}$ $(\sigma'_j \circ \sigma_k = \sigma'_i)$. This uniquely determines a signature morphism $\sigma' : D\Sigma \to D\Sigma'$ and a transition graph morphism $h' : TG_{\mathbf{M}'} \to TG_{\mathbf{M}}$ with $\sigma' \circ \kappa_i = \sigma'_i$ and $\pi^i_{TG} \circ h' = h'_i$ for all $i \in |I|$. Due to the limit property of $(\mathbb{D}_{D\Sigma}, (\mathbb{D}_{\kappa_i})_{i\in|I|})$ also $\mathbf{m} \circ h' = \mathbb{D}_{\sigma'} \circ \mathbf{m}'$, thus $((D\Sigma, (TG_{\mathbf{M}}, \mathbf{m})), (\kappa_i, \pi^i_{TG})_{i\in|I|})$ is a limit of D in $\mathbf{TF}$.

5.4 Compositional Semantics

The construction of limits in the global category of transformation systems yields the composition operation within the semantic domain, which has been interpreted as compositionality in the sense of structural transparency. If the semantic composition operation is compatible with the composition of signatures by colimits this yields compositionality of the semantics w.r.t. the syntax, in the sense of a compositional denotational semantics. An instance of this is the amalgamation property that has been used above to construct data states and transformations of composed systems, since amalgamation is a composition operation on semantic objects (algebras, action sets, etc.) that is induced by the (syntactic) composition of their signatures.

The amalgamation property also holds for transformation systems, provided the diagrams concerned satisfy the conditions used above and, in addition, are connected. This means that in this case, we have compositionality of the semantics w.r.t. the syntax, too. Pushouts with injective signature morphisms as obtained by the connection relations for example satisfy these properties; thus they also induce an amalgamation operation on transformation systems.

Technically the amalgamation property is a special case of the construction of limits in the global category **TF**, since these already contain colimits of signatures as a part of the construction.

Theorem 5.19 (Amalgamation Property). *Let $D : I \to$ **DSig** be a diagram of data space signatures such that*

- *I is a partial order,*
- *I is connected, i.e., for each pair of objects $i, j \in |I|$ there is a chain of morphisms $k_1, \ldots, k_n$ in I that connects i and j, like $i \xrightarrow{k_1} \bullet \xleftarrow{k_2} \cdots \xrightarrow{k_n} k$,*
- *$D(k)$ is injective for each $k : i \to j$ in I.*

*Furthermore, let $(D\Sigma, (\kappa_i)_{i\in|I|})$ be a colimit of D. Then $(\mathbf{TF}(D\Sigma), (V_{\kappa_i})_{i\in|I|})$ is a limit of the diagram $((\mathbf{TF}(D\Sigma_i))_{i\in|I|}, (V_{\sigma_k})_{k:i\to j\in I})$ in **Cat**.*

That means, for each family $(D\Sigma_i, \mathbf{M}_i)_{i\in|I|}$ of transformation systems with $V_{\sigma_k}(D\Sigma_j, \mathbf{M}_j) = (D\Sigma_i, \mathbf{M}_i)$ for each $k : i \to j$ in I, there is a transformation system $(D\Sigma, \mathbf{M}) = \sum_I (D\Sigma_i, \mathbf{M}_i)$, the amalgamation of $(D\Sigma_i, \mathbf{M}_i)_{i\in|I|}$, that satisfies $V_{\kappa_i}(D\Sigma, \mathbf{M}) = (D\Sigma_i, \mathbf{M}_i)$ for all $i \in |I|$ and is uniquely determined by this property.

Analogously, there is an amalgamation of compatible families $(\mathbf{h}_i)_{i\in|I|}$ of morphisms of transformation systems $\mathbf{h}_i : (D\Sigma_i, \mathbf{M}_i) \to (D\Sigma'_i, \mathbf{M}'_i)$, which means that there is an amalgamated morphism $\mathbf{h} = \sum_I \mathbf{h}_i : \sum_I (D\Sigma_i, \mathbf{M}_i) \to \sum_I (D\Sigma'_i, \mathbf{M}'_i)$ that satisfies $V_{\kappa_i}(\mathbf{h}) = \mathbf{h}_i$ for all $i \in |I|$ and is uniquely determined by this property.

Proof. Let **C** be a category and $(F_i : \mathbf{C} \to \mathbf{TF}(D\Sigma))_{i\in|I|}$ be a family of functors such that $V_{\sigma_k} \circ F_j = F_i$ for all $k : i \to j$ in I (where, as above, $\sigma_k := D(k)$).

Let $A \in |\mathbf{C}|$. Since $V_{\sigma_k}(F_j(A)) = F_i(A)$ for all $i \in |I|$ and I is connected the transition graphs of all transformation systems $F_i(A)$ coincide. Denote this transition graph by $TG_{\mathbf{M}} = (CS, T, in, id)$.

Due to the amalgamation properties of partial algebras, tracking relations, and action sets, the transition graph morphism $\mathbf{m} : TG_{\mathbf{M}} \to I\!D_{D\Sigma}$ given by

$$\mathbf{m}(c) = \sum_I \mathbf{m}_i(c) \qquad\qquad (c \in CS)$$
$$\mathbf{m}(t) = \sum_I \mathbf{m}_i(t) \;=\; (\sum_I act_t^{\mathbf{m_i}}, \sum_I \sim_t^{\mathbf{m_i}}) \quad (t \in T)$$

is well defined, and the transformation system $(D\Sigma, \mathbf{M})$ with $\mathbf{M} = (TG_{\mathbf{M}}, \mathbf{m})$ is uniquely determined by the property $V_{\kappa_i}(D\Sigma, \mathbf{M}) = F_i(A)$ for all $i \in |I|$.

This yields the object definition $F(A) = (D\Sigma, \mathbf{M})$ of the desired mediating functor $F : \mathbf{C} \to \mathbf{TF}(D\Sigma)$.

To define $F(f) : F(A) \to F(B)$ for some $\mathbf{C}$-morphism $f : A \to B$ recall that transformation system morphisms are transition graph morphisms that are compatible with the label mappings $\mathbf{m}$ and $\mathbf{n}$ of $F(A) = (D\Sigma, \mathbf{M})$ and $F(B) = (D\Sigma, \mathbf{N})$ respectively. Since the transition graph morphisms $F_i(f)$ are all identical for each $i \in |I|$ we can define $F(f) = F_i(f)$ for any $i \in |I|$. Since $I\!D_{\kappa_i} \circ (\mathbf{n} \circ F(f)) = \mathbf{n}_i \circ F_i(f) = \mathbf{m}_i = I\!D_{\kappa_i} \circ \mathbf{m}$ for all $i \in |I|$, the compatibility requirement $\mathbf{n} \circ F(f) = \mathbf{m}$ follows pointwise again from the amalgamation properties of partial algebras, tracking relations, and action sets. The uniqueness of $F(f)$ w.r.t. $V_{\kappa_i}(F(f)) = F_i(f)$ for all $i \in |I|$ is obvious.

5.5 Compositionality of Properties

The composition of transformation systems by limits also induces compositionality of their data space properties, i.e., data invariants and transformation rules. That means, if a local system satisfies a data invariant or a transformation rule (w.r.t. its local signature), then the global system satisfies it, too. Technically this is due to the fact that morphisms reflect these properties (see Lemmas 4.31 and 4.34) and that there are the projection morphisms from the global to the local systems. Due to the generic treatment of control flow logics a corresponding statement cannot be made, however. In general, the global behaviours of systems are not compositional. In the following theorem arbitrary conditional equations ce are considered to specify properties of the data states of a system. The corresponding satisfaction relation $\mathbf{M} \models ce$ for transformation systems $\mathbf{M} = (TG_{\mathbf{M}}, \mathbf{m})$ and conditional equations ce is defined by $\mathbf{M} \models ce$ if $\mathbf{m}(c) \models ce$ for each control state $c \in CS_{\mathbf{M}}$.

Theorem 5.20 (Compositionality of Properties). *Let $((D\Sigma, \mathbf{M}), (\pi_i)_{i \in |I|})$ be a limit of a diagram $D : I \to \mathbf{TF}$, with $\pi_i = (\kappa_i, \pi_{TG}^i)$ and $D(i) =: (D\Sigma_i, \mathbf{M}_i)$.*

1. For each $ce \in CEqns_{\Sigma_i}$,

$$\text{if } \mathbf{M}_i \models ce \text{ then } \mathbf{M} \models \kappa_i(ce) \,.$$

2. For each anonymous $D\Sigma_i$-transformation rule $r_0 = (L \to R)$,

$$\text{if } \mathbf{M}_i \models r_0 \text{ then } \mathbf{M} \models \kappa_i(r_0) \,.$$

3. For each $D\Sigma_i$-transformation rule $r = (\alpha \hat{=} L \to R)$,

$$\text{if } \mathbf{M}_i \models r \text{ and } \kappa_i \text{ is injective } \text{ then } \mathbf{M} \models \kappa_i(r) \ .$$

Proof. 1.   Let $c \in CS_{\mathbf{M}}$. Due to the satisfaction condition for partial algebras

$$\mathbf{m}(c) \models \kappa_i(ce) \ \Leftrightarrow \ V_{\kappa_i}(\mathbf{m}(c)) \models ce \ .$$

Since $V_{\kappa_i}(\mathbf{m}(c)) = \mathbf{m}_i(\pi^i_{TG}(c))$ and $\mathbf{M}_i \models ce$ the assertion follows.
The proof for 2 and 3 follows from Lemmas 4.31 and 4.34, since the projections are transformation system morphisms.

As mentioned above, a corresponding general result for control flow formulae cannot be shown, due to the general abstract definition of control flow logics. Even if it is an institution local control flow properties might not be preserved, since the local systems need not *coincide* with the restrictions of the global system to the local signatures. Instead, they are related by transition graph morphisms that need not preserve or reflect the properties of the global behaviour of a system.

The situation is different, however, if the amalgamation of transformation systems w.r.t. connected diagrams of signatures is considered, because in this case all local transition graphs must coincide.

Theorem 5.21. *Let $D : I \to \mathbf{DSig}$ be a diagram of data space signatures that satisfies the conditions of Theorem 5.19 and let $CL = (CF, \models)$ be a control flow logic that satisfies the satisfaction condition. Furthermore, let $(D\Sigma, \mathbf{M})$ be the amalgamation of a compatible family $(D\Sigma_i, \mathbf{M}_i)_{i \in |I|}$ of transformation systems. Then for each formula $\varphi \in CF(D\Sigma_i)$,*

$$\mathbf{M}_i \models_{D\Sigma_i} \varphi \text{ if and only if } \mathbf{M} \models_{D\Sigma} \kappa_i(\varphi) \ .$$

Proof. The assertion follows immediately from the satisfaction condition of CL, since $\mathbf{M}_i = V_{\kappa_i}(\mathbf{M})$ by definition of an amalgamation.

5.6 Compositionality of Developments

Based on the composition-by-limits of transformation systems the development operations and relations discussed in the previous chapter can also be composed. This means that each compatible family of developments of local components induces a global development of the same kind on the global system that includes the local ones.

First the compositionality of development relations for the binary connection of transformation systems via connection relations is discussed. The precondition for the desired compositionality result is that the local developments are compatible with each other w.r.t. the sharing and synchronisation expressed by the connection relations. The development relations considered for this elementary case are morphisms, uniform reductions, extensions, and sequential refinements. The last ones include sequential implementations. General refinements and implementations are treated in Section 5.10, where the corresponding compositionality conditions are given.

Definition 5.22 (Compatibility of Connections). *Let*

$$((D\Sigma_1, \mathbf{M}_1), \mathrm{con}, (D\Sigma_2, \mathbf{M}_2)) \quad and \quad ((D\Sigma_1', \mathbf{M}_1'), \mathrm{con}', (D\Sigma_2', \mathbf{M}_2'))$$

be connections of transformation systems, with $\mathrm{con} = (\mathrm{id}, \mathrm{s})$ *and* $\mathrm{con}' = (\mathrm{id}', \mathrm{s}')$.

1. *Two morphisms* $\mathbf{h}_i = (\sigma_i, h_i) : (D\Sigma_i, \mathbf{M}_i) \to (D\Sigma_i', \mathbf{M}_i')$ $(i = 1, 2)$ *are compatible with the connections* con *and* con' *if*
   - x_1' id' $x_2' \Rightarrow \sigma_1(x_1')$ id $\sigma_2(x_2')$ *for all* $x_i' \in S_i' \cup F_i' \cup A_i'$ $(i = 1, 2)$ *and*
   - x_1 s $x_2 \Rightarrow h_1(x_1)$ s' $h_2(x_2)$ *for all* $x_i \in CS_i \cup T_i$ $(i = 1, 2)$.
2. *Two reductions* $r_i = (g_i, \gamma_i) : (D\Sigma_i, \mathbf{M}_i) \to (D\Sigma_i', \mathbf{M}_i')$ $(i = 1, 2)$ *are compatible with* con *and* con' *if the morphisms* $r_i = (\gamma_i, g_i) : (D\Sigma_i', \mathbf{M}_i') \to (D\Sigma_i, \mathbf{M}_i)$ $(i = 1, 2)$ *are compatible with* con *and* con'.
3. *Two extensions* $e_i = (g_i, \gamma_i) : (D\Sigma_i, \mathbf{M}_i) \to (D\Sigma_i', \mathbf{M}_i')$ $(i = 1, 2)$ *are compatible with* con *and* con' *if*
   - x_1 id $x_2 \Rightarrow \gamma_1(x_1)$ id' $\gamma_2(x_2)$ *for all* $x_i \in S_i \cup F_i \cup A_i$ $(i = 1, 2)$ *and*
   - x_1 s $x_2 \Rightarrow g_1(x_1)$ s' $g_2(x_2)$ *for all* $x_i \in CS_i \cup T_i$ $(i = 1, 2)$.
4. *Two sequential refinements* $\mathbf{r}_i = (r_i, \sigma_i) : (D\Sigma_i, \mathbf{M}_i) \to (D\Sigma_i', \mathbf{M}_i')$ $(i = 1, 2)$ *are compatible with* con *and* con' *if*
   - x_1 id $x_2 \Rightarrow \sigma_1(x_1)$ id' $\sigma_2(x_2)$ *for all* $x_i \in S_i \cup F_i \cup A_i$ $(i = 1, 2)$,
   - c_1 s$_{CS}$ $c_2 \Rightarrow r_1(c_1)$ s$'_{CS}$ $r_2(c_2)$ *for all* $c_i \in CS_i$ $(i = 1, 2)$, *and*
   - *if* t_1 s$_T$ t_2

     then there are $t_{1,1}', \ldots, t_{1,n}' \in T_1'$

     and $t_{2,1}', \ldots, t_{2,n}' \in T_2'$

     such that $r_1(t_1) = t_{1,1}'; \ldots; t_{1,n}', \ r_2(t_2) = t_{2,1}'; \ldots; t_{2,n}'$

     and $t_{1,j}'$ s$'_T$ $t_{2,j}'$ *for each* $j \in \{1, \ldots, n\}$

     for all $t_i \in T_i$ $(i = 1, 2)$.

Concerning the compatibility condition for sequential refinements, recall that paths $t_1; \ldots; t_n$ are used to denote transitions in the sequential closure. Since the t_i's may also be idle transitions, i.e., neutral elements w.r.t. the sequential composition, this representation is not unique. Thus the requirement that refinements of synchronous transitions t_1 and t_2 be refined by paths with the same number of transitions ($t_{1,1}'; \ldots; t_{1,n}'$ and $t_{2,1}'; \ldots; t_{2,n}'$) is no restriction, since appropriate idle transitions can be added to the shorter path. The only requirement is that these be synchronous.

The following theorem on the compositionality of developments is formulated in terms of connections and compatibilities as defined above. In Lemma 5.24 below it is shown that this kind of compatibility is equivalent to the usual categorical definition of compatibility w.r.t. all morphisms of given diagrams, where in this case the diagrams are given by the cospans induced by the connection relations. Thus Theorem 5.23 follows from the more general Theorem 5.25.

Theorem 5.23 (Binary Compositionality). *Let*

$$((D\Sigma_1, \mathbf{M}_1), \mathsf{con}, (D\Sigma_2, \mathbf{M}_2)) \ \ and \ \ ((D\Sigma'_1, \mathbf{M}'_1), \mathsf{con}', (D\Sigma'_2, \mathbf{M}'_2))$$

be connections of transformation systems and let $\mathbf{q}_i = (\sigma_i, q_i) : (D\Sigma_i, \mathbf{M}_i) \rightarrow (D\Sigma'_i, \mathbf{M}'_i)$ *for* $i = 1, 2$ *be two morphisms / reductions / extensions / sequential refinements that are compatible with the connections* con *and* con'. *Furthermore, let* $(D\Sigma, \mathbf{M})$ *and* $(D\Sigma', \mathbf{M}')$ *be the corresponding global views with renamings* ρ_i *and* ρ'_i *respectively. Then there is a unique morphism / reduction / extension / sequential refinement* $\mathbf{q} = (\sigma, q) : (D\Sigma, \mathbf{M}) \rightarrow (D\Sigma', \mathbf{M}')$ *such that the corresponding diagrams (see below) commute.*

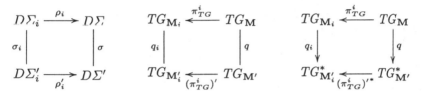

The corresponding lemma is formulated only for morphisms. The other cases (reduction, extension, refinement, implementation) follow immediately from this case.

Lemma 5.24. *Let*

$$((D\Sigma_1, \mathbf{M}_1), \mathsf{con}, (D\Sigma_2, \mathbf{M}_2)) \ \ and \ \ ((D\Sigma'_1, \mathbf{M}'_1), \mathsf{con}', (D\Sigma'_2, \mathbf{M}'_2))$$

be connections of transformation systems and

$$(D\Sigma_1, \mathbf{M}_1) \xrightarrow{\ \mathbf{k}_1 = (\kappa_1, k_1)\ } (D\Sigma_{\mathsf{id}}, \mathbf{M}_{\mathsf{con}}) \xleftarrow{\ \mathbf{k}_2 = (\kappa_2, k_2)\ } (D\Sigma_2, \mathbf{M}_2)$$

and

$$(D\Sigma'_1, \mathbf{M}'_1) \xrightarrow{\ \mathbf{k}_1 = (\kappa'_1, k'_1)\ } (D\Sigma'_{\mathsf{id}'}, \mathbf{M}'_{\mathsf{con}'}) \xleftarrow{\ \mathbf{k}_2 = (\kappa'_2, k'_2)\ } (D\Sigma'_2, \mathbf{M}'_2)$$

their induced cospans.

Each pair of morphisms $\mathbf{h}_i = (\sigma_i, h_i) : (D\Sigma_i, \mathbf{M}_i) \rightarrow (D\Sigma'_i, \mathbf{M}'_i)$, $i = 1, 2$, *that is compatible with* con *and* con' *induces a morphism*

$$\mathbf{h}_{\mathsf{con}} = (\sigma_{\mathsf{id}}, h_{\mathsf{s}}) : (D\Sigma_{\mathsf{id}}, \mathbf{M}_{\mathsf{con}}) \rightarrow (D\Sigma'_{\mathsf{id}'}, \mathbf{M}'_{\mathsf{con}'})$$

with $\mathbf{k}'_i \circ \mathbf{h}_i = \mathbf{h}_{\mathsf{con}} \circ \mathbf{k}_i$ $(i = 1, 2)$.

$$(D\Sigma_1, \mathbf{M}_1) \xrightarrow{\ \mathbf{k}_1 = (\kappa_1, k_1)\ } (D\Sigma_{\mathsf{id}}, \mathbf{M}_{\mathsf{con}}) \xleftarrow{\ \mathbf{k}_2 = (\kappa_2, k_2)\ } (D\Sigma_2, \mathbf{M}_2)$$

$$\mathbf{h}_1 = (\sigma_1, h_1) \Big\downarrow \qquad\qquad \mathbf{h}_{\mathsf{con}} = (\sigma_{\mathsf{id}}, h_s) \Big\downarrow \qquad\qquad \Big\downarrow \mathbf{h}_2 = (\sigma_2, h_2)$$

$$(D\Sigma'_1, \mathbf{M}'_1) \xrightarrow{\ \mathbf{k}'_1 = (\kappa'_1, k'_1)\ } (D\Sigma'_{\mathsf{id}'}, \mathbf{M}'_{\mathsf{con}'}) \xleftarrow{\ \mathbf{k}'_2 = (\kappa'_2, k'_2)\ } (D\Sigma'_2, \mathbf{M}'_2)$$

Proof. The compatibility conditions for morphisms immediately imply that the signature morphism $\sigma_{\mathsf{id}} : D\Sigma'_{\mathsf{id}'} \to D\Sigma_{\mathsf{id}}$, $\sigma_{\mathsf{id}}(x'_1, x'_2) := (\sigma_1(x'_1), \sigma_2(x'_2))$, is well defined and satisfies

$$\kappa_i \circ \sigma_{\mathsf{id}} = \sigma_i \circ \kappa'_i : D\Sigma'_{\mathsf{id}'} \to D\Sigma_i \quad (i = 1, 2).$$

Furthermore the transition graph morphism $h_s : TG_s \to TG'_{s'}$ given by $h_s([x]_s) = [h_i(x)]_{s'}$ if $x \in CS_i \cup T_i$, is well defined and satisfies

$$h_s \circ k_i = k'_i \circ h_i : TG_i \to TG'_{s'} \quad (i = 1, 2).$$

Finally, by definition of $\mathbf{m}_{\mathsf{con}}$ and $\mathbf{m}'_{\mathsf{con}'}$ and since $\mathbf{h}_i$ is a transformation system morphism, we have

$$\begin{aligned}
\mathbf{m}'_{\mathsf{con}'}(h_s([c]_s)) &= \mathbf{m}'_{\mathsf{con}'}([h_i(c)]_{s'}) \\
&= V_{\kappa'_i}(\mathbf{m}'_i(h_i(c))) \\
&= V_{\kappa'_i}(V_{\sigma_i}(\mathbf{m}_i(c))) \\
&= V_{\sigma_{\mathsf{id}}}(V_{\kappa_i}(\mathbf{m}_i(c))) \\
&= V_{\sigma_{\mathsf{id}}}(\mathbf{m}_{\mathsf{con}}([c]_s))
\end{aligned}$$

for each $c \in CS_i, i = 1, 2$. Analogously

$$act^{\mathbf{m}'_{\mathsf{con}'}}_{h_s([t]_{s'})} = \sigma_{\mathsf{id}}^{-1}(act^{\mathbf{m}_{\mathsf{con}}}_{[t]_s})$$

and

$$\sim^{\mathbf{m}'_{\mathsf{con}'}}_{h_s([t]_{s'})} = V_{\sigma_{\mathsf{id}}}(\sim^{\mathbf{m}_{\mathsf{con}}}_{[t]_s})$$

for each $t \in T_i, i = 1, 2$. Thus $\mathbf{h}_{\mathsf{con}}$ is a transformation system morphism.

Now the main theorem for the compositionality of development relations for arbitrary diagrams of transformation systems that have limits is shown. If the local development relations are given by compatible morphisms there is nothing to be shown, since limits are functorial. This means that each family of morphisms that commutes (i.e., is compatible) with the morphisms in the diagram induces a morphism on the global systems. This induced morphism is, moreover, compatible with the projections to the local systems and uniquely determined by this property. The other cases can be reduced to this basic one by putting together the signature morphisms and colimits, and transition graph morphisms and limits, appropriately. For the refinements the compatibility of sequential closure with limits also has to be shown.

Theorem 5.25 (Compositionality of Developments). *Let $D, D' : I \to$* **TF** *be two diagrams of transformation systems such that I is a partial order and the morphisms $D(k), D'(k)$ for all $k : i \to j$ in I are injective. Furthermore, let $((D\Sigma, \mathbf{M}), (\pi_i)_{i \in |I|})$ and $((D\Sigma', \mathbf{M}'), (\pi'_i)_{i \in |I|})$ be limits of D and D' respectively, where $\pi_i = (\kappa_i, \pi^i_{TG})$ and $\pi'_i = (\kappa'_i, (\pi^i_{TG})')$ for $i = 1, 2$, and let $D(i) =: (D\Sigma_i, \mathbf{M}_i)$, $D'(i) =: (D\Sigma'_i, \mathbf{M}'_i)$ for all $i \in |I|$, and $D(k) =: \mathbf{h}_k = (\sigma_k, h_k)$, $D'(k) =: \mathbf{h}'_k = (\sigma'_k, h'_k)$, for all $k : i \to j$ in I.*

1. *Let $r_i = (g_i, \rho_i) : (D\Sigma_i, \mathbf{M}_i) \to (D\Sigma'_i, \mathbf{M}'_i)$ $(i \in |I|)$ be a compatible family of uniform reductions, i.e.,*

$$\rho_i \circ \sigma_k = \sigma'_k \circ \rho_j \text{ and } h_k \circ g_i = g_j \circ h'_k$$

for all $k : i \to j$ in I. Then there is a unique uniform reduction $r = (g, \rho) : (D\Sigma, \mathbf{M}) \to (D\Sigma', \mathbf{M}')$ with

$$\rho \circ \kappa_i = \kappa'_i \circ \rho_i \text{ and } \pi^i_{TG} \circ g = g_i \circ (\pi^i_{TG})'$$

for all $i \in |I|$ (see Figure 5.2).

2. *Let $e_i = (g_i, \rho_i) : (D\Sigma_i, \mathbf{M}_i) \to (D\Sigma'_i, \mathbf{M}'_i)$ $(i \in |I|)$ be a compatible family of uniform extensions, i.e.,*

$$\rho_i \circ \sigma_k = \sigma'_k \circ \rho_j \text{ and } h'_k \circ g_i = g_j \circ h_k$$

for all $k : i \to j$ in I. Then there is a unique uniform extension $e = (g, \rho) : (D\Sigma, \mathbf{M}) \to (D\Sigma', \mathbf{M}')$ with

$$\rho \circ \kappa_i = \kappa'_i \circ \rho_i \text{ and } (\pi^i_{TG})' \circ g = g_i \circ \pi^i_{TG}$$

for all $i \in |I|$.

3. *Let $\mathbf{r}_i = (r_i, \rho_i) : (D\Sigma_i, \mathbf{M}_i) \to (D\Sigma'_i, \mathbf{M}'_i)$ $(i \in |I|)$ be a compatible family of uniform sequential refinements, i.e.,*

$$\rho_i \circ \sigma_k = \sigma'_k \circ \rho_j \text{ and } (h'_k)^* \circ r_i = r_j \circ h_k$$

for all $k : i \to j$ in I. Then there is a unique uniform sequential refinement $\mathbf{r} = (r, \rho) : (D\Sigma, \mathbf{M}) \to (D\Sigma', \mathbf{M}')$ with

$$\rho \circ \kappa_i = \kappa'_i \circ \rho_i \text{ and } (\pi^i_{TG})'^* \circ r = r_i \circ \pi^i_{TG}$$

for all $i \in |I|$.

Proof. 1.   Each reduction $r_i : (D\Sigma_i, \mathbf{M}_i) \to (D\Sigma'_i, \mathbf{M}'_i)$ is a morphism $r_i : (D\Sigma'_i, \mathbf{M}'_i) \to (D\Sigma_i, \mathbf{M}_i)$ in **TF**. Due to the functoriality of limits this induces a unique morphism $r : (D\Sigma', \mathbf{M}') \to (D\Sigma, \mathbf{M})$ in **TF** with the stated properties, which is a reduction $r : (D\Sigma, \mathbf{M}) \to (D\Sigma', \mathbf{M}')$.

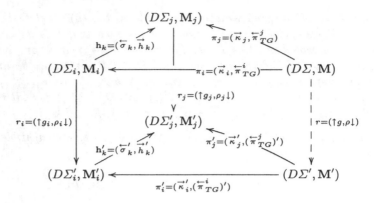

Fig. 5.2. Composition of uniform reductions

2.   The limits

$$((D\Sigma, \mathbf{M}), (\pi_i)_{i\in|I|}) \text{ and } ((D\Sigma', \mathbf{M}'), (\pi'_i)_{i\in|I|})$$

are given by colimits $(D\Sigma, (\kappa_i)_{i\in|I|})$ and $(D\Sigma', (\kappa'_i)_{i\in|I|})$ of signatures and limits $(TG_{\mathbf{M}}, (\pi^i_{TG})_{i\in|I|})$ and $(TG_{\mathbf{M}'}, ((\pi^i_{TG})')_{i\in|I|})$ of transition graphs. Thus there are a unique signature morphism $\sigma : D\Sigma \to D\Sigma'$ and a unique transition graph morphism $g : TG_{\mathbf{M}} \to TG_{\mathbf{M}'}$ that satisfy the equations. Furthermore, for each $x \in TG_{\mathbf{M}}$,

$$\begin{aligned}
& \mathbb{D}_{\kappa_i} \circ \mathbb{D}_\rho(\mathbf{m}'(g(x))) && (\rho \circ \kappa_i = \kappa'_i \circ \rho_i) \\
= {} & \mathbb{D}_{\rho_i} \circ \mathbb{D}_{\kappa'_i}(\mathbf{m}'(g(x))) && (\pi'_i = (\kappa'_i, (\pi^i_{TG})') \text{ is a } \mathbf{TF}\text{-morphism}) \\
= {} & \mathbb{D}_{\rho_i}(\mathbf{m}'_\mathbf{i}((\pi^i_{TG})'(g(x)))) && ((\pi^i_{TG})' \circ g = g_i \circ \pi^i_{TG}) \\
= {} & \mathbb{D}_{\rho_i}(\mathbf{m}'_\mathbf{i}(g_i(\pi^i_{TG}(x)))) && (e = (g_i, \rho_i) \text{ is an extension}) \\
= {} & \mathbf{m}_i(\pi^i_{TG}(x))
\end{aligned}$$

for all $i \in |I|$.

Since $\mathbf{m}(x)$ is given by the amalgamation $\mathbf{m}(x) = \sum_I \mathbf{m}_i(\pi^i_{TG}(x))$ in $\mathbb{D}_{D\Sigma}$ we obtain

$$\mathbb{D}_\rho(\mathbf{m}'(g(x))) = \mathbf{m}(x) ,$$

i.e., $e = (g, \rho) : (D\Sigma, \mathbf{M}) \to (D\Sigma', \mathbf{M}')$ is an extension.

3.   To reduce the assertion to the one of 2 it suffices to show that the sequential closure $(TG^*_{\mathbf{M}'}, (\pi^i_{TG}{}'^*)_{i\in|I|})$ of the limit of the diagram of local transition graphs $TG_{\mathbf{M}_i}$ coincides (up to isomorphism) with the limit $(TG, (p_i)_{i\in|I|})$ of the sequential closures $TG^*_{\mathbf{M}_i}$ and h^*_k of the diagram of local transition graphs and morphisms.

For that purpose the standard constructions for limits are used:

$$TG_{\mathbf{M'}} = (CS_{\mathbf{M'}}, T_{\mathbf{M'}}, in_{\mathbf{M'}}, id_{\mathbf{M'}}) \quad \text{with}$$

$$CS_{\mathbf{M'}} = \{(c_i)_{i \in |I|} \mid \forall i \in |I| \; c_i \in CS_i, \; \forall k : i \to j \text{ in } I \; h_k(c_i) = c_j\}$$

$$T_{\mathbf{M'}} = \{(t_i)_{i \in |I|} \mid \forall i \in |I| \; t_i \in T_i, \; \forall k : i \to j \text{ in } I \; h_k(t_i) = t_j\}$$

$$in_{\mathbf{M'}} = (in_i)_{i \in |I|}$$

$$id_{\mathbf{M'}}((c_i)_{i \in |I|}) = (id_i(c_i))_{i \in |I|}$$

and

$$TG = (CS, T, in, id) \quad \text{with}$$

$$CS = \{(c_i)_{i \in |I|} \mid \forall i \in |I| \; c_i \in CS_i, \; \forall k : i \to j \text{ in } I \; h_k(c_i) = c_j\}$$

$$= CS_{\mathbf{M'}}$$

$$T = \{(p_i)_{i \in |I|} \mid \forall i \in |I| \; p_i \in T_i^*, \; \forall k : i \to j \text{ in } I \; h_k^*(p_i) = p_j\}$$

$$in = (in_i)_{i \in |I|} = in_{\mathbf{M'}}$$

$$id((c_i)_{i \in |I|}) = (id_i(c_i))_{i \in |I|} = id_{\mathbf{M'}}((c_i)_{i \in |I|}) .$$

It remains to be shown that there are bijections on the sets of transitions. Let the mapping $f_T : T_{\mathbf{M'}}^* \to T$ be defined by

$$(t_i^1)_{i \in |I|}; \ldots ; (t_i^n)_{i \in |I|} \; \mapsto \; (t_i^1; \ldots ; t_i^n)_{i \in |I|} .$$

To define its inverse let $(p_i)_{i \in |I|} \in T$. For each $k : i \to j$ in I we have $h_k^*(p_i) = p_j$, whence there are representations $p_i = t_i^1; \ldots, t_i^{n_i}$ and $p_j = t_j^1; \ldots, t_j^{n_j}$ with $n_i = n_j$. If i and j are not connected by morphisms in I, then—using appropriate idle transitions—there are also representations $p_i = t_i^1; \ldots, t_i^{n_i}$ and $p_j = t_j^1; \ldots, t_j^{n_j}$ with $n_i = n_j$. Thus the mapping

$$(p_i)_{i \in |I|} \; \mapsto \; (t_i^1)_{i \in |I|}; \ldots ; (t_i^n)_{i \in |I|}$$

with $n = n_i = n_j$ and the presentations of p_i as given above are well defined and yield the desired inverse f_T^{-1}.

Example 5.26 (Comparison of the Alternating Bit Protocol Specifications). Trying to apply the compositionality Theorem 5.25 to the alternating bit protocol specifications and their semantic relations discussed in Examples 4.14 and 4.30 reveals the following incompatibility between them. There is a reduction $\mathbf{ch} : \mathbf{CCS}_{CH} \to \mathbf{U}_{CH}$ (i.e. a morphism $\mathbf{ch} : \mathbf{U}_{CH} \to \mathbf{CCS}_{CH}$) and a refinement $\mathbf{r}_S : \mathbf{CCS}_S \to \mathbf{U}_S$. But since these are different kinds of relations none of the assertions of the theorem applies to both comparisons. As already indicated in Examples 4.14 and 4.30, there is no reduction $\mathbf{U}_{CH} \to \mathbf{CCS}_{CH}$ and no refinement $\mathbf{U}_S \to \mathbf{CCS}_S$. Furthermore, there is also no morphism $\mathbf{s} : \mathbf{U}_S \to \mathbf{CCS}_S$, because $\mathbf{U}_S$ has much more observable transitions than $\mathbf{CCS}_S$. In particular, the state mappings $\langle b, a, s, c \rangle \mapsto s_{b, first(a)}$ and $\langle b, a, s, c \rangle \mapsto s'_{b, first(a)}$ whose data parts hide the internal queues of the UNITY sender cannot be extended to transition graph morphisms, because in a state $S_{b,d}$ the CCS sender refuses all acknowledgements and in a state $S'_{b,d}$ it refuses any sending. For the same reasons as discussed in Example 4.14 there is also no refinement $\mathbf{CCS}_{CH} \rightarrow \mathbf{U}_{CH}$. Thus there is altogether no pair of development relations of the same kind either from the CCS to the UNITY models or in the reverse direction. But what does this mean?

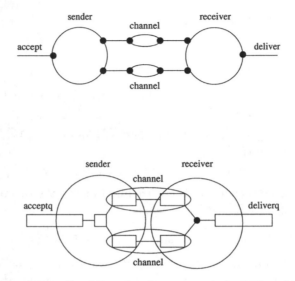

Fig. 5.3. Alternating bit protocol components in CCS and UNITY

Consider again the partitions of the two specifications and the distributions of the behaviours onto the components, for instance the *send* and *in* actions. In the CCS specification *send* and *in* are externally observable actions of the sender and channel, respectively, that are synchronised when connecting the two components. In contrast, the connection of the UNITY sender and channel is given by sharing the variables *sendq* and *inq*, thus also synchronising their *enq* and *deq* operations. The corresponding synchronisation pairs of transitions are *offer* and *in*, *send* and *transmit*, and *send* and *lose*. Thus an internal action of one component—transmitting an element from the input to the output queue of the channel, or losing an element—is synchronised with an observable action of the other one, sending an element. Furthermore, *transmit* will be synchronised with the read action of the receiver when it is connected to the channel at its output port, i.e., at the end some actions of the sender and the receiver are synchronised, as opposed to the CCS model where they are decoupled. Concerning the visibility of the composed UNITY system, all queues except the *accept* queue of the sender and the *deliver* queue of the receiver are internal variables of the sender or the receiver. Since the channels act on them they cannot be isolated entirely as components as in the CCS model (see Figure 5.3). That means therfore, that the distribution of the behaviour onto the components in the UNITY specification is also significantly different from the one in the CCS specification. Thus there *cannot* be a compositional comparison *in this example*.

The distribution of the behaviour onto the components and the mediated synchronisation of (internal) actions of the sender and the receiver in the UNITY specification partly depend on the fact that it has been designed as a whole, not in components. On the other hand, the shared variable communication model induces design decisions that may have an impact on several components. For instance, within the sender specification there is no need to model the variable *sendq* that holds the bit/data pairs that are communicated to the channel as a queue. This typing is induced by its sharing with the input variable of the channel, which must be a queue in order to allow for permanent writing to the channel input. Thus a more compositional design of a shared variable interconnection would lead to a non-trivial alteration of the given specification that would also significantly influence its behaviour.

5.7 Morphisms of Transformation Systems with Distributed Data

Up to now morphisms of transformation systems have been defined as morphisms of their transition graphs that *preserve* the data space labels, up to the restriction to the smaller data space signature via the forgetful functor. (Among others this has led to the restrictions on the composition of transformation systems (Theorem 5.18) that guarantee that the action sets are preserved by the projections from a global system to the local components.) In this section a more general definition of morphisms is given that allows more flexibility w.r.t. the data space labels. In a *d-morphism* the data states belonging to control states that are mapped to each other need not coincide, but may be related by a homomorphism. Analogously, the action sets and tracking relations may be subsets of their corresponding counterparts.

This generalisation allows the composition of transformation systems that have different carrier sets (data sets) and functions (function definitions) also in corresponding (synchronous) control states, as opposed to the composition condition in the previous sections, where identified sorts and functions must be identical in all components. This means in the more general case, that even the data elements of one sort may be distributed over the local components. Consider for example a family of Petri nets that should be composed. If their data states (markings) are defined as algebras with sorts of places and transitions, then each local Petri net will have different carrier sets of places and transitions. Using morphisms this fact would forbid their composition. With d-morphisms, however, they could be related by appropriate mappings. Analogous to the data states, actions may occur in one component but not in another, although they are synchronised. In the global view the unions of these sets, functions, and actions are taken then.

Considered as development relations d-morphisms realise a finer *part of* relation between transformation systems than morphisms, in that the target of the mapping may have smaller data states, action sets, and tracking relations. A d-morphism $\mathbf{h} : \mathbf{M} \to \mathbf{N}$ specifies how the system $\mathbf{N}$ contributes to the behaviour of $\mathbf{M}$ in that it indicates which parts of the data level of $\mathbf{M}$ are covered by $\mathbf{N}$ within each carrier set, function, and action set. To define this the transition graph of $\mathbf{M}$ is mapped to the transition graph of $\mathbf{N}$, and then for each state c of $\mathbf{M}$ a homomorphism h_c from the underlying data state of $h(c)$ in $\mathbf{N}$ to the data state of c in $\mathbf{M}$ is given (e.g., an inclusion) that represents the contribution of $\mathbf{N}$ to this state. Furthermore, each pair of state homomorphisms h_c and h_d corresponding to a transition $t : c \to d$ in $\mathbf{M}$ must map the action set and tracking relation of $h(t)$ in $\mathbf{N}$ to subsets of the corresponding action set and tracking relation of t in $\mathbf{M}$ respectively (see Figure 5.4). If $\mathbf{M}$ is composed of a collection of systems $\mathbf{N}_i$, then the corresponding d-morphisms $\mathbf{h}_i : \mathbf{M} \to \mathbf{N}_i$ act as projections from the global behaviour to the local components as above. In the construction of compositions-by-limits in this more general setting the data space parts are then composed using colimits of partial algebras, action sets and tracking relations instead of amalgamations.

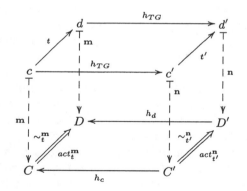

Fig. 5.4. D-morphism of transformation systems

D-morphisms are defined first within a local category $\mathbf{TF}(D\Sigma)$ of transformation systems of one given data space signature $D\Sigma$. The global category is introduced in the next section.

Definition 5.27 (D-Morphism). *Let $D\Sigma$ be a data space signature and $\mathbf{M} = (TG_{\mathbf{M}}, \mathbf{m})$ and $\mathbf{N} = (TG_{\mathbf{N}}, \mathbf{n})$ be $D\Sigma$-transformation systems with $TG_{\mathbf{M}} = (CS, T, in, id)$. A $D\Sigma$-d-morphism $H = (h_{TG}, h_{St}) : \mathbf{M} \to \mathbf{N}$ is given by*

- *a transition graph morphism $h_{TG} : TG_{\mathbf{M}} \to TG_{\mathbf{N}}$ and*
- *a family of Σ-homomorphisms $h_{St} = (h_c : \mathbf{n}(h_{TG}(c)) \to \mathbf{m}(c))_{c \in CS}$,*

- such that $(h_c \times h_d)(\mathbf{n}(h(t))) \subseteq \mathbf{m}(t)$ for each $t : c \to d$ in $TG_{\mathbf{M}}$.

In more detail the latter condition can be stated as

$$a(h_c(\bar{c}); h_d(\bar{d})) \in act_t^{\mathbf{m}} \text{ for each } a(\bar{c}; \bar{d}) \in act_{h_{TG}(t)}^{\mathbf{n}}$$

and

$$h_c(\bar{c}) \sim_t^{\mathbf{m}} h_d(\bar{d}) \text{ whenever } \bar{c} \sim_{h_{TG}(t)}^{\mathbf{n}} \bar{d}$$

for all $a \in A_{w,w'}$, $t : c \to d \in TG_{\mathbf{M}}$, $\bar{c} \in \mathbf{n}(h(c))_w, \bar{d} \in \mathbf{n}(h(d))_{w'}$.

Transition graph morphisms and homomorphisms of partial algebras can be composed, and these compositions obviously also preserve actions and tracking relations. Moreover, there are (the component-wise) identities w.r.t. this composition. We thus obtain categories of transformation systems with d-morphisms that will serve as frames for the local composition operations with distributed data.

Definition and Fact 5.28 (Data Category). Let $D\Sigma$ be a data space signature. The category $\mathbf{TF}^d(D\Sigma)$ is given by the class of all $D\Sigma$–transformation systems as objects and the $D\Sigma$-d-morphisms. Composition and identities are inherited from $\mathbf{TG}$ and $\mathbf{PAlg}(\Sigma)$.

The category $\mathbf{TF}(D\Sigma)$ is obviously a subcategory of $\mathbf{TF}^d(D\Sigma)$, whose morphisms have identities as data state morphisms $h_c = id_{\mathbf{m}(c)} : \mathbf{n}(h_{TG}(c)) \to \mathbf{m}(c)$.

The subcategory of $\mathbf{TF}^d(D\Sigma)$ given by the d-morphisms whose data state homomorphisms are isomorphisms is equivalent to $\mathbf{TF}(D\Sigma)$, but allows the preservation of data space labels *up to isomorphism*. Thus it is more flexible than $\mathbf{TF}(D\Sigma)$ but has the same categorical properties. Note that the equivalence requires a choice of representatives of equivalence classes of isomorphic algebras.

Analogous to the composition of transformation systems as discussed above, now local transformation systems are composed by taking limits of transition graphs, but colimits (pushouts, coproducts) instead of amalgamations of the data states (partial algebras), action sets, and tracking relations are used. (Coproducts and pushouts of partial algebras have been discussed in Section 4.4 for the definition of the parallel closure of transformation systems. Under certain compatibility conditions they are given by the unions of the carrier sets and the partial functions of the two algebras respectively.)

In Theorem 5.30 below it is shown that all limits of transformation systems connected via d-morphisms exist. Before that an example is given, however, that shows how the local data space parts are combined via coproducts of partial algebras.

Example 5.29. As an example of the parallel composition (without synchronisation, but) with composition of data states by coproducts, consider the following extension of the *program* example introduced in the Examples 2.3, 2.5, and 2.7. It models pointers to natural numbers and their incrementation.

First, a second designated pointer is introduced, which yields the signature

p,q-prog = **nat** +
sorts pointer
funs p,q : → pointer
      ! : pointer → nat
acts inc : pointer, nat

Then two *p,q-prog*-transformation systems $\mathbf{Y} = (TG_{\mathbf{Y}}, \mathbf{y})$ and $\mathbf{Z} = (TG_{\mathbf{Z}}, \mathbf{z})$ are constructed similarly to the *prog*-model $\mathbf{X}$ given in Example 2.7. Each one has access to one of the two pointers and increments its value with its local action *inc*. That means the set of pointers is distributed to the two components, and—correspondingly—the dereferencing function (environment) is also distributed. The corresponding data states Y_n and Z_m for $n, m \in I\!N$ are the partial $\Sigma_{p,q\text{-}prog}$-algebras given by

	Y_n	Z_m
nat	$I\!N$	$I\!N$
pointer	$\{Y\}$	$\{Z\}$
p	Y	$-$
q	$-$	Z
!	$Y \mapsto n$	$Z \mapsto m$

The transition graphs $TG_{\mathbf{Y}}$ and $TG_{\mathbf{Z}}$ are defined like the one of $\mathbf{X}$:

$$CS_{\mathbf{Y}} = CS_{\mathbf{Z}} = I\!N \cup \{\Delta\}$$

$$T_{\mathbf{Y}}(n, n+k) = T_{\mathbf{Z}}(n, n+k) = \begin{cases} \{k\} & (k > 0) \\ \{0, idle\} & (k = 0) \end{cases}$$

$$T_{\mathbf{Y}}(\Delta, n) = T_{\mathbf{Z}}(\Delta, n) = \begin{cases} \{init\} & (n = 0) \\ \emptyset & (n > 0) \end{cases} .$$

$$T_{\mathbf{Y}}(n, \Delta) = T_{\mathbf{Z}}(n, \Delta) = \emptyset$$

The data level is given by

	Y	**Z**
data states	$\mathbf{y}(n) = Y_n$	$\mathbf{z}(n) = Z_n$
	$\mathbf{y}(\Delta) = \emptyset$	$\mathbf{z}(\Delta) = \emptyset$
actions	$act_k^{\mathbf{y}} = \{inc(Y, k)\}$	$act_k^{\mathbf{z}} = \{inc(Z, k)\}$
	$act_{idle}^{\mathbf{y}} = \emptyset$	$act_{idle}^{\mathbf{z}} = \emptyset$
	$act_{init}^{\mathbf{y}} = \emptyset$	$act_{init}^{\mathbf{z}} = \emptyset$
track. rel.s	$\sim_k^{\mathbf{y}} = (id_{I\!N}, id_{\{Y\}})$	$\sim_k^{\mathbf{z}} = (id_{I\!N}, id_{\{Z\}})$
	$\sim_{idle}^{\mathbf{y}} = (id_{I\!N}, id_{\{Y\}})$	$\sim_{idle}^{\mathbf{z}} = (id_{I\!N}, id_{\{Z\}})$
	$\sim_{init}^{\mathbf{y}} = \emptyset$	$\sim_{init}^{\mathbf{z}} = \emptyset$

The systems $\mathbf{Y}$ and $\mathbf{Z}$ should be composed now in such a way that they still manipulate their pointers independently of each other. Only the initialisations should be synchronised, i.e., in the initial state of the composed system both pointers should have contents 0. This is achieved by the synchronisation relation $\mathsf{s} = (\mathsf{s}_{CS}, \mathsf{s}_T)$ on $TG_{\mathbf{Y}}$ and $TG_{\mathbf{Z}}$ given by

$$
\begin{array}{lll}
\Delta & \mathsf{s}_{CS} & \Delta \\
n & \mathsf{s}_{CS} & m \quad (n, m \in I\!\!N) \\[4pt]
init & \mathsf{s}_T & init \\
idle & \mathsf{s}_{I'} & idle \\
k & \mathsf{s}_T & idle \quad (k \in I\!\!N) \\
idle & \mathsf{s}_T & l \quad (l \in I\!\!N) \\
k & \mathsf{s}_T & l \quad (k, l \in I\!\!N) .
\end{array}
$$

Categorically this synchronisation is represented by the mappings $h_{\mathbf{Y}}$: $TG_{\mathbf{Y}} \to TG_{\mathbf{S}}$ and $h_{\mathbf{Z}} : TG_{\mathbf{Z}} \to TG_{\mathbf{S}}$ given by

$$
TG_{\mathbf{S}} : \quad \circlearrowleft \Delta \xrightarrow{\ init\ } * \circlearrowright
$$

$$
\begin{aligned}
h_{\mathbf{Y}} \quad &: \Delta \mapsto \Delta, n \mapsto * \quad (n \in I\!\!N) \\
&: idle \mapsto idle, init \mapsto init, n \mapsto idle_* .
\end{aligned}
$$

The morphism $h_{\mathbf{Z}}$ is defined analogously.

Now let $N = (I\!\!N, \emptyset, \emptyset, \emptyset, \emptyset)$ be the partial $\Sigma_{p,q\text{-}prog}$-algebra with all entries except the natural number part empty. Using it for the second data state, the transition graph $TG_{\mathbf{S}}$ with the labels $\mathsf{s}(\Delta) = \emptyset$, $\mathsf{s}(*) = N$, and $\mathsf{s}(init) = (\emptyset, \emptyset)$ yields a $p, q - prog$-transformation system $\mathbf{S} = (TG_{\mathbf{S}}, \mathsf{s})$. Moreover, $h_{\mathbf{Y}}$ and $h_{\mathbf{Z}}$ together with the homomorphisms $h_{\Delta}^{\mathbf{Y}} = h_{\Delta}^{\mathbf{Z}} = \emptyset$ and the inclusions $h_*^{\mathbf{Y}}$: $N \to Y_n$ and $h_*^{\mathbf{Z}} : N \to Z_m$ yield d-morphisms $\mathbf{h}_{\mathbf{Y}} : \mathbf{Y} \to \mathbf{S}$ and $\mathbf{h}_{\mathbf{Z}} : \mathbf{Z} \to \mathbf{S}$.

The composition $\mathbf{Y} \times_{\mathbf{h}_{\mathbf{Y}}, \mathbf{h}_{\mathbf{Z}}} \mathbf{Z} =: \mathbf{P} = (TG_{\mathbf{P}}, \mathbf{p})$ of the systems $\mathbf{Y}$ and $\mathbf{Z}$, given by the pullback of $\mathbf{h}_{\mathbf{Y}}$ and $\mathbf{h}_{\mathbf{Z}}$ in $\mathbf{TF}^d(p, q\text{-}prog)$, is then given by the pullbacks of their transition graphs, for each control state the coproduct of the component data states, and for each transition the union of their action sets and tracking relations. Explicitly this means $\mathbf{P}$ is given as in Table 5.2, where the partial $\Sigma_{p,q\text{-}prog}$-algebras $Y_n + Z_m$ are given by

$$
Y_n + Z_m|_{\text{nat}} = I\!\!N \ , \ (Y_n + Z_m)_{pointer} = \{Y, Z\} \ ,
$$

$$
p^{Y_n + Z_m} = Y \ , \qquad q^{Y_n + Z_m} = Z \ ,
$$

$$
!^{Y_n + Z_m}(Y) = n \ , \qquad !^{Y_n + Z_m}(Z) = m \ ,
$$

i.e., $Y_n + Z_m$ is the state in which Y has the value n and Z has the value m. Note that the shared function $!^{Y_n + Z_m} : \{Y, Z\} \to I\!\!N$ (the environment) is indeed given by the union of the local environments $!^{Y_n} : \{Y\} \to I\!\!N$ and $!^{Z_m} : \{Z\} \to I\!\!N$. A part of the behaviour of $\mathbf{P}$ is depicted in Figure 5.5.

$$CS_{\mathbf{P}} = (I\!N \times I\!N) \cup \{(\Delta, \Delta)\}$$

$$T_{\mathbf{P}}((\Delta, \Delta), (\Delta, \Delta)) = T_{\mathbf{Y}}(\Delta, \Delta) \times T_{\mathbf{Z}}(\Delta, \Delta) = \{(idle, idle)\}$$

$$T_{\mathbf{P}}((\Delta, \Delta), (n, m)) = T_{\mathbf{Y}}(\Delta, n) \times T_{\mathbf{Z}}(\Delta, m)$$
$$= \begin{cases} \{(init, init)\} & (n = m = 0) \\ \emptyset & \text{else} \end{cases}$$

$$T_{\mathbf{P}}((n, m), (n + k, m + l)) = T_{\mathbf{Y}}(n, n + k) \times T_{\mathbf{Z}}(m, m + l)$$
$$= \begin{cases} \{(k, l)\} & (k > 0, l > 0) \\ \{(0, l), (idle, l)\} & (k = 0, l > 0) \\ \{(k, 0), (k, idle)\} & (k > 0, l = 0) \\ \{(0, 0), (0, idle), (idle, 0), (idle, idle)\} & (k = 0, l = 0) \end{cases}$$

$$T_{\mathbf{P}}((n, m), (\Delta, \Delta)) = T_{\mathbf{Y}}(n, \Delta) \times T_{\mathbf{Z}}(m, \Delta) = \emptyset$$

$$\begin{aligned} \mathbf{p}(n, m) &= Y_n + Z_m \\ \mathbf{p}(\Delta, \Delta) &= \emptyset \end{aligned}$$

$$\begin{aligned} act^{\mathbf{P}}_{(k,l)} &= act^k_y \cup act^l_z = \{inc(Y, k), inc(Z, l)\} \\ act^{\mathbf{P}}_{(k,idle)} &= act^k_y = \{inc(Y, k)\} \\ act^{\mathbf{P}}_{(idle,l)} &= act^l_z = \{inc(Z, l)\} \\ act^{\mathbf{P}}_{(init,init)} &= \emptyset \end{aligned}$$

$$\begin{aligned} \sim^{\mathbf{P}}_{(k,l)} &= (id_{I\!N}, id_{\{Y,Z\}}) \\ \sim^{\mathbf{P}}_{(k,idle)} &= \sim^{\mathbf{P}}_{(idle,l)} = \emptyset \\ \sim^{\mathbf{P}}_{(init,init)} &= \emptyset \end{aligned}$$

Table 5.2. Explicit definition of the product system **P**

The following theorem shows that in a category of transformation systems with d-morphisms all limits exist, without the constraints that were necessary in Section 5.3.

Theorem 5.30 (Local Limits). *For each data space signature $D\Sigma$ the category $\mathbf{TF}^d(D\Sigma)$ is complete.*

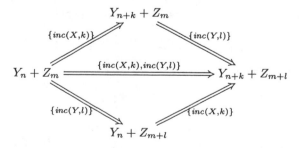

Fig. 5.5. The parallel composition $\mathbf{P} = \mathbf{Y} \times \mathbf{Z}$

Proof. Let $D : I \to \mathbf{TF}^d(D\Sigma)$ be a diagram of $D\Sigma$-transformation systems and d-morphisms with $D(i) =: \mathbf{M}_i = (TG_{\mathbf{M}_i}, m_i)$ and $D(k) =: H_k = (h_{TG}^k, (h_{c_i}^k)_{c_i \in CS_i})$. A limit $(\mathbf{M}, (\pi_i)_{i \in |I|})$ of D in $\mathbf{TF}^d(D\Sigma)$, with $\mathbf{M} = (TG_{\mathbf{M}}, \mathbf{m})$, can be constructed as follows (cf. Figure 5.6).

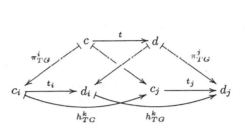

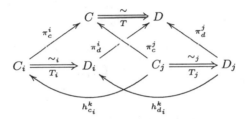

Fig. 5.6. Limit of transformation systems

Let $(TG_{\mathbf{M}}, (\pi_{TG}^i)_{i \in |I|})$ be a limit of the transition graphs $TG_{\mathbf{M}_i}$. For any control state c in $TG_{\mathbf{M}}$ the data state $C = \mathbf{m}(c)$ is defined as the colimit $(C, (\pi_c^i)_{i \in |I|})$ of the diagram $D_c : I^{op} \to \mathbf{PAlg}(\Sigma)$, given by $D_c(i) = m_i(\pi_{TG}^i(c))$ and $D_c(k : i \to j) = h_{c_i}^k : m_j(\pi_{TG}^j(c)) \to m_i(\pi_{TG}^i(c))$.

The tracking relations and action sets are given by the corresponding unions, which are colimits in the powersets considered as partial order categories. That means, for any $t : c \to d$ in $TG_{\mathbf{M}}$,

$$\sim_t^{\mathbf{m}} = \bigcup_{i \in |I|} (\pi_c^i \times \pi_d^i)(\sim_{\pi_{TG}^i(t)}^{m_i})$$

$$act_t^{\mathbf{m}} = \bigcup_{i \in |I|} (\pi_c^i \times \pi_d^i)(act_{\pi_{TG}^i(t)}^{m_i}) .$$

This completes the definition of the $D\Sigma$-transformation system $\mathbf{M} = (TG_{\mathbf{M}}, \mathbf{m})$. The d-morphisms $\Pi_i : \mathbf{M} \to \mathbf{M}_i$ $(i \in |I|)$ are given by $\Pi_i = (\pi_{TG}^i, (\pi_c^i)_{c \in CS})$. These preserve the action sets and tracking relations by definition.

Now the universal property has to be shown. Let $F_i = (f_{TG}^i, f_{St}^i) : \mathbf{N} \to \mathbf{M}_i$ $(i \in |I|)$ be a family of d-morphisms with $F_j = H_k \circ F_i$ for all $k : i \to j$

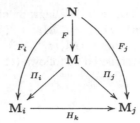

Fig. 5.7. Comparison morphism for the limit **M**

in I (see Figure 5.7). Since $(TG_{\mathbf{M}}, (\pi_{TG}^i)_{i \in |I|})$ is a limit of the transition graphs there is a unique transition graph morphism $f_{TG} : TG_{\mathbf{N}} \to TG_{\mathbf{M}}$ with $\pi_{TG}^i \circ f_{TG} = f_{TG}^i$ for all $i \in |I|$. For any control state c_N in $TG_{\mathbf{N}}$ the homomorphisms

$$f_{c_N}^i : \mathbf{m}_i(f_{TG}^i(c_N)) \to \mathbf{n}(c_N) \ (i \in |I|)$$

yield a cocone (natural transformation) from the diagram $D_{f_{TG}(c_N)}$ to $\mathbf{n}(c_N)$; thus there is also a unique Σ-homomorphism

$$f_{c_N} : \mathbf{m}(f_{TG}(c_N)) \to \mathbf{n}(c_N)$$

with $f_{c_N} \circ \pi_{f_{TG}(c_N)}^i = f_{c_N}^i$ for all $i \in |I|$. Since $(f_{c_N}^i \times f_{d_N}^i)(\mathbf{m}_i(f_{TG}^i(t_N))) \subseteq \mathbf{n}(t_N)$ for all $t_N : c_N \to d_N$ in $TG_{\mathbf{N}}$ and $i \in |I|$ also

$$
\begin{aligned}
&(f_{c_N} \times f_{d_N})(\mathbf{m}(f_{TG}(t_N))) \\
&= (f_{c_N} \times f_{d_N})(\textstyle\bigcup_{i \in |I|}(\pi_{f_{TG}(c_N)}^i \times \pi_{f_{TG}(d_N)}^i))(\mathbf{m}_i(f_{TG}^i(t_N)))) \\
&= \textstyle\bigcup_{i \in |I|}(f_{c_N}^i \times f_{d_N}^i)(\mathbf{m}_i(f_{TG}^i(t_N))) \\
&\subseteq \mathbf{n}(t_N) \,,
\end{aligned}
$$

i.e., $F = (f_{TG}, (f_{c_N})_{c_N \in CS_{\mathbf{N}}}) : \mathbf{N} \to \mathbf{M}$ is a d-morphism.

Compatibility with the projections and uniqueness w.r.t. the property $\Pi_i \circ F = F_i$ for all $i \in |I|$ follows from the corresponding properties of the components f_{TG} and f_{St}.

5.8 Construction of General Compositions by Global Limits

The two approaches of composition-by-limits with amalgamation of data states and composition-by-limits with distributed data and local colimits of data states can be subsumed in a global category of transformation systems that combines the corresponding definitions of morphisms. As a prerequisite the extension of the forgetful functor of transformation systems (see Definition 4.17) has to be extended to d–morphisms.

Definition and Fact 5.31 (Forgetful Functor). Let $\sigma = (\sigma_\Sigma, \sigma_A) : D\Sigma \to D\Sigma'$ be a data space signature morphism. The *forgetful functor*

$$V_\sigma^d : \mathbf{TF}^d(D\Sigma') \to \mathbf{TF}^d(D\Sigma)$$

is defined by

$$V_\sigma^d(\mathbf{M}') = (TG_{\mathbf{M}'}, I\!D_\sigma \circ \mathbf{m}')$$
$$V_\sigma^d(H') = (h'_{TG}, (V_{\sigma_\Sigma}(h'_{c'}))_{c' \in CS'})$$

for $H' = (h'_{TG}, (h'_{c'})_{c' \in CS'})$.

Proof. It is to be shown that V_σ is well defined on $D\Sigma'$-d-morphisms.

Since the transition graphs of $\mathbf{M}'$ and $V_\sigma(\mathbf{M}')$ coincide the transition graph component h'_{TG} of $V_\sigma(H')$ is well defined, and also the family $(V_{\sigma_\Sigma}(h'_{c'}))_{c' \in CS'}$ has the right functionality. Furthermore

$$V_{\sigma_\Sigma}(\sim_{h'_{TG}(t')}^{\mathbf{n}'})_s = (\sim_{h'_{TG}(t')}^{\mathbf{n}'})_{\sigma_\Sigma(s)} \subseteq (\sim_{t'}^{\mathbf{m}'})_{\sigma_\Sigma(s)} = V_{\sigma_\Sigma}(\sim_{t'}^{\mathbf{m}'})_s$$

and

$$act_{h'_{TG}}^{\mathbf{n}'} \subseteq act_{t'}^{\mathbf{m}'} \Rightarrow \sigma_A^{-1}(act_{h'_{TG}}^{\mathbf{n}'}) \subseteq \sigma_A^{-1}(act_{t'}^{\mathbf{m}'})$$

thus

$$V_\sigma(\mathbf{n}'(h'_{TG}(t'))) \subseteq V_\sigma(\mathbf{m}'(t')) ,$$

i.e., $V_\sigma^d(H')$ is a $D\Sigma$-d-morphism. Preservation of composition and identities follow from the corresponding properties of V_{σ_Σ}.

When putting signature morphisms and d-morphisms of local transformation systems together in the global category, the opposite directions of transition graph morphisms and data space morphisms have to be taken into account again. Since signatures are composed by colimits they occur in a global transformation system morphism in the reverse direction (see Figure 5.8).

Definition and Fact 5.32 (Global Category with d-Morphisms). The *global category of transformation systems with d-morphisms*, denoted by $\mathbf{TF}^d$, is defined as follows.

- Its objects are pairs $(D\Sigma, \mathbf{M})$, where $D\Sigma$ is a data space signature and $\mathbf{M}$ is a $D\Sigma$-transformation system.
- Its morphisms $\mathbf{H} : (D\Sigma, \mathbf{M}) \to (D\Sigma', \mathbf{N}')$ are pairs $\mathbf{H} = (\sigma, H)$, where $\sigma : D\Sigma' \to D\Sigma$ is a data space signature morphism (in the reverse direction) and $H : V_\sigma(\mathbf{M}) \to \mathbf{N}'$ is a $D\Sigma'$-d-morphism.
- Composition of morphisms $(\sigma, H) : (D\Sigma, \mathbf{M}) \to (D\Sigma', \mathbf{N}')$ and $(\sigma', H') : (D\Sigma', \mathbf{N}') \to (D\Sigma'', \mathbf{K}'')$ is given by

$$(\sigma', H') \circ (\sigma, H) = (\sigma \circ \sigma', H' \circ V_\sigma(H)) .$$

- The identities are given by $Id_{(D\Sigma, \mathbf{M})} = (id_{D\Sigma}, id_{TG_\mathbf{M}})$.

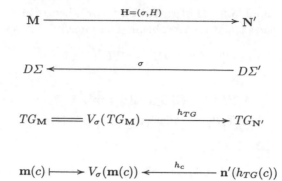

Fig. 5.8. Global morphism $\mathbf{H} = (\sigma, H) : (TG_{\mathbf{M}}, \mathbf{m}) \to (TG_{\mathbf{N}'}, \mathbf{n}')$

Proof. Taking the dualisation into account, this construction corresponds to the usual flattening construction of an indexed category $TF : \mathbf{DSig} \to \mathbf{Cat}^{op}$, given by the model functor TF^d of transformation systems $TF^d(D\Sigma) = \mathbf{TF}^d(D\Sigma)$, $TF^d(\sigma) = V^d_\sigma$.

Global limits of transformation systems with d-morphisms can be constructed by combining the local limit construction of Theorem 5.30 with a change of signature given by *right adjoint* functors F_σ of the forgetful functors V_σ (see Lemma 5.34). These allow the transport of all local systems into the category of the composed (global) signature and construct the local limit there.

Theorem 5.33 (Global Limits of Transformation Systems with d-Morphisms). *The global category of transformation systems $\mathbf{TF}^d$ is complete.*

Proof. The construction of limits in $\mathbf{TF}^d$ corresponds to the one for indexed categories, see [TBG87, Her94], but has to be adapted to the specific construction of the flattening and the transition *graphs* instead of categories.

Let $D : I \to \mathbf{TF}^d$ be a diagram of transformation systems $D(i) = (D\Sigma_i, \mathbf{M}_i)$ and global d-morphisms $D(k) = (\sigma_k, H_k)$. To obtain a limit first a colimit $(D\Sigma, (\kappa_i)_{i\in|I|})$ of the data space signatures is constructed. In the following lemma it is shown that each signature morphism $\kappa_i : D\Sigma_i \to D\Sigma$ induces a right adjoint $F_{\kappa_i} : \mathbf{TF}^d(D\Sigma_i) \to \mathbf{TF}^d(D\Sigma)$ to the forgetful functor $V_{\kappa_i} : \mathbf{TF}^d(D\Sigma) \to \mathbf{TF}^d(D\Sigma_i)$. It leaves the transition graphs unchanged, like the forgetful functor. At the data space level it associates free algebras as data states to the control states, and (unions of) images of action sets and tracking relations to the transitions. This means that at the data space level it is given by left adjoints.

As shown in the following, these right adjoints allow us to transport the whole diagram D into the local category $\mathbf{TF}^d(D\Sigma)$, where a local limit can be constructed as in Theorem 5.30. Each local transformation system $(D\Sigma_i, \mathbf{M}_i)$ is thereby mapped to $F_{\kappa_i}(D\Sigma_i, \mathbf{M}_i) \in |\mathbf{TF}^d(D\Sigma)|$.

Let $D(k) = (\sigma_k, H_k) : (D\Sigma_i, \mathbf{M}_i) \to (D\Sigma_j, \mathbf{M}_j)$ be a morphism in the diagram, with $H_k = (h_{TG}, h_{St})$. Furthermore, let $c_i \in CS_i$ be a control state with $\mathbf{m}_i(c_i) = C_i$ and $\mathbf{m}_j(h_{TG}(c_i)) = C_j$. Each morphism

$$h_{c_i} : C_j \to V_{\sigma_k}(C_i)$$

of h_{St} has a free extension

$$h_{c_i}^* : F_{\sigma_k}(C_j) \to C_i$$

whose image under F_{κ_i}

$$F_{\kappa_i}(h_{c_i}^*) : F_{\kappa_j}(C_j) \to F_{\kappa_i}(C_i)$$

yields a member of the family $F_{\kappa_i}(h_{St}^*)$ of the morphism

$$(h_{TG}, F_{\kappa_i}(h_{St}^*)) : F_{\kappa_i}(\mathbf{M}_i) \to F_{\kappa_j}(\mathbf{M}_j)$$

in $\mathbf{TF}^d(D\Sigma)$ (see Figure 5.9).

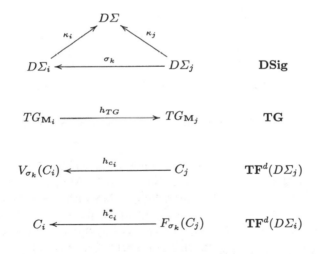

Fig. 5.9. Transporting the diagram to $\mathbf{TF}^d(D\Sigma)$

According to Theorem 5.30 the diagram $D_{D\Sigma} : I \to \mathbf{TF}^d(D\Sigma)$, given by

$$D_{D\Sigma}(i) = F_{\kappa_i}(D\Sigma_i, \mathbf{M}_i) \quad \text{(where } (D\Sigma_i, \mathbf{M}_i) = D(i))$$
$$D_{D\Sigma}(k) = (h_{TG}, F_{\kappa_i}(h_{St}^*)) \text{ (as given above)} ,$$

has a local limit $(\mathbf{M}, (\pi_i)_{i \in |I|})$ in $\mathbf{TF}^d(D\Sigma)$, where $(TG_{\mathbf{M}}, (\pi^i_{TG})_{i \in |I|})$ is a limit of the diagram of transition graphs and $(\mathbf{m}(c), (\epsilon^i_c)_{i \in |I|})$, for each $c \in CS_{\mathbf{M}}$, is a colimit of the partial algebras $F_{\kappa_i}(C_i)$ in $\mathbf{PAlg}(\Sigma)$, where $C_i = \mathbf{m}_i(\pi^i_{TG}(c))$ (see Figure 5.10). Via the adjunction the colimit injections $\epsilon^i_c :$ $F_{\kappa_i}(C_i) \to C$, where $C = \mathbf{m}(c)$, then also yield the data state components

$$\pi^i_c = V_{\kappa_i}(\epsilon^i_c) \circ \eta^{\kappa_i}_{C_i} : C_i \to V_{\kappa_i}(C)$$

of the projections $\mathbf{\Pi}_i = (\kappa_i, \pi^i_{TG}, (\pi^i_c)_{c \in CS}) : (D\Sigma, \mathbf{M}) \to (D\Sigma_i, \mathbf{M}_i)$. This completes the construction of the limit $((D\Sigma, \mathbf{M}), (\mathbf{\Pi}_i)_{i \in |I|})$ (see also Figure 5.10).

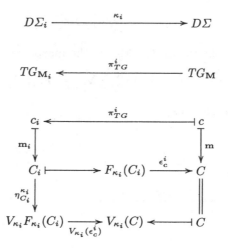

Fig. 5.10. The construction of the local limit in $\mathbf{TF}^d(D\Sigma)$

Its universal property is shown as follows. Let $(D\Sigma_N, \mathbf{N})$ be a transformation system and $(\sigma_i, F_i) : (D\Sigma_N, \mathbf{N}) \to (D\Sigma_i, \mathbf{M}_i)$, $F_i = (f^i_{TG}, f^i_{St})$, a family of global morphisms that are compatible with the diagram D, i.e., $\sigma_i \circ \sigma_k = \sigma_j$ for all $k : i \to j$ in I (where again $D(k) = (\sigma_k, H_k)$ and $V_{\sigma_k}(f^i_{c_N}) \circ h_{f^i_{TG}(c_N)} = f^j_{c_N}$ for all $c_N \in CS_N$. Let in the following $f_i := f^i_{c_N}$, $f_j := f^j_{c_N}$, and $h_i := h_{f^i_{TG}(c_N)}$ as in Figure 5.11. The morphisms σ_i and f^i_{TG} induce a unique compatible signature morphism $\sigma : D\Sigma \to D\Sigma_N$ and a unique compatible transition graph morphism $f_{TG} : TG_N \to TG_M$. The family of data state homomorphisms

$$f_i : C_i \to V_{\sigma_i}(C_N) = V_{\kappa_i} \circ V_\sigma(C_N)$$

for $c_N \in CS_N$, where $C_i = \mathbf{m}_i(f^i_{TG}(c_N))$ and $C_N = \mathbf{n}(c_N)$, induces a family of Σ-homomorphisms

$$f^*_i : F_{\kappa_i}(C_i) \to V_\sigma(C_N) \,,$$

which is compatible with $D_{D\Sigma}$, i.e., $f_i^* \circ F_{\kappa_i}(h_i^*) = f_j^*$, since

$$V_{\kappa_j}(f_i^* \circ F_{\kappa_i}(h_i^*)) \circ \eta_{C_j}^{\kappa_i}$$
$$\overset{1}{=} V_{\kappa_j}(f_i^* \circ F_{\kappa_i}(h_i^*)) \circ V_{\sigma_k}(\eta_{F_{\sigma_k}(C_j)}^{\kappa_i}) \circ \eta_{C_j}^{\sigma_k}$$
$$\overset{2}{=} V_{\sigma_k}(V_{\kappa_i}(f_i^*) \circ V_{\kappa_i}F_{\kappa_i}(h_i^*) \circ \eta_{F_{\sigma_k}(C_j)}^{\kappa_i}) \circ \eta_{C_j}^{\sigma_k}$$
$$\overset{3}{=} V_{\sigma_k}(V_{\kappa_i}(f_i^*) \circ \eta_{C_i}^{\kappa_i} \circ h_i^*) \circ \eta_{C_j}^{\sigma_k}$$
$$= V_{\sigma_k}(f_i \circ h_i^*) \circ \eta_{C_j}^{\sigma_k}$$
$$= V_{\sigma_k}(f_i) \circ h_i$$
$$\overset{4}{=} f_j$$
$$= V_{\kappa_j}(f_j^*) \circ \eta_{C_j}^{\kappa_j}$$

where $\eta_{C_j}^{\kappa_i} : C_j \to V_{\kappa_i}F_{\kappa_i}(C_j)$ is the unit of the adjunction $F_{\kappa_i} \dashv V_{\kappa_i}$ at C_j. The equations 1, 2, 3, and 4 hold because

$$1\ \ \eta_{C_j}^{\kappa_j} = V_{\sigma_k}(\eta_{F_{\sigma_k}(C_j)}) \circ \eta_{C_j}^{\sigma_k}$$
$$2\ \ V_{\kappa_j} = V_{\sigma_k} \circ V_{\kappa_i}$$
$$3\ \ V_{\kappa_i} \circ F_{\kappa_i}(h_i^*) \circ \eta_{F_{\sigma_k}(C_j)}^{\kappa_i} = \eta_{C_j}^{\kappa_i} \circ h_i^*$$
$$4\ \ \text{compatibility of } (f_i)_{i \in |I|} .$$

Since $C = \mathbf{m}(f_{TG}(c_N))$ is a colimit object of $D_{D\Sigma}$ this yields a unique Σ-homomorphism $f : C \to V_\sigma(C_N)$ with $f \circ \epsilon_i = f_i^*$. The family of the Σ-homomorphisms $f = f_{c_N} : C \to V_\sigma(C_N)$ also preserves the tracking relations and action sets, since $(\mathbf{M}, (\pi_{TG}^i, \epsilon_{St}^i))$ is a limit in $\mathbf{TF}^d(D\Sigma)$.

Furthermore, f is compatible with the f_i because

$$f_i = V_{\kappa_i}(f_i^*) \circ \eta_{C_i}^{\kappa_i}$$
$$= V_{\kappa_i}(f) \circ V_{\kappa_i}(\epsilon_i) \circ \eta_{C_i}^{\kappa_i}$$
$$= V_{\kappa_i}(f) \circ \pi_C^i .$$

It is furthermore uniquely determined by the equations $f_i = V_{\kappa_i}(f) \circ \pi_c^i$ since

$$f_i = V_{\kappa_i}(\tilde{f}) \circ \pi_c^i$$
$$\Rightarrow V_{\kappa_i}(f_i^*) \circ \eta_{C_i}^{\kappa_i} = f_i = V_{\kappa_i}(\tilde{f}) \circ V_{\kappa_i}(\epsilon_i) \circ \eta_{C_i}^{\kappa_i}$$
$$\Rightarrow f_i^* = \tilde{f} \circ \epsilon_i$$
$$\Rightarrow \tilde{f} = f$$

q.e.d.

It remains to be shown that the right adjoints of the forgetful functors of transformation exist.

Lemma 5.34 (Right Adjoint of the Forgetful Functor). *For each signature morphism* $\sigma = (\sigma_\Sigma, \sigma_A) : D\Sigma \to D\Sigma'$ *the forgetful functor* $V_\sigma : \mathbf{TF}^d(D\Sigma') \to \mathbf{TF}^d(D\Sigma)$ *has a right adjoint* $F_\sigma : \mathbf{TF}^d(D\Sigma) \to \mathbf{TF}^d(D\Sigma')$.

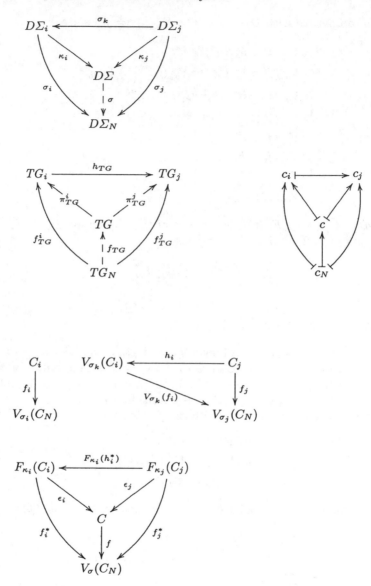

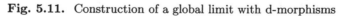

Fig. 5.11. Construction of a global limit with d-morphisms

Proof. Let $\mathbf{M} = (TG_{\mathbf{M}}, \mathbf{m}) \in |\mathbf{TF}^d(D\Sigma)|$. Define $\mathbf{M}' = (TG_{\mathbf{M}'}, \mathbf{m}') \in |\mathbf{TF}^d(D\Sigma')|$ by

$$TG_{\mathbf{M}'} = TG_{\mathbf{M}} =: (CS, T, in, id)$$

$$\mathbf{m}'(c) = F_{\sigma_\Sigma}(\mathbf{m}(c)) \quad (c \in CS)$$

$$(\sim_t^{\mathbf{m}'})_{s'} = \bigcup_{s : \sigma_\Sigma(s) = s'} ((\eta_{\mathbf{m}(c)})_s \times (\eta_{\mathbf{m}(d)})_s)((\sim_t^{\mathbf{m}})_s)$$

$$act_t^{\mathbf{m}'} = \{\sigma_A(a)(\eta_{\mathbf{m}(c)}(\bar{c}); \eta_{\mathbf{m}(d)}(\bar{d})) \mid a(\bar{c}; \bar{d}) \in act_t^{\mathbf{m}}\}$$

$$= (\sigma_A \times \eta_{\mathbf{m}(c)} \times \eta_{\mathbf{m}(d)})(act_t^{\mathbf{m}})$$

where $\eta_{\mathbf{m}(c)} : \mathbf{m}(c) \to V_{\sigma_\Sigma} F_{\sigma_\Sigma}(\mathbf{m}(c))$ is the unit of the adjunction $F_{\sigma_\Sigma} \dashv V_{\sigma_\Sigma} : \mathbf{PAlg}(\Sigma) \to \mathbf{PAlg}(\Sigma')$ at $\mathbf{m}(c)$. (The same for $\mathbf{m}(d)$.)

The counit $H_{\mathbf{M}} : V_\sigma F_\sigma(\mathbf{M}) \to \mathbf{M}$ is given by the identity $id_{TG_{\mathbf{M}}}$ and the units $\eta_{\mathbf{m}(c)}$. These preserve the tracking relations and action sets since

$$\bar{c} (\sim_t^{\mathbf{m}})_s \bar{d} \quad \Rightarrow \quad \eta_{\mathbf{m}(c)}(\bar{c}) \, (\sim_t^{\mathbf{m}'})_{\sigma_\Sigma(s)} \, \eta_{\mathbf{m}(d)}(\bar{d})$$

$$\Leftrightarrow \quad \eta_{\mathbf{m}(c)}(\bar{c}) \, (V_{\sigma_\Sigma}(\sim_t^{\mathbf{m}'}))_s \, \eta_{\mathbf{m}(d)}(\bar{d})$$

$$a(\bar{c}; \bar{d}) \in act_t^{\mathbf{m}} \quad \Rightarrow \quad \sigma_A(a)(\eta_{\mathbf{m}(c)}(\bar{c}); \eta_{\mathbf{m}(d)}(\bar{d})) \in act_t^{\mathbf{m}'}$$

$$\Rightarrow \quad a(\eta_{\mathbf{m}(c)}(\bar{c}); \eta_{\mathbf{m}(d)}(\bar{d})) \in \sigma_A^{-1}(act_t^{\mathbf{m}'}) \, ,$$

i.e., $H_M = (id_{TG_{\mathbf{M}}}, (\eta_{\mathbf{m}(c)})_{c \in CS})$ is a $D\Sigma$-d-morphism.

Let $H = (h_{TG}, h_{St}) : V_\sigma(\mathbf{N}') \to \mathbf{M}$ be a $D\Sigma$-d-morphism.

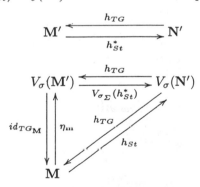

Its unique extension to a $D\Sigma'$-d-morphism $H^* = (h_{TG}, h_{St}^*) : \mathbf{N}' \to \mathbf{M}'$ is given as follows. The transition graph component is given by h_{TG} itself. Each of the Σ-homomorphisms

$$h_{c'} : \mathbf{m}(h_{TG}(c')) \to V_{\sigma_\Sigma}(\mathbf{n}'(c'))$$

induces via the adjunction $F_{\sigma_\Sigma} \dashv V_{\sigma_\Sigma}$ a Σ'-homomorphism

$$h_{c'}^* : F_{\sigma_\Sigma}(\mathbf{m}(h_{TG}(c'))) \to \mathbf{n}'(c') \, ;$$

these yield $h_{St}^* = (h_{c'}^*)_{c' \in CS_{\mathbf{N}'}}$.

The uniqueness of H^* w.r.t. $H_M \circ V_\sigma(H^*) = H$ is obvious. It remains to be shown that H^* is well defined, i.e., it preserves action sets and tracking relations.

Let $t_N : c_N \to d_N$ be a transition in $TG_{N'}$ with $h_{TG}(t_N : c_N \to d_N) =: (t : c \to d)$, and $a'(\tilde{c}, \tilde{d}) \in act_t^{m'}$. Then there are

$$a \in A_{w,w'}, \bar{c} \in \mathbf{m}(c)_w, \bar{d} \in \mathbf{m}(d)_{w'}$$

such that

$$a(\bar{c}; \bar{d}) \in act_t^{\mathbf{m}}, \sigma_A(a) = a', \eta_{\mathbf{m}(c)}(\bar{c}) = \tilde{c}, \eta_{\mathbf{m}(d)}(\bar{d}) = \tilde{d} \ .$$

Now $H = (h_{TG}, h_{St}) : V_\sigma(\mathbf{N'}) \to \mathbf{M}$ is a $D\Sigma$-d-morphism, i.e.,

$$a(h_{c_N}(\bar{c}); h_{d_N}(\bar{d})) \in \sigma_A^{-1}(act_{t_N}^{\mathbf{n'}})$$

for each $a(\bar{c}; \bar{d}) \in act_t^{\mathbf{m}}$. This yields

$$a(h_{c_N}(\bar{c}), h_{d_N}(\bar{d})) \in \sigma_A^{-1}(act_{t_N}^{\mathbf{n'}})$$
$$\Rightarrow \sigma_A(a)(h_{c_N}(\bar{c}), h_{d_N}(\bar{d})) \in act_{t_N}^{\mathbf{n'}}$$
$$\Rightarrow \sigma_A(a)(V_{\sigma_\Sigma}(h_{c_N}^*) \circ \eta_{\mathbf{m}(c)}(\bar{c}); V_{\sigma_\Sigma}(h_{d_N}^*) \circ \eta_{\mathbf{m}(d)}(\bar{d})) \in act_{t_N}^{\mathbf{n'}}$$
$$\Rightarrow a'(V_{\sigma_\Sigma}(h_{c_N}^*)(\tilde{c}), V_{\sigma_\Sigma}(h_{d_N}^*)(\tilde{d})) \in act_{t_N}^{\mathbf{n'}} \ ,$$

i.e., H^* preserves the action sets.

Analogously let $\tilde{c} \sim_{h_{TG}(t_N)}^{\mathbf{m'}} \tilde{d}$ for some $\tilde{c} \in \mathbf{m'}(h_{TG}(c_N))_{s'} = F_{\sigma_\Sigma}(\mathbf{m}(c))_{s'}$ and $\tilde{d} \in \mathbf{m'}(h_{TG}(d_N))_{s'} = F_{\sigma_\Sigma}(\mathbf{m}(d))_{s'}$. Then there are

- $s \in S, \bar{c} \in \mathbf{m}(c)_s, \bar{d} \in \mathbf{m}(d)_s$

with

- $s' = \sigma_\Sigma(s), \tilde{c} = \eta_{\mathbf{m}(c)}(\bar{c}) , \tilde{d} = \eta_{\mathbf{m}(d)}(\bar{d}),$

and

- $\bar{c} \sim_t^{\mathbf{m}} \bar{d}.$

Again,

$$h_{c_N}(\bar{c}) \sim_{t_N}^{\mathbf{n'}} h_{d_N}(\bar{d})$$
$$\Rightarrow V_{\sigma_\Sigma}(h_{c_N}^*) \circ \eta_{\mathbf{m}(c)}(\bar{c}) \sim_{t_N}^{\mathbf{n'}} V_{\sigma_\Sigma}(h_{d_N}^*) \circ \eta_{\mathbf{m}(d)}(\bar{d})$$
$$\Rightarrow V_{\sigma_\Sigma}(h_{c_N}^*)(\tilde{c}) \sim_{t_N}^{\mathbf{n'}} V_{\sigma_\Sigma}(h_{d_N}^*)(\tilde{d}) \ ,$$

whence H^* also preserves the tracking relations.

Example 5.35. In the global category $\mathbf{TF}^d$ the construction of the composition $\mathbf{P} = \mathbf{Y} \times_{\mathbf{S}} \mathbf{Z}$ from Example 5.29 can be reformulated in such a way that the independence of the two incrementation processes is already documented on the syntactic level. That means the models $\mathbf{Y}$ and $\mathbf{Z}$ can be reconstructed as models of a signature that contains only one pointer—the pointer the model has access to—and their composition can be reconstructed as a pullback in $\mathbf{TF}^d$.

According to the definition of global morphisms for this reconstruction, first an appropriate pushout diagram of transformation signatures has to be given:

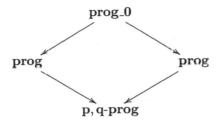

Here **prog** is defined as in Example 2.3, introducing only one designated pointer and the incrementation method. The signature **prog_0** defining the shared part is given by **prog** without the pointer p:

> **prog_0 = nat** +
>   **sorts** pointer
>   **funs** !: pointer → nat
>   **acts** inc: pointer, nat

The morphisms **prog_0** → **prog** are inclusions. Then the data space signature **p,q-prog** of Example 5.29, together with the inclusion morphisms, is a pushout of this diagram. There are two copies of the pointer, because it is not shared in **prog_0**.

The **prog**-transformation system $\mathbf{X}$ defined in Example 2.7 obviously coincides with the restrictions to **prog** of $\mathbf{Y}$ and $\mathbf{Z}$. The image $V(\mathbf{X})$ under the forgetful functor V induced by the inclusion **prog_0** → **prog** is the same as $\mathbf{X}$, except that in the data states $V(X_n)$ the program variable X is no longer designated by the constant p.

The transition graph $TG_{\mathbf{P}}$ is given by the pullback of $h_{\mathbf{X}} : TG_{\mathbf{X}} \to TG_{\mathbf{S}}$ with itself, as in Example 5.29, where $h_{\mathbf{X}}$ is defined analogously to $h_{\mathbf{Y}}$ and $h_{\mathbf{Z}}$.

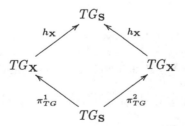

The sharing of the data states must be expressed by appropriate pushouts. In each state of the system the natural numbers should be shared, whereas the sets of pointers and the action sets should be united disjointly. This is obtained by the data state homomorphisms $h_n : (I\!N, \emptyset, \emptyset) \to (I\!N, \{X\}, !^{X_n}(X) = n) = X_n$ in $\mathbf{PAlg}(\Sigma_{prog\_0})$.

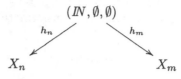

The data states of the initialisation states are related by the empty homomorphisms. Transporting these homomorphisms to the signature $\Sigma_{p,q\text{-}prog}$ yields the pushout diagram

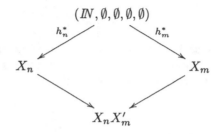

where the $\Sigma_{p,q\text{-}prog}$-algebras $X_n X'_m$ are given by

$$X_n X'_m = (I\!N, \{X, X'\}, X, X', !^{X_n X'_m}(X) = n, !^{X_n X'_m}(X') = m)$$

The resulting pullback system $(prog, \mathbf{X}) \times_{\mathbf{hx}, \mathbf{hx}} (prog, \mathbf{X})$ is obviously isomorphic to the system $(p, q\text{-}prog, \mathbf{P})$ constructed in Example 5.29.

In order to show that the composition-by-limits with distributed data is indeed a generalisation of the former composition-by-limits in the category $\mathbf{TF}$ it remains to be shown that the embedding $\mathbf{TF} \to \mathbf{TF}^d$ preserves limits. That means, for each diagram in $\mathbf{TF}$ whose limit exists, the construction of Theorem 5.33 yields an isomorphic result.

Theorem 5.36. *The embedding* $\mathbf{TF} \to \mathbf{TF}^d$ *preserves limits.*

Proof. (Throughout the proof the notation of Theorem 5.33 and its proof is used.)

It is to be shown that whenever each component h_{c_i} of a morphism $D(k) = (\sigma_k, h_{TG}, (h_{c_i})_{c_i \in CS_i})$ is an identity $h_{c_i} = id_{V_{\sigma_k}(C_i)} = id_{C_j}$, then the amalgamation $C = \sum_I C_i$ is a colimit of the diagram

$$((F_{\kappa_i}(C_i))_{i \in |I|}, (F_{\kappa_i}(h^*_{c_i}))_{k:i \to j \in I}) .$$

This is done in the following.

The colimit injections $F_{\kappa_i}(C_i) \to C$ are given by the free extensions $id_{C_i}^{\kappa_i}$ of the identities $id_{C_i} : C_i \to V_{\kappa_i}(C)$. In the diagram below showing the limit construction the following notational conventions are used: for each signature morphism s the unit of the induced adjunction of partial algebras $F_s \dashv V_s$ is denoted by η^s and the free extension of a morphism $f : A \to V_s(B)$ is denoted by $f^s : F_s(A) \to B$.

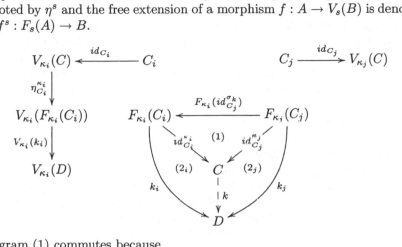

Diagram (1) commutes because

$$V_{\kappa_j}(id_{C_i}^{\kappa_i} \circ F_{\kappa_i}(id_{C_j}^{\sigma_k})) \circ \eta_{C_j}^{\kappa_j}$$
$$= V_{\sigma_k}(V_{\kappa_i}(id_{C_i}^{\kappa_i}) \circ V_{\kappa_i}(F_{\kappa_i}(id_{C_j}^{\sigma_k}))) \circ \eta_{F_{\sigma_k}(C_j)}^{\kappa_i}) \circ \eta_{C_j}^{\sigma_k}$$
$$= V_{\sigma_k}(V_{\kappa_i}(id_{C_i}^{\kappa_i}) \circ \eta_{C_i}^{\kappa_i} \circ id_{C_j}^{\sigma_k}) \circ \eta_{C_j}^{\sigma_k}$$
$$= V_{\sigma_k}(id_{C_j}^{\sigma_k}) \circ \eta_{C_j}^{\sigma_k}$$
$$= id_{C_j}^{\sigma_k}$$
$$= V_{\kappa_j}(id_{C_j}^{\kappa_j}) \circ \eta_{C_j}^{\kappa_j} .$$

Given compatible Σ-homomorphisms $(k_i : F_{\kappa_i}(C_i) \to D)_{i \in |I|}$ the amalgamation

$$k = \sum_I (V_{\kappa_i}(k_i) \circ \eta_{C_i}^{\kappa_i})$$

yields a Σ-homomorphism $k : C \to D$. Since $V_{\kappa_i}(id_{C_i}^{\kappa_i}) \circ \eta_{C_i}^{\kappa_i} = id_{C_i}^{\kappa_i}$, all diagrams (2_i) commute. Furthermore, $k \circ id_{C_i}^{\kappa_i} = k_i$ for all $i \in |I|$ implies

$$V_{\kappa_i}(k) = V_{\kappa_i}(k) \circ V_{\kappa_i}(id_{C_i}^{\kappa_i}) \circ \eta_{C_i}^{\kappa_i} = V_{\kappa_i}(k_i) \circ \eta_{C_i}^{\kappa_i}$$

whence by the amalgamation property k is the unique solution of these equations.

5.9 Sequential Composition

In the parallel composition-by-limits the global control flow always resides in all components. That means a control state of the composed system is given by a collection of control states of the components (exactly one in each component), and a transition is given by transitions in all components, some of which might be idle. The dual notion of *sequential* composition-by-colimits then means that the control flow of the composed system always resides in exactly one component, but may jump into other ones at certain states. Thus in this case components are composed sequentially. Formally this dualisation is supported by the fact that the (local and global) categories of transformation systems also have all colimits. As the discussion below will show, however, this construction of sequential composition by colimits only makes sense in the special case of transformation systems of the same signature, where, in addition, the control flow is only passed to another system in control states with identical data states. Alternatively, sequential composition can be reduced to parallel composition, where the disposal of the control flow to another component is realised by a synchronisation.

In the following the formal dualisation that yields the colimits of transformation systems as a formal operation representing their sequential composition is presented. A more detailed intuitive interpretation of colimts is given afterwards. For the construction of the colimits it is first shown that the local categories of transformation systems with d-morphisms have colimits.

Lemma 5.37 (Local Colimits). *For each data space signature $D\Sigma$ the category of transformation systems $\mathbf{TF}^d(D\Sigma)$ is cocomplete.*

Proof. The proof is essentially the same as that of Theorem 5.30, up to dualisation. However, the construction of the diagrams D_c that yield the data states cannot be dualised.

So let $D : I \to \mathbf{TF}^d(D\Sigma)$ be a diagram and let $(TG_{\mathbf{M}}, (\iota^i_{TG})_{i\in|I|})$ be a colimit of the diagram of underlying transition graphs $TG_i = (CS_i, T_i, in_i, id_i)$. Furthermore, let $D(i) = \mathbf{M}_i$ for $i \in |I|$ and $D(k) = H_k = (h^k_{TG}, (h^k_{c_i})_{c_i \in CS_i})$ for $k : i \to j$ in I. The local diagram $E_c : J^{op}_c \to \mathbf{PAlg}(\Sigma)$ for a control state $c \in CS_{\mathbf{M}}$, whose limit object yields the data state of c, is now constructed as follows:

$$
\begin{aligned}
|J_c| &= \{\langle i, c_i \rangle \mid i \in |I|, c_i \in CS_i, \iota^i_{TG}(c_i) = c\} \\
Mor_{J_c}(\langle i, c_i \rangle, \langle j, c_j \rangle) &= \{k : i \to j \in I \mid h^k_{TG}(c_i) = c_j\} \\
E_c(i, c_i) &= \mathbf{m}_i(c_i) \\
E_c(k : \langle i, c_i \rangle \to \langle j, c_j \rangle) &= h^k_{c_i} : \mathbf{m}_j(c_j) \to \mathbf{m}_i(c_i) \ .
\end{aligned}
$$

Then

$$
\mathbf{m}(c) = C
$$

where $(C, (\kappa_{\langle i, c_i \rangle})_{\langle i, c_i \rangle \in |J_c|})$ is a limit of E_c and

$$
\mathbf{m}(t : c \to d) = \bigcap_{\gamma(t)} (\kappa_{\langle i, c_i \rangle} \times \kappa_{\langle i, d_i \rangle})^{-1}(\mathbf{m}_i(t_i : c_i \to d_i))
$$

where $\gamma(t) = \{\langle i, t_i \rangle \mid \iota^i_{TG}(t_i) = t, t_i : c_i \to d_i \in T_i\}$. The colimit injections $\iota_i : \mathbf{M}_i \to \mathbf{M}$ ($i \in |I|$) are given by $\iota_i = (\iota^i_{TG}, (\kappa_{\langle i, c_i \rangle})_{c_i \in CS_i})$. By definition they preserve the transition labels, i.e., they are d-morphisms.

The universal property is shown as follows. Let $F_i : \mathbf{M}_i \to \mathbf{N}$ $(i \in |I|)$ with $F_i = (f_{TG}^i, (f_c^i)_{c \in CS_i})$ be a family of d-morphisms with $F_j \circ H_k = F_i$ for all $k : i \to j$ in I. This induces a unique transition graph morphism $f_{TG} : TG_{\mathbf{M}} \to TG_{\mathbf{N}}$ with $f_{TG} \circ \iota_{TG}^i = f_{TG}^i$ for all $i \in |I|$.

Now let $c \in CS_{\mathbf{M}}$. For each $\langle i, c_i \rangle \in |J_c|$ the morphism F_i contains a Σ-homomorphism

$$f_{c_i}^i : \mathbf{n}(f_{TG}(c)) \to \mathbf{m}_i(c_i)$$

since $f_{TG}^i(c_i) = f_{TG}(\iota_{TG}^i(c_i)) = f_{TG}(c)$.

Furthermore, for each $k : \langle i, c_i \rangle \to \langle j, c_j \rangle$ in J_c

$$h_{c_i}^k \circ f_{c_i}^i = f_{c_j}^j$$

since $F_j \circ H_k = F_i$.

Thus there is a unique Σ-homomorphism

$$f_c : \mathbf{n}(f_{TG}(c)) \to \mathbf{m}(c)$$

such that $\kappa_{\langle i, c_i \rangle} \circ f_c = f_{c_i}^i$ for all $\langle i, c_i \rangle \in |J_c|$, and, for the same reason, $\kappa_{\langle i, c_i \rangle} \circ f_c = f_{c_i}^i$ for all $c_i \in CS_i$ and all $i \in |I|$. The latter also shows the uniqueness of f_c w.r.t. the equations $\kappa_{\langle i, c_i \rangle} \circ f_c = f_{c_i}^i$ $(c_i \in CS_i, i \in |I|)$.

Theorem 5.38 (Global Colimits of Transformation Systems). *The global category of transformation systems $\mathbf{TF}^d$ is cocomplete.*

Proof. Since all local categories $\mathbf{TF}^d(D\Sigma)$ are cocomplete and the forgetful functors $V_\sigma : \mathbf{TF}^d(D\Sigma') \to \mathbf{TF}^d(D\Sigma)$ are left adjoints the dual constructions of the proof of Theorem 5.33 yield global colimits.

Sequential composition-by-colimits works as follows. Consider first systems $\mathbf{M}_1$ and $\mathbf{M}_2$ of a common data space signature. Without any connection the transition graph of the sequential composition is given by the disjoint union of $TG_{\mathbf{M}_1}$ and $TG_{\mathbf{M}_2}$, identifying only the initialisation states. The data space labels are inherited from $\mathbf{M}_1$ and $\mathbf{M}_2$ respectively. In this case the control flow can never pass from one component to the other. This means that one of the components is entered initially (via a transition from the initialisation state) and can be left only via a finalisation, i.e., a transition to the initialisation state.

Control states can be glued together to allow for an intermediate handing over of the control flow by taking a pushout w.r.t. a gluing graph TG_0 with transition graph morphisms $h_{TG}^i : TG_0 \to TG_i$ $(i = 1, 2)$. These morphisms identify all pairs of states $c_1 \in CS_1$ and $c_2 \in CS_2$ with $c_1 = h_{TG}^1(c_0)$ and $c_2 = h_{TG}^1(c_0)$ for some $c_0 \in CS_0$. In general this leads to a non-deterministic choice between the two components at state $c_1 = c_2$, but if c_1 for instance has no outgoing transition in TG_1 the thread of control must proceed in $\mathbf{M}_2$ (see Figure 5.12). Also transitions can be identified in this way. If the underlying data states $\mathbf{m}_1(c_1)$ and $\mathbf{m}_2(c_2)$ of identified control states coincide

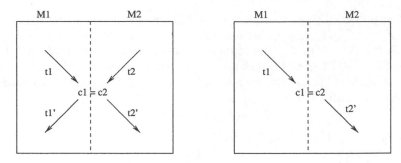

Fig. 5.12. Sequential composition of systems M_1 and M_2

with $m_0(c_0)$ this also yields the data state in the sequential composition, taking the pullback of the identity id_C with itself. Otherwise, the construction of the sequential composition-by-colimit yields a pullback of the local data states, i.e., a subalgebra of the cartesian product. However, there seems to be no appropriate interpretation for such non-trivial pullbacks. Correspondingly, equal action sets as labels of identified transitions yield the action set in the sequential composition, whereas in the general case intersections are obtained. Considering colimits in the global category, furthermore, pullbacks (limits) of the local data space signatures would be constructed to obtain the global signature. Also for this construction there seems to be no appropriate interpretation. Thus, pragmatically, sequential composition-by-colimits seems to be restricted to the local case (w.r.t. one given data space signature) and identical data states for all shared control states.

However, the initialisation states of transformation systems allow us to realise a similar form of sequential composition—without the gluing of control states—as a special case of parallel composition(-by-limits). The basic idea is to synchronise (some of) the finalisations of the first system with appropriate initialisations of the second one. Thereby the information of the final data state of the first system is used to select the initial state of the second one (see Figure 5.13 showing the synchronisation relation and its induced cospan of transition graph morphisms). Note, however, that this information is lost as soon as the second system is entered, as opposed to the parallel composition with idle steps on a (non-initialisation) state, where the last state is stored. This means that in a sequential composition, the first system (object) is destroyed when passing the control flow (the thread) to the second one.

This reduction of sequential to parallel composition was introduced for the process calculus CCS in [Mil89], Chapter 8, as the synchronisation of a designated action *done* for the successful termination of a process with the first actions of the subsequent process.

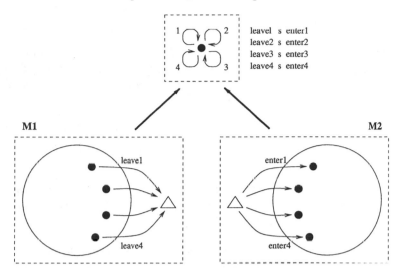

Fig. 5.13. Sequential composition as parallel composition with synchronisation of finalisations and initialisations

5.10 Composition w.r.t. Other Specification Frameworks

In this section the composition of transformation systems is generalised to arbitrary specification frameworks for the data spaces. Composition is modelled directly at the categorical level, via limits and colimits as in the previous sections. That means, connections are given by diagrams of transformation systems and their global views by (co)limits. A reduction to (or presentation at) a more elementary level in terms of identification and synchronisation relations is not worked out here. Whereas the latter are independent of the data space specification formalism and can be taken over directly to the more general case, the former would require further explicit structure of the signatures and models. Thus it seems to be more appropriate to formulate the concrete presentation of compositions (diagrams) for concrete instances rather than on the general abstract level.

The structure of this section follows the categorical presentation in the previous sections. First composition-by-limits with colimits of signatures and data space amalgamation is discussed, followed by the compositionality results for the semantics, properties, and developments. Then d-morphisms and composition with distributed data are presented, and finally sequential composition-by-colimits. Thus in each case the conditions on the employed specification framework are stated that are needed to obtain the desired results. Due to their categorical structure the proofs given above can be adapted easily to the general cases, and are mostly just cited.

Throughout this section let $\mathbb{F} = (Ins, AS, I, \epsilon)$ be a generic specification framework, whose concrete properties will be made precise in due course.

Composition-by-Limits

To compose transformation systems of different signatures a colimit of the diagram of the underlying local data space signatures in the category $\mathbf{DSig}^{Ins}$ is used (see Definition 4.40). For that purpose colimits of signatures in the institution that delivers the data spaces are needed.

Proposition 5.39 (Colimits of Signatures). *If the category* $\mathbf{Sig}$ *of the institution Ins in* $\mathbb{F}$ *is cocomplete then the category* $\mathbf{DSig}^{Ins}$ *of data space signatures w.r.t.* $\mathbb{F}$ *is also cocomplete.*

Proof. (Cf. Proposition 5.16.) $\mathbf{DSig}^{Ins}$ is equivalent to the comma category $(Id_{\mathbf{Set}} \downarrow (sorts^* \times sorts^*))$. Since $\mathbf{Set}$ and $\mathbf{Sig}$ are cocomplete and $Id_{\mathbf{Set}}$ preserves colimits the assertion holds.

The main technical result for the composition-by-limits is that the data space construction is co-continuous w.r.t. the composition of signatures by colimits. That means the data space $\mathbb{D}_{D\Sigma}^{\mathbf{F}}$ (Definition 2.15) and the forgetful functors $D_{\kappa_i}^{\mathbf{F}}$ (Definition 4.42) induced by a colimit $(D\Sigma, (\kappa_i)_{i \in |I|})$ of signatures are a limit in the category of transition graphs. For this property data states and transformations are required to satisfy the corresponding amalgamation properties and these must be compatible.

Lemma 5.40 (Data Space Amalgamation). *Let* $D : I \to \mathbf{DSig}^{\mathbf{F}}$ *be a diagram of data space signatures such that a colimit* $(D\Sigma, (\kappa_i)_{i \in |I|})$ *of* D *exists. Let* $D\Sigma = (\Sigma, A)$, $\kappa_i = (\kappa_{\Sigma}^i, \kappa_A^i)$, $D(i) = (\Sigma_i, A_i)$ *for all* $i \in |I|$, *and* $D(k) = \sigma_k = (\sigma_{\Sigma}^k, \sigma_A^k)$ *for all* $k : i \to j$ *in* I. *If*

- *Ins has amalgamations for* D, *i.e.,* $(Mod(\Sigma), (V_{\kappa_{\Sigma}^i})_{i \in |I|})$ *is a limit of the diagram*

$$((Mod(\Sigma_i))_{i \in |I|}, (V_{\sigma_k})_{k:i \to j \in I}) \text{ in } \mathbf{Cat}$$

  and
- *AS preserves amalgamations for* D, *i.e.,*

  if $C = \sum_I C_i$ *and* $D = \sum_I D_i$ *are amalgamations of families of* Σ_i-*models* $(C_i)_{i \in |I|}$ *and* $(D_i)_{i \in |I|}$ *respectively that satisfy* $V_{\sigma_k}(C_j) = C_i$ *and* $V_{\sigma_k}(D_j) = D_i$ *for all* $k : i \to j$ *in* I,

  then $(AS_{D\Sigma}(|C|, |D|), (AS_{\kappa_i, |C|, |D|})_{i \in |I|})$ *is a limit of the diagram*

$$(AS_{D\Sigma_i}(|C_i|, |D_i|)_{i \in |I|}, (AS_{\sigma_k, |C_i|, |D_i|})_{k:i \to j \in I})$$

  in $\mathbf{Set}$,

then $(\mathbb{D}_{D\Sigma}^{\mathbf{F}}, (\mathbb{D}_{\kappa_i}^{\mathbf{F}})_{i \in |I|})$ *is a limit of the diagram* $((\mathbb{D}_{D\Sigma_i}^{\mathbf{F}})_{i \in |I|}, (\mathbb{D}_{\sigma_k}^{\mathbf{F}})_{k:i \to j \in I})$ *in the category* $\mathbf{TG}$ *of transition graphs.*

Proof. (Cf. Lemma 5.17.) Due to the stated preconditions the amalgamations of data sates and action structures exist. Since furthermore the diagram

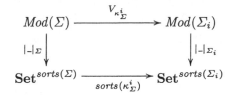

commutes by definition (see Section 2.3, p. 50), i.e., amalgamated models have amalgamated carrier sets, also the amalgamation $\sim\; =\; \sum_{i \in |I|} \sim_i$ of tracking relations given by

$$\sim_s \;=\; \sim^i_{s_i} \quad \text{if } sorts(\kappa^i_\Sigma)(s_i) = s$$

is well defined. Thus the proof of Lemma 5.17 can be carried over to this more general case.

Lemma 5.40 can now be used again to show that limits of diagrams of transformation systems in the global category $\mathbf{TF}^F$ exist (see Definition 4.43), provided a colimit of the underlying diagram of signatures exists.

Theorem 5.41 (Limits of Transformation Systems). *Let $D : I \to \mathbf{TF}^F$ be a diagram of transformation systems and $\Pi_{Sig} : \mathbf{TF}^F \to \mathbf{DSig}^F$ be the projection functor that maps transformation systems to their signatures. If $\Pi_{Sig} \circ D : I \to \mathbf{DSig}^F$ has a colimit, Ins has amalgamations for $\Pi_{Sig} \circ D$ and AS preserves them, then D has a limit in $\mathbf{TF}^F$.*

Proof. See Theorem 5.18.

Compositional Semantics

As a special case of limits of transformation systems we obtain again the amalgamation property of transformation systems, i.e., compositionality of the semantics w.r.t. the composition of signatures by colimits.

Theorem 5.42 (Amalgamation of Transformation Systems). *Let I be a connected schema category and $D : I \to \mathbf{DSig}^F$ be a diagram of data space signatures. If D has a colimit $(D\Sigma, (\kappa_i)_{i \in |I|})$, Ins has amalgamations for D and AS preserves them, then $(\mathbf{TF}^F(D\Sigma), (V^F_{\kappa_i})_{i \in |I|})$ is a limit of the diagram $((\mathbf{TF}^F(D\Sigma_i))_{i \in |I|}, (V^F_{\sigma_k})_{k:i \to j \in |I|})$.*

Proof. See Theorem 5.19.

Compositionality of Properties

Data space properties of the local components of a composition are preserved, i.e., they also hold in the global view of the composition, since the projections reflect them (see Proposition 4.48 and Proposition 4.52).

Theorem 5.43 (Compositionality of Properties). *Let $D : I \to \mathbf{TF}^F$ be a diagram of transformation systems such that Ins has amalgamations for $\Pi_{Sig} \circ D$ and AS preserves them. Furthermore, let $((D\Sigma, \mathbf{M}), (\pi_i)_{i \in |I|})$ be a limit of D, with $\pi_i = (\kappa_i, \pi_{TG}^i)$ and $D(i) = (D\Sigma_i, \mathbf{M}_i)$.*

1. For each $\varphi \in Sen(\Sigma_i)$,

$$\text{if } \mathbf{M}_i \models \varphi \text{ then } \mathbf{M} \models \kappa_i(\varphi) \ .$$

2. For each anonymous $D\Sigma_i$-transformation rule $r_0 = (L \to R)$,

$$\text{if } \mathbf{M}_i \models r_0 \text{ then } \mathbf{M} \models \kappa_i(r_0) \ .$$

3. For each $D\Sigma_i$-transformation rule $r = (\alpha \doteq L \to R)$,

$$\text{if } \mathbf{M}_i \models r \text{ and } AS_{\kappa_i}^{\sharp} \text{ and } AS_{\kappa_i} \text{ are isomorphisms then } \mathbf{M} \models \kappa_i(r) \ .$$

Proof. The assertions follow (1) from the satisfaction condition of the institution *Ins* and (2,3) from Proposition 4.48 and Proposition 4.52.

Control flow properties of the components are not preserved in general. If only the data spaces are amalgamated, however, and the control flow logic is functorial, preservation holds.

Theorem 5.44. *Let $D : I \to \mathbf{DSig}^{Ins}$ be a diagram of data space signatures that satisfies the conditions of Theorem 5.43 and let $CL = (CF, \models^{CL})$ be a functorial control flow logic. Furthermore, let $(D\Sigma, \mathbf{M})$ be the amalgamation of a compatible family $(D\Sigma_i, \mathbf{M}_i)_{i \in |I|}$ of transformation systems w.r.t. $\mathbb{F}$. Then for each formula $cf \in CF(D\Sigma_i)$*

$$\mathbf{M}_i \models_{D\Sigma_i} cf \text{ if and only if } \mathbf{M} \models_{D\Sigma} \kappa_i(cf) \ .$$

Proof. See Theorem 5.21.

Compositionality of Developments

Composition-by-limits implies that each compatible family of morphisms on the components uniquely determines a morphism of the composed systems that is compatible with the projections to the components. Since reductions are morphisms this immediately yields the compositionality of reductions. For the compositionality of extensions the two constructions for transition graphs and signatures just have to be put together in the opposite order. Concerning refinements and implementations, compatibility of the closure operation with the limits of transition graphs is required.

Theorem 5.45 (Compositionality of Developments). *Let $D, D' : I \to \mathbf{TF}^F$ be two diagrams of transformation systems such that Ins has amalgamations for $\Pi_{Sig} \circ D$ and $\Pi_{Sig} \circ D'$ and AS preserves them. Furthermore, let $((D\Sigma, \mathbf{M}), (\pi_i)_{i \in |I|})$ and $((D\Sigma', \mathbf{M}'), (\pi'_i)_{i \in |I|})$ be limits of D and D' respectively, where $\pi_i = (\kappa_i, \pi_{TG}^i)$ and $\pi'_i = (\kappa'_i, (\pi_{TG}^i)')$ for $i = 1, 2$, and let $D(i) = (D\Sigma_i, \mathbf{M}_i)$, $D'(i) = (D\Sigma'_i, \mathbf{M}'_i)$ for all $i \in |I|$, and $D(k) =: \mathbf{h}_k = (\sigma_k, h_k)$, $D'(k) =: \mathbf{h}'_k = (\sigma'_k, h'_k)$, for all $k : i \to j$ in I.*

1. *Let $r_i = (g_i, \rho_i) : (D\Sigma_i, \mathbf{M}_i) \to (D\Sigma'_i, \mathbf{M}'_i)$ $(i \in |I|)$ be a compatible family of uniform reductions, i.e.,*

$$\rho_i \circ \sigma_k = \sigma'_k \circ \rho_j \text{ and } h_k \circ g_i = g_j \circ h'_k$$

for all $k : i \to j$ in I. Then there is a unique uniform reduction $r = (g, \rho) : (D\Sigma, \mathbf{M}) \to (D\Sigma', \mathbf{M}')$ with

$$\rho \circ \kappa_i = \kappa'_i \circ \rho_i \text{ and } \pi^i_{TG} \circ g = g_i \circ (\pi^i_{TG})'$$

for all $i \in |I|$.

2. *Let $e_i = (g_i, \rho_i) : (D\Sigma_i, \mathbf{M}_i) \to (D\Sigma'_i, \mathbf{M}'_i)$ $(i \in |I|)$ be a compatible family of uniform extensions, i.e.,*

$$\rho_i \circ \sigma_k = \sigma'_k \circ \rho_j \text{ and } h'_k \circ g_i = g_j \circ h_k$$

for all $k : i \to j$ in I. Then there is a unique uniform extension $e = (g, \rho) : (D\Sigma, \mathbf{M}) \to (D\Sigma', \mathbf{M}')$ with

$$\rho \circ \kappa_i = \kappa'_i \circ \rho_i \text{ and } (\pi^i_{TG})' \circ g = g_i \circ \pi^i_{TG}$$

for all $i \in |I|$.

3. *Let $\mathbf{r}_i = (r_i, \rho_i) : (D\Sigma_i, \mathbf{M}_i) \to (D\Sigma'_i, \mathbf{M}'_i)$ $(i \in |I|)$ be a compatible family of uniform refinements, i.e.,*

$$\rho_i \circ \sigma_k = \sigma'_k \circ \rho_j \text{ and } (\bar{h}'_k) \circ r_i = r_j \circ h_k$$

for all $k : i \to j$ in I.

If the closure $(\overline{TG}_{\mathbf{M}'}, (\bar{\pi}^{i'}_{TG})_{i \in |I|})$ of the limit $(TG_{\mathbf{M}'}, (\pi^{i'}_{TG})_{i \in |I|})$ of the diagram of transition graphs $((TG_{\mathbf{M}'_i})_{i \in |I|}, (\bar{h}'_k)_{k : i \to j \in I})$ is a limit of the closures $((\overline{TG}_{\mathbf{M}'_i})_{i \in |I|}, (h'_k)_{k : i \to j \in I})$, then there is a unique uniform refinement $\mathbf{r} = (r, \rho) : (D\Sigma, \mathbf{M}) \to (D\Sigma', \mathbf{M}')$ with

$$\rho \circ \kappa_i = \kappa'_i \circ \rho_i \text{ and } (\bar{\pi}^i_{TG})' \circ r = r_i \circ \pi^i_{TG}$$

for all $i \in |I|$.

Proof. See Theorem 5.25.

Full compatibility of the closure operation used in the refinement with the limits of transition graphs has been required to have a unique induced refinement of the composed systems that is compatible with the local ones. A weaker result, the existence of an induced compatible refinement, but not uniqueness, can be obtained under the condition that there is a morphism from the limit of the closures to the closure of the limit of the transition graphs.

Distributed Data

As in Section 5.7 an extended definition of morphisms can be given that allows the comparison of the data states associated with related control states by morphisms instead of coincidence (see Definition 5.27 and Figure 5.4). To extend this to action structures a comparison relation is needed, generalising the set inclusion used in Definition 5.27. For that purpose the category **PO** of partial orders is used instead of **Set**.

Definition 5.46 (Ordered Action Structure). *An* ordered action structure *AS w.r.t. a concrete institution Ins is given by an action structure (family of functors)*

$$AS_{D\Sigma} : \mathbf{Set}^S \times \mathbf{Set}^S \to \mathbf{PO}$$

for each $D\Sigma = (\Sigma, A) \in |\mathbf{DSig}^{Ins}|$ with $S = sorts(\Sigma)$, and a natural transformation

$$AS_\sigma : AS_{D\Sigma'} \Rightarrow AS_{D\Sigma} \circ (V_{\sigma_S} \times V_{\sigma_S}) : \mathbf{Set}^{S'} \times \mathbf{Set}^{S'} \to \mathbf{PO}$$

for each $\sigma : D\Sigma \to D\Sigma'$ in $\mathbf{DSig}^{Ins}$, such that

$$AS_{id_{D\Sigma}} = id_{AS_{D\Sigma}} \text{ and } AS_{\sigma' \circ \sigma} = AS_\sigma \circ AS_{\sigma'}$$

for all $D\Sigma \in |\mathbf{DSig}^{Ins}|$ and $\sigma : D\Sigma \to D\Sigma'$ and $\sigma' : D\Sigma' \to D\Sigma''$ in $\mathbf{DSig}^{Ins}$.

The definition of the translations $AS_\sigma^\sharp$ (see Definition 4.50) remains the same, too, where accordingly the functions $AS_{\sigma,M,N}^\sharp$ are now monotone functions.

Definition 5.47 (D-Morphism). *Let $D\Sigma \in |\mathbf{DSig}^{Ins}|$ be a data space signature and $\mathbf{M} = (TG_\mathbf{M}, \mathbf{m})$ and $\mathbf{N} = (TG_\mathbf{N}, \mathbf{n})$ be transformation systems in $\mathbf{TF}^F(D\Sigma)$ with $TG_\mathbf{M} = (CS, T, in, id)$. A $D\Sigma$-d-morphism $H = (h_{TG}, h_{St}) : \mathbf{M} \to \mathbf{N}$ is given by*

- *a transition graph morphism $h_{TG} : TG_\mathbf{M} \to TG_\mathbf{N}$, and*
- *a family of Σ-morphisms $h_{St} = (h_c : \mathbf{n}(h_{TG}(c)) \to \mathbf{m}(c))_{c \in CS}$,*
- *such that*

$$AS_{D\Sigma}(h_c, h_d)(act_{h_{TG}(t)}^\mathbf{n}) \leq act_t^\mathbf{m}$$

and

$$(h_c \times h_d)(\sim_{h_{TG}(t)}^\mathbf{n}) \subseteq \sim_t^\mathbf{m}$$

for each $t : c \to d$ in $TG_\mathbf{M}$.

$D\Sigma$-transformation systems and d-morphisms form the category $\mathbf{TF}_d^F(D\Sigma)$.

Theorem 5.48 (Local Limits of Transformation Systems with d-Morphisms). *Let $D\Sigma = (\Sigma, A)$ be data space signature in $\mathbf{DSig}^F$. If $Mod(\Sigma)$ is cocomplete and $AS_{D\Sigma}(M, N)$ has suprema (is cocomplete) for all $M, N \in |\mathbf{Set}^S|$, then the category $\mathbf{TF}_d^F(D\Sigma)$ is complete.*

Proof. The proof of Theorem 5.30 can be carried over directly, replacing colimits in $\mathbf{PAlg}(\Sigma)$ by colimits in $Mod(\Sigma)$ and unions of action sets by suprema (colimits) of action structures.

Also the forgetful functor for d-morphisms can be carried over to the general case, since the mappings AS_σ that occur in $I\!\!D_\sigma^F$ are monotone by definition (cf. Fact 5.31).

Definition 5.49 (Forgetful Functor). *Let* $\sigma = (\sigma_\Sigma, \sigma_A) : D\Sigma \to D\Sigma'$ *be a data space signature morphism. The* forgetful functor $V_{d,\sigma}^F : \mathbf{TF}_d^F(D\Sigma') \to \mathbf{TF}_d^F(D\Sigma)$ *is defined by*

$$V_{d,\sigma}^F(\mathbf{M'}) = (TG_{\mathbf{M'}}, I\!\!D_\sigma^F \circ \mathbf{m'})$$
$$V_{d,\sigma}^F(H') = (h'_{TG}, (V_{\sigma_\Sigma}(h'_{c'}))_{c' \in CS'})$$

for $H' = (h'_{TG}, (h'_{c'})_{c' \in CS'})$.

To obtain global limits the whole diagram is transported into the category of the colimit signature (see Theorem 5.33). Therefore right adjoints of the forgetful functors are needed that are based on left adjoints in the model categories of the data state institution. (That means *Ins* is required to be liberal.) The proof of Lemma 5.34 can be carried over due to the conditions in the definitions of ordered action structures and translations.

Lemma 5.50 (Right Adjoint of the Forgetful Functor). *Let* $\sigma = (\sigma_\Sigma, \sigma_A) : D\Sigma \to D\Sigma'$ *be a signature morphism in* $\mathbf{DSig}^{Ins}$. *If Ins is liberal, i.e., each forgetful functor* $V_{\sigma_\Sigma} : Mod(\Sigma') \to Mod(\Sigma)$ *has a left adjoint* $F_{\sigma_\Sigma} : Mod(\Sigma) \to Mod(\Sigma')$, *and* $|\_|_{\Sigma'} \circ F_{\sigma_\Sigma} = F_{sorts(\sigma_\Sigma)} \circ |\_|_\Sigma$ *for all* $\sigma_\Sigma : \Sigma \to \Sigma'$ *in* $\mathbf{DSig}^{Ins}$, *then the forgetful functor* $V_\sigma : \mathbf{TF}_d^F(D\Sigma') \to \mathbf{TF}_d^F(D\Sigma)$ *has a right adjoint* $F_\sigma : \mathbf{TF}_d^F(D\Sigma) \to \mathbf{TF}_d^F(D\Sigma')$.

Proof. Let $\mathbf{M} = (TG_{\mathbf{M}}, \mathbf{m}) \in |\mathbf{TF}_d^F(D\Sigma)|$. Define $\mathbf{M'} = (TG_{\mathbf{M'}}, \mathbf{m'}) \in |\mathbf{TF}_d^F(D\Sigma')|$ by

$$TG_{\mathbf{M'}} = TG_{\mathbf{M}} =: (CS, T, in, id)$$
$$\mathbf{m'}(c) = F_{\sigma_\Sigma}(\mathbf{m}(c)) \quad (c \in CS)$$
$$(\sim_t^{\mathbf{m'}})_{s'} = \bigcup_{s:\sigma_\Sigma(s)=s'}((\eta_C)_s \times (\eta_D)_s)((\sim_t^{\mathbf{m}})_s)$$
$$act_t^{\mathbf{m'}} = AS_{\sigma,|C|,|D|}^\sharp(\eta_C, \eta_D)(act_t^{\mathbf{m}})$$

where $C = \mathbf{m}(c)$, $D = \mathbf{m}(d)$, and $\eta_C : C \to V_{\sigma_\Sigma}F_{\sigma_\Sigma}(C)$ and $\eta_D : D \to V_{\sigma_\Sigma}F_{\sigma_\Sigma}(D)$ are the components of the unit η of the adjunction $F_{\sigma_\Sigma} \dashv V_{\sigma_\Sigma} : Mod(\Sigma) \to Mod(\Sigma')$ at C and D respectively. This yields a right adjoint as in Lemma 5.34.

Theorem 5.51 (Global Limits of Transformation Systems with d-Morphisms). *If the conditions of Lemma 5.50 hold the global category of transformation systems* $\mathbf{TF}_d^F$ *is complete.*

Proof. See Theorem 5.33.

Sequential Composition-by-Colimits

The usage of colimits for the sequential composition of transformation systems was discussed in Section 5.9. Here the formal requirements on the specification framework for the data spaces are recorded that allow the results to be carried over to other specification frameworks.

- If the category **Sig** of signatures of the institution *Ins* is complete and the functors *sorts* : **Sig** → **Set** preserve limits, then the corresponding category **DSig**^{Ins} of data space signatures is also complete, because

$$\mathbf{DSig}^{Ins} \cong (Id_{\mathbf{Set}} \downarrow (sorts^* \times sorts^*))$$

(see Proposition 5.39).

As discussed in Section 5.9 the limits of algebraic signatures and action signatures are hardly used for the sequential composition of (algebra) transformation systems. But w.r.t. other signatures this might make sense.

- If the model category $Mod(\Sigma)$ in *Ins* has limits—for the composition of the data states—and the partial order $AS_{D\Sigma}$ has infima (limits)—for the composition of the action structures—then the local category $\mathbf{TF}_d^{\boldsymbol{F}}(D\Sigma)$ of $D\Sigma$-transformation systems has colimits. The tracking relations and action structures of the colimits are given by

$$\sim_t^{\mathbf{m}} = \bigcap_{\gamma(t)} (\kappa_{\langle i,c_i \rangle} \times \kappa_{\langle j,c_j \rangle})^{-1} (\sim_{t_i}^{\mathbf{m_i}}),$$
$$act_t^{\mathbf{m}} = \sqcap_{\gamma(t)} AS_{D\Sigma}(\kappa_{\langle i,c_i \rangle}, \kappa_{\langle j,c_j \rangle})(act_{t_i}^{\mathbf{m_i}})$$

(using the notation of Lemma 5.37).

- If **DSig**^{ns} and the local categories $\mathbf{TF}_d^{\boldsymbol{F}}(D\Sigma)$ are cocomplete then the global category $\mathbf{TF}_d^{\boldsymbol{F}}$ is also cocomplete, because the forgetful functors are left adjoints (cf. Theorem 5.38).

5.11 Discussion

Composition of systems has been introduced at the semantic level as an operation on transformation systems. The definition follows their structure, given by transition graphs for the behaviour and data state models and action structures for the static structure. For that purpose corresponding composition operations for graphs, algebras, and structured sets have been combined. Composition of transformation systems can be defined directly via identification and synchronisation relations, or, more generally, in categorical terms via diagrams and limits. In both cases first connection relations are defined, modelling the way in which the systems are connected and interrelated, and then the result of these connections as a single new system can be obtained. Thus both the architecture of a composed system and its abstraction represented as a global unstructured view are covered. This general approach to composition can be instantiated in many ways by defining specific connection relations or specific kinds of diagrams. That means composition-by-limits yields a schema for the definition of composition operations, rather than a composition operation itself. The advantage is that composition is defined independently of any specific language, following the general semantic approach pursued by the transformation system reference model. With respect to the integration of specifications, this property can be used to obtain compositional integrations. The example of the two different specifications of the alternating bit protocol in CCS and UNITY has shown such a compositional comparison of heterogeneous specifications in the semantic domain.

Beyond the integration of single specifications the reference model can also be used to integrate specification languages. The construction of the institution of transformation systems from a data institution, an action structure framework, and a control flow logic in Section 4.7 has shown the interfaces and integration tasks that are necessary for that purpose. In this case, the composition operations of the considered languages also have to be reconstructed in terms of the composition operations of the reference model. In this book no complete mappings of languages have been defined, but the examples and discussions have shown the principal ideas for the mappings concerned.

In some cases a composition operation of a language is mapped to a composed composition and development operation. The parallel composition of CCS for example is given by a pullback (a limit of two transformation systems and an induced connection relation) followed by the exclusion of the synchronous parallel steps. This is enforced by the interleaving semantics of CCS. This observation, as well as a more complete mapping of CCS to a category of labelled transition systems, has been given in [WN97]. Data states are not considered there, however, so a comparison with other languages like the one discussed here is not supported by this approach.

In the interpretation of the language UNITY, which does not provide composition operations, composition of transformation systems has been reflected in the language. Interface variables that can be written by the environment have been designated by introducing actions that effect these updates. Corresponding transformation steps have been added to the behaviour of the components to account for the possible actions of the environment. Via composition with another system, appropriate actions are selected and then realised. An analogous extension of UNITY called ComUnity (for communicating UNITY) has been introduced in [FM97]. This extension is also based on a categorical analysis of composition, especially the composition of theories via diagrams, theory morphisms, and colimits (see [GG78]). The distinction of control flow and data states advocated with the transformation system approach is not considered there, however. This is also the reason why colimits instead of limits are used.

An application of the transformation system approach to composition of graph transformation systems has been worked out in [Koc99]. In the former definitions of composition graph transformation rules could be amalgamated, but their application could not be synchronised. This means that whenever some rules are applicable, their amalgamation is also applicable. According to the Parallelism Theorems (see [CMR$^+$97]) this means that the union with (uncontrolled) structural identification but without explicit synchronisation is used. In [Koc99] this is extended by a synchronisation relation in the abstract categorical version introduced in [Gro97b, Gro98a] that allows the combination of identification and controlled synchronisation as introduced here for transformation systems.

As a further study an application to the composition of Petri nets has been investigated in [Gri00]. Operations like union and fusion of Petri nets (see [HJS90, PER95]) allow the identification of data state parts (places) and actions (transitions) in the sense of transformation systems. Again, an explicit synchronisation beyond the common enabledness and the identification of transitions had not been supported. With a dual approach using limits instead of colimits (see [Win87]) synchronisation can be modelled, but not gluing. The idea of [Gri00] is to use the composition operations of transformation systems and then try to find syntactic representations in terms of Petri net compositions that yield the same behaviour as the composed transformation systems. Some results are stated, in particular an operation called *or-synchronisation* that allows the synchronisation of a transition with one member of a specified set of transitions. But a more systematic investigation is still open. It should also be noted that algebras as data states with homomorphisms for the data state composition-by-colimits does not take into account the monoidal structure of Petri nets. Thus not all Petri net compositions can be reconstructed as transformation system limits. Another institution for the data spaces could lead to a more concise reconstruction and extension.

The categorical definition of the composition of transformation systems shows the relationship of composition w.r.t. the semantics, the properties of systems, and the development relations. In particular, the results for the compositionality of developments are immediate results of the categorical treatment and yield general schemes for the checking of compatibilities. These results are at a very abstract level, since both composition and development are treated schematically rather than w.r.t. operations or relations of given languages. Concerning the compositionality of properties, the distinction of structure and behaviour yields the expected results, also corresponding to the generic treatment of behaviour specifications. In general structure is compositional, whereas behaviour is not.

An approach to a composition of behaviour models that is compositional in this sense has been presented in [LSW95]. Modal transition systems are used to distinguish required and admissible transitions, i.e., transitions that the system must execute and transitions it may execute. This yields more flexible specifications and makes the descriptions more compositional. Based on this distinction the composition can be described as the conjunction of specifications as suggested in [ZJ93]. The precondition for a compositional composition of specifications is then that the components are independent, which means that each required transition of one component corresponds to exactly one admissible transition of the other one. Other approaches to compositional properties and compositional verification are presented in [DFG98, ASW98, XS98], for example. Indeed, compositionality of behaviour specifications has become a research issue in its own right (see for instance [RLP98]).

An interesting topic for further research w.r.t. the application of transformation system composition is software specification languages, especially object-oriented approaches like UML. These lack both compositionality and precise concepts for refinements that are definitely required for software systems development. A more detailed discussion of this topic is given in Section 6.3; a sketch of a broader application was presented in [Gro00]. Furthermore, in [Joh99] an investigation concerning the compositionality of object-oriented statecharts (like the ones used in UML, see [HG97, BRJ98, UML]) has been undertaken. Similar to the Petri net composition presented in [Gri00], a syntactic presentation of the semantic composition of the corresponding transformation systems in the syntax of statecharts is sought. It was shown in [Joh99] that the parallel composition of statecharts (using the given statecharts as parallel regions of a new root state) in fact yields a pullback of their transformation system semantics. Thus the implicit identification of actions via their global names is made explicit by means of a cospan of signatures as in the categorical representation of identification relations introduced in Section 5.2. An extension of the approach in [Joh99] to data states and more elaborate transition labels (closer to the full UML definitions) is discussed in [Gro01].

6

Applications to UML Software Specifications

The domain of transformation systems has been introduced to provide a general integration framework for formal specifications. In this chapter an application of the integration approach to less formal software specifications is discussed. For that purpose models given in the Unified Modeling Language (UML) are considered: class diagrams for the specification of the structure and architecture of the system, and statechart and sequence diagrams for the specification of its behaviour. Analogous to the applications to specification formalisms presented in the previous chapters, the basic idea here is to interpret specifications semantically by sets of transformation systems, exhibit their correspondences, and thereby to check whether a common interpretation of all considered specifications is possible. As opposed to the former examples, however, the investigation cannot be completely formal, since the semantics of the given UML languages is not formally defined. That means the correctness of the transformation system semantics cannot be formally proved. To cope with this situation the interpretation will be open w.r.t. certain semantic decisions, which is then treated as parameters of possible admissible interpretations. On the other hand, the interpretation in the transformation system reference model provides the means for the formalisation and thus precision of the considered software specification languages.

Concerning state machines, for example, no solutions are given here for more subtle open semantic questions such as the resolution of conflicting transition sets with priorities (see [Joh01] for a discussion). Instead, the proposed semantics starts with a state machine that is already flattened, i.e., hierarchy and concurrency are resolved. This preprocessing of the original state machine has to be given separately. It is considered as a parameter in the transformation system semantics of state machines, which is independent of the different possible ways to flatten a state machine. On the other hand, the transformation system approach will show that an integrative interpretation of state machines and other UML models also includes semantic interpretations of these specifications that might not have been considered explicitly before. For example, even a flat state machine and a class diagram, whose semantics seem to be entirely clear and unique, still allow many interpretations when considered explicitly as viewpoint specifications. This effect is due to the viewpoint model itself: each single specification is only a specification of a certain aspect of the system; all other aspects of the system are not constrained by this specification. The latter can be interpreted arbitrarily, and all systems that conform to the specification in the aspect concerned are admissible interpretations of the specification. Viewpoint specifications, by definition, are partial, incomplete specifications. Thus a state machine in general also allows more than one interpretation.

In the further sections of this chapter the semantics of the three considered specification techniques is discussed in more detail. That is, their sets of admissible interpretations and transformations of these sets that semantically reflect the correspondences are defined. Beyond the formal semantics given in this way, a major contribution of this investigation is the compositionality for software models. It is carried over from the formal framework of transformation systems and allows us for example to consider a collection of objects as a single entity and to compose state machines (see Section 6.3.1). The former supports compositionality as an abstraction means that allows the focusing on arbitrary levels of granularity. The latter gives a formal semantics to the construction of systems by composing objects. In particular, it clarifies the interaction of state machines that is usually defined only very metaphorically. In Section 6.6 further methodological questions that arise from the conceptual integration are discussed.

6.1 Class Diagram Semantics

The semantics of UML class diagrams seems to be sufficiently clear at first sight, whence no formalisation would be required. However, the effort of a formalisation shows a number of issues that still need to be made precise. For example, there is still an ongoing discussion on what precisely the meaning of associations is, i.e., what kinds of properties or constraints they express. Roughly, an association represents a relation of the objects of the classes it connects. Second, associations are preconditions for interactions: objects may only communicate directly with each other if they have a link, which can only exist if there is an association between the corresponding classes. These are roughly the static and the dynamic aspects of associations (see [Ste01, Rum98]). Finally, associations are used for navigation. That means they yield expressions as elements of a language that can be used to denote objects that are related to a given object via a single link or a chain of links. More subtle and yet unclear issues, however, are the inheritance of associations and multiplicities of n-ary associations for example (see [Ste01, GLM01]).

It is important to realise that the meaning of associations also depends very much on the development stage the model is used in. In a more abstract model, as in requirements analysis or domain modelling for example, the relational aspect of associations is stressed, i.e., they are only used to express that there are relations of some classes. In more concrete models, in the design stage for example where an implementation is developed, the abstract logical concept of a relation must be implemented. For that purpose usually references are used, i.e., local internal data that makes it possible to access other objects. Thus collections of objects also have to be implemented that arise from associations with multiplicity $n > 1$. These distinctions in the interpretation of associations also appear in the corresponding languages. At the logical level associations can be used to navigate in a model, described by appropriate navigation expressions provided by the language, whereas in concrete realisations reference expressions must be used.

A very detailed and concise analysis of associations is given in [Ste01]. The association part of the formalisation presented here essentially follows the interpretations introduced in that paper. In particular, associations are considered as classifiers that can be instantiated (by links), have their own identity, and determine relations of objects, but do not coincide with these relations. Furthermore, associations can be extended to association classes and are generalisable. References and navigation, which are also essential features of associations, are not discussed in [Ste01], however.

To define the formal integrative semantics of a class diagram the set of its admissible interpretations as transformation systems has to be given. Since class diagrams focus on the static structure, first the data spaces of such transformation systems are defined. That means the *data states* describing instantaneous states of collections of objects and the *action sets* that indicate a step from one state to another are determined. The former are called system states in this context; their formal construction is more complex and treated in the following five subsections. Action sets are basically sets of operation calls, they are treated in Section 6.1.7.

The formal definition of the data state signatures and data states of class diagrams, which in this context are better called system signature and system state respectively, is presented in three steps. First the *architectural* aspect of a class diagram is covered by introducing class graphs and object graphs to represent the classifier and instance levels respectively. The former constitute a part of the system signature, the latter belong to the system states themselves. An object graph states how many objects there are and how they are linked. In the second step the *internal structure* of classes and objects is addressed, given by their attributes and query operations. The latter are conceived as static modelling elements here, too, because query operations do not change the state of a system. In fact they can be considered as attributes with parameters. The internal structure of a class is thereby represented as an algebraic signature, whence object states can be reconstructed as partial algebras of these signatures. Architecture and internal structure are then combined in the third step: The nodes of a class graph are labelled by the class signatures and the nodes of an object graph are labelled by the corresponding partial algebras. This yields the complete formal definition of system signatures and states respectively.

In Figure 6.1 a class diagram for a network protocol is shown. The example is an adaptation of the UML model of the DHCP protocol [IET97] given in [Tsi01]. Servers, clients, and IP-addresses are introduced. A server can be discovered by a client. If the server offers it an IP-address the client can then request it; the request is answered by an acknowledgement (ack) or not (nak), depending on the actual availability of the requested address. Later on the client can release the IP-address again for further dynamic network connections. Furthermore, a server can check whether it has free IP-addresses and get references to them. Note that servers do not have attributes in this model. Their data states are given by their actual links to *IPAddress* and *Client* objects. *IPAddress* objects can be bound or unbound, the address itself is modelled as a string. Finally, clients have operations for connecting to or disconnecting from the network.

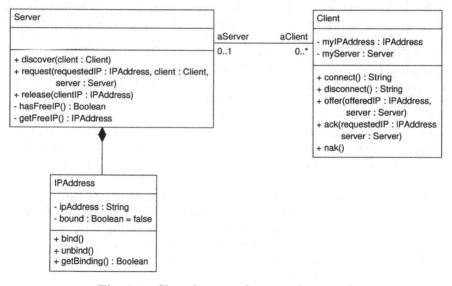

Fig. 6.1. Class diagram of a network protocol

6.1.1 Architecture: Class Graphs and Object Graphs

Class graphs are the formal counterparts of the classes and relationships (associations and generalisations) of class diagrams. A class graph has two kinds of nodes, representing classes and data types respectively, and three kinds of edges for the representation of associations, generalisations, and the inclusion of data types in classes or other data types. The latter are made explicit as edges here, too, as opposed to class diagrams where they are only represented textually. Generalisations and data type inclusions are represented by directed edges, associations as undirected hyper-edges, i.e., edges that have an arbitrary number of incident nodes, corresponding to n-ary associations.

First the structure of class graphs is defined independently of class diagrams, then the construction of the class graph of a given class diagram is introduced.

Definition 6.1 (Class Graph). A class graph $CG = (CN, DN, AE, GE, IE)$ with

- $AE = (AE(\mathbf{C}))_{\mathbf{C} \in CN^*}$,
- $GE = (GE(C', C))_{C', C \in CN}$, and
- $IE = (IE(D, C))_{D \in DN, C \in (CN \cup DN)}$

is given by

- two sets CN and DN, the class nodes and the data type nodes,
- for each list of class nodes $\mathbf{C} = (C_1, \ldots, C_n) \in CN^*$ a set $AE(\mathbf{C})$, the association hyper-edges,
- for each pair of class nodes $C', C \in CN$ a set $GE(C', C)$, the generalisation edges, and
- for each data type node $D \in DN$ and class or data type node $C \in CN \cup DN$ a set $IE(D, C)$, the data type inclusion edges,

such that

- there is at most one generalisation/data type inclusion edge between two nodes, i.e., $\sharp(GE(C', C)) \leq 1$ for all $C', C \in CN$ and $\sharp(IE(D, C)) \leq 1$ for all $D \in DN$ and $C \in CN \cup DN$.

An association edge $A \in AE(C_1, \ldots, C_n)$ is also denoted by $A : C_1, \ldots, C_n$, a generalisation edge $G \in GE(C', C)$ by $G : C' \longrightarrow C$, and a data type inclusion edge $I \in IE(D, C)$ by $I : D \dashrightarrow C$.

In order to construct the class graph of a given class diagram the names of the model elements of the class diagram are used. These are assumed to be unique throughout the class diagram. Then the class graph is essentially given by the sets of class names, association names, and generalisation names as class nodes, association hyper-edges, and generalisation edges respectively. The edges are connected with the class nodes as in the class diagram. As mentioned above, the data types and their occurrence in the classes are made explicit, too. Data types are assumed to be given via some data type library. A data type may occur in a class as a type of an attribute or a parameter (argument or return parameter) of an operation of that class. A data type may also occur in another data type. For example, Int occurs in $String$ if there is a function $length : String \rightarrow Int$, for instance. The occurrence relations among data types are assumed to be given with the data type library, too.

Definition 6.2. *The class graph $CG = CG(\text{CD})$ of a class diagram* CD, *with* $CG = (CN, DN, AE, GE, IE)$, *is given as follows.*

- *The set CN of class nodes is given by the set of class names of* CD.
- *The set DN of data type nodes is given by the set of all names of data types that occur in* CD *as a type of an attribute or a parameter (including the return parameters) of an operation of one of the classes in* CD.
- *Each set $AE(C_1, \ldots, C_n)$ of association hyper-edges is given by the set of names of associations of the classes $C_1, \ldots, C_n$.*
- *Each set $GE(C', C)$ of generalisation edges contains exactly one element $G : C' \longrightarrow C$ if C' is a direct subclass of C, i.e., there is a generalisation G in* CD *with child C' and parent C. Otherwise $GE(C', C)$ is empty.*
- *Each set $IE(D, C)$ of data type inclusion edges contains exactly one element $I : D \dashrightarrow C$ if*
  - *C and D are data types and D occurs in C,*
  - *C is a class and D occurs as a type of an attribute or parameter of an operation in C.*
  Otherwise $IE(D, C)$ is empty.

The class graph of the network protocol class diagram is shown on the left of Figure 6.2.

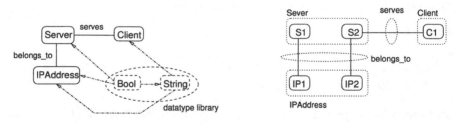

Fig. 6.2. The class graph of the *network protocol* class diagram with an object graph

The possible instantiations of a class graph are given by *object graphs*. The instantiation relations are given by graph homomorphisms (structure preserving mappings) from object graphs to class graphs. The structure of object graphs is similar to that of class graphs. Classes and associations can be instantiated by objects and links respectively. This is represented by the object nodes and link hyper-edges of object graphs and their mapping to class nodes and association hyper-edges respectively. Data types cannot be instantiated; they will be interpreted by static sets of values (see Section 6.1.2).

An object is considered first of all as an object of one class, its direct classifier. To consider an object O' of a class C' as an object of a superclass C of C' subclass inclusion edges are introduced. Such an edge is used to connect O' with an appropriate object O of class C representing 'O' considered as a

C-object'. The whole arrow $O' \longrightarrow\!\!\!\triangleright O$ can then be considered as representing one object with dynamic type, including the more detailed information on which classes the object may belong to via its source and target nodes. More generally, directed chains of objects and subclass inclusion edges $O_1 \longrightarrow\!\!\!\triangleright$ $O_2 \longrightarrow\!\!\!\triangleright \ldots \longrightarrow\!\!\!\triangleright O_n$ yield objects with dynamic types. This distinction of the direct class of an object and all classes it can be considered to belong to is discussed again in Section 6.1.4. There the subclass inclusion edges are used to *navigate* to the superclass that contains some required information, e.g., an association end.

We define first the general structure of object graphs, then the classification of an object graph w.r.t. a given class graph. The latter definition also gives the essential constraints on the instantiation of generalisation edges by subclass inclusion edges.

Definition 6.3 (Object Graph). *An object graph $OG = (ON, LE, SE)$ with $LE = (LE(\mathbf{O}))_{\mathbf{O} \in ON^*}$ and $SE = (SE(O, Q))_{O, Q \in ON}$ is given by*

- *a set ON, the object nodes,*
- *for each list of object nodes $\mathbf{O} = (O_1, \ldots, O_n) \in ON^*$ a set $LE(\mathbf{O})$, the link hyper-edges, and*
- *for each pair of object nodes $O, Q \in ON$ a set $SE(O, Q)$, the subclass inclusion edges, such that $\#(SE(O, Q)) \leq 1$.*

Analogous to association and generalisation edges a link hyper-edge $L \in LE(O_1, \ldots, O_n)$ is also denoted by $L : O_1, \ldots, O_n$ and a subclass inclusion edge $S \in SE(O, Q)$ by $S : O \longrightarrow\!\!\!\triangleright Q$.

A classification of an object graph is given by a graph homomorphism from the object graph to a class graph. The preservation of the corresponding graph structure, i.e., the node and edge kinds and the incidence relations, thereby realises the constraint that for each link there must be a corresponding association. The instantiation of generalisations by subclass inclusion edges, moreover, must make sure that each object of the subclass of a generalisation can indeed be considered as an object of the superclass. More precisely, it must determine a total injective function from the objects of the subclass to the objects of the superclass for each generalisation.

Definition 6.4 (Object Graph Classification). *A classification $c = (cl, as, ge)$ of an object graph $OG = (ON, LE, SE)$ w.r.t. a class graph $CG = (CN, DN, AE, GE, IE)$ is given by*

- *a mapping $cl : ON \to CN$ that assigns a class to each object,*
- *for each list of object nodes $\mathbf{O} \in ON^*$, a mapping*

$$as(\mathbf{O}) : LE(\mathbf{O}) \to AE(cl^*(\mathbf{O}))$$

that assigns an association hyper-edge between the class nodes of $\mathbf{O}$ to each link hyper-edge of $\mathbf{O}$, and

- *for each pair of objects $O, Q \in ON$ a mapping*

$$ge(O, Q) : SE(O, Q) \rightarrow GE(cl(O), cl(Q))$$

  that assigns a generalisation edge between the classes of O and Q to each subclass inclusion edge between O and Q,

such that

- *for each generalisation edge* $G : C' \longrightarrow C$
  and each object $O' \in ON$
  of class C', i.e., $cl(O') = C'$
  there is exactly one object $O \in ON$
  of class C, i.e., $cl(O) = C$
  and exactly one subclass inclusion edge $S : O' \longrightarrow O$
  such that $ge(S) = G$.

An object graph for the network protocol is shown on the right of Figure 6.2. Its classification is indicated by the dotted boxes and ovals surrounding the corresponding object nodes and link edges respectively.

The definition of object graph classification still admits different links of the same association connecting the same objects. As discussed in [Gen99] this might be useful. If it should not be allowed the following constraint has to be added:

$$\forall \mathbf{O} \in ON^* \; \forall L, L' : \mathbf{O} \in LE \, . \, as(L) = as(L') \Rightarrow L = L' \, .$$

6.1.2 Internal Structure: Class Signatures and Object States

Class graphs, objects graphs, and their classification represent the architectural part of a class diagram. Next, the internal structure of classes and data types is considered. The former is given by the attributes and query operations of a class. It may be given directly in the class, or indirectly, i.e., in one of the ancestors of the class. The set of all features (attributes and operations) of a class is given by its *full descriptor* that collects the information from all ancestors of the class. (We dispense with a formal definition of the full descriptor here, see [UML03], 2–69, for example.) A class structure is then represented by an algebraic signature $\Sigma = (S, F)$ with sort names S and function and constant names $F = (F_{w,s})_{w \in S^*, s \in S}$. Within the set S of sorts class sorts are distinguished, since they will be interpreted by sets of mutable object references, as opposed to the static values of the data types. Beyond attributes and query operations, return value place holders are also introduced. They represent the return values of operations in a state after their execution. If an operation has not been executed recently the corresponding return value is undefined.

Definition 6.5 (Class Signature). *A class signature $\Sigma = (S, CS, F)$ is given by an algebraic signature (S, F) with a designated subset $CS \subseteq S$ of* class sorts. *The signature $\Sigma C = (S, CS, F)$ of a given class C is defined as follows.*

- *The set S of sort names is given by the class name of C and all names of classes or data types that occur in the full descriptor of C as a type of an attribute or a parameter of an operation.*
- *CS is the subset of S given by all class names in S.*
- *The set F of (constant and) function names is given by*
  - *the attributes in the full descriptor of C with their types, i.e., for each attribute a with type t there is a constant $a : t$ in F,*
  - *a return value place holder $ret\_op : t$ for each operation op in the full descriptor of C with return type t,*
  - *the query operations in the full descriptor of C with their parameter type lists, and*
  - *the function signatures of the included data types.*

An internal state of an object O of class C is now represented by a partial ΣC-algebra St_O, as shown for example in Figure 6.3. A carrier set $(St_O)_s$ of a data type sort s contains the static values of sort s. A carrier set $(St_O)_{C'}$ of a class sort C' contains local references that an object holds internally to refer to objects of class C'. Note that these need not coincide with the nodes of the object graphs, i.e., the local view of the system from the point of view of a single object might not coincide with the global view of the system. Partial algebras as object states allow the representation of undefined attributes, query operations, and return values of operations, as well as partial functions in data types.

The full state of an object is then given by its internal state, its links—that are given in the object graph—and the values of the references if holds. The last ones are given within a system state, which is introduced next.

ΣClient		C1
sorts	String	A*
class sorts	Client	{0}
	IPAddress	{2}
	Server	{s}
functions attributes	myIPAddress : IPAddress	2
	myServer : Server	s
return values	ret_connect :String	–
	ret_disconnect : String	–

Fig. 6.3. State of the *Client* object $C1$ as partial Σ*Client*-algebra

6.1.3 Signature Diagrams and System States

Class graphs and class signatures are now combined to represent the architectural and structural information of a class diagram. In this way the the data state signature of the transformation systems that might be interpretations of a class diagram is defined. Such a data state (system) signature is not an algebraic signature; instead, a specific specification framework for class diagrams is defined. A system signature for a class diagrams is obtained by labelling the nodes of the class graph with class and data type signatures. The latter are assumed to be given by the data type library. The structural information of generalisations and data type inclusions is also represented by appropriate labels: each generalisation/data type inclusion edge is labelled by a signature morphism.[1] This can be considered as a correctness condition. Whenever there is a generalisation/data type inclusion edge between two class or data type nodes the corresponding smaller signature must be contained in the larger one. In the case of a generalisation the superclass has the smaller (contained) signature; if a data type D occurs in a class or another data type, then D has the smaller signature.

As above we define signature diagrams in general first and afterwards the construction of a signature diagram of a given class diagram.

Definition 6.6 (Signature Diagram). *A signature diagram* $\mathbf{SD} = (CG, l)$ *is given by a class graph* $CG = (CN, DN, AE, GE, IE)$ *and a labelling function* l *that assigns a class signature* $l(C)$ *to each class node* $C \in CN$, *an algebraic data type signature* $l(D)$ *to each data type node* $D \in DN$, *a signature morphism* $l(G) : l(C) \to l(C')$ *to each generalisation edge* $G : C' \longrightarrow\!\!\triangleright$ $C \in GE$, *and a signature morphism* $l(I) : l(D) \to l(C)$ *to each data type inclusion edge* $I : D -\!\cdot\!-\!\triangleright C \in IE$.

Definition 6.7. *The* signature diagram $\mathbf{SD} = \mathbf{SD}(\mathsf{CD})$ *of a class diagram* CD *is constructed as follows.*

- *The underlying class graph* $CG = (CN, DN, NE, GE, IE)$ *of* $\mathbf{SD}$ *is the class graph* $CG = CG(\mathsf{CD})$ *of the class diagram* CD.
- *Each class node* $C \in CN$ *is labelled by the corresponding class signature* ΣC.
- *Each data type node* $D \in DN$ *is labelled by an algebraic data type signature* ΣD, *which is assumed to be given via the data type library.*
- *Each data type inclusion edge* $I : D -\!\cdot\!-\!\triangleright D \in IE$ *is labelled by the signature inclusion morphisms* $\Sigma D \to \Sigma C$.
- *Each generalisation edge* $GE : C' \longrightarrow\!\!\triangleright C \in GE$ *is labelled by the according signature inclusion morphism* $\Sigma C \to \Sigma C'$.

---

[1] According to the construction of signature diagrams this will always be an inclusion morphism, but for further extensions, packages for example, other signature morphisms might be required that also allow renaming elements.

The signature inclusion morphisms used as labels for the inclusion and generalisation edges exist by definition of the class signatures and according to the assumptions on the well-definedness of the data type library. The signature diagram of the network protocol class diagram is shown in Figure 6.4.

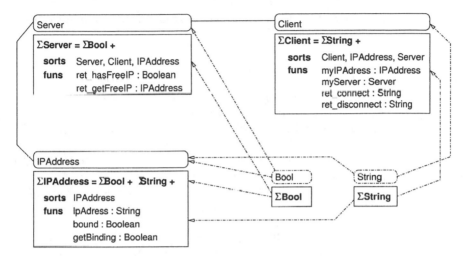

Fig. 6.4. The signature diagram induced by the network protocol class diagram

At the instance level the analogous combination of architectural and structural parts can now be defined. That means object graphs and internal object states are combined to represent system states. In addition, the object references inside the object states must be connected to the object nodes of the object graph. This is represented by a family of partial reference functions. Finally, the semantic interpretation of the data types by partial algebras of the data type signatures is given within a system state. The subclass and data type inclusion edges therefore induce constraints on the object states. Data types must be interpreted in all object states in the same way, and if an object O of class C is 'O' of a subclass of C considered as a C-object' via a subclass inclusion edge $O' \longrightarrow O$, then the restriction of the state of O' to the structure of the superclass C must coincide with the state of O. The same holds for the reference functions.

Definition 6.8 (System State). *Let* **SD** = **SD**(CD) *be a signature diagram of a class diagram* CD, *with* **SD** = (CG, l), $CG = (CN, DN, AE, GE, IE)$, *and* $l(C) = \Sigma C$ *for* $C \in CN$ *and* $l(D) = \Sigma D$ *for* $D \in DN$. *A system state SysState* = (DT, OG, c, OS, ref) *for* CD *is given by*

- *a family* $DT = (A_D)_{D \in DN}$ *of data type algebras, given by a partial* ΣD-*algebra* A_D *for each data type node* $D \in DN$,
- *an object graph* $OG = (ON, LE, SE)$ *with a classification* $c = (cl, as, ge)$: $OG \rightarrow CG$,

- *a family $OS = (St_O)_{O \in ON}$ of object states, given by a partial ΣC-algebra St_O for each object node $O \in ON$ with classifier $C = cl(O) \in CN$, and*
- *a family ref of reference functions, given by partial functions*

$$ref_{C'}^O : (St_O)_{C'} \dashrightarrow \{Q \in ON \mid cl(Q) = C'\}$$

for each class node $C \in CN$, each class sort C' in ΣC, and each object node $O \in ON$ with $cl(O) = C$,

such that

- *for each data type inclusion edge $I : D \dashrightarrow C$ and object state St_O with $cl(O) = C$ the restriction of St_O to the data type signature ΣD coincides with the given data type algebra A_D, i.e., $(St_O)|_{\Sigma D} = A_D$,*
- *for each subclass inclusion edge $S : O' \longrightarrow O \in SE$ with $ge(S) = G : cl(O') \longrightarrow cl(O)$*
  - *the restriction of the state of O' to the signature ΣC of $cl(O)$ coincides with the state of O, i.e., $(St_{O'})|_{\Sigma C} = St_O$, and*
  - *the reference functions of class sorts in $\Sigma C = (S_C, CS_S, F_C)$ coincide, i.e., $ref_{C''}^{O'} = ref_{C''}^{O}$ for all $C'' \in CS_C$.*

A state of the network protocol system is shown in Figure 6.5, with the underlying object graph as in Figure 6.2 and the internal state of the *Client* object C1 as shown in Figure 6.3. The reference functions are indicated by the arrows. Note that C1 has a reference to IP2 as value of the *myIPAddress* attribute, although there is no link between C1 and IP2, and no association between *Client* and *IPAddress*.

Remark 6.9. If only abstract system models are considered local object views and global system views need not be distinguished in the semantics. That is, as an abstraction it can be assumed that object identifiers are given globally and are uniformly used by all objects. In this case the reference functions of a system state can be replaced by the constraint that each carrier set of a class sort C' in an object state St_O is a subset of the corresponding set of object nodes, i.e., $(St_O)_{C'} \subseteq \{Q \in ON \mid cl(Q) = C'\}$ for each $C' \in CS$, where CS is the set of class sorts in the signature ΣC of the classifier $C = cl(O)$.

According to the different properties of system states, different levels of abstraction can be distinguished. In a fully abstract model references are not allowed: all possible connections of objects must be modelled by associations. This means that attributes of class sorts are excluded, like the *myServer* and *myIPSddress* attributes in the class *Client*. However, even without these attributes the class signature $\Sigma Client$ contains the class sorts *Server* and *IPAddress*, induced by the types of the parameters of the operations *offer* and *ack*. These should then be interpreted by sets of object nodes, as suggested in Remark 6.9.

When more concrete models are considered and both links and object references are allowed in system states, their relationship can be used for a

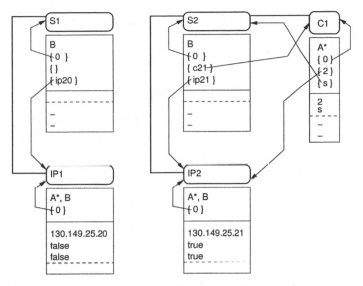

Fig. 6.5. A system state of the network protocol system

further characterisation. Consider first an association A from C to C' with multiplicity 0..1 at the C'-end. It is *realised* if there is an attribute a of type C', with the property that a has a value in a system state if and only if there is a corresponding link instantiating the association A in this state. That means $ref^O_{C'}(eval_O(a)) = O'$ if and only there is a link edge $L : O, O' \in LE$ with $as(L) = A$. Analogously, associations with multiplicity $n..m$ can be realised by m attributes such that at least n of them are defined in each state, and each one corresponds to a link of the association. Associations with multiplicities $n..m$ or $n..*$ can also be realised by attributes whose type is a collection type, like arrays, lists, or more complex data structures. The realisation relation then depends on the structure of the collection type. Note that the choice of the collection type introduces a new design decision. In particular, associations will not always be implemented by attributes of a set type, and also ordered associations will not always yield lists. This higher flexibility is also supported by the formal semantics proposed here in that the relation of links and references is not fixed.

A model is completely realised in this sense if all associations are realised. Intermediate models may contain both links and references, the former coming from the abstract model, the latter aiming at the implementation. At the other end of the development spectrum there are then the fully concrete models that no longer contain (unrealised) associations. The network protocol system represents an intermediate development stage, where some but not all associations are realised.

As mentioned above, associations not only define relations on objects but also yield navigation expressions. In the remainder of this section the corresponding language of class diagrams is defined. The definition of the transformation system semantics of class diagrams is continued in Section 6.1.7, where transformations of system states are introduced.

6.1.4 A Language for Object Systems

Based on the signature diagrams as formal representations of class diagrams a formal language for object systems can now be introduced. The basic idea is again to combine elementary mathematical constructs, according to the combination of graphs and algebraic signatures in signature diagrams. Class and data type signatures yield algebraic terms, with variables, constants, and function application, to denote values of data types and object references within one data type or class. The extension to object referencing that may yield objects of other classes is semantically covered by the reference functions of the system states. For their syntactic representation the usual dot notation will be employed. Furthermore, associations can be used to navigate in a system state. To define the syntactic navigation expressions first the undirected n-ary associations are resolved into directed binary navigation edges. Since associations essentially determine relations, navigation is interpreted as computing with relations in the sense of relational algebra. This is the main difference with the object constraints language OCL of UML (see [WK98, OCL, Ric01]). There a single navigation step yields a set (or list, if the association is ordered), whereas two or more steps yield a bag. The advantages of using sets throughout are that restructuring is supported, e.g., a new association can be introduced as an abbreviation for two consecutive ones, and that the analogy of associations in OO-models and relations in ER-models is preserved.

In this section only *expressions* are defined that denote elements of a system model. To specify its properties *formulae* are used, like equations, predicate instances, and other logical formulae based on these atomic formulae. However, this second step of the definition of an object language is straightforward, provided the expressions are defined. The new aspects, references and navigation, are already covered in it. Therefore the definition of the formulae of the object language is not given explicitly here.

Syntax of Expressions

In a UML class diagram navigability is modelled by the association ends and their navigability properties. From this information in the class diagram a function nav_{AE} can be derived for the formalisation that maps an association hyper-edge to a list of association end names and (positive or negative) values for their navigabilities. Thus, in addition to the signature diagram **SD**, we assume we have a set of association end names $AEnd$ and a function $nav_{AE} : AE \to (AEnd \times \{+, -\})^*$ with $nav_{AE}(A) = ((A_1, n_1), \dots, (A_k, n_k))$ that yields the association end names $A_i \in AEnd$ and navigability values

$n_i \in \{+, -\}$ for each association hyper-edge $A : C_1, \ldots, C_k \in AE$. Association end names are assumed to be unique, i.e., an association end (name) belongs to at most one association in a diagram.

For the graph-theoretic representation of navigation *navigation edges* are added to the class graph. These are binary directed edges that can be derived from the associations and the navigability information. Since the same derivation of binary navigation edges is needed for link hyper-edges in object graphs below, the corresponding link navigation edges are already defined here, too. Accordingly, we will also assume that in addition to an object graph, navigability information on its links is given by a set of link end names $LEnd$ and a function $nav_{LE} : LE \rightarrow (LEnd \times \{+, -\})^*$ with $nav_{LE}(L) = ((L_1, m_1), \ldots, (L_k, m_k))$ that yields the link end names L_i and navigability values $m_i \in \{+, -\}$ for each link hyper-edge $L : O_1, \ldots, O_k \in LE$. Thus the classification of the object graph must be compatible with the navigability, i.e., if $as(L) = A$ with $nav_{AE}(A) = ((A_1, n_1), \ldots, (A_k, n_k))$ and $nav_{LE}(L) = ((L_1, m_1), \ldots, (L_k, m_k))$ then $n_i = m_i$ for all $i = 1, \ldots, k$.

Definition 6.10 (Navigation Edges). *Let $CG = (CN, DN, AE, GE, IE)$ be a class graph, $OG = (ON, LE, SE)$ an object graph with a classification $cl = (cl, as, ge) : OG \rightarrow CG$, and nav_{AE} and nav_{LE} be navigability functions for CG and OG respectively that are compatible with cl.*

- *For each pair of class nodes $C, C' \in CN$ the set of* association navigation edges $ANE(C, C')$ *is given by*

$$ANE(C, C') = \{\ \tilde{A} \in AEnd\ |$$
$$\exists\, A : C_1, \ldots, C_k \in AE$$
$$\exists\, A_1, \ldots, A_k \in AEnd,\ n_1, \ldots, n_k \in \{+, -\}$$
$$\exists\, i, j \in \{1, \ldots, k\}\ .$$
$$nav_{AE}(A) = ((A_1, n_1), \ldots, (A_k, n_k))\ \wedge$$
$$C = C_i \wedge C_j = C' \wedge A_j = \tilde{A} \wedge n_j = +\ \ \}.$$

- *For each pair of object nodes $O, Q \in ON$ the set of* link navigation edges *is given by*

$$LNE(O, Q) = \{\ \tilde{L} \in LEnd\ |$$
$$\exists\, L : O_1, \ldots, O_k \in LE$$
$$\exists\, L_1, \ldots, L_k \in LEnd,\ m_1, \ldots, m_k \in \{+, -\}$$
$$\exists\, i, j \in \{1, \ldots, k\}\ .$$
$$nav_{LE}(L) = ((L_1, m_1), \ldots, (L_k, m_k))\ \wedge$$
$$O = O_i \wedge O_j = Q \wedge O_j = \tilde{L} \wedge m_j = +\ \ \}.$$

The derived classification ane : $LNE(O, Q) \rightarrow ANE(cl(O), cl(Q))$ of link navigation edges is then given by $ane(L_j) = A_j$ if L_j is a link end of the link L with $nav(L) = ((L_1, n_1), \ldots, (L_k, n_k))$ and $as(L) = A$ with $nav(A) = ((A_1, n_1), \ldots, (A_k, n_k))$.

Link end names are also assumed to be unique, whence the link navigation edge classification is well defined.

Variables may be used in expressions, too, and must therefore be declared corresponding to a given class or signature diagram. Thus both the type of the variable and the context where it is to be evaluated (i.e., the class or the data type) must be declared. Let $\mathbf{SD}$ be a signature diagram with underlying class graph $CG = (CN, DN, AE, GE, IE)$. A variable declaration for $\mathbf{SD}$ is then given by a family $X = (X_{C,t})_{C \in (CN \cup DN), t \in S_C}$, where S_C is the set of sorts in the signature $\Sigma C = (S_C, CS_C, F_C)$ of C. An element x of $X_{C,t}$ is also denoted by $x : t \in X_C$.

The components needed for the definition of the set $Exp_{\mathsf{CD}}(X)$ of expressions of a class diagram CD are thus

- the signature diagram $\mathbf{SD} = \mathbf{SD}(\mathsf{CD})$,
- the navigability function $nav_{AE} = nav_{AE}(\mathsf{CD}) : AE \rightarrow (AEnd \times \{+, -\})^*$, and
- a variable declaration $X = (X_{C,t})_{C \in (CN \cup DN), t \in S_C}$ for $\mathbf{SD}$.

Analogous to the variables expressions have a context and a type. The context states where the expression can be evaluated (i.e., basically, by objects of which classes it can be evaluated); the type of the expression is the type of its value, as usual. Thus $Exp_{\mathsf{CD}}(X) = (Exp_{C,t}(X))_{C \in (CN \cup DN), t \in S_C}$. As above, an expression $e \in Exp_{C,t}(X)$ is also denoted by $e : t \in Exp_C(X)$.

The first three rules for the definition of $Exp_C(X)$ are the usual definitions of algebraic or first-order logical terms. They introduce variables, constants, and function application.

variables
    if $x : t \in X_C$
    then $x : t \in Exp_C(X)$

constants
    if $c : t \in F_C$ (with $\Sigma C = (S_C, CS_C, F_C)$)
    then $c : t \in Exp_C(X)$

function application
    if $f : t_1, \ldots, t_n \rightarrow t \in F_C$
    and $e_1 : t_1 \in Exp_C(X), \ldots, e_n : t_n \in Exp_C(X)$
    then $f(e_1, \ldots, e_n) : t \in Exp_C(X)$.

An expression $r : C'$, where C' is a class sort, denotes a reference to an object of class C'. Attributes or query operations of this object are denoted with the usual dot notation , given by a further expression e. The latter may also contain references or navigations.

object referencing
    if $r : C' \in Exp_C(X)$ (where C' is a class sort in ΣC)
    and $e : t \in Exp_{C'}(X)$
    then $r.e : t \in Exp_C(X)$.

Navigation expressions are essentially given by paths of association navigation edges, i.e, association end names. Recall that the association hyper-edges in the class graph are only incident to the classes that are directly connected by the corresponding association in the class diagram. They are not incident to any subclasses of it. Inheritance of associations is now resolved in that paths of generalisation edges are used that allow navigation to an appropriate ancestor (superclass), where the desired association end is found. These paths of generalisation edges are implicit, i.e., they are not recorded in the syntactic navigation expression. The latter only records the names of the association ends that are (explicitly) used.

The type of a navigation expression is 'set of associated class'. This holds for a single association as well as for a chain of associations.

association navigation

if $G_1; \ldots; G_k \in GE^*$ with $G_i : C_{i-1} \longrightarrow\!\!\!\!\triangleright\, C_i$ $(i = 1, \ldots, k)$
and $A_1; \ldots; A_l \in ANE^*$ with $A_j : C_{k+j-1} \rightarrow C_{k+j}$ $(j = 1, \ldots, l)$
then $A_1; \ldots; A_l : \mathbf{set}(C_{k+l}) \in Exp_{C_0}(X)$

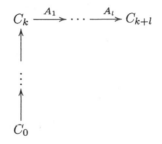

Finally, expressions of class types or data types can be lifted to sets by applying them to all elements of the set. If, for example, a navigation N yields a set of objects of class C and $a : t$ is an attribute of class C, then $N \rightarrow a$ yields the set of values of the attribute a of the objects in this set.

set expressions

if $N : \mathbf{set}(C') \in Exp_C(X)$
and $e : t \in Exp_{C'}(X)$
then $N \rightarrow e : \mathbf{set}(t) \in Exp_C(X)$

Further set-theoretic operations are not elaborated here, but are of course necessary for an object language. These would be defined as usual.

Remark 6.11. In the rule for the construction of navigation expressions generalisation paths are only allowed in front of the association path. That means the source of a navigable association is inherited by the subclasses, whereas the target is not inherited. (According to the UML definition all association ends are inherited, but, as advocated in [Ste01], *this cannot quite be taken literally.*) If an object O of class C has access to objects of class D according to the existence of a navigable association from C to D, then each object of a subclass of C also has access to objects of class D. But it may never expect to obtain an object of any subclass D' of D. Even if it obtained some object Q of class D', it would only know (i.e., could only use) it as an object of class D. The advantage of the model proposed here is that Q as an object of its class D' and 'Q considered as an object of the superclass D' can be distinguished. Models with global sets of object identifiers where class generalisation is represented by inclusion of object identifier sets like the one proposed in [OCL] do not support this distinction.

6.1.5 Evaluation of Expressions

To evaluate an expression $e \in Exp_{CD}(X)$ that is defined w.r.t. a signature diagram **SD**, a navigability function nav_{AE}, and a variable declaration X, the following instance level components are required.

- A system state $SysState = (DT, OG, c, OS, ref)$ w.r.t. **SD**, with $OG = (ON, LE, SE)$,
- a navigability function $nav_{LE} : LE \rightarrow (LEnd \times \{+, -\})^*$ for the object graph OG,
- a valuation v of the variables X, and
- an object $O \in ON$, where the evaluation starts.

Thus variables are evaluated according to their contexts in a data type algebra or in all object states corresponding to the context class. The latter must be compatible, i.e., a variable of data type sort in the context of a class must be mapped to the same value in all objects. Thus, a variable valuation is given by functions

$$v_{O,t} : X_{C,t} \rightarrow (St_O)_t \quad C \in CN \text{ with } \Sigma C = (S_C, CS_C, F_C)$$
$$t \in S_C, O \in ON, cl(O) = C$$

$$v_{D,t} : X_{D,t} \rightarrow (A_D)_t \quad D \in DN, \text{ with } \Sigma D = (S_C, F_C), t \in S_D$$

such that for all $O, O' \in ON$ with $cl(O) = cl(O') = C$ we have $v_{O,t} = v_{O',t}$ if $t \in S_D$ for some data type node D with signature $\Sigma D = (S_D, F_D)$.

The system state $SysState$, the navigability function nav_{LE}, and the variable valuation v are fixed for the evaluation of expressions. However, due to object referencing and navigation, the actual object where the evaluation takes place may change in the process of evaluation. Instead of indexing the evaluation function by all components $SysState$, nav_{LE}, v, and O, it is thus simply denoted by $eval_O(e)$.

Evaluation is a *partial* function, because the functions of the data types may be partial, attributes, return values of operations, or query operations may not be defined, or object references may be void or do not belong to the right object. It is defined along the definition of expressions as follows.

variables $(x : t \in X_C)$

$$eval_O(x) = v_{C,t}(x)$$

constants $(c : t \in F_C)$

if c^{St_O} is defined

then $eval_O(c) = c^{St_O}$

function application $(f : t_1, \ldots t_n \to t \in F_C, e_i : t_i \in Exp_C(X))$

if $f^{St_O}(eval_O(e_1), \ldots, eval_O(e_1))$ is defined

then $eval_O(f(e_1, \ldots, e_n)) = f^{St_O}(eval_O(e_1), \ldots, eval_O(e_1))$.

Note that the argument types of a function f may also be class types and that the subexpressions e_i of the function application $f(e_1, \ldots, e_n)$ may contain object references. Thus, depending on the state of the system, especially the reference functions, it might happen that the evaluation of e_i yields an object reference that does not belong to the actual object O, i.e., O cannot dereference it. This partiality is also covered by the definedness condition.

To evaluate an expression $r.e$ first the object reference expression r is evaluated, which yields the reference $i := eval_O(r) \in (St_O)_{C'}$. With the corresponding reference function $ref_{C'}^O$, the object node $Q := ref_{C'}^O(i)$ is determined, where the evaluation of the remainder e of the expression is continued.

object referencing $(r : C' \in Exp_C(X), e : t \in Exp_{C'}(X))$

if $eval_{ref_{C'}^O(eval_O(r))}(e)$ is defined

then $eval_O(r.e) = eval_{ref_{C'}^O(eval_O(r))}(e)$.

A navigation expression $A_1; \ldots; A_l$ yields the set of all object nodes that are accessible from O via a path of subclass inclusion edges $S_1; \ldots; S_k$ followed by a path of link navigation edges $L_1; \ldots; L_l$ that matches $A_1; \ldots; A_l$.

association navigation $(G_1; \ldots; G_k \in GE^*, A_1; \ldots; A_l \in ANE^*)$

$$eval_O(A_1; \ldots; A_l) = \{Q \in ON \mid$$
$$\exists S_i : O_{i-1} \dashrightarrow O_i \in SE \quad . \; ge(S_i) = G_i \quad (i = 1, \ldots k) \; \wedge$$
$$\exists L_j : O_{k+j-1} \to O_{k+j} \in LNE \; . \; ane(L_j) = A_j \quad (j = 1, \ldots l) \; \wedge$$
$$O = O_0 \wedge O_{k+l} = Q \; \}$$

$$O_k \xrightarrow{L_1} \cdots \xrightarrow{L_l} O_{k+l}$$

$$\vdots$$

$$O_0$$

Evaluation is defined for all navigations, but might yield the empty set.

Finally set expressions are evaluated by iterating the set and collecting all values.

set expressions $(N : \mathbf{set}(C') \in Exp_C(X), e : t \in Exp_{C'}(X))$.

> if $eval_Q(e)$ is defined for all $Q \in eval_O(N)$
> then $eval_O(N \to e) = \{eval_Q(e) \mid Q \in eval_O(N)\}$

Remark 6.12. If abstract system states without reference functions but global object identifiers in the local object states are considered (see Remark 6.9), the following definitions have to be changed accordingly.

The evaluation of **variables** $(x : C' \in X_C)$ for class sorts C' also becomes partial:

> if $v_{C,C'}(x) \in (St_O)_{C'} \subseteq \{O \in ON \mid cl(O) = C'\}$
> then $eval_O(x) = v_{C,C'}(x)$.

The evaluation of variables of data type sorts is total as before.

In the **object referencing** $(r : C' \in Exp_C(X), e : t \in Exp_{C'}(X))$ the reference functions are omitted:

> if $eval_{eval_O(r)}(e)$ is defined
> then $eval_O(r.e) = eval_{eval_O(r)}(e)$.

Remark 6.13. In a navigation expression only the used association ends are recorded, not the generalisations that lead to the appropriate class. Figure 6.6 shows an example where navigation along an association A with multiplicity $0..1$ yields two objects $(eval_{O_{12}}(A_1) = \{O_0, Q_0\})$, although the system state seems to conform to the class diagram, including the multiplicity 1 of the association A. This is of course due to the strange combination of multiple inheritance and a ternary association in this example.

But the formal model yields at least an unambiguous semantics for this situation, whether that corresponds to an intuitive understanding of associations, multiplicities, and generalisation in this case or not. (Is there any good intuition for such cases, anyway?)

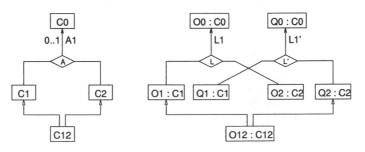

Fig. 6.6. Navigation with multiple inheritance and a ternary association

Remark 6.14. Internal navigation with subclass inclusion edges could also be used to define the inheritance of attributes and operations. This means, instead of using the full descriptor of a class to define the class signature, only its direct (incomplete) signature corresponding to the segment descriptor is taken. To evaluate an expression, an attribute $a : t$ for example, an object navigates to the superclass where this attribute is declared and looks up its value in the corresponding object state algebra. The formal definition of this construction, however, becomes more complicated than the definition of the full descriptor, so it has not been used here.

6.1.6 Further Static Features of Class Diagrams

In the formal model just defined the basic modelling concepts for the static structure of systems can be represented. Further features can now be added easily. **Multiplicities** have not been treated explicitly, but, obviously, a class multiplicity $n..m$ just constrains the number of objects of a class for each system state. This means system states are constrained by

$$n \leq \#\{O \in ON \mid cl(O) = C\} \leq m \,.$$

A multiplicity $k..m$ of an end of an n-ary association can be interpreted analogously. According to the UML standard ([UML03] 2–64) it specifies the number of possible links in a state for each fixed collection of objects at the other $n-1$ ends. That is

$$\forall O_1, \ldots, O_{j-1}, O_{j+1}, \ldots, O_n \in ON \,.$$
$$k \leq \#\{O_j \in ON \mid \exists L : O_1, \ldots, O_n \in LE \,.\, as(L) = A\} \leq m$$

where A_j is the constrained end of the association A. (For a discussion of some consequences and alternatives of this definition see [GLM01].) Other multiplicity ranges for classes and associations are treated analogously.

Next, **association classes** can be represented by labelling the association hyper-edges by corresponding class signatures, just like class nodes are labelled by class signatures. System states then also contain the states of the links, i.e., the instances of the association classes, given by partial algebras of the corresponding signatures, as attributes of the link hyper-edges, like object states are attributes of object nodes. Navigation edges from association classes to the incident classes of the association are derived corresponding to the definition in the UML standard. Analogously navigation edges are introduced at the instance level, i.e., the object graphs.

Also, **generalisation of associations** can be represented analogously to the generalisation of classes. Generalisation edges between the corresponding association hyper-edges are introduced into the class graph, and sub-association inclusion edges into the object graph, like the generalisation edges and subclass inclusion edges for classes and objects respectively. With the corresponding constraints (see Definition 6.4) the inclusion edges guarantee that the set of links corresponding to a subassociation corresponds to a subset of the set of links of the superassociation.

6.1.7 State Transformations

The set of all system states for a class diagram as defined in Definition 6.8 yields the set of data states for each transformation system that is an admissible interpretation of the class diagram. To complete the definition of admissible interpretations the possible transformations of data states have to be given.

By definition, a transformation step in a data space is given by two data states representing the commencing and the ending state of the step, and an action structure indicating the observable actions corresponding to this step. A pair of system states as the commencing and ending state of a transformation step shows

- how many objects have been created and destroyed (this is represented by the changes of the sets of object nodes in the system states),
- how the states of the (not destroyed) objects have changed and what the states of the newly created objects are,
- how the links and references have changed.

An action structure for a transformation step from one system state to another is given by a set of operation calls. That means parallel actions are considered, corresponding to the possible concurrency of the objects in the system. Each operation call is decorated with a target that allows one to determine the object that executes the operation. For that purpose the global object indexes are employed, using the dot notation $O.op(p_1, \ldots, p_n)$ as introduced in Section 6.1.4 to indicate that the object O is called to execute its operation op with the actual parameters $p_1, \ldots, p_n$. Formally operation call expressions, which are induced by the action signature of a class, are defined as follows.

Definition 6.15 (Operation Call Expressions). *The action signature A_C of a class C is given by the set of all non-query operation names of C with their parameter type lists. Return types that are recorded in the class signature, are nor taken up into the action signature. That is, if $op(x_1 : t_1, \ldots, x_n : t_n)$ or $op(x_1 : t_1, \ldots, x_n : t_n) : t$ is an operation of C, then $op : t_1, \ldots, t_n$ is an element of A_C.*

Let $\mathbf{SD} = \mathbf{SD}(CG)$ be a signature diagram of a class diagram CD, $\mathbf{SD} = (CG, l)$, $CG = (CN, DN, AE, GE, IE)$, and let nav_{AE} be a navigability function for $\mathbf{SD}$. Furthermore, let $OG = (ON, LE, SE)$ be an object graph with a classification $c = (cl, as, ge) : OG \to CG$. An operation call expression $O.op(p_1, \ldots, p_n)$ w.r.t. this structure is given by

- *an object node $O \in ON$, the target of the call,*
- *an operation name $op : t_1, \ldots, t_n \in A_C$, where $C = cl(O)$, and*
- *expressions $p_i : t_i \in Exp_C(\emptyset)$ for $i = 1, \ldots, n$, the actual parameters of the call.*

A transformation step of the network example is sketched in Figure 6.7.

Fig. 6.7. A transformation step in the network protocol

With system snapshots as data states and sets of operation calls as action structures each class diagram yields in this way a data space, i.e., a space of possible system states and state transformations. Since there is no behaviour specification the set of admissible interpretations of the class diagram is then given by all transformation systems with this data space. That means arbitrary transition graphs can be chosen and labelled with elements of this data space.

6.2 State Machine Semantics

After the modelling of the static structure and the architecture of object-oriented systems with class diagrams we now consider the UML modelling technique for the specification of the intra-object behaviour. State machines specify how objects of a given class react to operation calls or other events in their environment. The reaction may therefore depend on the state of the object, whereby a state machine state is an abstraction that need not coincide with the data state of the object, i.e., the values of its attributes.

Basically, a state machine is an automaton with events as input, actions as output, and guards as further transition labels. Events and actions are specified in detail in the UML standard. For the discussion here it is sufficient to consider operation calls to the object concerned and operation calls to other objects, i.e., call events and call actions. The transitions of a state machine may be constrained in addition by guards, i.e., boolean expressions specifying conditions on the data state of the object. State machines include several further features, like hierarchical states, parallel regions, history markers, etc. Their semantics has been defined in several approaches by reducing it to some kind of labelled transition system with event–guard–action labels (see for instance [HN95, DJHP97, LBC00, EW00]). The different semantics corresponds to the different variants of statecharts and state machines and to the different interpretations of the concepts defined only informally in the UML standard or the expository papers on statecharts (see [Bee94] for a survey). As a starting point for the definition of the transformation system semantics we may assume therefore a representation of a first-level operational semantics in terms of appropriate labelled transition systems. This decouples the specific issues of the transformation system semantics from the more operational questions concerning some state machine features whose meanings have not yet been entirely clarified. (In [Joh01] for example the interference of parallel regions, inter-level transitions, and maximal response to events is discussed and compared with the different solutions proposed in [UML, EW00, HG97, Joh99, MK98] and by the Rhapsody tool.) The first-level operational semantics, i.e., the translation of a state machine into a transition system with guard–event–action labels, can thus be considered as a parameter of the transformation system semantics that can be set independently of the remaining definitions.

As an example throughout this section the state machine of the *Server* class shown in Figure 6.8 is used. It is a flat labelled transition already. The transitions represent the different behaviours of the public operations of this class, depending on the control states of the objects and guards checking the parameters. In the figure the transitions labels are abbreviated, but their proper labels are given below.

In a state machine the order of the steps is defined, i.e., the overall reactive behaviour of an object, but the effect of the actions on its data state are not specified. To a certain extent this is complementary to class diagrams, where data states and transformation steps are specified, but the overall behaviour is left open.

The basic idea of the interpretation of a state machine by a set of transformation systems is to add the data states and transformations to its control states and transitions respectively in all possible ways. (Compare the interpretation of class diagrams, where transition graphs could be added arbitrarily to the data space induced by the class diagram.) This will then yield the set of admissible interpretations of a state machine.

Dual to the construction of the class diagram semantics we consider now the transition graphs of the admissible transformation system interpretations. That means control states and transitions are determined first. However, these will already incorporate the data states and action structures. They can be then recovered from the transition graph via suitable projections, which yields the labelling.

6.2.1 Control and Data States

First the data states of the transformation systems that might be admissible interpretations of a state machine are defined. Such a data state consists of a data state of a focal object O, i.e., one prototypical object that is fixed to define the semantics of the state machine. This is defined as in the interpretation of class diagrams above as a partial algebra of the signature induced by the class C of O. The class is supposed to be known; in UML terms it is the *context* of the state machine. In addition to the data state of the focal

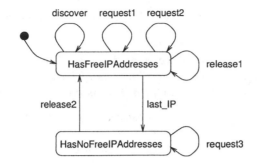

discover   request1   request2

HasFreeIPAddresses   release1

release2   last_IP

HasNoFreeIPAddresses   request3

Full labels for the transitions:

discover : *discover(client)*   (event)
            [self.hasFreeIP()=true]   (guard)
            /   client.offer(getFreeIP(),self)   (action)

request1 : *request(reqIP,client,server)*
            [(server−self)   and   (reqIP.getBinding()=false)]
            /   reqIP.bind();client.ack(reqIP,self)

request2 : *request(reqIP,client,server)*
            [(server=self)   and   (reqIP.getBinding()=true)]
            client.nak

request3 : *request(reqIP,client,server)*
            [(server=self)]
            /   client.nak

last_IP : *—*
            [self.hasFreeIP=false]
            / —

release1 : *release(clientIP)*
            [—]
            /   clientIP.unbind()

release2 : *release(clientIP)*
            [—]
            /   clientIP.unbind()

Fig. 6.8. State machine for *Server* objects

object, some information on its local environment is needed for the semantic interpretation of the state machine. It may contain for instance calls to other objects, whereby these objects are denoted by object references. Furthermore, conditions may refer to the publicly visible part of the state of other objects. Thus the objects that are known to the focal object, their visible data states, and the connection of the internal object references of the focal object to the external objects must be represented in a data state. Such an environment can be represented by an object graph with one designated node for the focal object.

Definition 6.16 (Data State of a State Machine). *Let SM be a state machine that models the behaviour of objects of a class C in a class diagram* CD. *A data state $D = (A, E, St, ref)$ of SM is given as follows.*

- *A is a partial ΣC-algebra; it represents the data state of a focal object O.*
- *The environment $E = (OG, s, c)$ is given by an object graph $OG = (ON, LE, SE)$ with a designated node $s \in ON$ for the focal object and a classification $c = (cl, as, ge)$ of ON w.r.t. the class graph of* CD.
- *$St = (St_O)_{O \in ON}$ is a family of partial $p\Sigma C$-algebras, where $p\Sigma C$ is the signature induced by the public attributes of class C and $C = cl(O)$; these represent the parts of the data states of the objects in the environment of O that are visible for O.*
- *$ref = (ref_{C'} : A_{C'} \to \{Q \in ON \mid cl(Q) = C'\})_{C' \in CS}$, where CS is the set of class sorts of ΣC, is a family of partial functions; these yield the external object nodes corresponding to the internal object references in O.*

A state of the server object $S2$ with its local environment, given by the objects $C1$ and $IP2$ and the referencing $0 \mapsto S2$, $c21 \mapsto C1$, $ip21 \mapsto IP2$, is shown in Figure 6.9. Since the class *Client* and *IPAddress* do not have public attributes the data states of the objects $C1$ and $IP2$ are void. Obviously, this data state is a part of the system state shown in Figure 6.5.

A control state of a state machine is now given by pair (s, D), where s is a configuration of the state machine, i.e., a maximal set of states that the state machine can be in simultaneously ([HN95]), and D is a data state of the state machine, i.e. the focal object and its local environment. This realises the addition of all possible data states to the state machine configurations mentioned above. (A similar construction of states as pairs of control states and data states has been used in the abstract object model introduced in [Web97].) The data state of the *Server* object $S2$ shown in Figure 6.9 together with the state *HasFreeIPAddresses* of the *Server* state machine in Figure 6.8, for example, yields a control state of a transformation system interpretation. The data space label of a control state (s, D) is finally given by the projection to D.

6.2.2 Transitions and Transformations

The second step in the definition of admissible interpretations of state machines by transformation systems concerns the transitions and transformations. As mentioned above, we assume that the state machine under consideration already has a flat structure, i.e., hierarchical states and concurrence are resolved. Moreover, action sequences are assumed to be modelled with individual consecutive transitions instead of labelling a single transition with a

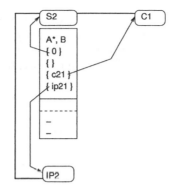

Fig. 6.9. A state of the *Server* object $S2$ with a local environment

sequence of actions. According to the run-to-completion semantics, this specifies the same behaviour. Finally, we assume that all expressions that occur as
events, guards, or actions in the state machine are instantiated, which means
that single transitions are replaced by (possibly infinite) sets of transitions
where the variables of the expressions are instantiated by all possible values.
This instantiation of expressions with all possible values for their variables is
also used in process calculi for the definition of the semantics of process expressions with variables. In the context of state machines this step is a non-trivial
one, since it requires a definition of scopes of variables that is compatible with
the complex structure of state machines. Since the problems that have to be
solved thereby do not essentially contribute to the integrative semantics that
is addressed here, instantiation is not defined formally here. Due to these preconditions the transitions of a state machine to be interpreted are thus all of
the form $e[g]/a : s_1 \rightarrow s_2$, where the event e, the guard g, and the action a
are ground expressions. Each component may also be empty.

The basic idea is to combine the transitions of the state machine with
arbitrary data state transformations, corresponding to the combination of
state machine configurations with arbitrary data states.

However, in view of the composition of state machines, which is discussed
in the following section, some preprocessing of these flat state machines is necessary. It prepares the treatment of asynchronous and synchronous operation
calls within one framework.

The first step of the preprocessing consists of the separation of event and
action transitions. Thus each state machine transition $e[g]/a : s_1 \rightarrow s_2$ yields
two consecutive transitions $e[g] : s_1 \rightarrow s'$ and $/a : s' \rightarrow s_2$. In the second
step of the preprocessing explicit return actions are introduced that represent
the termination of the execution of an operation. The aim is to have for each
operation call event op a set of corresponding return actions $/r_{op}$ that indicate
the end of the relevant part of the execution of op by sending a message back
to the calling object. The return action need not be the final action of the
operation, but it is the last one with which return values can be sent back to

the calling object. If return actions are not explicitly provided by the state machine they may be deduced via the run-to-completion semantics. That is, when the called state machine reaches a stable state after the event of an operation call, this state is expanded by an entry action that issues the return message.

If there is exactly one return action reachable from the operation call event in the state machine of the executing object the operation is deterministic. But operations may also be non-deterministic, indicated by several return actions reachable from the corresponding call event, or they may diverge. In this case there is no return action on any path starting from the call event.

Dually, return events are added immediately after each synchronous operation call action. That means each transition with a synchronous operation call action $/op : s_1 \rightarrow s_2$ is replaced by two consecutive transitions $/op : s_1 \rightarrow s'$ and $r_{op} : s' \rightarrow s_2$, where r_{op} is the return event corresponding to the call action op. Asynchronous operation call actions do not receive additional return events.

These transitions are now combined with data state transformations, which then yields the possible transitions for transformation systems as interpretations of the state machine considered. In this step two options are possible, corresponding to a strict and a loose interpretation of the state machine respectively. In a strict interpretation the only transitions that may be combined with a transformation that changes the data state are synchronous operation calls and internal actions like assignments, create, and delete actions. Communication actions or events, i.e., asynchronous operation call actions and operation call events, may not change the data state. The combination of a synchronous operation call action with a data state transformation represents the side effects on the objects in the environment and the calling object itself that may occur during the execution of the operation.

A loose interpretation on the other hand assumes that certain internal actions might not be visible in the state machine, i.e., it is considered as modelling essentially the communication of the object, without going into the details of the internal activities. In this case, sending or receiving messages may be accompanied by changes of the internal data state. Thus any transition $t : (s_1, D_1) \rightarrow (s_2, D_2)$ with arbitrary data states D_1 and D_2 is an admissible interpretation of a transition $t : S_1 \rightarrow s_2$ of the state machine in the loose interpretation. The only constraint is that D_1 must satisfy g if $t = e[g]$ is an event transition with guard g. The combination of an operation call event with a data state transformation represents the execution of the operation as a single transition. In a strict interpretation it is assumed that the data state changes triggered by an incoming operation call are modelled explicitly, for instance as internal actions.

Representing all possible call events of the environment to the object within the semantics of the object is often called an *open semantics*, since it not only reflects what the object performs actively but already includes all possible behaviours of the environment. With open semantics the composition of systems (objects, state machines) amounts to a restriction of the local behaviour to the one that the other system permits or realises.

Based on the definitions of strict and loose interpretations of transitions, the corresponding notions for transformation systems can be defined. A transformation system is a loose admissible interpretation of a state machine if

- its data states are pairs (s, D) of state machine configurations and data states as defined in Section 6.2.1,
- the data state labels are given by $\mathbf{m}(s, D) = D$,
- all of its transitions are loose admissible interpretations of the preprocessed state machine's transitions,
- the action structures of the transitions are given by $\mathbf{m}(e[g]) = e$ and $\mathbf{m}(a) = a$, i.e., event–guard pairs are mapped to the event and actions are mapped identically.

A transformation system is a strict interpretation of a state machine if furthermore

- all interpretations of the state machine's transitions are strict and
- for each event transition $e[g] : s_1 \to s_2$ and each data state D_1 that satisfies g the transition $e[g] : (s_1, D_1) \to (s_2, D_1)$ is present in the transformation system.

The latter condition means that enabled transitions cannot be neglected in a strict interpretation. In a loose interpretation it may happen that a transition is enabled according to its state machine description, but the operation that is executed blocks the transition. This blocking might also be documented in the precondition of the operation, but it might not be contained in the state machine.

Strict interpretations of the *request1* transition in the *Server* state machine are shown for example in the central column of Figure 6.10. There the object state D_{S2} of $S2$ is given as in Figure 6.9. Note that in this example the operation *request* does not change the state of the server, but only triggers further actions.

Note that even in a strict interpretation the combination of state machine transitions with data state transformations may yield a transition graph whose structure is different from the one of the state machine. If an internal operation is non-deterministic for example, a single transition $/op : s_1 \to s_2$ in the state machine may be interpreted by several transitions $/op : (s_1, D_1) \to (s_2, D_2^{(1)}), \ldots, /op : (s_1, D_1) \to (s_2, D_2^{(n)})$, representing the different possible behaviours of op. This applies for example to underspecified operations like the ones whose behaviours depend on the environment or system parts that have not been specified.

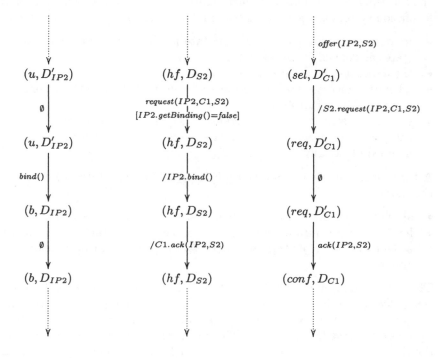

Abbreviations used for the state machine states:

u	=	*Unbound*	b	=	*Bound*
sel	=	*Selecting*	*req*	=	*Requesting*

hf = *HasFreeIPAddresses*
conf = *Configured*

Fig. 6.10. Synchronous steps of *IPAddress*, *Server*, and *Client* objects

6.3 Composition of State Machines

A state machine specifies the behaviour of a generic single object of a given class. A system is composed by creating a set of objects and letting them interact with each other according to their specifications. The interaction may occur between objects of the same or different classes and is determined by the mutual operation calls. When state machines are used for the specification of the intra-object behaviour this inter-object behaviour is already addressed and determined, too, in that the relation of call events and call actions within each object is specified. Putting state machines together, this determines the interaction of the objects: the call action of one object is a call event for the called object.

At the semantic level this can be reflected by the composition operations for transformation systems introduced in Chapter 5. As discussed in Section 5.1, a composition of transformation systems is defined by an identification relation that establishes the syntactic correspondences of the systems and a synchronisation relation that states which states and transitions are compatible with each other in the sense that they can be combined to obtain a global state or transition. The basic idea for the composition of state machines is now to derive identification and synchronisation relations for transformation systems that are admissible interpretations of the state machines. In this way a formal semantics for the state machine composition is defined that reflects the synchronisation of call actions and call events.

6.3.1 Asynchronous Communication

Asynchronous communication is the simpler case of composition. With the assumptions and the preprocessing made above, the synchronisation relation is immediately given by the synchronisation of call actions and corresponding call events.

Consider as an example the steps of the *IPAddress*, *Server*, and *Client* objects $IP2$, $S2$, and $C1$ shown in Figure 6.10. These correspond to the state machines shown in Figure 6.8 and 6.11 and represent admissible behaviours in a situation where the client $C1$ has been offered the IP address managed by the *IPAddress* object $IP2$ and now requests it. $IP2$ is still unbound, i.e., its initial local data state D'_{IP2} is given as in Figure 6.5, except that $bound = false$. It only knows itself under the reference 0, i.e.,

$$I'_{IPAddress} = \{IP2\}, I'_{Server} = I'_{Client} = \emptyset, ref'^{IPAddress}_{IP2,IPAddress}(0) = IP2 \ .$$

The initial state D'_{C1} of $C1$ is also as in Figure 6.5, except that it does not yet have an IP address. It only knows the server object $S2$ under its reference $s \in C1_{Server}$ and itself as 0. The initial state D_{S2} of $S2$ is the one given in Figure 6.5.

The induced *identification relation* for the composition of the transformation systems is now defined as follows. To reflect the sharing of pervasive static data types like *Strings* and *Booleans* these are identified in the components. This implies that they must always be interpreted identically. Attributes are never shared, corresponding to data encapsulation. On the other hand, all operation names are shared to make possible the communication between the objects. Object nodes of corresponding sorts may be identified to represent overlappings of the local environments of the objects, but the identifications have to be declared explicitly for the interconnection. They cannot be derived from the state machines since objects are not explicitly mentioned there. (In fact, this may depend on the actual language used for the action expressions.)

Now the *synchronisation relation* on the transition graphs has to be derived. Control states (s, D) and (s', D') of two transformation systems for

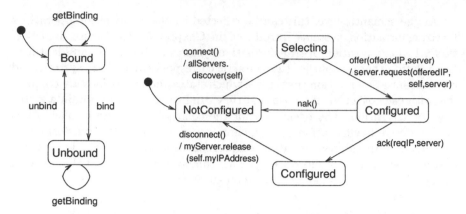

Fig. 6.11. State machines for *IPAddress* and *Client* objects

state machines are synchronous if the public parts of the data states of the objects in the identified parts of the local environments coincide. Concerning the transitions, we assume in this section that all operation call actions are asynchronous. Then two transitions are synchronous if one belongs to an object $O \in ON$ and consists of an operation call action $/O'.op$, and the other one belongs to the referred object O' and consists of the complementary operation call event op. That means the call action is synchronised with the call event, provided the guards allow it. Beyond these synchronisations the idle transitions are synchronous with all those transitions whose guards are satisfied in the commencing and ending states of the idle transition.

Consider again the steps of the *IPAddress*, *Server*, and *Client* objects $IP2$, $S2$, and $C1$ shown in Figure 6.10. In the first step $C1$ performs the action $S2.request(IP2, C1, S2)$, i.e., it sends a request to the server $S2$ that offered the IP address. According to the definition above, this transition is synchronous with the first transition of $S2$: the called object is $S2$, the operation call in the action of $C1$ and the event of $S2$ coincide ($request(IP2, C1, S2)$), and the guard of the $S2$-transition does not refer to $C1$.

The first transition of $S2$ is also synchronous with the first transition of $IP2$, since the guard of the $S2$-transition is true in the data state D'_{IP2}. Computing in this way the whole synchronisation relation for this example yields that all states and transitions shown on the same horizontal lines in Figure 6.10 are synchronous.

The composition operations of transformation systems also now yield a global view of the interaction of objects (i.e. the corresponding state machines) as a single entity. This is given by the result of the composition operation as defined in Section 5.1 that was defined there as follows.

- Its control states and transitions are given by pairs of synchronous control states and transitions of the local systems respectively.

- Its data space signature is given by the union (pushout) of the local signatures w.r.t. the identifications declared with the identification relation.
- Its data states and action structures are given by the amalgamations of the local data states and action structures respectively. The overlapping is therefore again given by the identifications expressed by the identification relation.

The global view of the interaction of the *IPAddress*, *Server*, and *Client* objects *IP2*, *S2*, and *C1* according to their state machines is thus given as follows. Its transition graph is given by the triples of synchronous control states and transitions, as defined above (the horizontal correspondences in Figure 6.10). The data states of the global view are given by the amalgamations of the object states as shown in Figure 6.12, for example. Thus object nodes with identical names are shared, i.e., the union of the environments of the three objects is taken. (This corresponds to the implicit identification relation on object node sets given by $\{(C1, C1), (S2, S2), (IP2, IP2)\}$.) Finally, the action structures are given by the unions of the local action structures.

For the steps shown in Figure 6.10 this yields the following three global steps:

$$\{ \ (request(IP2, C1, S2)[IP2.getBinding() = false],$$
$$/S2.request(IP2, C1, S2)) \ \} \ ;$$
$$\{ \ (bind(), /IP2.bind()) \ \} \ ;$$
$$\{ \ (/C1.ack(IP2, S2)), ack(IP2, S2)) \ \} \ .$$

Apart from the more complex notation this corresponds exactly to the *complementary actions* of the *synchronisation algebra* of a process calculus like CCS.

6.3.2 Synchronous Communication

The basic difference of asynchronous and synchronous operation calls in terms of composition of transformation systems is that in the first case the operation call action is synchronised with the call event, whereas in the second case the operation call must be synchronised with the whole execution of the called operation.

For the definition of the synchronisation relation, first a sequential and parallel closure of the preprocessed state machine is required (see Definitions 4.21 and 4.24). Sequential compositions of transitions provide operation executions as single transitions, based on the introduction of return actions for operation call events. Parallel transitions are required for recursive calls such as callbacks. For a pair of consecutive transitions $/op : s_1 \rightarrow s_2$ and $r_{op} : s_2 \rightarrow s_3$, given by a synchronous operation call and the corresponding return event as introduced in the preprocessing, their sequential composition will be denoted by $/\overline{op} = (/op); (r_{op}) : s_1 \rightarrow s_3$. It represents the synchronous operation call

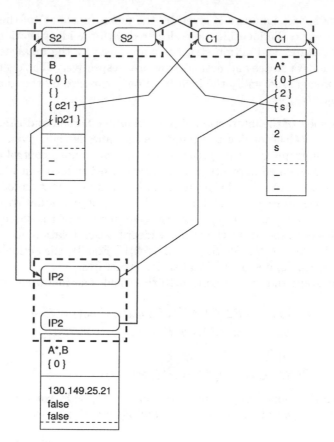

Fig. 6.12. Amalgamation of object states induced by shared local environments

action in the calling object as a single step. Analogously, the sequential composition of transitions from an operation call event to a corresponding return action will be denoted by $\overline{op} = op; \ldots; r_{op}$. Any such sequence represents a complete execution of the operation in the called object as a single step.

Now let SM_1 and SM_2 be two state machines that specify the behaviours of two objects o_1 and o_2. Both state machines may contain synchronous and asynchronous operation call actions. The synchronisation relation for SM_1 and SM_2 is defined as follows (see also Figure 6.13).

- Each operation call event transition $op : s_1 \to s_2$ in SM_1 is in synchronisation relation with each corresponding asynchronous call action $/o_1.op : s'_1 \to s'_2$ of SM_2 and vice versa.
- Let $\{/o_2.op_1, \ldots, /o_2.op_n\}$ be the set of all call-backs in the execution of an operation op by o_1, i.e., the operation call actions to o_2 that are on a path from the call event $op : s_1 \to s_2$ to a corresponding return action $/r_{op}$ in SM_1. Then each operation execution transition $\overline{op} : s_1 \to$

s_2 in SM_1 is in synchronisation relation with each parallel composition $/ \overline{op} \, \|o_2.\widetilde{op}_1\| \cdots \|o_2.\widetilde{op}_n$ in SM_2, where $o_2.\widetilde{op}_i = o_2.op_i$ if the call-back action $/o_2.op_i$ is asynchronous and $o_2.\widetilde{op}_i = o_2.\overline{op}_i$ if the call-back action $/o_2.op_i$ is synchronous.

- Each return action $r_{op} : s_1 \to s_2$ that ends an operation call event is in synchronisation relation with the idle transitions of all states that are in synchronisation relation with s_1.

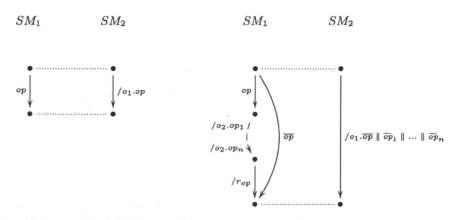

Fig. 6.13. Synchronisation relation (indicated by dotted lines) for asynchronous (left) and synchronous (right) communications

Binary compositions of state machines can of course be iterated to obtain compositions of arbitrary numbers of state machines. A composition is complete if all operation call actions that occur on a path triggered by some call event are synchronised with the corresponding call events in the state machine for the called object.

The diagram in Figure 6.14 shows a simple sequencing of operation calls via the sequence diagram and the corresponding three state machines for the objects concerned. Assume all operation calls are synchronous. When object o_1 receives the operation call op_1 it calls op_2 of o_2, which in turn calls op_3 of o_3. When o_3 finishes the execution of op_3 it sends its return message, whence o_2 signals o_1 that it has finished op_1. The sequence of return messages is, as usual, not shown in the sequence diagram.

Figure 6.15 shows the steps of the state machines with the explicit return actions and events, and the synchronous operation call action and operation execution transitions. The synchronous call action transition $/o_2.\overline{op}_2$ of o_1 is synchronised with the operation execution transition $\overline{op}_2$ of o_2. Analogously the synchronous call action transition $/o_3.\overline{op}_3$ of o_2 is synchronised with the operation execution transition $\overline{op}_3$ of o_3. This yields, as a result, the transition system shown in the top line of Figure 6.15. The projections to the three local

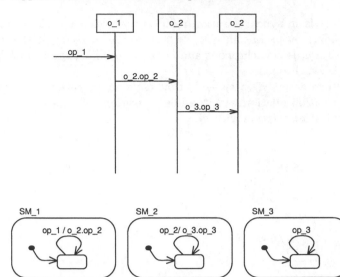

Fig. 6.14. Sequence diagram and state machines for consecutive synchronous operation calls

systems, represented by the dotted lines, also indicate the synchronisation relation again. The first step of the composed system corresponds to the first step of o_1, the call of op_1 arrives, o_2 and o_3 are still idle. In the second step o_1 synchronously calls op_2 at o_2 and waits for the return event $(/op_2.\overline{op}_2)$. Within this step o_2 completely executes op_2, which includes the execution of op_3 by o_3. In the last step o_2 and o_3 are idle again, while o_1 sends back the return message $/r_1$.

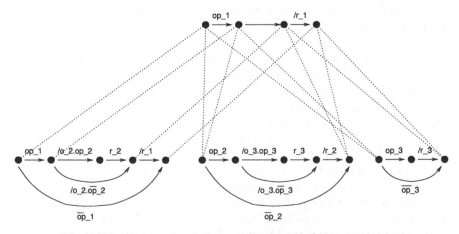

Fig. 6.15. Preprocessed state machines and their composition

Figure 6.16 shows a sequence diagram with a call-back and state machines for the two involved objects. While executing op_0 object O calls object Q to perform op_1, which in turn during the execution of op_1 calls back O to perform op_2. When O signals Q that it has finished op_2, Q can send the return message r_1 back to O to signal that it has finished op_1, whence O also finishes op_0. The state machine of O shows that it is capable of executing op_2 in parallel with op_0, i.e., the call-back can be served.

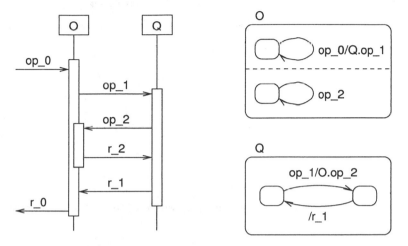

Fig. 6.16. Sequence diagram of a call-back

The steps of the corresponding preprocessed state machines are shown in Figure 6.17. The transition system for object O on the left is represented as a product of its two threads, one for the execution of op_0 and one for the execution of op_2. The horizontal and vertical curved transitions indicate the synchronous call action $/Q.\overline{op}_1$ and operation execution $\overline{op}_2$ respectively. The diagonal curved transition indicates their parallel composition $/Q.\overline{op}_1 \parallel \overline{op}_2$. This parallel transition is synchronised with the transition $\overline{op}_1$ in the transition system of Q, because the execution of op_1 includes the synchronous call-back action $O.\overline{op}_2$. Furthermore, the op_0 event transitions and the $/r_0$ actions are synchronised with the idle transitions on the first and last state of Q's transition system respectively.

One of the preconditions for the reduction of state machine composition to the composition operations of transformation systems has is separation of operation executions via the introduction of return actions and operation execution transitions as sequential compositions. A similar separation of operation execution and overall control flow or communication via message exchange has been suggested in [TS03]. There reflexive operation calls and call-backs are considered from a more methodological point of view. Supported by a concise formal analysis, separate state machines for operation executions and

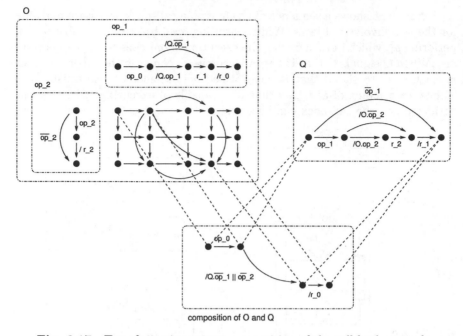

Fig. 6.17. Transformation system composition of the call back example

communications are suggested. Thus, as opposed to the suggestion developed here, the modelling method is changed, but based on the same underlying concept.

6.4 Integration of Class Diagrams and State Machines

There are several ways to integrate the class diagram and state machine semantics. The first one is given by looking at single objects. That is, the system behaviours corresponding to the class diagram are projected to the behaviour of a single object of the class the state machine refers to. On the side of the state machine interpretations the information on the local environments of the objects has to be removed, i.e., the object indexes it refers to in the states and the guards and actions corresponding to other objects that occur in the action structures of its transformation steps. The formal definitions of such projections to an object of class C are shown in Table 6.1. Note that they can also be defined as views in the sense of Definition 4.3.

The intersection of the projections yields the transformation systems that are admissible interpretations for both the class diagram and the state machine. Looking at the local semantics, i.e., the sets of transformation systems corresponding to the class diagram and the state machine, this yields a relation of consistent interpretations: a class diagram interpretation is consistent

class diagram	projection to	single object
system state (DT, OG, c, OS, ref)	$\mapsto$	object state $St_O \in OS$
set of operation calls AS	$\mapsto$	operation calls to O $\{a \in AS \mid a = O.op(p_1, \ldots, p_n)\}$

state machine	projection to	single object
state machine state $(c, (A, E, St, ref))$	$\mapsto$	focal object state A
transition t	$\mapsto$	operation call event for O $\{O.op\}$ if $t = O.op[g]$, else $\{\}$

Table 6.1. The projection of system and state machine interpretations to a single object

with a state machine interpretation if they have the same projection (see also Figure 1.3). That means they must have the same transition graphs and for each control state and transition the state and operation calls to the considered object must coincide. If for each class of a class diagram a state machine is given, corresponding binary consistency checks have to be performed for each one.

Another way of integrating class diagrams and state machines is given by the opposite construction. Instead of projecting systems to single objects, single objects (with local environments) are composed to systems, as discussed in the previous section. The composition of state machines then makes possible a formal comparison with the class diagram semantics, because both sets of admissible interpretations are now sets of transformation systems of the same data space signature. However, the action structures of the composed state machine transformation system still contain the communication information. If a composition of state machines is considered as complete (i.e., sufficiently many instances of the classes concerned are given) and should be compared or integrated with the class diagram semantics, the additional composition information has to be hidden. That means the labels have to be projected to the event components, augmented by the index of the executing object. The intersection of the class diagram and composed state machine semantics then yields the interpretations that are admissible from both points of view. This excludes for instance all class diagram interpretations where the operations are not executed in the order specified by the state machines, and all composed state machine interpretations where a client has more than one server or IP addresses are not bound to servers. These constraints are specified in the class diagram but not in the state machine diagram.

6.5 Sequence Diagram Semantics

Sequence and collaboration diagrams in UML specify the interaction of objects, i.e., the inter-object behaviour, via the exchange of messages. Sequence diagrams graphically stress the temporal order, whereas collaboration diagrams show the system architecture realised by the instances of a class diagram, i.e., the objects and their links. Semantically the two kinds of diagram are equivalent. They can be integrated into the transformation system framework easily, following the constructions and interpretations for collections of objects as discussed in the previous sections.

As a starting point for the definition of the set of admissible interpretations of a sequence diagram we again assume a transition system semantics, as given for instance in [DH99, KW01] for *life sequence charts* that are a conservative extension of sequence diagrams. The semantics is based on the partial order of operation call actions and events that are specified in a sequence diagram via the life lines of the instances and the messages, and in a collaboration diagram via the enumeration of messages.

For the construction of the transformation system semantics consider for example the sequence diagram in Figure 6.18 that shows a successful attempt by a user to connect her notebook (the client) to the network. This yields tran-

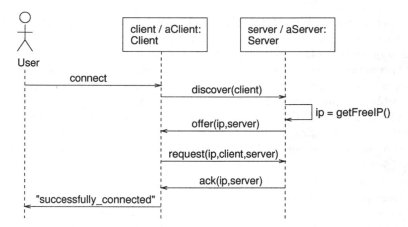

Fig. 6.18. A sequence diagram for the network protocol

sition graphs with system states and action structures for the transformation steps as follows.

The object instances yield the classified sets of object nodes; in the example these are $ON_{Client} = \{client\}$ and $ON_{Server} = \{server\}$. The user is not represented here, since she is not part of the system. Arbitrary data states for the objects, i.e., partial $\Sigma Client$- and $\Sigma Server$-algebras, and links and *ref-*

functions can be added. These are not constrained by the sequence diagram, except that the sender and receiver of a message must be linked.

The object graphs, object states, and the referencing functions yield parts of system states as in the state machine semantics, but with several objects as in the class diagram semantics. They may be incomplete due to the messages sent to or received from the environment.

Each sending or receipt of a message yields an action for a corresponding transformation system. In order to retain the complete information of a message the sender, the receiver, and the direction must be recorded in the action structure. As in the formalisation introduced for LSCs in [DH99] we use the notation $(i, m, i', !)$ and $(i, m, i', ?)$ for the sending and reception respectively of a message m from instance i to instance i'. This yields the action structures that may be used as transition labels in a transformation system interpretation of the sequence diagram.

To define the admissible transition graphs consider first the possible control states of a sequence diagram. A *location* $loc = (i, k)$ in a sequence diagram consists of an instance i of the diagram and a number $k \in \{0, \ldots, max_i\}$ that indicates a position on i's life line. In the example of Figure 6.18 the set of locations is given by $\{client, server\} \times \{0, \ldots, 6\}$ since both happen to have seven positions on their life lines. (The initial points of the life lines are locations, too.) The relations

- $(i, k) < (i, k + 1)$ for all $i \in I$ and $k < max_i$

and

- $(i, k) < (j, l)$ if there is a message m sent from the location (i, k) and received at the location (j, l)

induce a partial order on the locations that represents the causal and temporal dependencies modelled by the sequence diagram. Life lines represent the temporal order $((i, k) < (i, k+1))$ and a message must be sent before it can be received. Now a control state of a sequence diagram is given by a *cut* of its set of locations, i.e., a maximal set of locations that does not contain any pair of dependent locations. In a sequential scenario like the one of Figure 6.18 each cut contains exactly one location, because every other action must have happened before or after the considered one. In general, however, scenarios need not be sequential and, consequently, cuts can have more than one element.

Analogous to the construction of the control states for the state machines we can now define a control state of a transformation system interpretation of a sequence diagram as a pair $(c, SysSt)$, where c is a cut of the sequence diagram and $SysSt$ is a system state. The data space label of $(c, SysSt)$ is then given by the projection to the data state $SysSt$.

Finally, there may be a transition $t : (c, SysSt) \rightarrow (c', SysSt')$ in a transformation system if

- there is an independent set Act of send and receive actions in the sequence diagram that leads from c to c', and

- at most the state (object state and referencing) of the concerned object has changed from *SysSt* to *SysSt′* and the objects to be created and destroyed according to create and destroy action in *Act* are created and destroyed.

The action label of *t* is given by the set *Act*. In the example we obtain in this way the sequence of steps

$$(\_, connect(), client, ?) \; ;$$
$$(client, discover(client), server, !) \; ;$$
$$(client, discover(client), server, ?) \; ;$$
$$(server, getFreeIP(), server, !) \; ;$$
$$(server, getFreeIP(), server, ?) \; ;$$
$$\ldots \; ;$$
$$(client, \text{successfully connected}, \_, !) \; .$$

The essential task in comparing the sequence diagram semantics with the class diagram semantics is to check whether the operation calls are syntactically correct, i.e., whether their occurrence in the sequence diagram conforms to their declaration in the class diagram. This is a check on the syntactic level, and, since the data space signature of the sequence diagram semantics is induced by the class diagram, holds by definition. Nevertheless, the sequence diagram semantics cannot simply be included in the class diagram semantics. The difference is that the interaction is specified at a finer level of granularity in a sequence diagram in that both the sending and the reception of a message are stated explicitly. Although there is a one-to-one correspondence of sending and receiving, this might not be directly visible in the temporal ordering of the activities, because other steps may be performed in between. Furthermore, sending and receiving are not distinguished in the class diagram semantics.[2] Therefore the action structures of a sequence diagram interpretation have to be transformed appropriately. Each message receipt $(i, m, i', ?)$ is interpreted as an operation call and mapped to the form $i'.m$ that is used in the class diagram semantics. The sending of a message $(i, m, i', !)$ is hidden because it is not represented in the transformations in the class diagram semantics. Formally the hiding is obtained by applying the corresponding hiding operation as defined in Section 4.1. The set of admissible sequence diagram interpretations transformed in this way can then be embedded into the class

---

[2] Note that if a communication medium like the event queue of state machines were represented in the transformation system semantics, too, this would have to be changed. That means operation call actions and events would have to be separated also in the class diagram semantics and treated as sending a call to and receiving a call from the medium respectively. This communication medium has not been taken into account here, because the simpler direct communication via the synchronisation of events and actions is closer to the intuitive understanding and also supported directly by the transformation system composition operations. Obviously, a communication medium and a centralised fine-grained communication structure could be modelled as well.

diagram semantics and designates there all systems that correspond exactly to the scenario specified by the sequence diagram. That is, all those transformation systems in the class diagram semantics would be considered as consistent with the sequence diagram that contain exactly the objects that occur in the scenario and perform exactly the sequences of steps specified there.

A broader consistency definition is given by projecting the class diagram semantics to the objects that occur in the sequence diagram. As in the integration of state machines and class diagrams, this means that only that part of a system is constrained that corresponds to the sequence diagram. The other objects may behave arbitrarily. Moreover, the scenario specified in the sequence diagram may be an abstraction in comparison with the class diagram interpretation, whence an appropriate abstract relation (as defined in Chapter 4) would have to be applied to the class diagram interpretation. In this way the scopes and abstraction levels can again be adjusted to obtain an appropriate integration and consistency relation. Of course, it is important then to store this information, since it documents relevant design decisions.

The integration of sequence and statechart diagrams proceeds analogously. On the one hand the sequence diagram interpretations can be projected to single objects to compare them with the state machines. This has been discussed for the corresponding integration of class and statechart diagrams in Section 6.4 (see especially Table 6.1). Note that in this case both the sending and reception of a message matter, since in the state machine semantics these are distinguished as actions and events respectively. (This comparison of sequence diagrams and state machines is worked out in more detail in [Özh01], cf, also [KW01].) On the other hand, state machine interpretations can be composed in order to reproduce the scenario specified by the sequence diagram. With an appropriate adjustment of the corresponding action structures we again then obtain a formal integration by intersection. Since the state machines specify constructively the capabilities of the objects, whereas the sequence diagrams specify requirements, this particular integration makes it possible to prove whether the objects are able to do—according to their construction—what they should do—according to the specified demands.

6.6 Discussion

In this section an application of the formal integration approach to semi-formal software specification techniques has been discussed. The idea was to use the framework of transformation systems to develop an understanding of UML models as viewpoint models and make precise the meaning of the models in this context. Transformation systems as an abstract formal domain support such an endeavour, in that they are general and generic and provide a sufficient structure. Generality thereby means that the semantic domain is independent of a particular specification paradigm or language. The approach is generic in that it supports the usage of arbitrary frameworks for the specification of its constituents: the data states, action structures, and overall behaviour. The internal structure of the domain of transformation systems furthermore yields abstract schemes of development relations and composition operations that can be used to relate and integrate the specifications.

In spite of these properties, however, the application to a complex language like UML does not simply amount to a pure instantiation in the sense of setting some parameters. The discussion in this chapter has shown some of the problems that arise in such an application. First of all, the semantics of the languages is not entirely clear. Although the UML standard contains detailed and thorough explanations of the concepts introduced in the meta model, many can still be interpreted in different ways. The detection of these problems, however, is the first main advantage of the formal approach. By looking for a mapping of the language into the semantic domain the gaps in the original semantics definition of the language become apparent. Second, UML is an extremely complex language, in terms of both its syntactic features and its number of basic semantic concepts. As opposed to the common estimation of UML as an intuitive and easy language, any study of its semantics reveals its true internal complexity. But even if the features are restricted to a set of more fundamental kernel features, the semantic complexity remains. (If the kernel is chosen in such a way that the other features can be reduced to it this is obvious, because the kernel language would have the same expressive power as the full language.)

The situation becomes even more complex if not just single languages are considered, but also an integration point of view is taken. In this case each specification has to be considered as a viewpoint specification of a system and, when defining semantics, the complete structure of systems has to be taken into account. As discussed in the introduction this means also that those aspects have to be defined in the semantics that are not addressed explicitly in the specification at all. If a class diagram is considered as a viewpoint specification its interpretations are systems comprising static structure *and* dynamic behaviour, even if the latter—*ex negatio*—is specified by not constraining it. But only this more general point of view allows us to combine and integrate the different specifications, for example, in the way suggested here by transformations and intersections representing the correspondences and consistency relations.

Furthermore, composition has been covered, too. Obviously, composition is necessary in system specification to allow the construction of specifications from smaller parts, just like systems are composed from their components. Nevertheless, composition is hardly supported by software specification languages like UML, except at a very metaphorical level. This leads to even more problems of course when attempting to define formal semantics for the languages and compare their support for composition. In this chapter for example the composition of state machines has been defined using the concept of *open semantics* and communication as composition. That means, in the semantics of an entity, the possible behaviour of its environment is already reflected.

Usually this amounts to representing input actions like the execution of operations that might be called from the environment as non-determinism. Then the communication is modelled as a restrictive composition whose effect is to choose from the possible behaviours those that are actually realised. In this way the environment constrains the behaviour of the entity in that it selects some of the behaviour that had been foreseen in its local semantics. This interpretation of composition reflects the intuitive idea of synchronisation of the operation calls of an active object that emits the calls with a passive object that receives the call. Thus it can be considered as an adequate formalisation of the intended meaning of object interaction. On the other hand, state machines have the concept of an event queue that, to a certain extent, plays the role of a communication medium. However, it is only used to describe the behaviour of a single state machine, so it is not clear to what extent it should be taken into account for object interaction by composition. Note, furthermore, that the modelling here should be understood as one possibility to make precise state machine composition, which has been chosen due to its abstractness and direct representation of interaction. But also composition with explicit communication media (like the event queue) could be represented of course as composition operations of transformation systems. It would just have to be introduced as a further system, and all state machine interpretations would have to be composed with this one instead of being composed directly with each other.

The brief discussion of the integrated semantics of UML languages presented in this chapter might have led to the impression that well-known relations have been rephrased with large technical overhead. Obviously, the investigation is far from a complete analysis of the languages considered and thus brings about just a limited view. Accordingly, it should be understood just as a sketch of how the approach works. For this reason, those parts of the integration have been stressed that are close to an intuitive understanding of the UML concepts and their relations. The idea has been to demonstrate that the formal concepts of the transformation system approach match these intuitions. Nevertheless, in the course of the discussion the overall benefit of the approach should have become clearer. First it yields a very concise guideline on how specifications can be integrated. By looking at the way data states, action structures, control states, and transitions are specified by the single specifications, a superordinated framework is given for the systematic comparison. The development relations provide systematic means to relate specifications according to their addressed scope, level of abstraction, and granularity. Then, looking at the semantics precisely, implicit properties of the specifications and redundancies are discovered that might not have been clear before. For instance, access to other objects can be specified behaviourally via a call to an operation that reads an attribute or statically via a navigation expression. Both may occur in the same specification, and it might not be clear what type the read operation, for example, is. The mapping to the domain of transformation systems makes the difference precise in that the navigation expression is interpreted inside a data state whereas the operation call is interpreted as one or more transformation steps.

The main benefit of using the transformation system approach can be seen in its stability and flexibility. As shown in the other chapters of this book, the approach can be applied to the integration of extremely different specification techniques. That means it is not biased towards any particular specification paradigm. Changes of a specification language, which are very likely in any applied specification language like UML, would not entail a completely new integration approach, but could be rephrased according to the same pattern. Thus also the exact place (or effect) of the changes can be identified. The same holds for extensions of the language, also a typical UML phenomenon, whose integration with the base language can be achieved along the lines of the integrations sketched here.

Investigations of a more delimited scope of languages, analogous to the discussions of this chapter, would also lead to more methodological support. In this book the general language-independent approach has been worked out and its generality and flexibility have been stressed. Therefore the integration concept also has been very generally defined as the transformation and intersection of sets of admissible interpretations. This defines the meaning of integration and consistency, but, obviously, does not yield a feasible methodology of how to proceed in concrete cases. In general one would not try to obtain a characterisation or complete description of the intersection, i.e., the full set of totally admissible interpretations. Instead, one common model for a set of specifications would suffice to show their consistency w.r.t. the correspondences that are developed and fixed in the search for or construction of the common model.

In the consideration of the specifications their role in the model development process may also determine in which way they are considered in the integration. For example, a class diagram to the greater part defines the signature of a system. It may contain further information like cardinalities, multiplicities, or indications of derived attributes, for example, that are constraints rather than signature information. Other specifications like state machines or collaboration diagrams are syntactically based on it, i.e., their contexts and the expressions that may be used in them for actions, event, guards, etc., are determined by the class diagram. In this sense the class diagram is a syntactic precondition for the construction of the all other specifications. Accordingly, class diagrams have been interpreted here as defining just a data space signature; arbitrary transition graphs could be added to the induced data space when considering the class diagram alone as a viewpoint specification. The role in the development process is of course to define admissible transition graphs (behaviours) via the behaviour modelling techniques, state machines, and collaboration or sequence diagrams. Nevertheless, the discussion in the previous sections has shown that when going into the details the addition of the behaviour specifications does not simply amount to an inclusion of the set of models in the sense that the models of the behaviour specifications define the subset of transition graphs that are admissible. Instead, they have to be adjusted (transformed) corresponding to the different ways in which certain data space elements are used in the behaviour specifications. For example, operation calls that are actions in the class diagram semantics are used in different ways in state machines and sequence diagrams, as actions, events, or contents of messages.

As mentioned in the introduction, however, more concrete or detailed methodological considerations of this kind are not within the scope of this book.

7

Conclusion

The aim of this book has been to introduce a theoretical foundation for the integration of heterogeneous software specifications. Since it is accepted that the use of different specification languages should be supported, or at least, cannot be avoided, the problem of integration occurs systematically in the development of software systems. Instead of hoping for one fixed and universal language that everybody agrees on, the use of specific languages that are adequate for some well-defined partial purposes is appreciated and, correspondingly, appropriate integration means are requested. In the Reference Model of Open Distributed Processing RM-ODP this multiple paradigm approach has been worked out in great detail and—being an ISO/ITU standard—also with great obligation. The viewpoint approach introduced therein has been highly influential in the field of software systems development, without necessarily being incorporated explicitly, and is nowadays broadly accepted in one form or another. In this sense also the different diagrammatic modelling techniques of the unified modelling language UML can be considered as an embodiment of the viewpoint approach, in that different aspects of system modelling are separated and the corresponding models are constructed by using different languages. Obviously, the classification of viewpoints and the corresponding aims of this separation of viewpoints in UML are very different from the ones of the RM-ODP. Nevertheless, at least the general multiparadigm approach is supported in both cases, and the result of having to deal with multiple models of one system that are heterogeneous in both form and contents is the same.

The idea of the transformation system approach to the integration of heterogeneous software specifications was to deliver fundamental notions and constructions that allow a semantic comparison of specifications. Accordingly, two basic principles determined the development of the approach:

Semantics first! Integration must be based on the semantics of the specifications. In particular, correspondences must be established based at the semantical level. Consistency is a semantic property by definition (existence of a common model) and should be made explicit as such.

No new language! Instead of introducing just another meta or integration modelling language, semantic concepts must be worked out as a precondition for the integration.

Although the distinction between syntax and semantics is in principle relative, and—as discussed in Section 7.4—there is no semantics without syntax, the second principle has been completely realised by using standard mathematical notions (including category theoretical ones) for the construction of the domain of transformation systems. In comparison with other approaches that use other specification languages for the integration, such as Z or Abstract State Machines, this elementary mathematical approach entails the least constraints and is not biased towards any specification paradigm.

7.1 Summary

The basic distinction provided by the transformation system approach is that of structure and behaviour. These are distinguished logically to separate and identify the semantic concepts. Methodologically the representation and specification of structure and behaviour will always be mixed, at least to a certain extent. Structure is represented in a transformation system by the data space, given by the sets of data states and data state transformations. Behaviour is represented as a graph that simply states how many states there are and how they are connected. In the following in informal description of these basic notions is given as a summary.

Data State

A data state represents the internal state of an entity at one point of time. The structure of a data state, i.e., the definition of what constitutes the data state of the entity, is given by a data state *signature*. All data states are instantiations of the signature, that can thus also be understood as a schema. To give an example, a data state of an object is given by the list of its attribute values, the corresponding signature is given by the list of attributes and their types. A class diagram can also be understood as a data state signature. Its instantiations are system states, i.e., the data states of a system that is given by a collection of objects. Each system state is given by the number of objects of each class, their states, and their links.

Data states need not contain the complete information about the further behaviour of the entity. This is represented in the *control states* (the nodes of the transition graph, see below). That means a data state is an abstraction w.r.t. a specific point of view that may be determined by the role of the specification language being interpreted. A data state may contain 'static' functions for example, i.e., functions that do not change the state but describe input–output relations.

The signatures that are used to define the data states furthermore induce languages that can be used to describe *properties of the data states*. For example, an algebraic or logical signature yields equations and logic formulae. A list of attributes of objects comes with the operations of the types of the attributes that induce a language like an algebraic signature. Properties that are required to hold in all states are *data invariants* like consistency conditions, definitions of derived attributes, etc. The specification of such properties allows the reduction of the set of all instances of the signature to the set of all those instances that satisfy the properties. Data state properties can also be used to select individual states, like initial or final states.

Transformation Step

A transformation step is given by a commencing and an ending data state that together represent a state change. The identities of the elements of the data states are formally given by a tracking relation. This may be induced by designated parts of the signature or by some frame assumption.

In addition to the commencing and ending states of a step, a data state transformation contains an *action structure* that represents the observable actions of the step. What is considered as observable thereby depends again on the point of view that may be induced by the specification considered. The action structure may denote the cause of the step, like the operations that are applied, or its controllable sign. The elements of an action structure, the *actions*, are the instances of an *action signature*, which introduces the action names and their parameter type lists. The actual parameters of the actions are elements of the data states. The action structure definition states which combinations of actions are considered as labels of single transformation steps. These could be sets of actions for parallel systems, where several actions can be performed in parallel in one step, lists for sequential compositions, tuples, representing for instance different roles like the distinction of actions and events, etc. Action structures thus also yield an abstraction mechanism in that collections of actions can be considered as labels of single steps.

The set of transformation steps contains all steps that are syntactically correct (*all* type correct action instances together with *all* pairs of data states as commencing and ending states). The set of transformation steps can be diminished by *transformation rules* that specify pre- and postconditions for action structures, analogous to the reduction of the set of data states by the data invariants.

Data Space

A data space is given by the collection of all data states and all transformation steps according to a given *data space signature* (= data state signature + action signature). It is uniquely determined by the data space signature since the data states and transformation steps are all possible instances of their signatures. If data state properties and/or pre- and postconditions for the transformation steps are specified this yields a *data space specification* and an according data space which is a subspace of the data space induced by the signature.

The data space is thus the collection of all possible data states and transformations. A data state in the data space might not be reachable in a system. This depends on the behaviour, which is modelled by the *transition graph* of a system. Analogously, a transformation step in the data space may never be performed by the system.

Transition Graph

The transition graph is an abstract representation of the dynamic behaviour of a system. Its nodes are given by the *control states* of the system that carry the information on the (re)active capability at some point in time. This may in general be independent of the information given in the data states. Each control state is labelled by a data state. Via this labelling those data states are selected from the data space that may actually be entered by the system. The control states also define at which points a system can be accessed, for instance for synchronisation, composition, or refinement, and where or when properties of its data states can be checked.

The edges of the transition graph are given by the *transitions* that represent the possibility to pass from one control state to another. Transitions are labelled by action structures, whereby the transformation steps the system is able to perform are selected from the data space.

The transition graph and its labelling mapping into the data space thus define how the system traverses its data space.

The transition graph defines a skeleton of the overall dynamic behaviour of the system. Paths in the transition graph denote the sequential execution of steps, branching denotes non-deterministic choice. Only the labelling by data states and action structures defines what is the case in the states and what happens in the transitions.

Development

Developments of system specifications are represented as relations on transformation systems as their semantic representations. According to the structure of transformation systems the transition graphs and the data spaces of the systems must be related. The former can be described by a mapping (graph homomorphism) that states how the behaviour of one system is embedded into the other one. This represents extensions or restrictions of behaviour (depending on the direction of the mapping) but also foldings or unfoldings (the mapping need not be injective). Using closure operations behavioural abstractions can be represented, for example by mapping a step of one system to a sequence of steps of the other system.

At the data space level *signature morphisms* are used to refine or extend the data states and action structures. This can be used to define specific views on a system or hide parts of it. The general definition of signature morphism allows the mapping of names to descriptions (terms), analogous to the mapping of single steps to composed steps at the behaviour level.

Transition graph mapping and data space signature morphism can be combined arbitrarily, i.e., in the same or in opposite directions. This yields a schema that can be instantiated to reconstruct the development relations defined in a given specification language, introduce new ones by reflection, and to relate specifications semantically for the definition of the appropriate transformations for their integration.

Composition

Analogous to the development of transformation systems, composition is based on their two-level structure. The behaviours of the systems are synchronised and their structures are superposed or amalgamated.

The connection of systems, i.e., the architecture of a system that is composed of subsystems or components, is defined by an *identification relation* that expresses which parts of the structure of the systems are shared and a *synchronisation relation* that states which states and transitions are compatible with each other in the sense that they can coexist and together form a global state or step of the composed system. Architecture thus comprises structure and behaviour, formally via the identification and the synchronisation relation. Synchronisation is thereby a *may* synchronisation, i.e., states and transitions that are in the synchronisation relation may be entered or executed at the same time. *Must* synchronisation can be obtained as a special case. If there is exactly one transition (state) in the other systems that is synchronous with the given one, then these must be synchronised.

Applying a composition operation to connected systems makes it possible to consider them as a single system, i.e., to abstract from the internal architecture of the composition. The global view of the composed system has one data space, which is given by the amalgamation of the local data spaces according to the identification relations, and one transition graph, given by all tuples of synchronous local states and transitions respectively. In this way full compositionality is supported.

Integration of specifications has been defined conceptually as the possibility to consider a collection of heterogeneous partial viewpoint specifications as a single specification of a single system. That means, neither a concrete syntactic integration of specification languages, nor a fixed method for the integration of specifications of some given languages, have been addressed primarily. Instead, the interpretation of arbitrary specifications in the common domain of transformation systems has been discussed and it has been shown how this supports the detection and declaration of correspondences and, based on these, how to check their consistency. This is defined semantically as

integration by **transformation** and **intersection** of sets of **admissible interpretations**

of the specifications considered. The transformations therefore allow the adjustment of the differences of the specifications concerning their name spaces, structures, scopes, and granularities. It is important to stress that correspondences must be defined explicitly, i.e., one cannot assume detection of them automatically. In larger developments this is obvious, because names and structures within specifications are designed locally and have to be brought together and unified only at the moment of their integration. But also in smaller developments, specification techniques might be used by different people or in different circumstances in different styles. Thus, even within a single explicit name space, equal types of model elements need not mean the same thing (and different model structures need not mean different things). This also implies of course that consistency checking of viewpoint specifications cannot be entirely automated, since it requires a declaration of the correspondences to specify in which way the specifications complement each other and how they are related to the target system.

The way in which the transformation system approach supports this kind of integration has been discussed in the examples in this book in detail. Applying it in larger contexts requires of course a worked-out methodology and a reformulation of the semantic integration concepts in the syntax of the concrete languages considered in this context. Examples of such reflections of semantic structures to their syntactic representations have been discussed here, too. A principal way of how to employ the approach for the *integration of languages* (instead of single specifications) has also been indicated. First in the discussion on the specification means for the different kinds of properties of transformation systems in Section 3.6 and then for the generic construction of institutions of transformation systems w.r.t. specification frameworks for data states, action structures, and control flow logics in Section 4.8. Guidelines for the mapping of several specification languages to the transformation system reference model have been discussed within the examples in all chapters, and in more detail in Section 2.5 for several specification formalisms and in Chapter 6 for UML specifications.

7.2 Further Developments and Applications

A couple of questions have been touched upon during the discussion of different integrations without being worked out so that they could be applied immediately. In this section some of the larger issues for further developments and applications of the integration approach are discussed.

7.2.1 UML Integration

In Chapter 6 an application of the integration approach to UML was sketched. Obviously, this would have to be worked out in more detail and larger scope in order to obtain an applicable methodology for the continuous usage of UML models in the sense of a semantically founded, integrated viewpoint method. The discussion in Chapter 6 has already shown, however, in which way the considered specification languages complement each other and how this determines the way they can be integrated. Class diagrams mainly yield the signature of the data space that is common to all admissible interpretations. Note, however, that class diagrams also may contain constraints like class cardinalities and association end multiplicities, i.e., they are data space specifications rather than pure signatures. The role of the behaviour models is then to specify the admissible transition graphs that define (with their labels in the data space) how the data states and transformations are traversed. Usually the collaborations are specified before the state machines, via sequence or collaboration diagrams, since they are used as refinements of use cases. As discussed above, however, the state machines also specify the intra–object behaviour completely, which means that the collaborations become pure reflexive specifications whose consistency with the constructive specification given by the state machines has to be checked. The conceptual integration framework defines the abstract means of how to check consistency here, too, but in the special case of consistency checking of behaviour specifications more algorithmic support can be given. Both the specifications considered are interpreted operationally as transition systems that can be constructed step by step, like a simulation or complete traversal of their behaviours. Accordingly, the consistency check can also be performed by checking stepwise whether the required steps of the collaboration are supported by the state machines involved. Such an algorithm is formulated in [Özh01] for UML sequence and state machine diagrams, and in [KW01] for life sequence charts to check their consistency with STATEMATE designs. Neiher of the two papers covers UML collaborations and state machines in sufficient detail, however, and both do not consider the possible effects of data state transformations.

In order to complete this particular method for consistency checking, first the semantics of state machines and collaborations has to be investigated further. The semantics of state machine compositions has been defined here by mapping it to the composition of transformation systems by connection relations. But the role of the event queue that is crucial in the UML semantics of single state machines has not yet been explicitly taken into account. For a sequence diagram a synchronous operation call is first of all an internal correctness criterion: the object that emitted the call must not perform any action before the return event has arrived. The precondition to check this is of course that the return action is modelled explicitly, otherwise a default has to be assumed.

The reference model, i.e., the domain of transformation systems with its predefined composition operations and development relations, offers the possibility to formalise different interpretations of the informal concepts of the UML meta model for example. This may also introduce new points of view, such as the open semantics of behaviour models like state machines for example, where all possible effects of the environment are represented in the formal semantics of the behaviour specification and communication is then represented as a selection of those behaviours the environment actually performs. (This interpretation has also been suggested in [EW00], for example.) The properties of the concepts made precise in this way, like the different forms of compositionality (w.r.t. syntactic composition operations, properties in the sense of the transformation system classification, and developments), can then be checked and formally proved and yield guidelines for design decisions concerning the fixation of the semantics of state machines and collaborations, for example. This does not mean that the presentation of the semantics must become formal. The results of the formally supported decisions can be stated again in natural language.

Analogous investigations might use the predefined development relations of the reference model to make precise different variants of behavioural conformance, for instance. These could then be used to define the behavioural meaning of inheritance, i.e., the constraints on state machines associated with sub- and superclasses of an inheritance relation could be formulated. Of course, a syntactic representation of such behavioural conformance conditions would be required. The semantic investigation just defines the contents of these rules, i.e., the correctness criterion, independently of whether all admissible relations can be formulated directly in the syntax of state machines.

As for the discussion of behaviour models, the transformation system reference model can also be used to investigate open questions of structural modelling concepts. The treatment of associations in Chapter 6.1 is an example. It provides suggestions for design decisions; other ones might be possible, too. The major contribution of the reference model should be seen again in the opportunity to make precise the different possibilities and check their compatibility with other semantic structures and properties. Indeed, the relation of associations, links, and references as defined above yields a stable ground to discuss the different variants, as opposed to completely informal discussions.

A formal semantic domain may not only be used to investigate, clarify, and suggest (informal) semantics definitions. It also offers the possibility to connect analyser tools to the investigated languages that are based on a formal logic. The integration approach sketched in [Ste97], for example, that is also based on a common semantic domain, aims especially at tool support. For example, theorem proving environments like HOL [HOL] or Isabelle [Isa] accept inputs in higher order logic languages and offer the possibility to prove theorems semi-automatically. Tool support in general has not been addressed in this book, although tools are the precondition for a wider use of specification methods. But it poses its own problems, specific both for the envisaged tools or their input languages and the specification languages considered. However, the formalisation supported by the transformation system approach is a step in this direction. Explicit mappings would have to be considered then that allow the use of such tools, for example in the context of objects with reference semantics (as opposed to a (simplistic) value semantics). Again, the formalisation of system states presented in Section 6.1.3 might serve as a first step.

7.2.2 Integration Methods

As already mentioned at the beginning, the integration framework does not provide a concrete methodology that could be applied immediately by developers of software specifications to integrate their specifications. Instead, it yields a formal foundation that delivers all the necessary semantic notions that need to be considered when an integration method is developed. That means the reference model can be used to develop such methods. As also already discussed, integration methods obviously depend on the languages that are considered. The more concretely the languages are given the more concretely the integration method can be formulated. On the other hand, classes of languages could also be considered that are classified w.r.t. their relations to the notions introduced in the reference model. These are, basically, static structure, dynamic behaviour, architecture, and development, whence the mapping to the reference model usually does not introduce further complexity in the analysis or usage of the languages. Rather, the way in which the languages address these fundamental aspects is made precise when mapping them to the reference model, formally or informally. Usually the basic aspects are not completely separated in specification languages.

The principal ways in which specifications can be related have also been discussed in the introduction. Specifications may supplement each other, i.e., one adds the information that has not been given by the previous ones since this particular aspect had not been considered by them. This might seem to be the ideal viewpoint model, but is hardly realistic. As mentioned above, viewpoint specification languages are seldom as pure as to (syntactically) exclude all overlappings or inconsistencies. Class diagrams contain constraints (cardinalities and multiplicities) that also concern and constrain the possible behaviours of objects. For example, certain create or destroy actions of behaviour models may be excluded since they would violate these constraints. Object constraints, as OCL-constraints for example, may interfere with all other specifications, due to their overall logic point of view of the whole system. (For instance, the OCL contains constructs like *oclInState* that directly addresses state machine states and allows their usage in other contexts.) Thus the second case of semantically overlapping specifications can be assumed as the generally interesting case and it has to be checked where and to what extent the considered viewpoint specifications can overlap and interfere. This then yields the dependencies of the viewpoint specifications or the corresponding development steps. In the methodology they should be reflected by corresponding integration steps that state when and where correspondences have to be made explicit and, based on that, consistency has to be checked. More concrete directions can then be formulated for these consistency checks, like stepwise algorithms for different behaviour specifications as discussed above, or theorem proving for example. (Theorem proving as a consistency check is suggested for example in [Tsi01] where sequence diagrams are enriched by OCL formulae to incorporate the information given in class and statechart diagrams as logical constraints, and consistency checking is reduced to checking the consistency of logical formulae at certain points within the sequence diagram.)

7.2.3 Architecture Description

Beyond the further applications to UML semantics and the development of integration methods for UML or other software specifications, the semantic definitions of the reference model can also be used to integrate software architecture descriptions (in the sense of [SG96], see also [Egy99, EM00] especially concerning the integration aspect). The composition operations for transformation systems are based on interconnections that represent architectures as discussed in Chapter 5. These could be described either by relations on the static structure and the dynamic behaviour levels respectively, or, more generally, as diagrams of local systems representing the components of the global system. Thus the synchronisation relation has been used to characterise the interaction mechanisms that can be based on complementary actions, designated ports, synchronisation points, etc. The advantage of the semantic approach realised by the transformation system reference model is again that all these different ways to define interconnections (or configurations) of components are described by *what* happens instead of giving specific mechanisms for describing *how* the interconnection can be achieved. This allows a comparison and integration of different architecture models, which may be based on such different description paradigms.

In a more detailed investigation this mapping of architecture description languages (see for instance [MT00] for a survey) to the reference model would make precise how the different underlying paradigms are related to each other. For that purpose the interconnection mechanisms defined via corresponding syntactic features in the architecture description languages must be reconstructed semantically by the semantic interconnection mechanisms of the reference model. Beyond the specification of the interconnection of the components, an architecture description also contains the specification of the components themselves, together with their interfaces, and the connectors. Corresponding semantic notions are provided abstractly within the reference model, too, presented within the discussion of development relations (for interfaces, implementations, refinements, and abstractions) and composition operations as defined above. The semantic modelling of interfaces especially supports specification approaches for component-based systems that goes far beyond the usual purely syntactical interface description languages. Moreover, the composition of components via connectors would be defined semantically, which allows the modelling and specification of dependencies.

The advantage of the semantic approach for the description of architectures is again that first the concepts can be made precise and analysed and then appropriate languages can be chosen for their description. Furthermore, specifications using given architecture description languages can be integrated according to the integration of system specifications. The construction of software systems by component composition can thus be lifted to the integration of component models, supporting system construction on a much higher level of abstraction. Using these semantic descriptions, finally the results of the categorical composition approach by Fiadeiro et al. mentioned in Section 7.3 could be made available without committing oneself to the specification language used there. This means that concepts like contracts as evolutionary construction and coordination mechanisms (see [Fia96, FLM97, AFG⁺00, AF01, WLF01]) could be detached from the concrete representation and reconstructed in the languages that are appropriate for the model development concerned.

7.3 Related Approaches

Transformation systems have been introduced as a reference model for the integration of heterogeneous software specifications. Corresponding requirements have been stated in Section 1.3 and the design of the reference model follows these requirements closely in order to deliver a general and fundamental integration theory. There are few other approaches that address the integration task as directly as the transformation system reference model, whence the full set of requirements as stated here is not covered in any of the approaches discussed below.

The comparison, beyond stating the conceptual and technical contributions to single aspects, amounts rather to discussing the main sources that influenced the development of the transformation system reference model. Individual comparisons, embeddings, and discussion of specific aspects of related works have already been given in the corresponding chapters where more concise statements have been made.

7.3.1 Integration of Static States and Dynamic Changes

Starting from either specification methods for abstract data types or process specification methods, many approaches have been developed to integrate the complementary part. In the former case, for instance, algebraic specifications have been extended to cover object-oriented features (e.g. in [Bre91, Gro91, Pie94, AB96]) including a notion of states and state changes. In these approaches the relevant structure is encoded into the static structure, however, instead of making it explicit in the logical framework. This also concerns the approaches that are based on transition systems specified as a part of the static structure to represent state changes and dynamic behaviour internally (see [AR96, CR97]). Not encoded into a single static model, but still on the same level, the use of the operational semantics of directed term rewriting used in the rewriting logic approach (see [Mes92, MM96, CDE$^+$98]) incorporates states into the static structure instead of adding a new level. In [ABR99] these approaches are called algebraic specifications of *dynamic data* types, in contrast with the algebraic specifications of dynamic *data types*. In the latter an algebra represents a single state of the system, not the whole system. The most prominent among these approaches are the abstract state machine approach (ASM, formerly called evolving algebras, see [Hug, Gur91, Gur94, BH98, BS03]) and *D-oids*, which have already been mentioned above.

ASMs are a rule-based specification framework in which states are represented by algebras. State transformations are described by elementary rules for the pointwise updating of function definitions. Rule composition operators allow the definition of the control flow. The ASM framework has been developed mainly for the definition of programming language semantics and, accordingly, to prove compiler correctness (see [BR92]). Meanwhile the semantics of specification languages like SDL ([SDL99, EGGP00, GGP99]) are also defined in terms of ASMs, whence they are also used as a semantic domain for integration (see e.g., [KNNZ00]). As opposed to the transformation system approach, however, ASMs pursue a more pragmatic approach. In particular, tool support has been developed to a large extent (see [CW00, Cas01, BS03]), whereas structural aspects are often handled in an ad hoc manner by encoding them into the algebras instead of making them explicit in the logic. Thus general compositionality results as presented in this book for example will be hard to formulate and prove for ASMs. Of course, a mapping of transformation systems to ASMs would be very beneficial as it would make available the concrete language design and ASM tools. On the other hand, much of the structure of transformation systems is not supported by ASMs, especially the distinction of control flow and data states. Moreover, the aim of the transformation system reference model is to deliver a semantic domain for the integration of given languages, not to develop a new language.

From a more theoretical point of view D-oids[1] address the integration of static states and dynamic state changes (see [AZ93, AZ95]). Among others, like the *algebraic specification with implicit state* introduced in [Dau92, DGM93, DG94], they have also been introduced to deliver an abstract formal foundation for ASMs. The basic idea is to use models of an arbitrary institution as models of the states of a system and to build dynamic models on top of them. For that purpose dynamic operations are introduced that use a state model as implicit input and elements of this model as explicit input parameters. The effect of a dynamic operation is given by the result-

---

[1] The name *D-oid* should resemble mathematical constructs like mon*oids* and group*oids*, and at the same time stand for an abbreviation of *dynamic object identities*.

ing state, representing the side effects of the operation, and—optionally—an output value, i.e., an element of the new state. D-oids do not support the separation of control states and data states, so control flow information must be encoded in the states as in the other algebras-as-states approaches. Furthermore, no refinement relations or composition operations have yet been defined. An embedding of the D-oid approach into transformation systems is discussed in Section 2.5.

A more orthogonal integration of algebras as states with behaviour modelling was introduced in [BW00]. The latter is thereby given by stream processing functions that are defined in terms of their effect on algebras. That means components and communication channels are defined, the states of the former are represented as algebras, and the latter specify which streams can flow in between these components. Thus in particular the composition aspect is addressed immediately. Moreover, refinement, based on the refinement of stream processing functions has been considered ([Bro93, Bro96, Bro97]). The fundamental idea is to refine the time model in each iteration step to proceed from more abstract to more concrete system models. Due to this overall structure, the approach has also already been used to discuss the integration of UML models ([GSB98, BS01]).

A sketch of a general abstract integration framework has been presented in [EO94, EO98, EOP99]. It introduces informally four levels: static data types, data states and transformations, processes, and system architecture (formerly called high-level operations), similar to the structure of the formal reference model presented here. Like the latter it should serve as a reference to integrate specifications or specification languages by investigating their semantic correspondences. In [ELO95] this framework is applied to graph transformation systems.

This leads to the dual approaches that start from process specification methods that are extended by explicit data states. Conceptually this is supported mostly by using some kind of extended transition systems as in [WC89], where also the states are labelled. As opposed to transformation systems, where data states and actions can be arbitrarily complex, usually a very simple notion of state is used, given by a list of (typed) variables whose values determine the data state. Thus the types are assumed to be globally given and immutable. In particular, data type specification is not considered as a domain that should be integrated, since types are considered just as given structured sets. One of the main contributions of transformation systems can actually be seen in closing this gap and integrating data type specification methods with their complex composition operations and refinement relations with transition systems as basic behaviour models as orthogonal as possible.

In addition to these conceptual approaches, integration of specification methods has of course also been addressed on the more concrete level of specification languages. In fact, most process specification languages that are based on atomic actions have been extended by parameterised states (agents) and actions, incorporating implicit or explicit data types and corresponding specification languages. Their specific integration concepts that have influenced the development of the transformation system reference model have also been discussed. In particular the relation of control states and transitions on the one hand and data states and transformations on the other hand are defined in very different ways in the different approaches. In the language μSZ for example (see [BDG$^+$96, BGK98]), the integration of statecharts and Z, data states and their transformations by operation applications are specified via corresponding Z schemata. They are then organised into processes via STATEMATE statecharts ([HN95]) that define the order of the operation invocation. The relation is thus obtained by putting a statechart on top of a Z specification of data states and transformations, where the data states and transformations become labels of the states and transition of the statechart. Thus this is an integration conceptually very close to the schema presented here.

Technically the μSZ integration is supported by a meta modelling approach (see [GKP98]) where the syntax and semantics of the languages are defined in a common object-oriented meta model. This also allows the precise specification of the overlapping of the languages and thereby indicates the integration task since it points to the parts of the languages that have to be replaced and connected. This meta modelling approach has also been applied to the integration of other languages (class diagrams, object-oriented programming languages, constraint language, statecharts) in [Kla99, MK98].

In the integrated language CSP/OZ (see [Fis97]), which combines the object-oriented extension ObjectZ ([DRS95, Smi00]) of the same data specification technique Z with the process specification language CSP, the relation of control flow and data state transformation is obtained in a completely different way. The basic idea here is to consider the Z-operations (= data state transformations) together as a single process that continuously offers all enabled operations. The selection of the steps that are actually performed is then obtained by using the process composition operation of CSP. Due to the open semantics of CSP, composition amounts to constraining the actions of a process to the ones that are actually required by the other process. In this way the composition of a CSP process with the Z-operation process can be used to define the control flow. Thus although the idea and technique of the integration is very different, the overall result is the same: a process is used to select specific operation applications that define the data state transformations. In terms of transformation systems this means that the label function from the transition graph to the data space is defined. Thus semantically CSP/OZ can be considered as a transformation system specification language.

Yet another way of relating behaviour and data states is given in the extension of Petri nets by algebraic data type specifications by algebraic high-level nets (AHL nets, see for instance [DHP91, Rei98]). In this approach the data states are not added orthogonally as in the above-mentioned approaches. Instead, the elementary data state concept of Petri nets, given by the markings of nets, is enhanced in that arbitrary distinguishable data elements are allowed as tokens. Thus, although algebraic specification is integrated, data states cannot be conceived immediately as algebras. The discussion on the embedding of AHL nets into the transformation system approach in Chapter 3 shows various ways of how to define data states for AHL nets as algebras, and how these different ways can be used to make explicit and compare different styles of using AHL nets. These more implicit data states resemble the extension of CCS by parameterised actions and agents as defined for instance in the process and protocol specification language LOTOS [LOT87, Bri89]. The basic idea is that the occurrence of a parameterised read or input action defines a scope for the formal parameters of the action. Within this scope the parameters can be bound to actual values by a parallel composition. Thereby implicitly local data states are defined.

Another development towards the integration of algebras as data states with dynamic state changes has been worked out by the author (see [Gro91, Gro95, Gro97a, Gro98a, Gro98b]), which finally led to the presentation given here.

7.3.2 Categorical Composition of Theories and Models

In [BG77, GG78, GB84] a categorical approach to the composition of theories has been introduced in the framework of general logics. For that purpose *institutions* have been introduced that provide a framework for the presentation of logics. Institutions abstract from their specific definitions, the concrete syntax of signatures and formulae, the models, deduction, and satisfaction relations. On this abstract level then the composition of theories and specifications is formulated, using the categorical concepts of morphisms to relate theories by structure preserving mappings, diagrams for their interconnection, and colimits to express the result of the composition as a global unstructured theory. In the special case of a binary composition the diagram is given by a binary relation, expressed as a span of two morphisms, and the result is given by a pushout.

This approach has been used in [EM85] to define the composition of algebraic specifications. First a formal parameter PAR of an algebraic specification is introduced as a designated subspecification that is formally included in the body BOD of the specification via an inclusion morphism $PAR \rightarrow BOD$. (This can be generalised to arbitrary specification morphisms instead of inclusions.) The actualisation of the formal parameter PAR by a parameter specification ACT is given by a specification morphism $act : PAR \rightarrow ACT$ that specifies by which sorts and functions of ACT the formal parameter sorts and functions are actualised. The textual substitution of the formal parts in BOD by their actualisations from ACT delivers the result of the actualisation. Since this yields a pushout in the category of algebraic specifications, it is indeed an instance of the general approach of putting theories together by colimits.

The syntactic composition by pushouts (actualisation) induces, moreover, a composition operation for the algebras of the corresponding specifications, called *amalgamation*. Thereby *ACT*- and *BOD*-algebras whose sorts and functions corresponding to the *PAR* specification coincide are glued and yield an algebra of the resulting actualised specification. This yields a compositional semantics for the actualisation of parameterised algebraic specifications. The amalgamation operation can be extended in two ways. It can be generalised to arbitrary institutions, abstracting from the concrete framework of algebraic specification (see [EG94]), and pushouts can be replaced by arbitrary colimits to express *n*-ary instead of binary relations. This also yields a general definition of compositional semantics: The syntactic composition of specifications by colimits is required to induce a semantic composition of models by amalgamation, i.e., the models are composed in the same way as the specifications. In categorical terms this means that the model functor is continuous. General amalgamations are used in the context of transformation systems for the composition of data states and action structures as well as for the composition of entire transformation systems.

The composition-by-colimits approach has been taken up in [FM92] to define modularisation units for concurrent system specifications. Thereby temporal logic theories are employed for the specification of the dynamic behaviour of systems. Their interconnection and interaction can then directly be expressed with the categorical composition technique, using morphisms, diagrams, and colimits. So in this case the general categorical approach instantiates to the interaction of dynamic concurrent units and yields a concise and well-structured approach to their specification and analysis.

Based on this general approach specific features of compositions that can be expressed via colimits of diagrams of theories have been investigated and worked out in a series of papers.[2] The general pattern is again given by the pushout construction: a relation of theories models a connector of components, and the resulting behaviour is given by the *superposition* of the components according to their connection via the connector (see [FR92, WLF00]). Thus the behaviours of the local components may be constrained, i.e., the connector implements a *contract* that specifies the permitted behaviour in the given context. Corresponding to the generality of the approach, applications have been worked out in a wide range of fields, like object-based systems [FM96], parallel program design [FM97], component-based systems [Fia96, FLM97], software architectures [WLF01], and coordination [AFG+00, AF01].

Starting with models of concurrent systems instead of their specifications yields a dual characterisation of composition. In the seminal paper [WN97] a categorical analysis of different semantic domains for concurrent systems has been given, including labelled transition systems (LTSs), synchronisation trees, trace languages, and event structures. It is shown there that parallel composition and synchronisation can be expressed by limits (products, pullbacks, cartesian liftings). The duality of limits and colimits for the represen-

---

[2] See http://www.fiadeiro.org/jose/papers/.

tation of composition corresponds to the duality of syntax and semantics, and the contravariance of the semantic interpretation.

In a transformation system structure and behaviour are separated and represented by static data state models that are instances of some signature and transition graphs (unlabelled transition systems) respectively. Correspondingly, the composition of transformation systems is given by composition-by-colimits for the structural part and composition-by-limits for the behavioural part. That means the analysis and constructions of [EM85, EG94] (amalgamation of static models), [FM92] (superposition), and [WN97] (parallel composition and synchronisation of dynamic models/LTSs) are integrated to obtain the composition for the integrated system models given by transformation systems. This combination and integration of composition techniques yields the required generality for transformation systems as a reference model, i.e., it supports the interpretation of many composition operations defined in specification languages.

7.3.3 Consistency and Integration of Viewpoint Specifications

The Reference Model of Open Distributed Processing RM-ODP has been mentioned above as one of the main sources for the viewpoint model. During its development the question of the consistency of viewpoint specifications was addressed in a series of research projects at the University of Kent at Canterbury.[3] Starting from the observation that traditional definitions of consistency cannot be applied in this context (compare the discussion in Section 1.2), a framework was developed for consistency checks and applied to specification languages that support the ODP viewpoints, essentially Z and LOTOS for the information and computational viewpoints. Beyond the specific consistency checks supported within single specification techniques as presented in [ACGW94, ZJ93], the following requirements are fulfilled in this framework (cited from [BSBD99]).

- The consistency definition is applicable *intra-language* for different formal description techniques, i.e., it can be applied to two (or more) Z specifications for example as well as to two LOTOS specifications.
- It is also applicable *inter-language* between different formal description techniques, i.e., it is possible to relate for example a Z specification and a LOTOS specification.
- It supports different classes of consistency checks, depending on the viewpoints considered and the relation between these viewpoints.
- It supports global consistency, i.e., checks of arbitrary numbers of specifications instead of only binary checks.
- It allows viewpoints to relate to the target system in different ways.

---

[3] See http://www.cs.ukc.ac.uk/research/groups/tcs/openviews/.

The clue to integration supported in this way is to consider different kinds of development relations, like refinement, implementation, and equivalences, and use these to find *unifications* of specifications. The existence of a common unification of a collection of specifications w.r.t. to a given development relation for each one of them then proves their consistency and at the same time shows in which way the features addressed in the specifications correspond to each other. An abstract formal framework for this approach has been worked out and instantiated with different given development relations of LOTOS and Z. Moreover, a translation of LOTOS to Z is given in [DBBS96] to support inter-language consistency checks. Considering the comparisons worked out in the framework of transformation systems, however, a single (non-parameterised) translation of languages seems to be too strict to support the general goal of inter-language consistency checks. For instance, using different LOTOS or Z styles is not supported when there is only one fixed translation.

The consistency approach starts by considering specification languages, with their given semantics and development relations. In this sense it is dual to the transformation system approach that starts with purely semantical investigations that are not bound to specific languages or specification paradigms. Only as a result of the semantical comparisons should syntactic representations within concrete languages be given. The ideas of the consistency approach nevertheless have influenced the development of the transformation system reference model and, since the approaches are complementary, there are good chances to bring the two views together finally.

7.3.4 Semantic Unification of Programming Languages

The usage of a semantic domain as a common reference level has also been applied in the area of unification of programming languages. As a reaction to the growing number of programming languages and to the weakness of their semantic definitions a common ground has been sought that clarifies the underlying concepts on a semantic level. Following [Mos92] these approaches can be classified as denotational semantics, algebraic frameworks, axiomatic frameworks, and operational semantics. The book contains a discussion of these classes of approaches in relation to Mosses' action semantics, and pointers to the literature.

The aims of semantic unifications of programming languages are twofold. First the semantics of programming languages is usually only vaguely defined. That means each compiler defines a semantics for the programs, but these are neither unique nor explicit. The problem therefore is the complexity of the languages on the one hand and the difficulty of finding the right abstractions for the definition of semantics on the other hand. The above-mentioned approaches differ accordingly by the semantic domains they use and the way they express the semantics of programs. The second issue is that it is rather obvious that different imperative languages for example do not differ in their fundamental semantic concepts, but it is very hard to make this observation precise and use it constructively for a precise comparison of programming languages. The problems are thus very similar to the problems found in software specification languages: weak definitions of semantics and unclear basic concepts.

A very concise set of concepts for the definition of formal semantics of programming languages has been developed with the framework of action semantics [Mos92]. Actions are distinguished by what kind of information they are concerned with. Functional actions are concerned with data flow, declarative actions with scoped information, imperative actions with stable information, and communicative actions with permanent information. Furthermore, there are reflective actions for abstractions of actions and their enactions, and actions include data. Information is related with storage; thus the structural aspect that complements the behavioural one is essentially concerned with the organisation of stores. Action semantics introduces a notation for actions, semantic descriptions, and the formal semantics. Thereby the formality is combined with good pragmatic features that make the framework applicable also to real programming languages.

Action semantics describes how states (of a storage) are changed. This is complementary to the transformation system approach that does not introduce specific sets of actions for state changes, but provides a framework that allows the descriptive representation of state changes of arbitrary structures. The difference is of course due to the fact that action semantics addresses programming languages that are concerned with the constructive change of data, whereas transformation systems address specification languages that are concerned with the description of structures and behaviours of systems. The complementary aspects of transformation systems and action semantics could be combined by applying the composition and development concepts of transformation systems to action semantics. In fact, action semantics describes mainly sequential programs, and does not take into account modularisation in the sense of software components or modules, and development relations.

Another approach to the unification of programming languages that stresses these aspects is presented in [HJ98]. Programs are considered semantically as relations of input and output values. Relational algebra is used for the composition of programs, which thus yields an algebra of programs. The development and the composition dimension are covered by the definition of a refinement calculus for programs and the explicit treatment of concurrency and communication. This yields the algebra of communicating processes (ACP) and the closely related process calculus Communicating Sequential Processes (CSP). The comparison with transformation systems yields analogous differences as above. The algebras of programs and communicating processes are concerned with the semantics of programming. That means the static structure can be considered as a set of variables or a family of sets of variables. On the behaviour level the questions of how states are changed and how state changes are combined are addressed. Software specifications, however, are concerned with the description of structure and behaviour, rather

than the constructive state changes. The way in which process calculi like
CSP or CCS can be reconstructed and embedded into the transformation system reference model has been shown in more detail in the examples given
throughout this book.

7.4 Methodological Remarks

In the discussion and presentation of the integration framework given by the
transformation systems reference model three layers can be distinguished (see
Figure 7.1). The formal basis is given by the *mathematical theory* that comprises the formal definitions of all notions and constructions and the assertions
of their relationships and properties with their formal proofs. The meanings
of the concepts are determined within this layer by their mutual relationships,
i.e., by the internal structure of the theory. The way in which a composition
operation refers to control states and data states for example determines the
meanings of the composition operation and the control states mutually.

applications to software specification languages
applications to specification formalisms
examples in the mathematical theory

Fig. 7.1. (Theory and) Presentation layers of the integration framework

The second layer is given by the *application* of the integration framework
to *specification formalisms*, i.e., specification languages with formal syntax
and semantics. By mapping these languages to the reference model and re-
constructing their semantics in this formal domain the meanings of their constructs that are established within their domain of usage are linked with the
formal concepts. That means the relationships of the concepts of the mathematical theory and the formal specification languages enrich the meaning of
the former (and, vice versa, the latter) in that an external structure (theory—
application) is established.

The integration approach is furthermore *applied to software specification
languages* that do not (necessarily) have formal semantics. On the one hand
this yields yet another interpretation of the formal concepts, i.e., it contributes
to the constitution of their meanings by establishing a further external structure comprising the mathematical theory and an informal application. On the
other hand it shows how the formal concepts can be applied to an informal

domain. The structuralist approach, defining meaning by structure, allows us to carry over results from one domain (the mathematical theory) to another one (software specification languages). Obviously, 'result' must not be misinterpreted as a mathematical theorem, but denotes a structural relationship. More concretely this means that the basic notions that are established as structure within the theoretical layer can be conceptualised and presented non-formally to carry them over and apply them.

The formal specification languages considered in this book cover a variety of different specification paradigms and corresponding different and sometimes incompatible elementary concepts. For instance, process calculi like CCS are based on the assumption of atomic (non-decomposable) actions, whose temporal ordering in a process is specified. Data states are abstracted, i.e., static structure is not considered. The communication paradigm is message exchange via the synchronisation of actions. The semantics is open in the sense that admissible actions of the environment that may have an impact on the considered process are modelled as part of its behaviour. Accordingly, composition constrains the behaviour of the process to the actions actually offered by the environment.

A completely different paradigm is exemplified by the parallel programming language UNITY [CM88]. It is a rule-based specification technique, whose basic actions are transformations of internally structured data states. In contrast to temporal orderings, causal relations are specified that are represented in the data states as well as in the application conditions of the rules. The communication paradigm is given by common access to shared variables. The semantics is closed, i.e., only actions performed (actively) by the process itself are specified. The possible impact of the environment is represented by its ability to change the state of some of the variables, whereby new transformations may be enabled. UNITY does not really support composition of specifications. In this book a UNITY example was treated in a compositional way nevertheless, applying the composition operations of transformation systems as if these were already contained in the language.

Other rule-based specification formalisms are considered, too, like graph grammars and Petri nets. Especially the latter introduce further concepts, like explicit causality on atomic actions and formal indistinguishability of data flow and control flow. These can be embedded into the reference model and compared with the other ones. Finally, also purely static (stateless) specification formalisms like algebraic specification can be considered. But obviously, these only reach a very limited part of the reference model, the data states. Recall, however, that dynamic behaviour can be encoded into algebras, for instance by specifying transition systems as parts of the algebras. The labelled transition logic approach [AR87, AR96, CR97] for example is based on this idea. Mapping such a specification to the reference model would make explicit this encoding and interpret the algebra as a transformation system. A schematic approach on the other hand would always map algebras to data states. As discussed in Section 1.2 this again shows that integrations cannot be automatised but constitute a (creative) design step.

The structural concepts of the reference model may also contribute to an enhanced understanding of the ones implemented in a particular specification technique. The categorical analysis of elementary notions of concurrency in [WN97] is a prominent example of this kind of reflection of semantic properties to the syntax of a specification language. The interpretation of a specification language in the reference model thus may have an additional value. Missing features (in comparison with the reference model) can be reflected to the language in that a syntactic presentation of the given semantic features in the syntax of the language is sought.

The integration approach is also applied to software modelling languages like UML. Obviously, this application is of a very different nature than the interpretation of the specification formalisms or formal methods. A specification formalism has well-defined formal syntax and semantics. A formal method offers more methodological support, but also its more elaborated concepts can be reduced to a set of basic ones the formal semantics is defined for. A software modelling technique or language usually does not have formal semantics, and also its syntax—although being formally defined—need not be presented in a traditional mathematical style. The UML meta model is a prominent example of a formal non-mathematical syntax definition in this sense. Also the meta model language MML [MML] that should be used to make precise the semantics of UML is defined by a class diagram, i.e., not a traditional mathematical type of definition.

Applying the transformation system reference model in this case thus means to discuss and relate concepts much more informally than in the application to specification formalisms or formal methods. In particular, it offers several possible interpretations of the software modelling concepts in precise formal terms of the reference model as discussed in Chapter 6, for instance, and makes possible a reflection of the semantic development relations and composition operations for transformation systems to the modelling languages. That means the semantics of development (refinement, conformance, implementation, etc.) and composition (object interaction, inter-object behaviour, communication, etc.) can be defined by choosing the appropriate construction from the reference model. Their compositionality properties are then inherited for free, since these are already established once and for all in the reference model.

Let me finally make a few further remarks on the development and design of the theory of transformation systems and its presentation in this book. As mentioned above, the main aim here is twofold. On the one hand, the mathematical definitions and properties of the domain of transformation systems, i.e., the mathematical theory, should be presented in detail to serve as a reference. On the other hand, the role of the transformation system domain *as* reference model should be explained, i.e., its application and use in the integration of heterogeneous software specifications. Since the latter task is the main motivation and the aim of the development of this theory, the exposition cannot be entirely mathematical but corresponding discussions and interpretations of the concepts need to be included. One of the consequences—w.r.t. a pure mathematical presentation—is that definitions for example are sometimes given step by step, proceeding from more elementary and more intuitive cases to the more general ones. The detailed presentation of transformation systems is in fact formulated for *algebra* transformation systems, a special case of transformation systems where data states are always given by partial algebras. In the general case, arbitrary data type models can be used as data states. This kind of presentation clearly deviates from the usual mathematical style of deducing special cases from the most general ones and giving examples only after the formal definitions. But hopefully this style enhances the readability of the book in view of the intended application of the theory. Nevertheless, mathematical rigour is not neglected. That is, all definitions and statements (theorems) are fully formalised and proved.

When developing the theory formal structuring and development means for the theory design turned out to be indispensable. They are necessary to obtain the right definitions and to reduce the complexity of the overall structure of the reference model that is implied by the requirements. The obvious choice for such theory structuring and development means—a *general theory design guide*—is category theory (cf. [Gog89, AM75, Mac71, EGW96, EGW98]). So for instance the proofs of the compositionality properties and the generalisation to transformation systems with arbitrary data state models and action structures would not have been achieved without categorical methods. Moreover, some of the specific categorical principles directly correspond to requirements of the application. The *locality principle* of category theory for example states that the internal ingredients of two different objects (by default) have nothing in common, independently of their local representations. If for example M and N are two sets, then an element of M that might be denoted by a is distinct from each element of N, even if some are denoted by the same symbol a. Names are local; thus $a \in M$ and $a \in N$ are just local statements which do not necessarily imply that M and N have an element in common. There is no implicit global name space or other background that would allow elements of different sets to be considered as identical. If identifications are required these have to be made explicit by defining appropriate mappings (morphisms) or relations (spans) between the objects that realise identifications independently of the local names. This locality principle is used for example in identification relations for the connection of transformation systems and the declaration of correspondences of local static structures. It is used furthermore in the definition of the development relations and composition operations on all levels, which should not rely on accidentally chosen local names but also support the statement of semantic correspondences.

Second, category theory supports structuralism, which, according to the discussion above, is crucial for the development of the theory. That means, first, elements are always conceived as elements of a local domain (category) and that they are always given with their relationships (the morphisms). The latter define the external structure, whereas the internal structure of the objects is completely hidden and only serves to establish the external structure (see also [Gro99] for a discussion). This *structure principle* obviously corresponds to the information hiding principle in software engineering, where objects can only be accessed by other objects via the external (export) interface. The internal structure (implementation) here also only serves to realise the external structure. It can be changed without changing the relevant behaviour of the object. In category theory this principle obviously applies to all categorical objects, not just models of objects in the sense of object-oriented methodology. The structure principle is mainly used here—beyond its general meaning—for the definition of the composition operations. The architectural part, the connection of units, is given by diagrams, as in [FM92]. The result of a composition operation is given by a limit of the diagram. Thus its external structure (its relation to all local components) is uniquely defined, but its internal realisation may be arbitrary. That means no naming conventions or conflict resolutions of any kind need to be fixed. Only this abstraction from realisation details (the definition 'up to isomorphism') allows the proofs of the compositionality properties for example.

But as mentioned above, this book is not an exercise in category theory. Therefore the categorical structure is only exhibited after the corresponding constructions have been given in elementary terms, and is worked out only as far as necessary for the given application.

The last methodological remark concerns the semantic approach, the development of a formal structure as a reference model, and syntactic presentations of instances in this reference model.

Transformation systems are used as semantic elements that serve to define the meaning of constructs from different specification languages. They are themselves defined in terms of sets and functions, using the general language of mathematics, but no specific presentation language for transformation systems has been introduced. Later on, in the definitions of the development relations and the composition operations, also more specific category-theoretic constructions (morphisms, limits, colimits, etc.) are used and denoted by the usual category-theoretic language, but still independently of specification languages. However, in the definition of the data states that are given by partial algebras (or models within an arbitrary institution) at least an abstract syntax of algebraic signatures is needed, because algebras and models cannot be defined without signatures. Also type-compatible bindings of attributes (variables) require structural information, the names and the types of the attributes, which is usually considered as abstract syntax. That means semantics cannot be defined without some abstract syntactic elements at least and also a purely semantical formal approach incorporates certain aspects of an abstract syntax.

Furthermore, different kinds of properties of transformation systems are distinguished and investigated, corresponding to their two-level structure. The data states of a system can be described by data invariants, i.e., properties that hold in each state. Data state transformations can be described by pre- and postconditions relating data state properties of their initial and final states. Finally, the dynamic behaviour of a transformation system can be specified by making statements about the temporal ordering of its steps. The representation of these descriptions must be based on the abstract syntax of the data states, introducing further layers of an abstract syntax of transformation systems. It is important to realise that this abstract syntax does not preclude any concrete specification language to be considered in the integration. When mapping a language to the reference model this means that its constructs may be mapped to semantic elements like transformation systems, development relations, or composition operations directly, or to abstract syntactic elements like signatures, data state invariants, or abstract pre- and postconditions, that are bound to the semantic elements.

Beyond the consideration of given specification formalisms, however, also the presentation of the examples in this book gave rise to some principle concepts for the syntactic presentation of transformation systems, which could be understood as first steps of a language design. Based on these principles a global schema could then be derived that allows the presentation of individual transformation systems, relations, and operations systematically. This aspect of language design has not been further developed in this book in order not to deviate from the openness of the reference model w.r.t. the interpretation of different specification languages. Nevertheless, in the presentation of the examples a certain system may be detected that arose from these considerations.

A

Partial Algebras and Their Specification

This appendix gives a survey on the basic definitions and properties of partial algebras and algebraic specifications with conditional equations. In particular, the structural properties that are needed to employ partial algebras as data states in a specification framework for transformation systems (as introduced in Section 2.3) are discussed. They are also presented in *institutional* terms at the end of this appendix.

An **algebraic signature** $\Sigma = (S, F)$ is given by a set S of sort names and a family $F = (F_{w,v})_{w,v \in S^*}$ of function names indexed by their arities. Function names $f \in F_{w,v}$ are denoted by $f : w \to v \in F$ as usual. Note that products of sorts are also allowed as targets of functions. Functions with target sort $s_1 \ldots s_k$ ($k > 1$) returning tuples or records of values could also be used in the traditional framework that provides only single sorts as targets by specifying product sorts explicitly. Thus this case does not enlarge the expressive power essentially. Functions with the empty string λ as target ($p : w \to \lambda \in F$), however, model predicates, which cannot be adequately represented using only functions with single sorts as targets.

A **partial Σ-algebra** $A = ((A_s)_{s \in S}, (f^A)_{f \in F})$ is given by an S-indexed family of sets A_s and for each function name $f : w \to v \in F$ a partial function $f^A : A_w \multimap A_v$, given by a subset $dom(f^A) \subseteq A_w$, the domain of f^A, and a total function $f_!^A : dom(f^A) \to A_v$. (Where $A_u = A_{s_1} \times \ldots \times A_{s_k}$ for all $u = s_1 \cdots s_k \in S^*$ and $A_\lambda \cong \{*\}$.) The interpretation A_p of a function name $p : w \to \lambda$ is thus given by $dom(p^A) \subseteq A_w$ and $p_!^A : dom(p^A) \to A_\lambda \cong \{*\}$. Since the latter is redundant—there is only one function whose codomain is a singleton—the semantics p^A of p can be considered as (the extension $dom(p^A)$ of) a predicate.

A **Σ-homomorphism** $h : A \to B$ of partial Σ–algebras A and B is given by a family $(h_s : A_s \to B_s)_{s \in S}$ of total functions that preserve domains and function application, i.e., $h_w(dom(f^A)) \subseteq dom(f^B)$ and $h_v(f_!^A(a)) = f_!^B(h_w(a))$ ($\forall a \in dom(f)^A$) for each $f : w \to v \in F$. (Where again $h_u = h_{s_1} \times \cdots \times h_{s_k}$ for $u = s_1 \ldots s_k \in S^*$.)

Partial Σ-algebras and Σ-homomorphisms with component-wise identities and composition constitute the category $\mathbf{PAlg}(\Sigma)$.

The $S^* \times S^*$-indexed set $Term_\Sigma = (Term_{\Sigma,w,v})_{w,v \in S^*}$ of **terms** is defined inductively as usual (see below), where, however, projections have to be taken into account due to product sorts in the targets of the function arities. Like function names, terms $t \in Term_{\Sigma,w,v}$ are also denoted by $t : w \to v \in Term_\Sigma$:

- variables
  $$x_i : s_1 \ldots s_n \to s_i \in Term_\Sigma \quad (s_i \in S, i = 1, \ldots, n)$$
- tuples
  If $\quad t_1 : v \to s_1, \ldots, t_n : v \to s_n \in Term_\Sigma$
  then $\langle t_1, \ldots, t_n \rangle : v \to s_1 \ldots s_n \in Term_\Sigma$.
- function application
  If $\quad \langle t_1, \ldots, t_n \rangle : v \to w \in Term_\Sigma$

  then $\begin{cases} f_i(t_1, \ldots, t_n) : v \to s'_i \in Term_\Sigma & (i = 1, \ldots, k) & \text{if } k > 1 \\ f(t_1, \ldots, t_n) : v \to s'_1 \in Term_\Sigma & & \text{if } k = 1 \\ f(t_1, \ldots, t_n) : v \to \lambda \in Term_\Sigma & & \text{if } k = 0 \end{cases}$

  for each $f : w \to s'_1 \ldots s'_k \in F$.

The **evaluation** of a term $t : w \to v \in Term_\Sigma$ in a partial Σ–algebra A is given by the partial function $t^A : A_w \overset{\circ}{\to} A_v$ defined as follows:

- variables
  $$dom(x_i{}^A) = A_{s_1} \times \cdots \times A_{s_n}$$
  $$(x_i)^A_!(\langle a_1, \ldots, a_n \rangle) = a_i$$
- tuples
  $$dom(\langle t_1, \ldots, t_n \rangle^A) = \bigcap_{1 \leq i \leq n} dom(t_i{}^A)$$
  $$\langle t_1, \ldots, t_n \rangle^A_!(a) = \langle t_1{}^A(a), \ldots, t_n{}^A(a) \rangle$$
- function application
  $$dom(f(t_1, \ldots, t_n)^A) = \{ a \in dom(\langle t_1, \ldots, t_n \rangle^A) \mid$$
  $$\langle t_1{}^A(a), \ldots, t_n{}^A(a) \rangle \in dom(f^A) \}$$

  $k > 1 : \quad f_i(t_1, \ldots, t_n)^A_!(a) = \pi_i(f^A_!((t_1)^A_!(a), \ldots, (t_n)^A_!(a)_!))$,

  the i-th component of $f^A_!((t_1)^A_!(a), \ldots, (t_n)^A_!(a))$

  $k = 1 : \quad f(t_1, \ldots, t_n)^A_!(a) = f^A((t_1)^A_!(a), \ldots, (t_n)^A_!(a))$

  $k = 0 : \quad f(t_1, \ldots, t_n)^A_!(a) = *$,

  the unique element of A_λ.

(The exclamation mark in $t^A_!$ will be omitted in the sequel.)

An **equation** e w.r.t. a signature Σ is given by a pair of parallel terms $t, t' : w \to v \in Term$, denoted by $e = (w : t = t')$. The string $w = s_1 \ldots s_n$ represents the declaration $x_1 : s_1, \ldots, x_n : s_n$ of the variables that may occur in t or t'. This representation abstracts from the (redundant) names of variables and replaces them by their position that determines the substitution behaviour. The set of Σ-equations is denoted by $Eqns_\Sigma$; the subset of all equations $e = (w : t = t')$ with domain w is denoted by $Eqns_{\Sigma,w}$.

A **conditional equation** ce w.r.t. Σ is given by two pairs of parallel terms $r, r' : w \to v'$, and $t, t' : w \to v \in Term_\Sigma$ with common source w, denoted by $ce = (w : r = r' \to t = t')$. These form the set $CEqns_\Sigma$.

The **solution set** e^A of an equation $e = (w : t = t')$ in a partial Σ-algebra A is defined by

$$e^A = \{a \in dom(t^A) \cap dom(t'^A) \mid t^A(a) = t'^A(a)\} ,$$

and A **satisfies** the conditional equation $ce = (w : r = r' \to t = t')$, denoted $A \models ce$, if

$$(w : r = r')^A \subseteq (w : t = t')^A .$$

Terms, equations, and conditional equations can also be defined with named variables that are given explicitly as families of sets $X = (X_s)_{s \in S}$. Then $Term_\Sigma(X) = (Term_{\Sigma,s}(X))_{s \in S \cup \{\lambda\}}$ is given by

- $X_s \subseteq Term_{\Sigma,s}(X)$ $(s \in S)$.
- If $t_1 \in Term_{\Sigma,s_1}(X), \ldots, t_n \in Term_{\Sigma,s_n}(X)$ and $f : s_1 \ldots s_n \to s'_1 \ldots s'_k \in F$ then

$$\begin{cases} f_i(t_1, \ldots, t_n) \in Term_{\Sigma,s'_i} & (i = 1, \ldots, k) \text{ if } k > 1 \\ f(t_1, \ldots, t_n) \in Term_{\Sigma,s'_1} & \text{if } k = 1 \\ f(t_1, \ldots, t_n) \in Term_{\Sigma,\lambda} & \text{if } k = 0 . \end{cases}$$

For the evaluation $t^{A,a}$ of such terms an instantiation a of the variables X in the algebra A is needed, i.e., a total S-indexed mapping $a = (a_s : X_s \to A_s)_{s \in S}$. Then

- $x^{A,a} = a_s(x)$ $(x \in X_s)$
- $f_i(t_1, \ldots, t_n)^{A,a} = \pi_i(f^A(t_1^{A,a}, \ldots, t_n^{A,a}))$ if $(t_1^{A,a}, \ldots, t_n^{A,a}) \in dom(f^A)$
  $f(t_1, \ldots, t_n)^{A,a} = f^A(t_1^{A,a}, \ldots, t_n^{A,a})$ if $(t_1^{A,a}, \ldots, t_n^{A,a}) \in dom(f^A)$
  $f(t_1, \ldots, t_n)^{A,a} = *$ if $(t_1^{A,a}, \ldots, t_n^{A,a}) \in dom(f^A) .$

If the corresponding condition is not satisfied $t^{A,a}$ is not defined, i.e., t is not in the domain of the evaluation function $\_^{A,a} : Term_\Sigma(X) \to |A|$.

Equations with explicit named variables are given by pairs of terms with variables, i.e.,

$$Eqns_\Sigma(X) = \{(X : t = t') \mid \exists \bar{s} \in S \cup \{\lambda\} . t, t' \in Term_{\Sigma,\bar{s}}(X)\} .$$

A solution set $Sol_\Sigma(e, A)$ of an equation $e = (X : t = t') \in Eqns_\Sigma(X)$ in a partial Σ-algebra A is then a subset of the variable instantiations

$$Sol_\Sigma(e, A) \subseteq |A|^X ,$$
$$Sol_\Sigma(e, A) = \{a : X \to |A| \mid t, t' \in dom(\_^{A,a}) \wedge t^{A,a} = t'^{A,a}\} .$$

Analogous to the definitions above then

$$CEqns_\Sigma(X) = \{ \; (X : t_1 = t'_1, \ldots, t_n = t'_n \to t = t') \; | $$
$$(X : t_1 = t'_1), \ldots, (X : t_n = t'_n), (X : t = t') \in Eqns_\Sigma(X) \; \}$$

and a partial Σ-algebra A satisfies $ce \in CEqns_\Sigma(X)$ if

$$\bigcap_{1 \le i \le n} Sol_\Sigma((X : t_i = t'_i), A) \subseteq Sol_\Sigma((X : t = t'), A) .$$

Of course, both versions are equivalent in the sense that they can be translated into each other. In the following the categorical variant with anonymous variables is used, while in the other chapters both versions are used.

It follows immediately from the definitions that **homomorphisms preserve term evaluation and solution sets**, that is, if $h : A \to B$ is a Σ-homomorphism then for each term $t : w \to v$ and each equation $e = (w : t = t')$ we have $h(t^A(a)) = t^B(h(a))$ for all $a \in dom(t^A)$, and $a \in e^A$ implies $h(a) \in e^B$ for all $a \in A_w$.

Using an equation that always holds, like $(w : \langle\rangle = \langle\rangle)$, each equation $e = (w : t = t')$ can be considered as a conditional equation $e^* = (w : \langle\rangle = \langle\rangle \to t = t')$. Since $(w : \langle\rangle = \langle\rangle)^A = A_w$ we have $A \models e^*$ iff $A_w \subseteq (w : t = t')^A$; that is, iff each element $a \in A_w$ is a solution of e. In this sense $A \models e$ will be used as short notation for $A \models e^*$. Furthermore, the common notation $A, a \models e$ is sometimes used for $a \in e^A$. According to the definition of a solution set and the above convention, we have $A \models (w : t = t)$ iff $t^A : A_w \rightarrowtail A_v$ is a total function. In particular, $A \models (\lambda : t = t)$ for a ground term $t : \lambda \to v$ iff the element $t^A := t^A(*) \in A_v$ is defined. In the following this *existence predicate* $(w : t = t)$ will be abbreviated as $(w : t \downarrow)$. By definition equations are *strict*; that means, if $A \models (w : t = t')$ then also $A \models (w : t \downarrow)$ and $A \models (w : t' \downarrow)$. Non-strict equations can be expressed by appropriate conditions, as in $(w : t \downarrow, t' \downarrow \to t = t')$. Note, furthermore, that terms comprise tuples of single sorted terms, $t = \langle t_1, \ldots, t_n \rangle$, whence equations comprise conjunctions of single sorted equations, $(w : t = t') \hat{=} (w : t_1 = t'_1 \wedge \cdots \wedge t_n = t'_n)$.

Applying partial equational specifications, it is often convenient to use the following notion of *strong equality* $(w : t \overset{s}{=} t')$ that is satisfied if either both terms t and t' are undefined, or both are defined and equal. Since $(w : t \overset{s}{=} t')$ is equivalent to $(w : t \downarrow \Rightarrow t = t') \wedge (w : t' \downarrow \Rightarrow t = t')$, strong equality can be reduced to existential equality as defined above.

A **partial equational specification** $\Gamma = (S, F, CE)$ is given by

- an algebraic signature $\Sigma = (S, F)$, and
- a set CE of conditional equations w.r.t. Σ.

A partial Σ-algebra A is a **partial Γ-algebra** if A satisfies all conditional equations in CE. A Σ-homomorphism $h : A \to B$ is a **Γ-homomorphism** if A and B are partial Γ-algebras. Partial Γ-algebras and Γ-homomorphisms yield the category **PAlg**(Γ).

Signature morphisms are defined as for the usual algebraic specifications: that is, a **signature morphism** $\sigma : \Sigma_1 \to \Sigma_2$ with $\Sigma_i = (S_i, F_i)$, $i = 1, 2$, is given by a pair of functions $\sigma = (\sigma_S : S_1 \to S_2, \sigma_F : F_1 \to F_2)$ that respects the arities of functions. That means $f \in (F_1)_{w,v}$ implies $\sigma_F(f) \in (F_2)_{\sigma_S^*(w), \sigma_S^*(v)}$. Signatures and signature morphisms with component-wise identities and composition form the category **AlgSig**.

Each signature morphism $\sigma : \Sigma_1 \to \Sigma_2$ induces a **forgetful functor**

$$V_\sigma : \mathbf{PAlg}(\Sigma_2) \to \mathbf{PAlg}(\Sigma_1)$$

that *forgets* those parts of Σ_2-algebras and homomorphisms that are not in the image of σ. The functor V_σ is defined by

$$V_\sigma(A_2)_{s_1} = (A_2)_{\sigma_S(s_1)} \quad (s_1 \in S_1) ,$$
$$f_1^{V_\sigma(A_2)} = \sigma_F(f_1)^{A_2} \quad (f_1 \in F_1) ,$$

for each partial Σ_2-algebra A_2, and

$$V_\sigma(h_2)_{s_1} = (h_2)_{\sigma_S(s_1)} \quad (s_1 \in S_1)$$

for each Σ_2-homomorphism h_2.

Moreover, each forgetful functor $V_\sigma : \mathbf{PAlg}(\Sigma_2) \to \mathbf{PAlg}(\Sigma_1)$ induced by a signature morphism $\sigma : \Sigma_1 \to \Sigma_2$ has a left adjoint

$$F_\sigma : \mathbf{PAlg}(\Sigma_1) \to \mathbf{PAlg}(\Sigma_2) .$$

The free partial Σ_2-algebra $F_\sigma(A_1)$ for some partial Σ_2-algebra A_1 is given by

$$(F_\sigma(A_1))_{s_2} = \sum_{s_1 \in S_1 : \sigma_S(s_1) = s_2} (A_1)_{s_1} \quad (s_2 \in S_2) ,$$
$$f_2^{(F_\sigma(A_1))} = \sum_{f_1 \in F_1 : \sigma_F(f_1) = f_2} f_1^{A_1} \quad (f_2 \in F_2) .$$

If σ is injective $F_\sigma(A_1)$ is thus given by extending A_1 by empty carrier sets and empty (totally undefined) functions.

A signature morphism $\sigma : \Sigma_1 \to \Sigma_2$ is a **specification morphism** $\sigma : (\Sigma_1, CE_1) \to (\Sigma_2, CE_2)$ if the forgetful image $V_\sigma(A_2)$ of each partial (Σ_2, CE_2)-algebra A_2 satisfies CE_1. That means $V_\sigma : \mathbf{PAlg}(\Sigma_2) \to \mathbf{PAlg}(\Sigma_1)$ restricts to $V_\sigma : \mathbf{PAlg}(\Sigma_2, CE_2) \to \mathbf{PAlg}(\Sigma_1, CE_1)$ if σ is a specification morphism. Also, these restricted forgetful functors (w.r.t. specification morphisms) have left adjoints $F_\sigma : \mathbf{PAlg}(\Sigma_1, CE_1) \to \mathbf{PAlg}(\Sigma_2, CE_2)$. In this case carrier sets and partial functions are constructed inductively, based on the sets and functions of A_1 and the conditional equations CE_2.

A signature morphism $\sigma : \Sigma_1 \to \Sigma_2$ can be used to *translate* Σ_1-terms and (conditional) Σ_1-equations, i.e., it induces functions $\sigma : Term_{\Sigma_1} \to Term_{\Sigma_2}$, $\sigma : Eqns_{\Sigma_1} \to Eqns_{\Sigma_2}$, and $\sigma : CEqns_{\Sigma_1} \to CEqns_{\Sigma_2}$ by

$$\sigma(x_i : s_1 \ldots s_n \to s_i) \quad = x_i : \sigma_S(s_1) \ldots \sigma_S(s_n) \to \sigma_S(s_i)$$
$$\sigma(\langle t_1, \ldots, t_n \rangle) \quad = \langle \sigma(t_1), \ldots, \sigma(t_n) \rangle$$
$$\sigma(f_i(t_1, \ldots, t_n)) \quad = \sigma_F(f)_i(\sigma(t_1), \ldots, \sigma(t_n))$$
$$\sigma(f(t_1, \ldots, t_n)) \quad = \sigma_F(f)(\sigma(t_1), \ldots, \sigma(t_n))$$
$$\sigma((w : t = t')) \quad = (\sigma_S^*(w) : \sigma(t) = \sigma(t'))$$
$$\sigma((w : r = r' \to t = t')) = (\sigma_S^*(w) : \sigma(r) = \sigma(r') \to \sigma(t) = \sigma(t')) .$$

This yields also an equivalent condition for specification morphisms. A signature morphism $\sigma : \Sigma_1 \to \Sigma_2$ is a specification morphism $\sigma : (\Sigma_1, CE_1) \to (\Sigma_2, CE_2)$ if the translated set of conditional equations $\sigma(CE_1)$ is derivable from CE_2, i.e., $CE_2 \models \sigma(CE_1)$.

One of the most important structural properties of the specification logic of partial algebras (beyond the existence of the free functors) is the **invariance of solution sets and satisfaction under translation.** (In institutional terms this is called the *satisfaction condition*.) For each signature morphism $\sigma : \Sigma_1 \to \Sigma_2$, term $t \in Term_{\Sigma_1}$, equation $e \in Eqns_{\Sigma_1}$, and conditional equation $ce \in CEqns_{\Sigma_1}$, we have

$$t_1^{V_\sigma(A_2)} \quad = \sigma(t_1)^{A_2}$$
$$e_1^{V_\sigma(A_2)} \quad = \sigma(e_1)^{A_2}$$
$$V_\sigma(A_2) \models ce_1 \Leftrightarrow A_2 \models \sigma(ce_1) .$$

These properties follow immediately from the (inductive) definitions given above.

Signatures (and specifications) can be **composed** by forming **colimits** of diagrams of signatures and signature morphisms. The category **AlgSig** is cocomplete, and so is **AlgSpec**, the category of specifications and specification morphisms. That means they have (small) colimits. (Thus, in particular, **AlgSig** has *pushouts*.) Composition of signatures (specifications) by colimits induces a composition of partial algebras and homomorphisms called **amalgamation.**

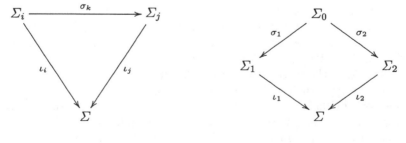

colimit   pushout

Let $(\Sigma, (\iota_i)_{i \in |I|})$ be a colimit of a diagram $D : I \to$ **AlgSig** (a pushout of $\Sigma_1 \leftarrow \Sigma_0 \to \Sigma_2$), and let $\Sigma_i := D(i)$ for $i \in |I|$ and $\sigma_k := D(k)$ for

$k : i \to j$ in I. The category $\mathbf{PAlg}(\Sigma)$, together with the forgetful functors $V_{\iota_i} : \mathbf{PAlg}(\Sigma) \to \mathbf{PAlg}(\Sigma_i)$ ($i \in |I|$), is then a limit of the diagram given by the categories $\mathbf{PAlg}(\Sigma_i)$ ($i \in |I|$) and the (forgetful) functors V_{σ_k} ($k : i \to j$ in I). In terms of institutions this amalgamation property means that the model functor is continuous. Spelling it out yields:

- For each family $(A_i)_{i \in |I|}$ of partial Σ_i-algebras A_i that satisfies $V_{\sigma_k}(A_j) = A_i$ for each $k : i \to j$ in I there is a partial Σ-algebra $A =: \sum_I A_i$ that satisfies $V_{\iota_i}(A) = A_i$ for all $i \in |I|$.
- If some partial Σ-algebra B satisfies $V_{\iota_i}(B) = A_i$ for all $i \in |I|$, then $B = \sum_I A_i$.
- The same holds for homomorphisms.

The **amalgamations** $A =: \sum_I A_i$ and $h =: \sum_I h_i$ in $\mathbf{PAlg}(\Sigma)$ are given by

$$A_s = (A_i)_{o_i} \quad \text{if } s = \iota_i(s_i) \quad \text{for some } i \in |I|$$
$$f^A = (f_i)^{A_i} \quad \text{if } f = \iota_i(f_i) \quad \text{for some } i \in |I|$$
$$h_s = (h_i)_{s_i} \quad \text{if } s = \iota_i(s_i) \quad \text{for some } i \in |I| .$$

The condition on the families of algebras and homomorphisms ensures that the amalgamations are well defined.

For the sake of reference the **institution of partial algebras** is finally given.

- The *category of signatures* **Sig** is given by $\mathbf{Sig} = \mathbf{AlgSig}$.
- The *sentence functor* $Sen : \mathbf{AlgSig} \to \mathbf{Set}$ is given by

$$Sen(\Sigma) = CEqns_\Sigma$$
$$Sen(\sigma : \Sigma_1 \to \Sigma_2) = \sigma : CEqns_{\Sigma_1} \to CEqns_{\Sigma_2} .$$

- The *model functor* $Mod : \mathbf{AlgSig} \to \mathbf{Cat}^{op}$ is given by

$$Mod(\Sigma) = \mathbf{PAlg}(\Sigma)$$
$$Mod(\sigma : \Sigma_1 \to \Sigma_2) = V_\sigma : \mathbf{PAlg}(\Sigma_2) \to \mathbf{PAlg}(\Sigma_1) .$$

- The *satisfaction relations* $(\models_\Sigma)_{\Sigma \in |\mathbf{PAlgSig}|}$ are the satisfaction relations for conditional Σ-equations in partial Σ-algebras, $A \models ce$.

The *satisfaction condition* has been shown above. Obviously this institution is concrete

$$sorts(S, F) = S , \quad |A|_\Sigma = (A_s)_{s \in S}$$

and has formulae $Form_\Sigma(X) = CEqns_\Sigma(X)$ with

$$Sol_\Sigma((X : r = r' \to t = t'), A) = \{a : X \to |A| \mid$$
$$a \in Sol_\Sigma((X : r = r'), A) \Rightarrow a \in Sol_\Sigma((X : t = t'), A)\} .$$

References

[AB96]   M. Aignier and G. Bernot. ÉTOILE-specifications: an object-oriented
           way of specifying systems. In J.-P. Bahsoun, J. Fiadeiro, D. Galmiche,
           and A. Yonezawa, editors, *Proc. of the ECOOP'96 Workshop on Proof
           Theory of Concurrent Object-Oriented Programming, Linz, Austria*,
           pages 50–57, 1996.

[Abr96]   J.R. Abrial. *The B-Book: Assigning Programs to Meanings*. Cambridge
           University Press, 1996.

[ABR99]   E. Astesiano, M. Broy, and G. Reggio. Algebraic specification of concur-
           rent systems. In E. Astesiano, H.-J. Kreowski, and B. Krieg–Brückner,
           editors, *Algebraic Foundations of System Specification*, IFIP State-of-
           the-Art Reports, chapter 13, pages 467–520. Springer-Verlag, Berlin,
           1999.

[AC92]   E. Astesiano and M. Cerioli. Relationships between Logical Frameworks.
           In *Recent Trends in Data Type Specification*, pages 126–143. LNCS 655,
           Springer-Verlag, Berlin, 1992.

[ACGW94]   M. Ainsworth, A.H. Cruickshank, L.J. Groves, and P.J.L. Wallis.
           Viewpoint specification and Z. *Information and Software Technology*,
           36(1):43–51, February 1994.

[AF01]   L. Andrade and J. Fiadeiro. Coordination technologies for managing
           information system evolution. In K. Dittrich, A. Geppert, and M. Norrie,
           editors, *Proc. CAiSE'01*, pages 374–387. LNCS 2068, Springer-Verlag,
           Berlin, 2001.

[AFG⁺00]   L. Andrade, J. Fiadeiro, J. Gouveia, A. Lopes, and M. Wermelinger. Pat-
           terns for coordination. In G. Gruia-Catalin and A. Porto, editors, *Proc.
           Coordination Languages and Models*, pages 317–322. Springer-Verlag,
           Berlin LNCS 1906, 2000.

[AM75]   M. Arbib and E.G. Manes. *Arrows, Structures, and Functors: The Cat-
           egorical Imperative*. Academic Press, New York, 1975.

[AR87]   E. Astesiano and G. Reggio. SMoLCS-driven concurrent calculi. In
           H. Ehrig, R. Kowalski, G. Levi, and U. Montanari, editors, *Proc. of
           TAPSOFT'87*, pages 169–201. LNCS 249, Springer-Verlag, Berlin, 1987.

[AR96]   E. Astesiano and G. Reggio. Labelled transition logic: An outline. Tech-
           nical Report DISI–TR–96–20, DISI – Università di Genova, Italy, 1996.

312   References

[ASW98]   R.A. Andersen, C. Stirling, and G. Winskel. A compositional proof system for the modal mu-calculus. Technical Report BRICS reports series RS-98-40, BRICS, Department of Computer Science, University of Aarhus, 1998.

[AZ95]   E. Astesiano and E. Zucca. D-oids: A model for dynamic data types. *Mathematical Structures in Computer Science*, 5(2):257–282, 1995.

[AZ96]   E. Astesiano and E. Zucca. A free construction of dynamic terms. *Journal of Computer and System Sciences*, 52(1):143–156, February 1996.

[AZ93]   E. Astesiano and E. Zucca. A semantic model for dynamic systems. *Springer Workshops in Computing*, pages 63–80, 1992/93.

[BBD+00]   E.A. Boiten, H. Bowman, J. Derrick, P.F. Linington, and M.W.A. Steen. Viewpoint consistency in ODP. *Computer Networks*, 34(3):503–537, 2000.

[BBDS99]   H. Bowman, E.A. Boiten, J. Derrick, and M.W.A. Steen. Strategies for consistency checking based on unification. *Science of Computer Programming*, 33:261–298, 1999.

[BD99]   H. Bowman and J. Derrick. A junction between state based and behavioural specification. In A. Fantechi, P. Ciancarini, and R. Gorrieri, editors, *Proc. Formal Methods for Open Object-based Distributed Systems*, pages 213–239. Kluwer, Dordrecht, 1999.

[BDG+96]   R. Büssow, H. Dörr, R. Geisler, W. Grieskamp, and M. Klar. μSZ – Ein Ansatz zur systematischen Verbindung von Z und Statecharts. Technical Report 96-32, Technische Universität Berlin, February 1996.

[Bee94]   M. von der Beeck. A comparison of Statechart variants. In H. Langmaack, W.-P. de Roever, and J. Vytopil, editors, *Third Int. School and Symp. on Formal Techniques in Real-time and Fault-tolerant Systems (FTRTFT'94)*, pages 128–148. LNCS 863, Springer-Verlag, Berlin, 1994.

[BG77]   R.M. Burstall and J.A. Goguen. Putting theories together to make specifications. In *Proc. Int. Conf. Artificial Intelligence*, 1977.

[BGK98]   R. Büssow, R. Geisler, and M. Klar. Specifying safety-critical embedded systems with statecharts and Z: a case study. In E. Astesiano, editor, *Proc. 1st Int. Conf. on Fundamental Approaches to SoftwareEngineering (FASE'98)*, pages 71–87. LNCS 1382, Springer-Verlag, Berlin, 1998.

[BH98]   E. Börger and J.K. Huggins. Abstract State Machines 1988–1998. *Bull. EATCS 64*, pages 71–87, 1998. Commented ASM Bibliography.

[BHK89]   J.A. Bergstra, J. Heering, and R. Klint. *Algebraic Specification*. Addison-Wesley, Reading, MA, 1989.

[BR92]   E. Börger and D. Rosenzweig. The WAM – definition and compiler correctness. Technical Report TR 14 – 92, Universita di Pisa, Dipartimento di Informatica, 1992.

[Bre91]   R. Breu. *Algebraic Specification Techniques in Object Oriented Programming Environments*. LNCS 562, Springer-Verlag, Berlin, 1991.

[Bri89]   E. Brinksma, editor. Information processing systems – Open Systems Interconnection – LOTOS – A formal description technique based on the temporal ordering of observational behaviour. ISO 8807, 1989.

[BRJ98]   G. Booch, J. Rumbaugh, and I. Jacobson. *The Unified Modeling Language, User Guide*. Addison-Wesley, Reading, MA, 1998.

[Bro93]   M. Broy. Interaction refinement: The easy way. In M. Broy, editor, *Program Design Calculi*, volume 118 of *NATO ASI Series F: Computer and System Sciences*. Springer-Verlag, Berlin, 1993.

[Bro96]   M. Broy. Specification and refinement of a buffer of length one. In
           M. Broy, editor, *Deductive Program Design*, volume 152 of *NATO ASI
           Series F: Computer and System Sciences*. Springer-Verlag, Berlin, 1996.

[Bro97]   M. Broy. Compositional refinement of interactive systems. *Journal of
           the Association for Computing Machinery*, 44(6), 1997.

[BS91]   Egon Börger and Peter H. Schmitt. A formal operational semantics for
           languages of type Prolog III. In E. Börger, editor, *CSL'90, 4th Workshop
           on Computer Science Logic*, pages 67–79. LNCS 533, Springer-Verlag,
           Berlin, 1991.

[BS01]   M. Broy and K Stolen. *Specification and Development of Interactive
           Systems — Focus on Streams, Interfaces, and Refinement*. Monographs
           in Computer Science. Springer-Verlag, Berlin, 2001.

[BS03]   E. Börger and R. Stärk. *Abstract State Machines. A Method for High-
           Level System Design and Analysis*. Springer-Verlag, Berlin, 2003.

[BSBD99]   H. Bowman, M.W.A. Steen, E.A. Boiten, and J. Derrick. A formal
           framework for viewpoint consistency. Computing Laboratory Technical
           Report 22-99, University of Kent at Canterbury, December 1999. URL
           http://www.cs.ukc.ac.uk/people/staff/jd1/pubs.html.

[BT96]   M. Bidoit and A. Tarlecki. Behavioural satisfaction and equivalence in
           concrete model categories. In H. Kirchner, editor, *Proc. 21st Coll. on
           Trees in Algebra and Programming (CAAP'96)*. LNCS 1059, Springer-
           Verlag, Berlin, 1996.

[Bur86]   P. Burmeister. *A Model Theoretic Oriented Approach to Partial Alge-
           bras*, volume 32 of *Mathematical Research — Mathematische Forschung*.
           Akademie-Verlag, Berlin, 1986.

[BW90]   J.C.M. Baeten and W.P. Weijland. *Process Algebra*. Cambridge Tracts
           in Theoretical Computer Science. Cambridge University Press, 1990.

[BW00]   M. Broy and M. Wirsing. Algebraic state machines. In T. Rus, editor,
           Proc. Algebraic Methodology and Software Technology (AMAST 2000),
           pages 89–118. LNCS 1816, Springer-Verlag, Berlin, 2000.

[Cas01]   G. del Castillo. The ASM workbench — a tool environment for com-
           puter aided analysis and validation of abstract state machine models. In
           T. Margaria and W. Yi, editors, *Proc. Tools and Algorithms for the Con-
           struction and Analysis of Systems (TACAS 2001), Genoa, Italy, April
           2001*, pages 578–581. LNCS 2031, Springer-Verlag, Berlin, 2001.

[CD00]   J. Cheesman and J. Daniels. *UML Components: A simple process for
           specifying component-based software*. Addison–Wesley, Reading, MA,
           2000.

[CDE+98]   M. Clavel, F. Duràn, S. Eker, P. Lincoln, N. Martí-Oliet, and
           J. Meseguer. Metalevel computation in Maude. In C. Kirchner and
           H. Kirchner, editors, *Int. Workshop on Rewriting Logic and its Applica-
           tions*, volume 15 of *Electronic Notes in Theoretical Computer Science*.
           Elsevier Science, Oxford, 1998.

[Cer93]   M. Cerioli. *Relationships between Logical Formalisms*. PhD thesis, Uni-
           versità di Pisa–Genova–Udine, 1993. TD-4/93.

[CGW95]   I. Claßen, M. Große-Rhode, and U. Wolter. Categorical concepts for pa-
           rameterized partial specifications. *Mathematical Structures in Computer
           Science*, 5(2):153–188, 1995.

[CM88]   K.M. Chandy and J. Misra. *Parallel Program Design - A Foundation*.
           Addison-Wesley, Reading, MA, 1988.

314   References

[CM93]   M. Cerioli and J. Meseguer. May I Borrow Your Logic? Technical report, SRI International, Menlo Park, CA, 1993.

[CMR+97]   A. Corradini, U. Montanari, F. Rossi, H. Ehrig, R. Heckel, and M. Löwe. Algebraic approaches to graph transformation I: basic concepts and double pushout approach. In G. Rozenberg, editor, *Handbook of Graph Grammars and Computing by Graph Transformation, Volume 1: Foundations*, chapter 3. World Scientific, Singapore, 1997.

[CR97]   G. Costa and G. Reggio. Specification of abstract dynamic data types: A temporal logic approach. *Theoretical Computer Science*, 173(2):513–554, 1997.

[CW00]   G. del Castillo and K. Winter. Model checking support for the ASM high–level language. In S. Graf and M. Schwartzbach, editors, *Proc. Tools and Algorithms for the Construction and Analysis of Systems (TACAS 2000), at ETAPS 2000*, pages 331–346. LNCS 1785, Springer-Verlag, Berlin, 2000.

[Dau92]   P. Dauchy. *Développement et exploitation d'une spécification algébrique du logiciel embarqué d'un métro*. PhD thesis, Université de Paris Sud, 1992.

[DBBS96]   J. Derrick, E. Boiten, H. Bowman, and M. Steen. Supporting ODP – Translating LOTOS to Z. In E. Najm and J.-B. Stefani, editors, *First IFIP Int. Workshop on Formal Methods for Open Object-Based Distributed Systems (FMOODS'96)*, pages 399–406. Chapman & Hall, 1996.

[DFG98]   M. Dam, L. Fredlund, and D. Gurov. Toward parametric verification of open distributed systems. In W.-P. de Roever, H. Langmaack, and A. Pnueli, editors, *Compositionality: The Significant Difference (COMPOS'97)*, pages 150–185. LNCS 1536, Springer-Verlag, Berlin, 1998.

[DG94]   P. Dauchy and M.C. Gaudel. Algebraic specifications with implicit states. Technical Report, Université de Paris Sud, 1994.

[DGM93]   P. Dauchy, M.-C. Gaudel, and B. Marre. Using algebraic specifications in software testing: a case study on the software of an automatic subway. *Journal of Systems and Software*, 21(3):229–244, 1993.

[DH98]   W. Damm and D. Harel. LSCs: Breathing life into message sequence charts. Technical Report CS98–09, The Weizmann Institute of Science, Rehovot, Israel, 1998.

[DH99]   W. Damm and D. Harel. LSCs: Breathing Life into Message Sequence Charts. In P. Ciancarini, A. Fantechi, and R. Gorrieri, editors, *Proc. 3rd IFIP Int. Conf. on Formal Methods for Open Object-Based Distributed Systems (FMOODS'99)*, pages 293–312. Kluwer Academic, Dordrecht, 1999. Abridged version of [DH98].

[DHP91]   C. Dimitrovici, U. Hummert, and L. Petrucci. Composition and net properties of algebraic high-level nets. In *Advances of Petri Nets*. LNCS 524, Springer-Verlag, Berlin, 1991.

[DJHP97]   W. Damm, B. Josko, H. Hungar, and A. Pnueli. A compositional real-time semantics of STATEMATE designs. In W.-P. de Roever, H. Langmaack, and A. Pnueli, editors, *Proc. COMPOS'97*. LNCS 1536, Springer-Verlag, Berlin, 1997.

[DMM89]   P. Degano, J. Meseguer, and U. Montanari. Axiomatizing Net Computations and Processes. In *Proc. LICS'89*, pages 175–185, 1989.

[DRS95]   R. Duke, G. Rose, and G. Smith. Object-Z: A specification language advocated for the description of standards. *Computer Standards and Interfaces*, 17:511–531, 1995.

[DW98]   D. D'Souza and A. Wills. *Objects, Components and Frameworks With UML: The Catalysis Approach.* Addison-Wesley, Reading, MA, 1998.

[EG94]   H. Ehrig and M. Große-Rhode. Functorial Theory of Parameterized Specifications in a General Specification Framework. *Theoretical Computer Science*, 135:221–266, 1994.

[EGGP00] R. Eschbach, U. Glässer, R. Gotzhein, and A. Prinz. On the formal semantics of SDL-2000: a compilation approach based on an abstract SDL machine. In Y. Gurevich, M. Odersky, P. Kutter, and L. Thiele, editors, *International Workshop on Abstract State Machines (ASM 2000)*, 2000.

[EGW96]   H. Ehrig, M. Große-Rhode, and U. Wolter. On the role of category theory in the area of algebraic specifications. In M. Haveraaen, O. Owe, and O.-J. Dahl, editors, *Recent Trends in Data Type Specification, Proc. 11th Int. Workshop on Algebraic Data Type Specification*, pages 17–48. LNCS 1130, Springer-Verlag, Berlin, 1996.

[EGW98]   H. Ehrig, M. Große-Rhode, and U. Wolter. Applications of category theory to the area of algebraic specification in computer science. *Applied Categorical Structures*, 6(1):1–35, 1998.

[Egy99]   A. Egyed. *Heterogeneous View Integration and its Automation.* PhD thesis, University of Southern California, Los Angeles, April 1999.

[EHK+97] H. Ehrig, R. Heckel, M. Korff, M. Löwe, L. Ribeiro, A. Wagner, and A. Corradini. Algebraic Approaches to Graph Transformation II: Single Pushout Approach and Comparison with Double Pushout Approach. In G. Rozenberg, editor, *Handbook of Graph Grammars and Computing by Graph Transformation, Volume 1: Foundations*, chapter 4, pages 247–312. World Scientific, Singapore, 1997.

[ELO95]   H. Ehrig, M. Löwe, and F. Orejas. Dynamic abstract data types based on algebraic graph transformations. In *ADT-Workshop'94*, pages 236–254. LNCS 906, Springer-Verlag, Berlin, 1995.

[EM85]   H. Ehrig and B. Mahr. *Fundamentals of Algebraic Specification 1: Equations and Initial Semantics*, volume 6 of *EATCS Monographs on Theoretical Computer Science*. Springer-Verlag, Berlin, 1985.

[EM90]   H. Ehrig and B. Mahr. *Fundamentals of Algebraic Specification 2: Module Specifications and Constraints*, volume 21 of *EATCS Monographs on Theoretical Computer Science*. Springer-Verlag, Berlin, 1990.

[EM00]   A. Egyed and N. Medvidovic. A formal approach to heterogeneous software modeling. In T. Maibaum, editor, *Fundamental Approaches to Software Engineering (FASE 2000)*, pages 178–192. LNCS 1783, Springer-Verlag, Berlin, 2000.

[Eme90]   E.A. Emerson. Temporal and modal logic. In J. van Leeuwen, editor, *Handbook of Theoretical Computer Science, Volume B: Formal Models and Semantics*, chapter 16, pages 995–1072. Elsevier and MIT Press, Amsterdam and Cambridge, MA, 1990.

[EO94]   H. Ehrig and F. Orejas. Dynamic abstract data types: An informal proposal. *Bull. EATCS 53*, pages 162–169, 1994. Also in [PRS01], pages 180–191.

316   References

[EO98]   H. Ehrig and F. Orejas. Integration Paradigm for Data Type and Pro-
          cess Specification Techniques. *Bull. EATCS 65, Formal Specification
          Column, Part 5*, 1998. Also in [PRS01], pages 192–201.
[EOP99]   H. Ehrig, F. Orejas, and J. Padberg. From Basic Views and Aspects to
          Integration of Specification Formalisms. *Bull. EATCS 69*, pages 98–108,
          1999.
[ER97]   J. Engelfriet and G. Rozenberg. Node replacement graph grammars. In
          G. Rozenberg, editor, *Handbook of Graph Grammars and Computing by
          Graph Transformation, Volume 1: Foundations*, chapter 1, pages 1–94.
          World Scientific, Singapore, 1997.
[ERT99]   C. Ermel, M. Rudolf, and G. Taentzer. The AGG-Approach: Language
          and Tool Environment. In H. Ehrig, G. Engels, H.-J. Kreowski, and
          G. Rozenberg, editors, *Handbook of Graph Grammars and Computing
          by Graph Transformation, volume 2: Applications, Languages and Tools*,
          pages 551–603. World Scientific, Singapore, 1999.
[EW00]   R. Eshuis and R. Wieringa. Requirements-level semantics for UML stat-
          echarts. In S.F. Smith and C.L. Talcott, editors, *Proc. FMOODS 2000*,
          pages 121–140. Kluwer Academic, Dordrecht, 2000.
[FC95]   J.L. Fiadeiro and J.F. Costa. Institutions for behaviour specification. In
          E. Astesiano, G. Reggio, and A. Tarlecki, editors, *Recent Trend in Data
          Type Specification*, pages 273–289. LNCS 906, Springer-Verlag, Berlin,
          1995.
[FF90]   N. Francez and I. Forman. Superimposition for interacting processes.
          In J.C.M. Baeten and J.W. Klop, editors, *Proc. CONCUR'90*, pages
          230–245. LNCS 458, Springer-Verlag, Berlin, 1990.
[Fia96]   J.L. Fiadeiro. On the emergence of properties in component-based sys-
          tems. In M. Wirsing and M. Nivat, editors, *Proc. AMAST'96*, pages
          421–443. LNCS 1101, Springer-Verlag, Berlin, 1996.
[Fis97]   C. Fischer. CSP–OZ: A combination of Object–Z and CSP. In H. Bow-
          man and J. Derrick, editors, *Formal Methods for Open Object-Based Dis-
          tributed Systems (FMOODS'97)*, volume 2, pages 423–438. Chapman &
          Hall, London, 1997.
[FLM97]   J.L. Fiadeiro, A. Lopes, and T. Maibaum. Synthesising interconnections.
          In R. Bird and L. Meertens, editors, *Proc. IFIP TC 2 Working Confer-
          ence on Algorithmic Languages and Calculi*, pages 240–264. Chapman
          & Hall, London, 1997.
[FM92]   J. Fiadeiro and T. Maibaum. Temporal theories as modularisation units
          for concurrent system specifications. *Formal Aspects of Computing*,
          4(3):239–272, 1992.
[FM96]   J.L. Fiadeiro and T. Maibaum. Design structures for object-based sys-
          tems. In S. Goldsack and S. Kent, editors, *Formal Methods and Object
          Technology*, pages 183–204. Springer-Verlag, Berlin, 1996.
[FM97]   J.L. Fiadeiro and T. Maibaum. Categorical semantics of parallel program
          design. *Science of Computer Programming*, 28(2–3):11–138, 1997.
[FR92]   J. Fiadeiro and G. Reichwein. A categorical theory of superposition.
          Technical Report 17/92, Instituto Superior Técnico, Universidade Tec-
          nica de Lisboa, 1992.
[FW99]   C. Fischer and H. Wehrheim. A hierarchy of subtyping relations (full
          version). Technical Report TRFC-99-1, Carl von Ossietzky Universität
          Oldenburg, 1999.

[GB84]   J.A. Goguen and R.M. Burstall. Introducing institutions. Proc. Logics of Programming Workshop, pages 221–256. LNCS 164, Springer-Verlag, Berlin, 1984.

[GB92]   J. Goguen and R.M. Burstall. Institutions: Abstract model theory for specification and programming. *Journal of the ACM*, 39(1):95–146, 1992.

[Gen99]   G. Genilloud. Informal UML 1.3 – remarks, questions and some answers. In *Proc. ECOOP Workshop on UML Semantics, Lisbon, Portugal*, 1999. Available from http://icawww.epfl.ch/genilloud/.

[GG78]   J Goguen and S. Ginali. A categorical approach to general systems theory. In G. Klir, editor, *Applied General Systems Research*, pages 257–270. Plenum, New York, 1978.

[GGP99]   U. Glässer, R. Gotzhein, and A. Prinz. Towards a new formal SDL semantics based on abstract state machines. In R. Dssouli, G.V. Bochmann, and Y. Lahav, editors, *SDL '99 - The Next Millenium, 9th SDL Forum Proc.*, pages 171–190. Elsevier Science, Amsterdam, 1999.

[GKP98]   R. Geisler, M. Klar, and C. Pons. Dimensions and Dichotomy in Meta-modeling. Technical Report 98–05, FB Informatik, TU Berlin, 1998.

[GLM01]   G. Génova, J. Llorens, and P. Martínez. Semantics of minimum multiplicity in ternary associations in UML. In M. Gogolla and C. Kobryn, editors, *UML 2001 - The Unified Modeling Language. Modeling Languages, Concepts, and Tools*, pages 329–341. LNCS 2185, Springer-Verlag, Berlin, 2001.

[Gog89]   J.A. Goguen. A categorical manifesto. Technical Monograph PRG–72, Oxford University Computing Laboratory, 1989.

[Gri98]   F. Griffel. *Componentware — Konzepte und Techniken eines Softwareparadigmas*. dpunkt Verlag, Heidelberg, 1998.

[Gri00]   L. Grigoriu. Transformation system semantics and compositionality of algebraic Petri nets. Master's thesis, TU Berlin, FB Informatik, 2000.

[Gro91]   M. Große-Rhode. Towards object-oriented algebraic specifications. In H. Ehrig, K.P. Jantke, F. Orejas, and H. Reichel, editors, *Recent Trends in Data Type Specification*, pages 98–116. LNCS 534, Springer-Verlag, Berlin, 1991.

[Gro95]   M. Große-Rhode. Concurrent state transformations on abstract data types. In M. Haveraaen, O. Owe, and O.-J. Dahl, editors, *Recent Trends in Data Type Specification*, pages 222–236. 11th Workshop on Specification of Abstract Data Types, LNCS 1130, Springer-Verlag, Berlin, 1995.

[Gro97a] M. Große-Rhode. Transition specifications for dynamic abstract data types. *Applied Categorical Structures*, 5:265–308, 1997.

[Gro97b] M. Große-Rhode. Sequential and parallel algebra transformation systems and their composition. Technical Report 97–07, Università di Roma *La Sapienza*, Dip. Scienze dell'Informazione, 1997.

[Gro98a] M. Große-Rhode. Algebra transformation systems and their composition. In E. Astesiano, editor, *Fundamental Approaches to Software Engineering (FASE'98)*, pages 107–122. LNCS 1382, Springer-Verlag, Berlin, 1998.

[Gro98b] M. Große-Rhode. First steps towards an institution of algebra replacement systems. *Applied Categorical Structures*, 6(4):403–426, 1998.

[Gro99]   M. Große-Rhode. Kategorielle Grundlagen. In *Mathematisch-strukturelle Grundlagen der Informatik, Part V*. Springer-Verlag, Berlin, 1999.

[Gro00]   M. Große-Rhode. Using a formal reference model for consistency checking and integration of UML diagrams. In M.M. Tanik and A. Ertas,
editors, *Proc. 5th World Conf. on Integrated Design and Process Technology (IDPT 2000)*. Society for Design and Process Science, Austin,
TX, 2000.

[Gro01]   M. Große-Rhode. Integrating semantics for object-oriented system models. In F. Orejas, P. G. Spirakis, and J. van Leeuwen, editors, *Proc.
Int. Coll. on Automata, Languages and Programming (ICALP 2001)*,
pages 40–60. LNCS 2076, Springer-Verlag, Berlin, 2001.

[GSB98]   R. Grosu, G. Stefanescu, and M. Broy. Visual formalisms revisited. In
L. Lavagno and W. Reisig, editors, *CSD '98, International Conference
on Application of Concurrency to System Design, Aizu-Wakamatsu City,
Fukushima*. IEEE Computer Society Press, Silver Spring, MD, 1998.

[Gur91]   Y. Gurevich. Evolving algebras, a tutorial introduction. In *Bull. EATCS
43*, pages 264–284. Springer-Verlag, 1991.

[Gur94]   Y. Gurevich. Evolving algebra 1993. In E. Börger, editor, *Specification
and Validation Methods*. Oxford University Press, 1994.

[Har87]   D. Harel. Statecharts: a visual formalism for complex systems. *Science
of Computer Programming*, 8:231–274, 1987.

[HEET99] R. Heckel, H. Ehrig, G. Engels, and G. Taentzer. A View-Based Approach to System Modeling based on Open Graph Transformation Systems. In H. Ehrig, G. Engels, J.-J. Kreowski, and G. Rozenberg, editors,
*Handbook of Graph Grammars and Computing by Graph Transforma-
tion, Volume 2: Applications, Languages and Tools*. World Scientific,
Singapore, 1999.

[Hen88]   M. Hennessy. *Algebraic Theory of Processes*. MIT Press, Cambridge,
MA, 1988.

[Her94]   C. Hermida. On fibred adjunctions and completeness for fibred categories. In *Recent Trends in Data Type Specification, Proc. 9th Workshop
on Specification of Abstract Data Types, Caldes de Malavella, Spain,
1992*, pages 235–251. LNCS 785, Springer-Verlag, Berlin, 1994.

[HG95]   D. Harel and E. Gery. Executable object modeling with Statecharts.
Technical Report 94-20, Weizman Institute of Science, 1995. http://-
www.wisdom.weizmann.ac.il/Papers/CSreports/reps94/94-20.ps.Z.

[HG97]   D. Harel and E. Gery. Executable object modeling with Statecharts. In
Proc. 18th International Conf. on Software Engineering, pages 246–257.
IEEE Computer Society Press, Silver Spring, MD, 1997.

[HJ98]   C.A.R. Hoare and H. Jifeng. *Unifying Theories of Programming*. Prentice Hall Series in Computer Science. Prentice Hall, London, 1998.

[HJS90]   P. Huber, K. Jensen, and R.M. Shapiro. Hierarchies in Coloured Petri
Nets. In G. Rozenberg, editor, *Advances in Petri nets*, pages 313–341.
LNCS 483, Springer-Verlag, Berlin, 1990.

[HN95]   D. Harel and A. Naamad. The STATEMATE semantics of statecharts.
Technical report, i-Logix, Inc., 1995.

[Hoa85]   C.A.R. Hoare. *Communicating Sequential Processes*. Prentice Hall, London, 1985.

[HOL]   Automated reasoning with higher–order logic. Automated Reasoning
Group , University of Cambridge, Computing Laboratory, HOL page
http://www.cl.cam.ac.uk/Research/HVG/HOL/.

[HPSS87]   D. Harel, A. Pnueli, J.P. Schmidt, and R. Sherman. On the formal semantics of Statecharts. In *Proc. Symp. on Logic in Computer Science II*, pages 54–64, 1987.

[Hug]   J.K. Huggins. Abstract state machine home page. EECS Department, University of Michigan, URL http://www.eecs.umich.edu/gasm/.

[Hum89]   U. Hummert. *Algebraische High-Level Netze*. PhD thesis, Technische Universität Berlin, 1989.

[HW89]   R. Holzapfel and G. Winterstein. VDM++ - a formal specification language for object-oriented designs. In *Ada in Industry, Proceedings of the Ada-Europe Conference 1988*, Great Britain, 1989. Cambridge University Press.

[IET97]   IETF, Networking Group. *Dynamic host configuration protocol*, March 1997. Available at http://www.ietf.org/rfc/rfc2131.txt.

[Isa]   Isabelle theorem proving environment. Cambridge University and Technische Universität München, Isabelle web page http://www.cl.cam.ac.uk/Research/HVG/Isabelle/.

[Jen92]   K. Jensen. *Coloured Petri Nets. Basic Concepts, Analysis Methods and Practical Use. Volume 1*. EATCS Monographs on Theoretical Computer Science. Springer-Verlag, Berlin, 1992.

[Jen94]   K. Jensen. *Coloured Petri Nets - Basic Concepts, Analysis Methods and Practical Use. Volume 2*. EATCS Monographs on Theoretical Computer Science. Springer-Verlag, Berlin, 1994.

[Joh99]   S. John. Zur kompositionalen Semantik von objekt-orientierten Statecharts. Master's thesis, TU Berlin, 1999.

[Joh01]   S. John. Transition selection algorithms for statecharts. In K. Bauknecht, W. Brauer, and T. Mück, editors, *Informatik 2001: Wirtschaft und Wissenschaft in der Network Economy — Visionen und Wirklichkeit, Proc. GI/OCG–Jahrestagung, 25.–28. September 2001, Wien, Austria*, volume 1, pages 622–627. Östereichische Computer-Gesellschaft, 2001.

[Jon86]   C.B. Jones. *Systematic software development using VDM*. Prentice-Hall International, London, 1986.

[Kla99]   M. Klar. *A Semantical Framework for the Integration of Object-Oriented Modeling Languages*. PhD thesis, TU Berlin, FB13, 1999.

[KNNZ00]   H.J. Köhler, U. Nickel, J. Niere, and A. Zündorf. Integrating UML diagrams for production control systems. In *Proc. 22th Int. Conf. on Software Engineering (ICSE), Limerick, Ireland*, 2000.

[Koc99]   M. Koch. *Integration of Graph Transformation and Temporal Logic for the Specification of Distributed Systems*. PhD thesis, TU Berlin, FB 13, 1999.

[KW01]   J. Klose and H. Wittke. An automata based interpretation of life sequence charts. In *Proc. Tools and Algorithms for the Construction and Analysis of Systems (TACAS 2001)*, pages 512–527. LNCS 2031, Springer-Verlag, Berlin, 2001.

[LBC00]   G. Lüttgen, M. von der Beeck, and R. Cleaveland. A compositional approach to statecharts semantics. Technical Report NASA/CR-2000-210086, ICASE Report No. 2000-12, Langley Research Center, 2000.

[LEW96]   J. Loeckx, H.-D. Ehrich, and M. Wolf. *Specification of Abstract Data Types*. Wiley–Teubner, Chichester, 1996.

[Lin91]   P.F. Linington. Introduction to the Open Distributed Processing basic reference model. In J. de Meer, V. Heymer, and R. Roth, editors, *Proc. IFIP TC6/WG6.4 Int. Workshop on Open Distributed Processing*, pages 3–13, 1991.

[LOT87]   LOTOS - A formal description technique based on temporal ordering of observational behaviour. Information Processing Systems - Open Systems Interconnection   ISO DIS 8807, July 1987   (ISO/TC 97/SC 21 N).

[Löw93]   M. Löwe. Algebraic Approach to Single-Pushout Graph Transformation. *Theoretical Computer Science*, 109:181–224, 1993.

[LSW95]   K.G. Larsen, B. Steffen, and C. Weise. A constraint oriented proof methodology based on modal transition systems. In E. Brinksma, W.R. Cleaveland, K.G. Larsen, T. Margaria, and B. Steffen, editors, *Tools and Algorithms for the Construction and Analysis of Systems (TACAS '95)*, pages 17–40. LNCS 1019, Springer-Verlag, Berlin, 1995.

[LT91]   K.G. Larsen and B. Thomsen. Partial specifications and compositional verification. *Theoretical Computer Science*, 88(1):15–32, 1991.

[LW98]   S. Lutz and M. Weber. Simulation and analysis of real-time concurrent object models. In *Proc. First Int. Symp. on Object-Oriented Real-Time Distributed Computing (ISORC'98)*, pages 318–326. IEEE Computer Society, Silver Spring, MD, 1998.

[LX91]   K.G. Larsen and L. Xinxin. Compositionality through an operational semantics of contexts. *Journal of Logic and Computation*, 1(6):761–795, 1991.

[Mac71]   S. MacLane. *Categories for the Working Mathematician*, volume 5 of *Graduate Texts in Mathematics*. Springer, New York, 1971.

[Mar99]   A. Martini. *Relating Arrows between Institutions in a Categorical Framework*. PhD thesis, TU Berlin, Fachbereich Informatik, 1999.

[Mes92]   J. Meseguer. Conditional rewriting logic as a unified model of concurrency. *Theoretical Computer Science*, 96:73–155, 1992.

[Mey88]   B. Meyer. *Object-Oriented Software Construction*. Prentice Hall International, Englewood Cliffs, NJ, 1988.

[Mil83]   Robin Milner. Calculi for synchrony and asynchrony. *Theoretical Computer Science*, 25, 1983.

[Mil89]   R. Milner. *Communication and Concurrency*. Prentice Hall International, 1989.

[MK98]   S. Mann and M. Klar. A metamodel for object-oriented statecharts. In *Proc. 2nd Workshop on Rigorous Object-Oriented Methods, ROOM 2*. University of Bradford, 1998.

[MM96]   N. Martí-Oliet and J. Meseguer. Rewriting logic as a logical and semantic framework. In J. Meseguer, editor, *First Int. Workshop on Rewriting Logic and its Applications*, volume 4 of *Electronic Notes in Theoretical Computer Science*. Elsevier Science, Oxford, 1996.

[MML]   Reports on the meta modelling language. http://www.cs.york.ac.uk/-puml/mml.html.

[Mos92]   P. Mosses. *Action Semantics*, volume 26 of *Cambridge Tracts in Theoretical Computer Science*. Cambridge University Press, 1992.

[MT00]   N. Medvidovic and R.N. Taylor. A classification and comparison framework for software architecture description languages. *IEEE Transactions on Software Engineering*, 26(1):70–93, January 2000.

[MW98]   A. Martini and U. Wolter. A systematic study of mappings between institutions. In F. Parisi-Presicce, editor, *Recent Trends in Algebraic Development Techniques*, pages 300–315. 12th International Workshop, WADT'97, Tarquinia, Italy, June 1997, Selected Papers, LNCS 1376, Springer-Verlag, Berlin, 1998.

[MW99]   A. Martini and U. Wolter. A Single Perspective on Arrows between Institutions. In A. M. Haeberer, editor, *Algebraic Methodology and Software Technology*, pages 486–501. 7th International Conference, AMAST'98, Amazonia, Brazil, January 1999, Proceedings, LNCS 1548, Springer-Verlag, Berlin, 1999.

[OCL]   OCL RfP (ad/2000-09-03), Initial submission, Version 1.0, August 20, 2001. *Response to the UML 2.0.* Available from http://www.klasse.nl/-ocl/subm-draft-text.html.

[ODP]   ISO/IEC International Standard 10746, ITU–T recommendation X.901–X.904: Reference model of open distributed processing – Parts 1–4.

[Özh01]   M. Özhan. Semantische Konsistenzanalyse von UML Sequenz- und Zustandsdiagrammen. Technical Report 2001/7, TU Berlin, 2001.

[Par81]   D. Park. Concurrency and automata on infinite sequences. In *Proc. 5th GI Conf.*, LNCS 104, Springer-Verlag, Berlin, 1981.

[Par01]   D. Parnitzke. Formal semantics of object systems with data- and object attributes. Master's thesis, TU Berlin, Fachbereich Informatik, January 2001.

[PER95]   J. Padberg, H. Ehrig, and L. Ribeiro. Algebraic high-level net transformation systems. *Mathematical Structures in Computer Science*, 5:217–256, 1995.

[Pet62]   C.A. Petri. *Kommunikation mit Automaten*. PhD thesis, Schriften des Institutes für Instrumentelle Mathematik, Bonn, 1962.

[Pho92]   W. Phoa. An introduction to fibrations, topos theory, the effective topos and modest sets. LFCS Report Series ECS-LFCS-92-208, Dept. of Computer Science, University of Edinburgh, April 1992.

[Pie94]   A. Pierantonio. Making static dynamic: Towards an axiomatization for dynamic ADT's. In *Proc. Int. Workshop on Communication Based Systems*, Berlin, 1994.

[PR91]   H. Plünnecke and W. Reisig. Bibliography of Petri Nets 1990. LNCS 524, Springer-Verlag, Berlin, 1991.

[PRS01]   G. Paun, G. Rozenberg, and A. Salomaa, editors. *Current Trends in Theoretical Computer Science: Entering the 21st Century*. World Scientific, Singapore etc., 2001.

[Que98]   J. Quemada. Final committee draft on enhancements to lotos. Technical Report Project 1.21.20.2.3, ISO/IEC JTC1/SC21/WG7, May 1998. URL ftp://ftp.dit.upm.es/pub/lotos/elotos/Working.Docs/.

[RE98]   W.P. de Roever and K. Engelhardt. *Data Refinement*. Cambridge Tracts in Theoretical Computer Science. Cambridge University Press, 1998.

[Rei85]   W. Reisig. *Petri Nets*, volume 4 of *EATCS Monographs on Theoretical Computer Science*. Springer-Verlag, 1985.

[Rei87]   H. Reichel. *Initial Computability, Algebraic Specifications, and Partial Algebras*. Oxford University Press, 1987.

[Rei98]   W. Reisig. *Elements of Distributed Algorithms: Modelling and Analysis with Petri Nets*. Springer-Verlag, Berlin, 1998.

[RG83]   W. Reisig and U. Goltz. Processes of place/transition nets. In *ICALP 83*, LNCS 154, Springer-Verlag, Berlin, 1983.

[Ric01]   M. Richters. *A Precise Approach to Validating UML Models and OCL Constraints*. PhD thesis, Universität Bremen, 2001.

[RLP98]   W.-P. de Roever, H. Langmaack, and A. Pnueli, editors. *Compositionality: The Significant Difference (Proc. COMPOS'97)*. LNCS 1536, Springer-Verlag, Berlin, 1998.

[Roz97]   G. Rozenberg, editor. *Handbook of Graph Grammars and Computing by Graph Transformations, Volume 1: Foundations*. World Scientific, Singapore, 1997.

[Rum98]   J. Rumbaugh. Modelling and design. *Journal of Object Oriented Programming*, 11(4):5–9, 1998.

[RV87]   W. Reisig and J. Vautherin. An algebraic approach to high level Petri nets. In *Proc. of the 8th Eur. Workshop on Petri Nets, Zaragoza*, 1987.

[Sch91]   A. Schürr. Progress: A VHL-language based on graph grammars. In *4th Int. Workshop on Graph Grammars and their Application to Computer Science*. LNCS 532, Springer-Verlag, Berlin, 1991.

[SDL99]   ITU Recommendation Z.100. *Specification and description language (SDL)*, 1999.

[SFC]   International Electrotechnical Commission. *International Standard 61131, Programmable Controllers, Part 3: Programming Languages*.

[SG96]   M. Shaw and D. Garlan. *Software Architecture: Perspectives on an Emerging Discipline*. Prentice Hall, Englewood Cliffs, NJ, 1996.

[Smi00]   G. Smith. *The Object-Z Specification Language*. Advances in Formal Methods Series. Kluwer Academic, Dordrecht, 2000.

[SNW93]   V. Sassone, M. Nielsen, and G. Winskel. A classification of models for concurrency. In E. Best, editor, *Proc. CONCUR'93*, pages 82–96. , LNCS 715, Springer-Verlag, Berlin, 1993.

[SP96]   C. Szyperski and C. Pfister. Why objects are not enough. In *Proc. Intl. Component Users Conf., Munich, Germany*. SIGS Publishers, July 1996. URL http://www.fit.qut.edu.au/~szypersk/pub/.

[Spi88]   J.M. Spivey. *Understanding Z: A Specification Language and its Formal Semantics*. Cambridge University Press, 1988.

[Spi92]   J.M. Spivey. *The Z Notation: A Reference Manual*. Prentice Hall, New York, NY, 1992.

[SS98]   D. Schmidt and B. Steffen. Program analysis as model checking of abstract interpretations. In G. Levi, editor, *Static Analysis 5th Int. Symp. (SAS'98), Pisa, Italy*, pages 351–380. LNCS 1503, Springer-Verlag, Berlin, 1998.

[Ste93a] B. Steffen. Generating data flow analysis algorithms from modal specifications. *International Journal on Science of Computer Programming*, 21:115–139, 1993.

[Ste93b] W. Steinmüller. *Informationstechnologie und Gesellschaft. Einführung in die angewandte Informatik*. Wissenschaftliche Buchgesellschaft, Darmstadt, 1993.

[Ste97]   B. Steffen. Unifying models. In R. Reischuk and M. Morvan, editors, *14th Symp. on Theoretical Aspects of Computer Science (STACS'97), Lübeck (Germany)*, pages 1–20. LNCS 1200, Springer-Verlag, Berlin, 1997.

[Ste01]   P. Stevens. On associations in the Unified Modeling Language. In
M. Gogolla and C. Kobryn, editors, *UML 2001 - The Unified Model-
ing Language. Modeling Languages, Concepts, and Tools*, pages 361–375.
LNCS 2185, Springer-Verlag, Berlin, 2001.

[Sti92]   C. Stirling. Modal and temporal logics. In *Handbook of Logic in Computer Science, volume 2, Background: Computational structures*. Claren-
don Press, Oxford, 1992.

[SWZ95]   A. Schürr, A.J. Winter, and A. Zündorf. Graph grammar engineering
with PROGRESS. In W. Schaefer and P. Botella, editors, *5th Eur.
Software Engineering Conf. (ESEC'95), Sitges*, pages 219–234. LNCS
989, Springer-Verlag, Berlin, 1995.

[Szy98]   C. Szyperski. *Component Software*. Addison-Wesley, Reading, MA,
1998.

[Tae00]   G. Taentzer. AGG: A Tool Environment for Algebraic Graph Transformation. In *Int. Workshop on Applications of Graph Transformations
with Industrial Relevance (AGTIVE'99)*, pages 481–490. LNCS 1779,
Springer-Verlag, Berlin 2000.

[TBG87]   A. Tarlecki, R.M. Burstall, and J.A. Goguen. Some fundamental algebraic tools for the semantics of computation. Part III: Indexed categories.
Technical report, University of Edinburgh, 1987.

[TBG91]   A. Tarlecki, R.M. Burstall, and J.A. Goguen. Some fundamental algebraic tools for the semantics of computation. Part III: Indexed categories. *Theoretical Computer Science* 91:239–264, 1991. Also appeared
as technical report ECS-LFCS-89-90, University of Edinburgh, 1989.

[TS03]   J. Tenzer and P. Stevens. Modelling recursive calls with UML state
diagrams. In M. Pezz, editor, *Fundamental Approaches to Software Engineering (FASE 2003)*, pages 135–149. LNCS 2621, Springer-Verlag,
Berlin, 2003.

[Tsi01]   A. Tsiolakis. Semantic analysis and consistency checking of UML sequence diagrams. Technical Report 2001/06, TU Berlin, 2001.

[UML]   OMG. *OMG Unified Modeling Language Specification, Version 1.3*,
March.

[UML03]   OMG. *OMG Unified Modeling Language Specification, Version 1.5*,
March 2003.

[Vau87]   J. Vautherin. Parallel System Specification with Coloured Petri Nets. In
G. Rozenberg, editor, *Advances in Petri Nets 87*, pages 293–308. LNCS
266, Springer-Verlag, Berlin, 1987.

[vVD89]   P. van Eijk, C. Vissers, and M. Diaz. *The formal description technique
LOTOS*. North-Holland, Amsterdam, 1989.

[WC89]   J.-P. Wu and S. Chanson. Translation from LOTOS and Estelle spec-
ifications to extended transition systems and its verification. In S.T.
Voung, editor, *Formal Description Techniques, II*, pages 533–549. North-
Holland, Amsterdam, 1989.

[Web97]   M. Weber. Abstract object systems – a three-layer model of concurrent
real-time object systems. Technical Report 97/12, TU Berlin, 1997.

[Win86]   G. Winskel. Event structures. In *Advances in Petri Nets 86 – Part II*,
pages 325–392. LNCS 255, Springer-Verlag, Berlin, 1986.

[Win87]   G. Winskel. Petri nets, algebras, morphisms, and compositionality. *Information and Computation*, 72:197–238, 1987.

324   References

[Win88a]   G. Winskel. Event Structures. In W. Brauer, W. Reisig, and G. Rozen-
            berg, editors, *Petri Nets: Applications and Relationships to Other Mod-
            els of Concurrency*, pages 324–392. LNCS 255, Springer-Verlag, Berlin,
            1988.
[Win88b]   G. Winskel. Introduction to Event Structures. In G. Rozenberg J.W. de
            Bakker, W.-P. de Roever, editors, *Linear Time, Branching Time, and
            Partial Order in Logics and Models of Concurrency*, pages 364–397.
            LNCS 354, Springer-Verlag, Berlin, 1988.
[WK98]   J. Warmer and A. Kleppe. *The Object Constraint Language: Precise
            Modeling with UML*. Addison-Wesley, Reading, MA, 1998.
[WLF00]   M. Wermelinger, A. Lopes, and J. Fiadeiro. Superposing connectors.
            In *Proc. 10h Int. Workshop on Software Specification and Design*, pages
            87–94. IEEE Computer Society Press, Silver Spring, MD, 2000.
[WLF01]   M. Wermelinger, A. Lopes, and J. Fiadeiro. A graph based architectural
            (re)configuration language. In *Proc. ESEC/FSE'01*. ACM Press, New
            York, 2001.
[WM97]   U. Wolter and A. Martini. Shedding New Light in the World of Logical
            Systems. In E. Moggi and G. Rosolini, editors, *Category Theory and
            Computer Science, 7th Int. Conf., CTCS'97*, pages 159–176. LNCS 1290,
            Springer-Verlag, Berlin, 1997.
[WN97]   G. Winskel and M. Nielsen. Categories in concurrency. In A.M. Pitts and
            P. Dybjer, editors, *Semantics and Logics of Computation*, Publications
            of the Newton Institute, pages 299–354. Cambridge University Press,
            1997.
[XS98]   Q. Xu and M. Swarup. Compositional reasoning using the assumption-
            commitment paradigm. In W.-P. de Roever, H. Langmaack, and
            A. Pnueli, editors, *Compositionality: The Significant Difference (COM-
            POS'97)*, pages 565–583. LNCS 1536, Springer-Verlag, Berlin, 1998.
[ZJ93]   P. Zave and M. Jackson. Conjunction as composition. *ACM Transactions
            on Software Engineering and Methodology*, 2(4):379–411, October 1993.

Index

Monographs in Theoretical Computer Science · An EATCS Series

Texts in Theoretical Computer Science · An EATCS Series

Former volumes appeared as
EATCS Monographs on Theoretical Computer Science